A2 Accounting for AQA

the complete resource for the A2 examination

David Cox

Michael Fardon

osborne BOOKS

Published by Osborne Books Limited
Unit 1B Everoak Estate
Bromyard Road
Worcester WR2 5HP
Tel 01905 748071
Email books@osbornebooks.co.uk
Website www.osbornebooks.co.uk

Graphic design by Richard Holt

Printed and bound in Malta by Gutenberg Press Limited

British Library Cataloguing in Publication Data
A catalogue record for this book is available from the British Library

ISBN 978 1905777 174

Contents

Introduction

A2 Accounting for AQA has been written to provide a study resource for students taking the Assessment and Qualifications Alliance's A2 examinations in Accounting. The A2 course is structured into two equally-weighted Units, as follows:

Unit 3 **Further Aspects of Financial** **Accounting**	**Unit 4** **Further Aspects of Management** **Accounting**

Unit 3 is designed to develop further the financial accounting techniques acquired in AS Unit 1 'Introduction to Financial Accounting'.

Unit 4 develops further the knowledge and understanding of management accounting techniques acquired in AS Unit 2 'Financial and Management Accounting'.

A2 Accounting for AQA has been designed to be user-friendly and contains:

- clear explanations and numerous worked examples

- chapter summaries to help with revision

- a wide range of questions, many from past AQA examinations

- answers to selected questions, set out in full at the end of the book

Resources for tutors – Tutor Zone

For the questions where answers are not given in this book, separate **tutor support material** provides the answers, together with a range of photocopiable layouts, a web directory and various electronic resources.

These resources are available to tutors in a password-protected area – a **Tutor Zone** – on the Osborne Books website. Tutors who would like access to this material should complete the online application form for membership; this form can be found on the tutor section of www.osbornebooks.co.uk

Use of Accounting Terminology

In past years it has been AQA practice in GCE Accounting question papers and mark schemes to operate a dual system where the new IAS (International Accounting Standards) term is given with the UK term in brackets, for example 'inventory (stock)'.

This practice is changing from the January 2013 examinations: AQA will no longer quote dual terminology for commonly used accounting terms, but use only the IAS wording. The relevant IAS terms are set out below, with the old terminology shown in brackets.

- Non-current assets (fixed assets)
- Non-current liabilities (long-term liabilities)
- Inventory (stock)
- Trade receivables (debtors)
- Trade payables (creditors)
- Income statement (trading and profit and loss account)
- Profit for year (net profit)
- Revenue (sales) [where used in income statements]
- Rate of inventory turnover (stock turnover)
- Trade receivables collection period (debtor collection period)
- Trade payables collection period (creditor payment period)

AQA have also stated that in instances where an IAS term has not yet been used in examinations, a new IAS term could be quoted followed by the UK term in brackets, for example 'Statement of Financial Position (Balance Sheet).' The terms that could be used in an examination are shown in the table below.

Current UK term	International term
Accruals	Other payables
Balance sheet	Statement of financial position
Bank and cash	Cash and cash equivalents
Interest payable	Finance costs
Interest receivable	Investment revenues
Investments	Investment property
Land and buildings	Property
Prepayments	Other receivables
Sundry expenses	Other operating expenses
Sundry incomes	Other operating incomes

For the latest information about the use of IAS terminology, please refer to the relevant book pages in the Products and Resources Section of www.osbornebooks.co.uk and www.aqa.org.uk for updating notices.

Acknowledgments

The publisher wishes to thank Jean Cox, Maz Loton, Jon Moore and Cathy Turner for their help with the reading and production of this book. Particular thanks go to Roger Petheram of Worcester College of Technology for his technical editorial work. AQA examination materials are reproduced by kind permission of the Assessment and Qualifications Alliance (AQA). Thanks are also due to Tesco PLC for their permission to reproduce extracts from their Annual Report & Accounts.

Authors

David Cox is a Certified Accountant with more than twenty years' experience teaching accountancy students over a wide range of levels. Formerly with the Management and Professional Studies Department at Worcester College of Technology, he now lectures on a freelance basis and carries out educational consultancy work in accountancy studies. He is author and joint author of a number of textbooks in the areas of accounting, finance and banking.

Michael Fardon has extensive teaching experience of a wide range of banking, business and accountancy courses at Worcester College of Technology. He now specialises in writing business and financial texts and is General Editor at Osborne Books.

Electronic Resources

Online Multiple Choice Tests for each chapter

At the beginning of the questions at the end of each chapter you will see a screen that indicates that an additional 'True or False' multiple choice test is available online to test understanding of the chapter. These tests can be accessed in the Products and Resources section of www.osbornebooks.co.uk

Online Resource Documents

Also available in the Products and Resources section of www.osbornebooks.co.uk are downloadable pdf files which will help with the practice questions in this book. These include:

- stores ledger record
- limited company income statement, balance sheet and cash flow statement
- cash budget

A2 Accounting Unit 3

Further Aspects of Financial Accounting

Unit 3 for AQA A2 Accounting is designed to develop further the financial accounting techniques you will have acquired in AS Unit 1 'Introduction to Financial Accounting'. The areas it covers include:

- sources of finance – the assessment of internal and external sources of finance which are essential to the running of a business

- incomplete records – the techniques used to draw up financial statements when some of the required accounting data is missing

- partnership accounts – the format of partnership final accounts and the implications of changes in partnerships

- published accounts of limited companies – the formats used and their relevance to user groups

- accounting standards – international rules of accounting for assets, liabilities and income

- inventory valuation – two different methods of valuing the inventory of a business and the situations in which they might be used

1 SOURCES OF FINANCE

Providing finance for a business is essential for its day-to-day operations and also for its future growth. Business owners and managers must always ensure that they plan well ahead to provide the necessary funds.

In this chapter we examine:

- internal sources of finance, for example capital provided by the owner and cash generated from the profits of a business
- external sources of finance, for example
  - bank loans, overdrafts and commercial mortgages
  - finance for limited companies, eg shares and debentures

We will examine the advantages and disadvantages of different forms of finance and show how to assess sources of finance in the light of the requirements of a business over a variety of time periods.

WHERE WILL THE FINANCE COME FROM?

A person starting up in business or expanding an existing business will need to know where to obtain finance. Some sources of funds are generally well-known, others may need to be researched. The banks are an obvious first point of contact, but as this chapter will show, if the business is a limited company there are many other options open.

This chapter will outline the wide range of sources of finance available and will then explain all the factors – advantages and disadvantages – that have to be taken into account when deciding between them.

The first distinction to be drawn is between **internal sources** and **external sources** of finance.

internal sources of finance

Internal sources of finance include:

- funds provided by the owner or owners – for example, capital from savings or loans from members of the family who want to help and possibly receive some return on their investment
- if the business is already established, funds generated from profits can be used to provide finance – for example new computers may be purchased using cash generated from the profits made by the business

The main drawback of internal sources of finance – and cash from profits in particular – is that after the initial investment has been made they cannot always be relied upon to provide money when it is required: for example, the owner may not have any further cash to spare and the business may be making a loss. More often than not, therefore, it is external sources of finance that business owners and managers rely on to provide finance for running and expanding a business.

external sources of finance

Before examining the advantages and disadvantages of specific forms of external finance we will first provide an overview of all the different institutions and individuals who can provide finance. We will then in the next section explain the different factors that have to be taken into account when deciding on a particular form of funding.

- **banks – loans, overdrafts and mortgages**

   The main commercial banks in the UK – 'high street' names such as Lloyds Banking Group, HSBC, RBS – are the traditional providers of business finance. Their products include overdrafts to finance day-to-day trading, and loans and mortgages for the purchase of assets such as computers, machinery and property. A study of the business services section of bank websites will reveal the very wide range of financial products they provide.

- **private equity capital**

   If a private limited company needs external financing, it can apply for funds from a 'private equity' company. The typical way this works is for the private equity company to provide finance and in return receive a percentage of the shares of the business and an active role in helping to run the business. This type of funding is obviously a very long-term commitment, but it can be very advantageous for a new business which will receive expertise as well as money from the investing company. Public limited companies receive similar assistance from 'venture capital' companies such as 3i ('Investors in Industry').

- **business angels**

   These 'angels' are wealthy individuals – often entrepreneurs or retired executives – who invest their own money. They provide finance and in return take a percentage stake in the business and help to run it.

forming a limited company to obtain additional finance

Banks and business angels provide finance for all forms of business: sole traders, partnerships and limited companies. Private equity and venture capital companies, on the other hand, provide finance specifically for limited companies. The reason for this is that the investing company will want to receive a percentage of the shares, profits and an element of control in return for the finance provided. Each proposition is judged very much in terms of investment potential and profit.

It follows that an entrepreneur who is ambitious and needs substantial financing may well form a limited company to take advantage of the additional financing available from private equity and venture capital firms.

The diagram on the next page shows the finance available to different forms of business.

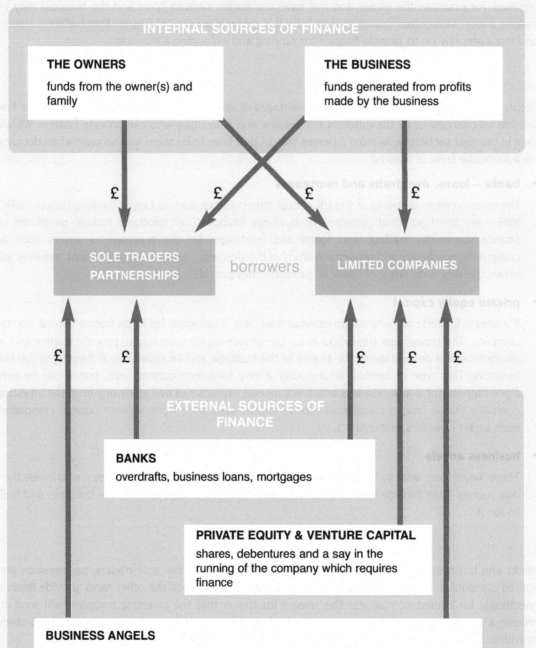

where will the finance come from?

INTERNAL SOURCES OF FINANCE

THE OWNERS

funds from the owner(s) and
family

THE BUSINESS

funds generated from profits
made by the business

£ £ £ £

**SOLE TRADERS
PARTNERSHIPS**

borrowers

LIMITED COMPANIES

£ £ £ £ £

**EXTERNAL SOURCES OF
FINANCE**

BANKS

overdrafts, business loans, mortgages

PRIVATE EQUITY & VENTURE CAPITAL

shares, debentures and a say in the
running of the company which requires
finance

BUSINESS ANGELS

investment in a business which requires finance, and a say in the way in which it
is run

FACTORS TO CONSIDER WHEN APPLYING FOR FINANCE

We will discuss all the different forms of finance in the next section, but it is important first to appreciate all the factors involved in choosing a source of finance.

Examination questions in the past have often asked you to make suggestions for sources of finance for an individual starting up in business. In order to provide a full answer you will need to know the different types of finance and their advantages and disadvantages; you will need to make recommendations and be able to justify your decision.

A starting point is to identify the financial needs of the individual. This can be done by remembering the mnemonic 'PARIS' which stands for **P**urpose, **A**mount, **R**epayment, **I**nterest and **S**ecurity:

- **purpose**

  You will need to identify the purpose for which the financing is required. Is it needed to purchase assets? Is it needed for day-to-day trading purposes as indicated on the cash budget you will have studied at AS level? The answer here is fairly simple – you will need some form of loan or mortgage for asset purchase and an overdraft for day-to-day requirements (working capital). These products are explained in detail later in the chapter.

- **amount**

  It is important to work out exactly how much you will need to borrow. This is straightforward when it comes to a loan for asset purchase; an overdraft requirement can be worked out from a cash budget.

- **repayment**

  It is also important to work out accurately the period over which the finance is needed and from this to draw up a schedule for the repayments that will be needed. Most loans are repaid by regular instalments of the amount borrowed, plus interest, but some may require payment in full at the end of the period. As you will know from the bottom line of the cash budget (the bank balance), overdrafts are variable and may be repaid from time-to-time when cash flow into the business is positive.

- **interest**

  Interest is the cost to the business of 'servicing' the loan or overdraft. Interest is often expressed as an annual rate, eg 5% p.a., and is a useful guide for comparing the cost to the business of raising different forms of finance. For example a bank loan to a partnership may be charged at 8% p.a. whereas a loan from one of the partners (internal financing) may only cost 5% p.a., in which case the partner's loan is the better (cheaper) choice.

  If you need to work out the amount of interest payable on a loan over a year, the formula is:

  $$\text{Amount of loan or overdraft} \times \frac{\text{interest rate}}{100}$$

  For example, a £10,000 loan with an interest rate of 5% p.a. will cost a business during the year

  $$£10,000 \times \frac{5}{100} = £500$$

- **security**

  Business finance from a bank will inevitably involve the business or business owners having to put down security for the borrowing. This security might comprise the business assets (eg the business property) or the homes of the owners/directors. What this means is that if the business fails and the finance has to be repaid to the bank, the business assets or homes of the owners/directors may have to be sold to repay the borrowing.

DIFFERENT SOURCES OF FINANCE

In this section we will describe the different sources of finance for businesses and examine:

- their features
- their advantages and disadvantages

You should note and memorise all these details carefully. Examination questions often ask you to assess the advantages and disadvantages of various sources of finance and require you to make recommendations for specific situations. The Worked Example that follows this section is based on an examination question and illustrates this process.

bank overdraft

features
- A bank overdraft is a flexible arrangement with a bank which allows a customer to borrow money on a current account up to a certain limit, eg £50,000. An overdraft is used to cover the day-to-day working capital requirements of a business, eg purchase of inventory at times when funds are low.
- Interest is paid – normally at a variable rate in line with market rates.
- An overdraft limit is normally reviewed with the business every year.
- An overdraft is repayable on demand if the bank wants the borrowing repaid.
- Security will be required from the business or business owner to safeguard the borrowing.

advantages
- A bank overdraft is very flexible: a business can borrow and repay whenever it likes.
- An overdraft can be economical to operate: interest is only payable when the business borrows, and is charged only the borrowed amount.

disadvantages
- Interest rates for bank overdrafts can be higher than bank loan rates.
- If the business gets into financial difficulties the bank can ask for immediate repayment of an overdraft.
- Security, including possibly the house of the business owner, is required for an overdraft.

bank loan

features
- A bank loan is finance provided by the banks for a specific purpose, often the purchase of an asset. Loan amounts can range from £1,000 to £100,000.
- Interest is paid, either at a rate fixed at the beginning of the loan, or at a variable rate in line with market rates during the lifetime of the loan.
- A bank loan is for a set time period, normally between 2 and 30 years.
- The loan is often repaid in regular instalments, but this may be varied, for example with a 'repayment holiday' – this is where the borrower is allowed to wait a year or so before starting to make repayments. Some loans can also be repaid in full at the end of the loan period rather than by instalments.
- Security, either the assets being purchased or the property of the business owner(s), is required for a bank loan.

advantages
- A bank loan is easy to budget for because the timing and the amount of the repayments is known.
- There may be flexibility in the repayment schedule, for example arranging to delay the early repayments (a 'repayment holiday')
- Favourable interest rates can be negotiated, often at a lower rate than an overdraft.

disadvantages
- A business loan is a long-term financial commitment which will need to be serviced.
- Security, including possibly the house of the business owner, is needed.

bank commercial mortgage

features
- A mortgage is an arrangement in which property is used as security for borrowing. If the borrower defaults on the loan, the lender can sell the property to obtain the funds. Amounts range from £25,000 to £500,000.
- Banks can provide finance for the purchase of commercial property, normally up to 70% of its market value. In principle a mortgage is basically the same for a business as it is for a house buyer.
- Interest is paid, either at a rate fixed at the beginning of the mortgage, or at a variable rate in line with market rates during the lifetime of the mortgage.
- A mortgage is for a set time period, normally up to 25 years.

advantages
- A mortgage is easy to budget for because the timing and the amount of the repayments is known.
- If a fixed rate mortgage is taken when rates are relatively low, the cost of borrowing is also relatively low.

disadvantages
- A mortgage is a long-term financial commitment which will need to be serviced. It also involves the putting down of security.

limited company ordinary shares

features
- When a limited company starts up for the first time, or expands its operations, it obtains finance by issuing ordinary shares to its owners and other investors who become its shareholders.
- Shares are issued in return for payment of a fixed amount per share and become the capital of the company.
- In return for investment in company ordinary shares the shareholders receive regular dividend payments, paid out of the profits of the company.
- It is possible to buy the shares of public limited companies (PLCs) on the Stock Exchange but the majority of limited companies are private limited companies (ltd's), often started by sole trader or family businesses. Their shares are not for public sale.
- If a limited company wishes to raise finance by issuing more shares, it can do so either by issuing them to the existing owners and shareholders or by applying to a private equity firm for an issue to outside investors. These investors will provide the finance, but will also want an element of control over the company because they have in practice become new part-owners.

advantages
- A limited company making a share issue can potentially raise more finance than a sole trader or partnership because outside investors are able to buy shares in the company.
- A limited company making a share issue can also attract new management with valuable skills and expertise.
- Dividends on most ordinary shares vary according to the level of profits; therefore the cost of the finance is effectively variable and will not be such a burden if the business profits are lower.

disadvantages
- If outside investors buy into the company by acquiring ordinary shares, they will have an element of control over the company which could prove disruptive for the existing management.
- With most shares, the finance is never 'paid off' as it is with a fixed term loan or overdraft because there will always be the need to pay dividends.
- If the company 'goes bust' the ordinary shareholders are normally the last people to get their money back – in fact they rarely get anything at all.

limited company preference shares

features
- Most shares issued by companies are ordinary shares. Preference shares, as the name suggests, have preference over ordinary shares because they have priority claim on the profits ahead of the other shareholders.
- Preference shares are often quoted as having a fixed percentage rate dividend, eg '3% Preference shares'.

| advantages | • Preference shareholders are unable to vote at shareholder meetings and so are unable to take part in the running of the company. |

• Preference dividends are normally at a fixed percentage rate – this makes budgeting easier for the company

disadvantages • If the profitability of the company is low ordinary shareholders (in many cases these are the company owners) may lose out completely on their dividend because preference shareholders have to be paid first.

debenture stock

features • Debenture stock is a fixed interest, fixed repayment date investment issued by a limited company which represents debt owed by that company.

• Debenture stock only relates to loans made to the company and does not give any rights of ownership of the company in the way that ordinary shares and preference shares do. It is sometimes secured on the company's assets.

• Debenture stock of larger companies can be traded on the stock markets.

• Debenture holders may require to have company assets charged as security.

advantages • Debenture stock holders are unable to vote at shareholder meetings and so are unable to take part in the running of the company.

• Interest is paid at a fixed percentage rate – this makes budgeting easier for the company.

disadvantages • If the company does not make a profit, the interest (which ranks ahead of dividends) will always have to be paid at the fixed rate on the due date.

• Debenture stock sometimes gives the holders better rights than ordinary shareholders to obtain repayment if the company 'goes bust'.

WORKED EXAMPLE: FINANCING A BUSINESS

We will now present a practical example of an individual, Toni, who is planning to set up a restaurant 'Perfetto'. He intends to rent premises but will need financing for everything else.

Toni has spoken to his accountant, who has worked out that he will need £200,000 for buying equipment, fitting out the restaurant and for working capital.

The accountant has taken Toni through the various options for raising finance, discussing with him all the advantages and disadvantages. Toni then makes a decision on the basis of this discussion.

The following points were raised at the start of the discussion:

• Toni will need a total of £200,000:
  – £120,000 for purchase of assets – furniture, ovens and refitting costs
  – £80,000 of working capital for day-to-day operation of the restaurant

• Toni has £30,000 of savings and his family have offered to lend him £20,000 interest free for five years, repayable at the end of that period.

The discussion then went on to cover the following areas:

internal or external finance?

Toni has a total of £50,000 available from his own resources and from the family: £30,000 savings of his own which will become the capital of his business and a £20,000 interest-free loan from the family. There are no profits yet to provide funding. This is all classed as internal finance.

This is very attractive as there is no interest cost to him on the loan. There are some risks: the family may want the money back before the end of the five years or they may want a say in the way the business is run. Toni decides that the risk is worth taking and decides to use the £50,000 of internal funding to finance the business

working capital finance?

Toni now has £150,000 (£200,000 – £50,000) to finance:

- £80,000 working capital requirement
- £70,000 asset purchase and refitting

The obvious choice for the working capital financing is a bank overdraft. It is flexible because Toni will only have to borrow when he needs to, and also it will prove cheaper because interest is only charged when the account is overdrawn

But . . . Toni will have to put down his house as security for the borrowing. He has no choice.

longer term finance?

Toni needs £120,000 in total for the purchase of assets – furniture, ovens and refitting costs. But as he is using £50,000 of internal financing for this purpose, he now has only £70,000 (£120,000 – £50,000) to finance over the long term.

His accountant points out that if Toni forms a limited company he could possibly attract outside investors such as private equity companies to help finance his business. He would then be able to issue shares. But his accountant also points out that the restaurant is a comparatively small business and so this step would not really be sensible at this stage. Toni could possibly form a company in years to come if he were planning a chain of restaurants which would require a larger amount of finance.

So Toni is left with £70,000 to raise. He is unlikely to attract the help of a business angel as the amount is relatively small and so the accountant recommends investigating bank finance. A commercial mortgage is effectively ruled out because Toni is only renting the business premises and cannot put it down as security.

conclusion

Toni is therefore left with the option of a bank loan, which is ideal for his purposes:

- it is easy to budget for because the timing and the amounts of the repayments will be known
- he may be able to choose the option of a fixed rate loan at a low rate
- he may be able to negotiate a repayment 'holiday' – a period at the beginning of the loan when he does not have to make repayments and when he may be short of cash flow

The only downside is that he will be asked by the bank for his house as security. This means that if the business fails, the bank may have to sell his home to repay the loan and the overdraft. Toni reckons that it is worth the risk as he is confident of making a success of his 'Perfetto' venture.

CHAPTER SUMMARY

- Businesses may be financed from a variety of sources, both internal and external.

- Internal sources include:
  - funds provided by the owner(s) – ie 'capital'
  - funds provided by the family of the owner(s) in the case of sole traders and partnerships
  - funds generated from the profits of the business

- External sources of finance include:
  - banks
  - private equity and venture capital companies (both for limited company borrowers only)
  - business angels

- The factors to consider when applying for different types of finance are (PARIS):
  - **P**urpose of the borrowing
  - **A**mount of the finance required
  - **R**epayment – when and how much, and over what period
  - **I**nterest – the cost of the finance
  - **S**ecurity needed

- A bank overdraft:
  - a flexible form of finance, normally for working capital (day-to-day trading purposes)
  - the business is able to borrow on its current account up to an agreed limit, as and when it wants
  - interest rates can be high but interest is only paid when the account goes overdrawn
  - security is normally required and the bank has the right to request repayment on demand

- A bank loan:
  - is normally for a period of years (usually between 2 to 30 years) for the purchase of assets
  - repayment is normally by regular instalments, although their timing can be varied
  - the interest rate is either fixed, or variable in line with market rates
  - security is normally required

- A bank commercial mortgage:
  - a loan for the finance of non-current assets – normally for property, which forms the security for the loan
  - for a fixed period of years (up to 25) and for up to 70% of the value of the asset
  - the interest rate is either fixed, or variable in line with market rates

- Limited company ordinary shares form the main capital of a company:
  - issued to the investors in the company (these could be the owners or outside investors)
  - dividends are paid regularly to shareholders out of the profits of the company

Limited company preference shares:

- receive dividends from profits in preference to ordinary shareholders
- often have a fixed percentage dividend and a fixed period
- preference shareholders cannot vote at company meetings (ordinary shareholders can)

Debenture stock:

- a fixed interest, fixed period investment issued by a limited company – normally traded on the Stock Exchange
- represents debt owed by the company; sometimes it has the company's assets as security
- gives no right of ownership over the company, but provides better rights to repayment than ordinary shareholders if the company 'goes bust'

In the next chapter we move on to the preparation of final accounts – a topic important at AS Level. For A2 Level, however, we will examine the preparation of accounts from incomplete records – where the owner of the business has not followed double-entry book-keeping principles.

QUESTIONS

> visit
> **www.osbornebooks.co.uk**
> to take an online test

An asterisk (*) after the question number means that the answer is given at the end of this book.

1.1* Businesses often make use of internal sources of finance.

(a) Describe the two main sources of internal financing for a business.

(b) Explain how these two main sources are suitable for a business in different stages of its development.

(c) Describe the disadvantages of relying on internal sources of finance. Give examples to support your answer.

1.2 Banks offer a wide range of sources of finance. You are to recommend the bank finance product which best fulfils the need of each of the three businesses described below. In each case you are to describe the main features of the product, give reasons for your choice and set out the advantages and disadvantages of the source of finance you have chosen for the business.

(a) Sajit is setting up a stationery shop and is looking for short-term finance which will see him through times when his working capital needs support. For example, he will need to pay his suppliers for his inventory and the wages of his two assistants before the sales from his shop have become fully established.

(b) Rachel is setting up a business which will make and market organic yoghurt to the supermarket chains. In order to get going she needs to purchase substantial manufacturing and refrigeration equipment which she estimates will cost her £85,000.

(c) Basil, who has spent twenty years in the hotel trade, wants to buy a house in Torquay to convert into a hotel. The property will cost him £450,000 and he has £150,000 as a deposit. He is therefore looking for finance totalling £300,000 for the property purchase.

1.3* Explain the meaning of the following terms:

(a) business angel

(b) private equity finance

In what ways are these forms of finance different from a bank loan?

1.4* Describe the three types of limited company finance listed below. Include in your description the ways in which they differ as far as the payment of dividends or interest is concerned.

(a) ordinary shares

(b) preference shares

(c) debenture stock

1.5 Tariq plans to set up a design consultancy business as a sole trader within the next six months. He will need total financing of £150,000 in addition to the money he is putting in himself (ie all his savings and available funds). His family have hinted that they might be willing to lend him money, interest-free, but he knows they want to help him in the business, and he is not sure if this is a good idea.

He plans to rent an office and needs £80,000 for non-current assets such as furniture and computer equipment. The remaining £70,000 he will need for working capital. He owns his house which has sufficient security value available for the finance.

REQUIRED

Discuss alternative methods of raising the required finance for

(a) the assets Tariq needs to purchase

(b) the working capital he will need

Your discussion should explain the options for Tariq's financial needs and come to a justified conclusion and firm recommendation in each case.

2 INCOMPLETE RECORDS

In our studies for the AS Accounting for AQA we have concentrated on the double-entry system and, from this, we have extracted a trial balance and prepared the income statement and balance sheet. However, many smaller businesses do not use the double-entry system, and no trial balance is available. Such businesses keep some records – but these are incomplete records – and, at the end of the year, it is the task of the accountant to construct the final accounts from these.

This chapter looks at:

● the information available when constructing final accounts from incomplete records

● how information that is required can be calculated, including the use of a statement of affairs

● preparing final accounts from incomplete records

● the use of gross profit mark-up and margin in incomplete records accounting

● the calculation of cash losses – cash missing as a result of poor cash handling procedures, or as a result of theft

● the calculation of inventory losses – goods 'lost' as a result of fire, flood or theft – for insurance purposes

● commenting on financial statements prepared from incomplete records

WHAT HAPPENS WHEN THERE'S NO DOUBLE-ENTRY?

Many small businesses do not run a double-entry system but, instead, rely on a cash book to record receipts and payments. At the same time they collect together – often in a box file – their paid invoices, credit notes, copies of invoices issued, bank statements and other bank documentation, notes and jottings, and bits and pieces. At the end of the financial year, it is the task of the accountant to use this 'box file' information – or incomplete records – to construct the income statement and balance sheet. The owner of the business can then see how much profit has been made during the year, and the assets, liabilities and owner's stake in the business at the end of the year.

Accounting Records

Incomplete records is the term used where the book-keeping system does not use double-entry principles and no trial balance is available. Some records are kept and the accountant will construct final accounts by

*   using the information available
*   seeing what information may not be available, and how 'missing' figures can be calculated

information available to the accountant

The basic financial record kept by most businesses is a cash book, often operated as a *single-entry* system. In practice, even if a cash book has not been kept, it is usually possible to reconstruct it from banking records, although this task can prove to be time-consuming. Other financial information will be available so that, in all, the accountant has the following to work from:

*   cash book – the basic record for any single entry system
*   banking details – statements, paying-in books, cheque counterfoils
*   invoices – both received (for purchases) and sent (for sales) during the year
*   expenses – during the year
*   records of assets and liabilities – non-current and current assets, non-current and current liabilities, both at the beginning and end of the year
*   records of non-current assets – bought or sold during the year

Information which may not be available, and will need to be calculated includes:

*   capital at the beginning of the financial year
*   purchases and sales for the year
*   cash book summary
*   profit for the year

the tools of accounting

In the two Worked Examples which follow we construct the accounts that are required by taking the financial information that is available and using the following accounting techniques:

*   the use of an opening trial balance, or a statement of assets and liabilities
*   the construction of a cash account and/or a bank account
*   the use of control accounts (also known as totals accounts) – sales ledger control account and purchases ledger control account

In addition, the following may be of use:

*   the accounting equation (assets – liabilities = capital)
*   gross profit mark-up and margin (see page 29)
*   the format of the income statement and balance sheet

The two Worked Examples make use of these accounting techniques, although it should be emphasised that no two incomplete records situations are the same; however practice will help to develop your skills in this aspect of accounting.

WORKED EXAMPLE: JAYNE PERRY – STATIONERY SUPPLIES

situation

The following information has been taken from the incomplete records of Jayne Perry, who runs a small stationery supplies business.

LIST OF ASSETS AND LIABILITIES		
	1 Jan 20-4	31 Dec 20-4
	£	£
Shop fittings	8,000	8,000
Inventory	25,600	29,800
Trade receivables	29,200	20,400
Bank balance	5,000	not known
Trade payables	20,800	16,000
Expenses owing	200	300

BANK SUMMARY FOR 20-4	
	£
Receipts from trade receivables	127,800
Payments to trade payables	82,600
Drawings	12,500
Expenses	30,600

solution

In the text which follows we shall see how Jayne Perry's accountant will construct the final accounts for 20-4 from incomplete records. The information to be calculated is:

- opening capital, at the beginning of the financial year
- cash book summary for the year
- purchases and sales for the year
- profit for the year
- year end balance sheet

OPENING CAPITAL

the statement of affairs

Opening capital is needed in Jayne Perry's case because a year end balance sheet is to be prepared. In other situations with incomplete records, opening capital may be stated, being the difference between assets and liabilities. To calculate the capital at the beginning of the financial year, we use the formula *assets – liabilities = capital.*

This is presented in a *statement of affairs* as follows:

	£	£
JAYNE PERRY		
STATEMENT OF AFFAIRS AS AT 1 JANUARY 20-4		
Assets		
Shop fittings		8,000
Inventory		25,600
Trade receivables		29,200
Bank balance		5,000
		67,800
Less Liabilities		
Trade payables	20,800	
Expenses owing	200	
		21,000
Capital at 1 January 20-4		46,800

Notes:

• Here, the bank balance is an asset, ie money in the bank; if it was marked as an overdraft, it would be included amongst the liabilities.

• Look out for the opening bank balance or overdraft being stated elsewhere in the information; for example, a bank summary may be given which starts with the bank figure at the beginning of the year – this figure must be included in the statement of affairs, which is used to calculate opening capital.

changes in capital over time

A statement of affairs can be used to calculate capital at the start of the year, as above. It can also be used to calculate capital at the end of the year (or at any other time). The change in capital over time shows the amount of profit or loss of the business after the owner has taken out any drawings.

For example, in the statement of affairs above, Jayne Perry's capital at 1 January 20-4 is calculated at £46,800. If her capital at 31 December 20-4 is calculated from a statement of affairs to be £49,000, then we can say that her retained profit for the year is:

	£
capital at start of year	46,800
capital at end of year	49,000
retained profit for year after drawings	2,200

If we then know that Jayne Perry's drawings for the year were £12,500, we can say that the profit for the year of her business was £2,200 + £12,500 = £14,700. Later on we will see from Jayne Perry's income statement (page 22) that £14,700 is her profit for the year.

Remember that changes in capital over time can indicate either a profit or a loss – a fall in the value of capital would show that the business has made a loss. Don't forget to allow for drawings taken by the owner to get to the profit or loss figure for the year.

CASH BOOK SUMMARY

A cash book summary enables us to find out the cash and bank balances at the year-end. (Sometimes this is not necessary, as a cash book may have been prepared already by the owner of the business.) In practice, the entries on the firm's bank statement can be used to produce a summary of receipts and payments for the year. In the case of Jayne Perry's business, the cash book (bank columns) are:

Dr		Cash Book (bank columns)		Cr
20-4	£	20-4		£
1 Jan Balance b/d	5,000	Payments to trade payables		82,600
Receipts from trade receivables	127,800	Drawings		12,500
		Expenses		30,600
		31 Dec Balance c/d		7,100
	132,800	*missing figure*		132,800
20-5		20-5		
1 Jan Balance b/d	7,100			

The bank balance of £7,100 on 31 December 20-4 is calculated by filling in the missing figure.

Notes:

- When preparing a cash book summary, look out for an opening bank balance that is *overdrawn*; this is entered on the credit side.

- At the end of the cash book summary, a credit balance brought down is an overdraft.

- In some incomplete records questions a cash book with cash columns may be needed.

Purchases and Sales

In calculating purchases and sales, we need to take note of the trade payables and trade receivables at both the beginning and the end of the year. The important point to note is that payments to trade payables are *not* the same as purchases for the year (because of the change in the level of trade payables). Likewise, receipts from trade receivables are not the same as sales (because of the change in trade receivables). Only in a business which trades solely on cash terms and has no trade receivables/trade payables would the receipts and payments be the figures for sales and purchases.

calculating purchases and sales

The method of calculating the purchases and sales figures is:

- **purchases for year** = payments to trade payables in year, *less* trade payables at the beginning of the year, *plus* trade payables at the end of the year

- **sales for year** = receipts from trade receivables in year, *less* trade receivables at the beginning of the year, *plus* trade receivables at the end of the year

When calculating purchases and sales, also take note of any cash discounts received and allowed, and – for sales – bad debts written off.

The figures from Jayne Perry's business are:

purchases	= £82,600 - £20,800 + £16,000	= £77,800
sales	= £127,800 - £29,200 + £20,400	= £119,000

use of control accounts

The use of control accounts (or total accounts) is recommended for calculating purchases and sales in incomplete records questions. We can use the information for purchases given in the Worked Example as follows:

Dr			Purchases Ledger Control Account			Cr
20-4		£	**20-4**			£
	Payments to trade payables	82,600	1 Jan	Balance b/d		20,800
31 Dec	Balance c/d	16,000		Purchases *(missing figure)*		?
		98,600				98,600
20-5			**20-5**			
			1 Jan	Balance b/d		16,000

The missing figure of purchases for the year is calculated as:

£98,600 – £20,800 = £77,800

In a similar way, the sales figure can be calculated:

Dr		Sales Ledger Control Account		Cr
20-4	£	**20-4**		£
1 Jan Balance b/d	29,200	Receipts from trade receivables		127,800
Sales (missing figure)	?	31 Dec Balance c/d		20,400
	148,200			148,200
20-5		**20-5**		
1 Jan Balance b/d	20,400			

The missing figure of sales for the year is £148,200 – £29,200 = £119,000

The control account method – which may be called for in examination questions – does bring a discipline to calculating the two important figures of purchases and sales. Do not forget that the control accounts give the figures for *credit* purchases and sales: *cash* purchases and sales need to be added, where applicable, to obtain total purchases and sales for the year.

purchases and sales – summary

Whichever method of calculating purchases or sales is used – calculation, or a control account – four pieces of information are usually required:

- opening balance
- closing balance
- payments or receipts for the year
- purchases or sales for the year

Provided that any three are known, the fourth can be calculated – the figure for purchases and sales was the missing figure in the examples above. However if, for example, we know the opening and closing trade receivables totals, together with sales for the year, then it is a simple matter to calculate the missing figure for receipts from trade receivables.

Remember that, if they are applicable, cash discounts allowed and received, and – for sales – bad debts written off, should also be incorporated into the control accounts.

PREPARATION OF THE FINAL ACCOUNTS

income statement

Having calculated the figures for purchases and sales, we can now prepare the income statement. The section as far as gross profit is:

JAYNE PERRY

INCOME STATEMENT FOR THE YEAR ENDED 31 DECEMBER 20-4

	£	£
Revenue (Sales)		119,000
Opening inventory	25,600	
Purchases	77,800	
	103,400	
Less Closing inventory	29,800	
Cost of sales		73,600
Gross profit		45,400

The expenses (overheads) section of the income statement follows but, before we are able to complete this, we need to know the figure for expenses for the year. The relevant information from the Worked Example is:

- bank payments for expenses during year, £30,600
- expenses owing at 1 January 20-4, £200
- expenses owing at 31 December 20-4, £300

Like the calculation of purchases and sales, we cannot simply use the bank payments figure for expenses; we must take note of cash payments, together with accruals and prepayments. The calculation is:

> **expenses for year** = bank and cash payments, less accruals/plus prepayments at beginning of year, plus accruals/less prepayments at end of year

Thus the figure for Jayne Perry's business expenses is:

> £30,600 – £200 + £300 = £30,700.

Alternatively, expenses can be calculated by means of a control account:

Dr			**Expenses Control Account**			Cr
20-4		£	20-4			£
	Cash/bank	30,600	1 Jan	Balance b/d		200
31 Dec	Balance c/d	300	31 Dec	Income statement *(missing figure)*		?
		30,900				30,900
20-5			20-5			
			1 Jan	Balance b/d		300

The missing figure is £30,900 – £200 = £30,700

Jayne Perry's income statement concludes as follows:

	£
Gross profit	45,400
Less:	
Expenses	30,700
Profit for the year	14,700

balance sheet

The balance sheet can now be prepared using the assets and liabilities from the Worked Example.

JAYNE PERRY
BALANCE SHEET AS AT 31 DECEMBER 20-4

	£	£	£
Non-current Assets			
Shop fittings			8,000
Current Assets			
Inventory		29,800	
Trade receivables		20,400	
Bank		7,100	
		57,300	
Less Current Liabilities			
Trade payables	16,000		
Accruals	300		
		16,300	
Net Current Assets			41,000
NET ASSETS			49,000
FINANCED BY			
Capital			
Opening capital			46,800
Add Profit for the year			14,700
			61,500
Less Drawings			12,500
			49,000

WORKED EXAMPLE: ELECTROPARTS

We will now look at a more comprehensive example of incomplete records accounting. This incorporates points on depreciation and the sale of a non-current asset and concludes with the production of final accounts. You may like to work through the Worked Example before comparing your solution with the one shown.

situation

John Anstey owns a small business, Electroparts, which supplies spare parts for a wide range of electrical goods – cookers, fridges, freezers, dishwashers, etc. Most of his customers are self-employed repairers who buy parts for specific jobs from his trade counter – John allows them credit terms; some sales are made to members of the public carrying out 'do-it-yourself' repairs – these customers pay in cash at the time of sale. All purchases from suppliers are made on credit.

John does not keep a full set of accounting records; however, the following statement of affairs has been produced for the year ended 31 December 20-4:

	ELECTROPARTS		
	STATEMENT OF AFFAIRS AS AT 1 JANUARY 20-4		
		£	£
ASSETS	Property at cost	100,000	
	Less provision for depreciation	10,000	
			90,000
	Fixtures and fittings at cost	15,000	
	Less provision for depreciation	7,500	
			7,500
			97,500
	Inventory	24,400	
	Trade receivables	21,650	
	Prepayment: general expenses	140	
	Cash	250	
			46,440
	TOTAL ASSETS		143,940
LIABILITIES	Trade payables	15,950	
	Bank overdraft	12,850	
	TOTAL LIABILITIES		28,800
CAPITAL			115,140

SUMMARY OF BANK ACCOUNT (YEAR ENDED 31 DECEMBER 20-4)

	£		£
Cash sales	45,280	Balance b/d	12,850
Receipts from trade receivables	177,410	Payments to trade payables	149,620
Sale proceeds of fixtures		General expenses	17,340
and fittings	1,950	Wages	18,280
		Drawings	25,390
		Balance c/d	1,160
	224,640		224,640
Balance b/d	1,160		

other information

– On 31 December 20-4, inventory was valued at £28,400

– Depreciation is calculated at the rate of 2% on the cost of property and 10% on the cost of fixtures and fittings held at the end of the financial year. No depreciation is calculated in the year of sale/disposal

– Fixtures and fittings purchased on 1 January 20-2 for £2,500 were sold on 30 September 20-4, the purchaser paying by cheque

– The proceeds from cash sales are placed in the till and paid into the bank account at the end of the day, apart from a cash float which is retained in the till; the amount of the cash float was £250 until October, when it was increased to £500

– On 31 December 20-4, trade payables were £18,210, trade receivables were £23,840 and £210 was owing for general expenses

– During the year, bad debts of £870 have been written off

John Anstey asks you to:

1   Calculate the amount of credit sales during the year, using a control account

2   Calculate the total sales during the year, using a control account

3   Calculate the amount of purchases during the year, using a control account

4   Calculate the profit or loss on the sale of fixtures and fittings

5   Calculate the figure for general expenses to be shown in the income statement for the year ended 31 December 20-4, using a control account

6   Prepare the income statement for the year ended 31 December 20-4

7   Prepare the balance sheet at 31 December 20-4

solution

1

Dr			Sales Ledger Control Account			Cr
20-4			£	20-4		£
1 Jan	Balance b/d		21,650		Receipts from trade receivables	177,410
	Credit sales				Bad debts written off	870
	(missing figure)		180,470	31 Dec Balance c/d		23,840
			202,120			202,120
20-5				20-5		
1 Jan	Balance b/d		23,840			

2

Dr		Sales Account			Cr
20-4		£	20-4		£
31 Dec Income statement				Credit sales (see above)	180,470
(sales for year)		226,000		Cash sales (from bank)	45,280
				Increase in cash float	250
		226,000			226,000

3

Dr		Purchases Ledger Control Account			Cr
20-4		£	20-4		£
	Payments to trade payables	149,620	1 Jan Balance b/d		15,950
31 Dec	Balance c/d	18,210		Purchases	
				(missing figure)	151,880
		167,830			167,830
20-5			20-5		
			1 Jan Balance b/d		18,210

4

Profit or loss on disposal of fixtures and fittings

Depreciation per year	£250	
Number of years' depreciation	2	(20-2, 20-3; no depreciation in year of sale)
Provision for depreciation	£500	

Dr			**Disposals Account**		Cr
20-4		£	20-4		£
30 Sep	Fixtures and fittings	2,500	30 Sep	Provision for depreciation	500
			30 Sep	Bank (sale proceeds)	1,950
			31 Dec	Income statement	
				(loss on sale)	50
		2,500			2,500

5

Dr		**General Expenses Control Account**			Cr
20-4		£	20-4		£
1 Jan	Balance b/d	140	31 Dec	Income statement	
	Bank	17,340		*(missing figure)*	17,690
31 Dec	Balance c/d	210			
		17,690			17,690
20-5			20-5		
			1 Jan	Balance b/d	210

6

JOHN ANSTEY, TRADING AS 'ELECTROPARTS'
INCOME STATEMENT FOR THE YEAR ENDED 31 DECEMBER 20-4

	£	£
Revenue (Sales)		226,000
Opening inventory	24,400	
Purchases	151,880	
	176,280	
Less Closing inventory	28,400	
Cost of sales		147,880
Gross profit		78,120
Less expenses:		
General expenses	17,690	
Loss on sale of fixtures and fittings	50	
Provision for depreciation: property	2,000	
fixtures and fittings	*1,250	
Bad debts written off	870	
Wages	18,280	
		40,140
Profit for the year		37,980

*Note

Fixtures and fittings at cost on 1 January 20-4	£15,000
Less cost price of fixtures and fittings sold 30 September 20-4	£2,500
Fixtures and fittings at cost on 31 December 20-4	£12,500
Depreciation at 10%	£1,250

7

JOHN ANSTEY, TRADING AS 'ELECTROPARTS'
BALANCE SHEET AS AT 31 DECEMBER 20-4

Non-current Assets	£ Cost	£ Provision for depreciation	£ Net book value
Property	100,000	12,000	88,000
Fixtures and fittings	12,500	*8,250	4,250
	112,500	20,250	92,250
Current Assets			
Inventory		28,400	
Trade receivables		23,840	
Bank		1,160	
Cash		500	
		53,900	
Less Current Liabilities			
Trade payables	18,210		
Accrual of expenses	210		
		18,420	
Net Current Assets			35,480
NET ASSETS			127,730
FINANCED BY			
Capital			
Opening capital (from assets and liabilities at 1 January 20-4)			115,140
Add Profit for the year			37,980
			153,120
Less Drawings			25,390
			127,730

*Note	
Provision for depreciation of fixtures and fittings at 1 January 20-4	7,500
Less provision for depreciation on asset sold	500
	7,000
Depreciation for year (see income statement)	1,250
Provision for depreciation of fixtures and fittings at 31 December 20-4	8,250

The Use of Gross Profit Mark-up and Margin

It is often necessary to use accounting ratios and percentages in the preparation of final accounts from incomplete records. The topic of ratios and percentages has already been covered in your studies in AS Accounting.

The two main percentages used for incomplete records accounting are:

- gross profit mark-up
- gross profit margin

It is quite common for a business to establish its selling price by reference to either a mark-up or a margin. The difference between the two is that:

- mark-up is a profit percentage added to *buying* or *cost* price
- margin is a percentage profit based on the *selling* price

For example, a product is bought by a retailer at a cost of £100; the retailer sells it for £125, ie

$$\text{cost price} + \text{gross profit} = \text{selling price}$$

$$£100 + £25 = £125$$

The **mark-up** is:

$$\frac{\text{gross profit}}{\text{cost price}} \times \frac{100}{1} = \frac{£25}{£100} \times \frac{100}{1} = \mathbf{25\%}$$

The **margin** is:

$$\frac{\text{gross profit}}{\text{selling price}} \times \frac{100}{1} = \frac{£25}{£125} \times \frac{100}{1} = \mathbf{20\%}$$

In incomplete records accounting, mark-up or the margin percentages can be used in a range of circumstances, as shown by the examples, below.

WORKED EXAMPLE: USING MARGINS AND MARK-UPS

example 1 - calculation of sales

- Cost of sales is £150,000
- Mark-up is 40%
- What is the sales amount?

Gross profit $= £150,000 \times \dfrac{40}{100} = £60,000$

Sales = cost of sales + gross profit, ie £150,000 + £60,000 = **£210,000**

example 2 – calculation of purchases

- Sales are £450,000
- Margin is 20%
- Opening inventory is £40,000; closing inventory is £50,000
- What is the purchases amount?

Gross profit $= £450,000 \times \dfrac{20}{100} = £90,000$

Cost of sales = sales – gross profit, ie £450,000 – £90,000 = £360,000

The purchases calculation is:

Opening inventory	£40,000
+ Purchases (missing figure)	?
– Closing inventory	£50,000
= Cost of sales	£360,000
Purchases =	**£370,000**

example 3 – converting from a mark-up to a margin

- Mark-up is 50%
- What is the margin?

Margin $= \dfrac{\text{mark-up \%}}{100 + \text{mark-up \%}} \times \dfrac{100}{1}$

$= \dfrac{50}{100 + 50} \times \dfrac{100}{1} =$ **33.33% margin**

example 4 – converting from a margin to a mark-up

- Margin is 33.33%
- What is the mark-up?

Mark-up $= \dfrac{\text{margin \%}}{100 - \text{margin \%}} \times \dfrac{100}{1}$

$= \dfrac{33.33}{100 - 33.33} \times \dfrac{100}{1} =$ **50% mark-up**

example 5 – late calculation of closing inventory

- Closing inventory was valued at £22,350 on 5 January, five days after the end of the financial year.
- For the period 1-5 January:

	£
sales	1,680
sales returns	175
purchases	970
purchases returns	55
goods taken for own use (valued at selling price)	42
goods stolen on 4 January (valued at selling price)	154

- Mark-up is 40%
- What was the value of closing inventory at the end of the financial year on 31 December?

		£
Inventory at 31 December		?
– sales at cost price	1,680 ÷ 1.4	1,200
+ sales returns at cost price	175 ÷ 1.4	125
+ purchases		970
– purchases returns		55
– owner's drawings at cost price	42 ÷ 1.4	30
– goods stolen at cost price	154 ÷ 1.4	110
Inventory valuation at 5 January		22,350

start your calculation here and then work upwards

By working up the calculation (adding the minuses and deducting the pluses), the inventory valuation at 31 December is found to be **£22,650**.

Notes:

- Any items at selling price must be brought back to cost price – here dividing by 1.4, ie 1.00 + 0.40 mark-up = 1.4.
- Items to adjust in this way are sales and sales returns and, where stated at selling price, owner's drawings and goods stolen.
- The effect on gross profit of a change in the valuation of inventory is summarised by the following rules:

  higher closing inventory = higher gross profit

  lower closing inventory = lower gross profit

This is because closing inventory is deducted from opening inventory and purchases to calculate cost of sales: an increase in the value of closing inventory reduces cost of sales which increases gross profit; a decrease in the value of closing inventory increases cost of sales which reduces gross profit.

CASH LOSSES

A cash loss may occur simply as a result of poor cash-handling procedures (eg by not banking cash regularly) or, more seriously, as a result of theft. The value of cash losses can be calculated either by preparing a cash book summary and/or using margins and mark-ups to work out how much cash should have been received. The Worked Example which follows shows the calculations of cash losses in two common situations.

WORKED EXAMPLE: CASH LOSSES

example 1 – cash book summary

There was a theft of cash from a business on 30 January. From the following information, calculate how much cash was stolen.

	£
Cash balance at 1 January	1,056
Cash balance at 31 January	955
Cash sales for January	12,112
Cash paid into bank in January	9,648
Expenses paid from cash in January	2,235

A summarised cash account is prepared for January:

Dr		£		Cash Account	Cr £
1 Jan	Balance b/d	1,056		Bank	9,648
	Cash sales	12,112		Expenses	2,235
			31 Jan	Balance c/d	955
			31 Jan	Amount of cash stolen	
				(missing figure)	330
		13,168			13,168
1 Feb	Balance b/d	955			

By preparing a summarised cash book and filling in the missing figure, the amount of cash stolen on 30 January is found to be **£330**.

example 2 – margins and mark-ups

The owner of a business thinks that some cash has been stolen during the month of April. From the following information, calculate how much cash was stolen.

- A mark-up of 50% is used for all goods.
- All takings are banked at the end of each day.
- The following figures are available:

	£
Inventory at 1 April	1,550
Inventory at 30 April	1,790
Purchases for April	4,560
Trade receivables at 1 April	2,075
Trade receivables at 30 April	2,695
Cash paid into bank in April	5,270

Step 1 Calculating cost of sales, gross profit and sales

	£
Opening inventory	1,550
Purchases	4,560
	6,110
Less Closing inventory	1,790
Cost of sales	4,320
Gross profit at mark-up of 50%	2,160
Sales	6,480

Note: the mark-up is applied to cost of sales rather than purchases.

Step 2 Using a sales ledger control account

Dr		Sales Ledger Control Account				Cr
		£				£
1 Apr	Balance b/d	2,075		Bank *(missing figure)*	5,860
	Sales	6,480	30 Apr	Balance c/d	2,695
		8,555			8,555
1 May	Balance b/d	2,695			

Step 3 Calculating the cash loss

	£
Cash expected to be banked (from control account)	5,860
Cash actually banked	5,270
Cash loss	**590**

measures to prevent cash losses

- maintaining accurate records of cash transactions
  - keeping a detailed cash book
  - keeping a copy of all cash receipts issued
  - use of a numbering system for all receipts and invoices
  - preparation of a bank reconciliation statement each time a bank statement is received
  - using margin and/or mark-up to compare expected sales with actual sales figures
- office procedures
  - recording cash transactions as they occur, eg by using tills that issue receipts
  - collecting cash from tills regularly, and placing the cash in a safe in the office
  - banking cash regularly, so that there is a low level of cash on the premises at any time
  - paying bills by cheque or bank transfer rather than in cash, so avoiding the need to carry cash when paying trade payables
  - dividing duties within the business, ensuring that no one person is responsible for all cash handling
  - carrying out cash checks at regular intervals, eg to ensure that the cash in tills balances against receipts
  - improving security, eg use of a safe in the office for cash to be banked, keeping the office door locked when the office is empty, use of security cameras
  - checking references for new employees
  - setting authorisation limits for employees who pay bills, to ensure that large amounts cannot be paid out by newer employees

INVENTORY LOSSES

A loss of inventory may occur as a result of an event such as a fire, a flood or a theft. When such a loss occurs, an estimate of the value of the inventory lost needs to be made in order for the business to make an insurance claim (always assuming that the inventory was adequately insured). The value is calculated by preparing an accounting summary to the date of the event, and often making use of margins and mark-ups. The calculations are best carried out in three steps:

1.	Opening inventory	
	+	Purchases
	=	Cost of inventory available for sale
2.	Sales	
	–	Gross profit (using normal gross profit margin)
	=	Cost of sales
3.	Cost of inventory available for sale (from 1, above)	
	–	Cost of sales (2, above)
	=	Estimated closing inventory
	–	Value of inventory remaining or salvaged
	=	Value of inventory lost through fire, flood or theft

WORKED EXAMPLE: CLOTHING SUPPLIES – THEFT OF INVENTORY

situation

Peter Kamara runs Clothing Supplies, a small clothing wholesalers. Peter is convinced that various items of clothing have been stolen during the year and he asks you to calculate, from the accounting details, the value of inventory stolen. The following information is available:

- sales for the year, £500,000
- opening inventory at the beginning of the year, £15,000
- purchases for the year, £310,000
- closing inventory at the end of the year, £22,000
- the gross profit margin achieved on all sales is 40 per cent

solution

CALCULATION OF INVENTORY LOSS FOR THE YEAR		
	£	£
Opening inventory		15,000
Purchases		310,000
Cost of inventory available for sale		325,000
Sales	500,000	
Less Normal gross profit margin (40%)	200,000	
Cost of sales		300,000
Estimated closing inventory		25,000
Less Actual closing inventory		22,000
Value of inventory loss		3,000

measures to prevent inventory losses

- maintaining accurate records of inventory transactions
  - using stores ledger records/inventory cards (see Chapter 8) for each inventory line
  - keeping a copy of all inventory receipts and issues documents
  - keeping records for the disposal of damaged inventory
  - carrying out inventory counts, either on a periodic or continuous basis (see Chapter 8)

- office procedures
  - improving security, eg controlling access to the inventory and inventory records
  - carrying out inventory reconciliations to compare the information from the inventory count with the inventory records
  - ensuring that discrepancies in inventory reconciliation are referred to the company's managers and any other people who may need to know, eg the firm's auditors
  - setting authorisation limits for the disposal of damaged inventory and the write-off of inventory discrepancies

DRAWBACKS OF INCOMPLETE RECORDS

Whilst the use of a double-entry system is the preferred way to keep business accounting records, there are many smaller businesses that choose to pay an accountant to sort out their incomplete records. The availability of cheap accounting software may encourage some businesses to switch to double-entry accounts, but there will still be a role for the accountant in the preparation of final accounts and especially to deal with the tax authorities. It is also true that many people, and often those setting up in business for the first time, have little understanding of the way to keep accounting records – hence the approach of incomplete records used in this chapter.

The main drawbacks of maintaining incomplete records include:

- cost – because it is time-consuming, an accountant usually charges more to prepare final accounts from incomplete records than from records kept using double-entry
- lack of up-to-date management information – details are not readily available of such things as trade receivables (how much are we owed?), bank (what is the bank balance?), sales (what have we sold this month?), expenses (how much have we spent on fuel for the vehicles this month?), etc
- statements of account sent to trade receivables may not be completely accurate – this will also make chasing payments from trade receivables difficult
- dangers of loss or theft of cash and inventory – may be difficult to verify if the accounting records are not up-to-date

- there may be a lack of accuracy – a number of amounts, such as sales and purchases, are calculated by means of a missing figure; there may be other items that should be included in the calculations

- additional costs may be incurred – eg the costs of obtaining duplicate bank statements and paid cheques from the bank

- reliability of figures may be questioned – eg by lenders and the tax authorities' (both for income tax and Value Added Tax) lack of independent verification (double-check) of figures – the assumption with incomplete records is that if something has been calculated, then it must be correct

- items may be missed from the final accounts – eg an asset or liability from the balance sheet

COMMENTING ON YEAR END FINANCIAL STATEMENTS

From time-to-time examination questions will ask you, after you have prepared financial statements from incomplete records, to make comments on the figures, or give advice to the owner of the business or other interested party. Questions asked can include a commentary on the profitability, liquidity and capital structure of the business. To answer these, you will need to make use of accounting ratios learned in AS Accounting, eg profit margins, return on capital employed, net current asset and liquid capital ratios, etc.

Be ready to make comparisons from one year to the next in order to indicate a trend – eg falling profitability, increasing expenses (overheads) – and to suggest ways in which adverse trends can be corrected – eg by increasing sales/sales prices, keeping a tight rein on expenses. Also, be prepared to make comparisons between two businesses – eg to compare the business whose financial statements you have prepared with those of a rival business, or with an industry average.

The owner of the business may seek advice such as, 'should I expand the business?'; if so, how should I finance the expansion?'; or, 'should I consider selling the business and retiring?' Make sure that the advice you give is backed up with financial figures – eg if the owner is thinking of selling up and retiring, see how much profit the business is currently making and compare this with the interest that could be earned from investing the sale proceeds in a savings account. For a business which is seeking to expand, you will need to suggest appropriate sources of finance – eg a bank overdraft or loan.

As always, with any 'commentary' question, ensure you finish with a conclusion that summarises your findings.

CHAPTER SUMMARY

○ Incomplete records is the term used where the book-keeping system does not follow double-entry principles.

○ In order to prepare final accounts, the accountant may well have to calculate:
- capital at the beginning of the financial year, using a statement of affairs
- purchases and sales for the year
- cash book summary
- profit for the year

○ The change in capital over time shows the profit or loss of the business after the owner has taken out any drawings.

○ On the basis of these calculations, the accountant can then construct the final accounts without recourse to a trial balance.

○ Two ratios and percentages used in incomplete records accounting are:
- gross profit mark-up, which is the profit percentage added to the buying price
- gross profit margin, which is the profit percentage based on the selling price

○ The value of cash losses and inventory losses may be calculated using margins and mark-ups.

○ The main drawbacks of maintaining incomplete records include:
- cost of accountant's time
- lack of up-to-date management information
- statements sent to trade receivables may be inaccurate
- dangers of loss or theft of cash and inventory
- lack of accuracy
- additional costs may be incurred
- reliability of the figures may be questioned
- lack of independent verification
- items may be missed from the final accounts

○ Commenting on year end financial statements prepared from incomplete records will often include consideration of the profitability, liquidity and capital structure of the business.

In the next chapter we will turn our attention to the year-end accounts of partnerships.

QUESTIONS

visit
www.osbornebooks.co.uk
to take an online test

An asterisk (*) after the question number means that the answer is given at the end of this book.

2.1* • Cost of sales for the year is £200,000.

• Mark-up is 30%.

What are sales for the year?

2.2 • Sales for the year are £100,000.

• Gross profit margin is 25%.

• Opening inventory is £10,000; closing inventory is £12,000.

What are purchases for the year?

2.3* You are preparing accounts from incomplete records. Trade receivables at the start of the year were £2,500, and at the end were £3,250. Cheques received from trade receivables total £17,850; cash sales total £2,500. What is the sales figure for the year?

2.4* James Harvey runs a stationery supplies shop. He is convinced that one of his employees is stealing stationery. He asks you to calculate from the accounting records the value of inventory stolen. The following information is available for the year ended 30 June 20-8:

• sales for the year, £180,000

• opening inventory at the beginning of the year, £21,500

• purchases for the year, £132,000

• closing inventory at the end of the year, £26,000

• the gross profit margin achieved on all sales is 30 per cent

You are to calculate the value of inventory stolen (if any) during the year ended 30 June 20-8.

2.5 Talib Zabbar owns a shop selling children's clothes. He is convinced that his customers are stealing goods from the shop. He asks you to calculate from the accounting records the value of inventory stolen.

The following information is available for the year ended 30 September 20-7:

• sales for the year, £160,000

• opening inventory at the beginning of the year, £30,500

• purchases for the year, £89,500

• closing inventory at the end of the year, £21,500

• the gross profit margin achieved on all sales is 40 per cent

You are to calculate the value of inventory stolen (if any) during the year ended 30 September 20-7.

2.6* Mary owns an electrical goods shop. Her goods are marked up by 40%. She was unable to value her inventory at the financial year end on 31 December 2006. However, she was able to take inventory on 8 January 2007 and she valued it at £14,569.

In the period 1 January - 8 January 2007 the following transactions took place.

	£
Sales	2,429
Purchases	1,320
Sales returns	350
Purchases returns	56
Goods for own use (valued at selling price)	84
Goods stolen on 7 January 2007 (valued at selling price)	322

REQUIRED

(a)   Calculate the value of inventory at 31 December 2006.

Mary had estimated her inventory value at 31 December 2006 at £12,000.

She used this figure to calculate her gross profit at £168,530.

REQUIRED

(b)   Calculate the correct gross profit.

Assessment and Qualifications Alliance (AQA), Specimen Paper for 2010

2.7 Pat Parker is a butcher. She marks up all goods sold in her shop by 100%. All takings are banked each evening after the shop is closed.

During the year ended 31 December 2004, £93,322 was banked. Pat believes that some cash is missing from the till on 31 December 2004. She is unable to determine the exact amount but provides the following information.

	£
Inventory at 1 January 2004	890
Inventory at 31 December 2004	950
Purchases	46,753
Trade receivables at 1 January 2004	2,786
Trade receivables at 31 December 2004	2,640

REQUIRED

Calculate the amount of cash missing from the till on 31 December 2004.

Assessment and Qualifications Alliance (AQA), 2005

2.8　Gordon McGuire does not keep a full set of accounting records for his business. On Saturday 29 May 2004, two days before his financial year-end, an amount of cash was stolen from the business.

Gordon provides you with the following information.

	£
Cash balance at 1 June 2003	229
Cash balance at 31 May 2004	160
Cash sales for the year	219,941
Cash paid into bank during the year	165,640
Expenses paid by cash	49,600

REQUIRED

(a)　Prepare a summarised cash account showing clearly the amount of cash stolen on 29 May 2004.

(b)　Advise Gordon on **two** measures he could use to prevent such a loss occurring in the future.

(c)　Advise Gordon on **two** ways to maintain accurate records of cash transactions.

Assessment and Qualifications Alliance (AQA), 2004

2.9*　Jane Price owns a fashion shop called 'Trendsetters'. She has been in business for one year and, although she does not keep a full set of accounting records, the following information has been produced for the first year of trading, which ended on 31 December 20-4:

Summary of the business bank account for the year ended 31 December 20-4:

	£
Capital introduced	60,000
Receipts from trade receivables	153,500
Payments to trade payables	95,000
Advertising	4,830
Wages	15,000
Rent	8,750
General expenses	5,000
Shop fittings	50,000
Drawings	15,020

Summary of assets and liabilities as at 31 December 20-4:

	£
Shop fittings at cost	50,000
Inventory	73,900
Trade receivables	2,500
Trade payables	65,000

Other information:

* Jane wishes to depreciate the shop fittings at 20% per year using the straight-line method
* At 31 December 20-4, rent is prepaid by £250, and wages of £550 are owing

You are to:

(a) Calculate the amount of sales during the year.

(b) Calculate the amount of purchases during the year.

(c) Calculate the figures for:

  * rent

  * wages

  to be shown in the income statement for the year ended 31 December 20-4

(d) Prepare Jane Price's income statement for the year ended 31 December 20-4.

(e) Prepare Jane Price's balance sheet at 31 December 20-4.

2.10 Colin Smith owns a business which sells specialist central heating parts to trade customers. He has been in business for a number of years. Although he does not keep a full set of accounting records, the following information is available in respect of the year ended 30 June 20-5:

Summary of assets and liabilities:

	1 July 20-4	30 June 20-5
	£	£
Assets		
Inventory	25,000	27,500
Fixtures and fittings (cost £50,000)	40,000	35,000
Trade receivables	36,000	35,000
Bank	1,500	1,210
Liabilities		
Trade payables	32,500	30,000
Accrual: expenses	500	700

Summary of the business bank account for the year ended 30 June 20-5:

	£
Expenses	30,000
Drawings	28,790
Receipts from trade receivables	121,000
Payments to trade payables	62,500

Other information:

- Fixtures and fittings are being depreciated at 10% per year using the straight line method
- Bad debts of £550 have been written off during the year

You are to:

(a)   Calculate the amount of sales during the year ended 30 June 20-5

(b)   Calculate the amount of purchases during the year ended 30 June 20-5

(c)   Calculate the figure for expenses to be shown in the income statement for the year ended 30 June 20-5

(d)   Prepare Colin Smith's income statement for the year ended 30 June 20-5

(e)   Prepare Colin Smith's balance sheet at 30 June 20-5

2.11   Sandrine does not keep proper books of account. She is able to provide the following information for the year ended 31 December 2006 (see next page):

Summarised Cash Book

	Cash	Bank		Cash	Bank
Balance b/d 1 January 2006	170		Balance b/d 1 January 2006		3,190
Receipts from trade receivables	163,729		Bank	133,130	
Cash		133,130	Payment to trade payables	720	61,700
Cash sales	65,324		Bank	24,000	
Cash		24,000	Wages	57,200	
Sale of equipment	1,200		Motor expenses		7,920
			General expenses	7,963	
			Motor vehicle		22,000
			Drawings	7,100	35,440
			Private holiday		2,400
			Loan repayment		30,000
			Loan interest		2,500
Balance c/d		8,020	Balance c/d	310	
	230,423	165,150		230,423	165,150
Balance b/d	310		Balance b/d		8,020

Additional information

(1) Assets and liabilities

	at 1 January 2006 £	at 31 December 2006 £
Inventory	4,987	5,038
Trade receivables	3,746	2,988
Trade payables	1,822	2,196
Wages owing	796	–
Loan interest paid in advance	500	–
Equipment at net book value	20,000	13,500
Vehicles at net book value	26,000	?

(2) No equipment was purchased during the year; equipment with a net book value of £5,000 was sold during the year.

(3) There were no disposals of vehicles during the year.

(4) Depreciation on vehicles is to be provided using the reducing balance method on year end balances of 25%.

REQUIRED

Using the information above, prepare an income statement for Sandrine for the year ended 31 December 2006. (A balance sheet is **not** required.)

Assessment and Qualifications Alliance (AQA), Specimen Paper for 2010

2.12* Michael Wong is the proprietor of a retail gift shop. He has one outlet and a small warehouse where he keeps his inventory.

Michael does not keep full accounting records, but he is able to provide the following information for the year ended 31 March 2006.

Summarised Bank Account for the year ended 31 March 2006

	£		£
1 April 2005 Balance b/fwd	784	Payments to trade payables	178,943
Cash banked	253,641	Warehouse rent	7,800
Received from trade receivables	2,356	Advertising and wrapping materials	12,340
		Rates and insurances	11,870
		Purchase of vehicle	30,000
		Motor expenses	12,659
31 March 2006 Balance c/fwd	4,393	General expenses	7,562
	261,174		261,174
		1 April 2006 Balance b/fwd	4,393

Additional Information

(1) Assets and liabilities

	at 1 April 2005	at 31 March 2006
	£	£
Property	103,600	100,800
Fixtures and fittings	12,000	10,000
Vehicles	20,000	28,500
Inventory	4,562	4,328
Trade payables	12,403	11,987
Trade receivables	458	476
Warehouse rent unpaid	700	–
Insurances paid in advance	760	840
Cash at bank	784	–
Bank overdraft	–	4,393
Cash in hand	260	320

(2) During March 2006, one of the vehicles, with a value of £12,000, was involved in an accident. The vehicle and all of the goods being carried in the vehicle had to be written off. The goods had cost £1,560.

The insurance company agreed to pay £7,200 for the loss of the vehicle; the payment was made at the end of April 2006.

Unfortunately, Michael was not insured for the loss of the goods.

(3)   On 1 September 2005, a new vehicle was purchased for £30,000.

(4)   Before paying the shop takings into the bank account, Michael used some of the cash received to pay the following.

	£
Cash for personal use	1,500 per calendar month
Staff wages	2,650 per calendar month

(5)   During December 2005, Michael took goods costing £368 to give as Christmas presents to his friends and relatives.

REQUIRED

(a)   Prepare the following accounts for the year ended 31 March 2006:
    (i)   a cash account;
    (ii)   a total trade receivables account (control account);
    (iii)   a total trade payables account (control account);
    (iv)   a vehicles account.

(b)   Prepare an income statement for the year ended 31 March 2006.

Over the past few years, there has been a growth in the number of retail outlets selling similar goods to those sold by Michael. As a result, Michael's profitability has been declining. This is shown in the following table.

Year ended 31 March	2003	2004	2005
Gross margin	45%	44%	44%
Net margin	19%	15%	14%

Michael, who is 62 years of age, is considering whether or not the time has come for him to sell his business and retire. An estate agent has recently valued the business and believes that it could be sold as a going concern for £150,000.

REQUIRED

(c)   Advise Michael whether or not he should sell his business and retire.
    Use ratios where appropriate to support your argument.

Assessment and Qualifications Alliance (AQA), 2006

2.13   *Tutorial note: This question incorporates aspects of AS Accounting into incomplete records.*

Cindy Tofe does not keep proper books of account. However, she keeps an accurate record of cash and bank transactions, except for personal drawings, in a cash book. She is able to provide the following information for the year ended 31 December 2005:

Assets and liabilities	at 1 January 2005	at 31 December 2005
	£	£
Equipment	24,000	20,000
Vehicles	60,000	56,000
Inventory	2,998	?
Trade receivables	6,546	7,219
Trade payables	5,982	5,433
Cash at bank	1,726	?
Cash in hand	142	169
Interest-free long-term loan	–	15,000
Rent paid in advance	160	420
Wages owing	831	762

Cindy has drawn a cheque from the bank each week for her own personal use. She is unsure of the exact amount withdrawn over the year, but she believes it to be between £17,000 and £18,000. All other bank transactions have been recorded accurately.

Cindy provides the following summary of her business bank transactions during the year ended 31 December 2005:

	£		£
Cash and cheques banked	186,784	General expenses	1,604
Loan from parent	15,000	Wages	23,110
(interest-free, to be repaid 2011)		Drawings	?
		New vehicle	13,500
		Payments to trade payables	142,911
		Rent	4,940
Total receipts	201,784	Total withdrawals except drawings	186,065

At the end of the financial year, the bank statement received from Cindy's bank showed that she was overdrawn by £668. Cindy knows there was an unpresented cheque for £291. She has also noted that takings of £1,084, paid into the bank on 31 December 2005, did not appear on the bank statement.

REQUIRED

(a) Prepare a bank reconciliation statement to determine the bank balance as per Cindy's cash book at 31 December 2005.

(b) Calculate the amount of Cindy's drawings from her bank account.

(c)

Cindy was unable to carry out an inventory count on 31 December 2005 because of illness. The inventory count was completed on 8 January 2006, when the inventory was valued at £2,986.

The following transactions took place in the period 1 January 2006 to the close of business on 7 January 2006:

	£
Purchases of goods for resale	1,036
Purchases returns	140
Sales (marked up by 40%)	2,520
Sales returns (marked up by 40%)	504
Sale to Frank Fearless, a fellow trader, at cost plus 10%	858

REQUIRED

Calculate the value of inventory at 31 December 2005.

(d)

During the year ended 31 December 2005, vehicle ZT52 SMH, book value £12,000, was accepted by Foxhall's garage in part exchange for a new vehicle PQ55 JJH costing £25,000. Cindy paid £13,500 by cheque.

REQUIRED

Calculate the profit or loss on disposal of vehicle ZT52 SMH.

(e)   Before banking her takings, Cindy paid £11,022 in cash during the year for the following:

	£
Motor expenses	3,040
General expenses	5,162
Cash purchases	740
Her own private use	2,080

REQUIRED

Prepare an income statement for the year ended 31 December 2005.

A balance sheet is **not** required.

Assessment and Qualifications Alliance (AQA), 2006

3 PARTNERSHIP FINAL ACCOUNTS

Partnerships, which were considered briefly as a type of business organisation in AS Accounting, can be found in the form of:

- sole traders who have joined together with others in order to raise finance and expand the business
- family businesses, such as builders, car repairers, gardeners
- professional firms such as solicitors, accountants, doctors, dentists

In this chapter we examine:

- the definition of a partnership
- the accounting requirements of the Partnership Act 1890
- the accounting requirements which may be incorporated into a partnership agreement
- the use of capital accounts and current accounts
- the appropriation of profits
- the layout of the capital section of the balance sheet
- the preparation of partnership final accounts from a trial balance

WHAT DOES A PARTNERSHIP INVOLVE?

The Partnership Act of 1890 defines a partnership as:

the relation which subsists between persons carrying on a business in common with a view of profit

Normally, partnerships consist of between two and twenty partners. Exceptions to this include large professional firms, eg solicitors and accountants, who sometimes set up what are known as 'limited liability partnerships' (LLPs). Partnerships are often larger businesses than sole traders because, as there is more than one owner, there is likely to be more capital. A partnership may be formed to set up a new business or it may be the logical growth of a sole trader taking in partners to increase the capital.

advantages and disadvantages

Partnerships are cheap and easy to set up; their advantages are:

- there is the possibility of increased capital
- individual partners may be able to specialise in particular areas of the business
- with more people running the business, there is more cover for illness and holidays

The disadvantages are:

- as there is more than one owner, decisions may take longer because other partners may need to be consulted
- there may be disagreements amongst the partners
- each partner is liable in law for the dealings and business debts of the *whole* firm – unless it is a 'limited liability partnership' (LLP) set up under the Limited Liability Partnerships Act 2000
- the retirement or death of one partner may adversely affect the running of the business

accounting requirements of a partnership

The accounting requirements of a partnership are:

- either to follow the rules set out in the Partnership Act 1890
- or – and more likely – for the partners to agree amongst themselves, by means of a partnership agreement (see page 53), to follow different accounting rules

Unless the partners agree otherwise, the Partnership Act 1890 states the following accounting rules:

- profits and losses are to be shared equally between the partners
- no partner is entitled to a salary
- partners are not entitled to receive interest on their capital
- interest is not to be charged on partners' drawings
- when a partner contributes more capital than agreed, he or she is entitled to receive interest at five per cent per annum on the excess

As noted above, the partners may well decide to follow different accounting rules – these will be set out in a partnership agreement (see page 53).

YEAR-END ACCOUNTS OF A PARTNERSHIP

A partnership prepares the same type of financial statements as a sole trader business:

- income statement
- balance sheet

The main difference is that, immediately after the income statement, follows an appropriation section (often described as a partnership appropriation account). This shows how the profit from the income statement is shared amongst the partners.

sharing profits

Ela, Fay and Gen are partners sharing profits and losses equally; for 20-4 their income statement shows a profit for the year of £60,000. The appropriation of profits appears as:

ELA, FAY AND GEN
INCOME STATEMENT APPROPRIATION ACCOUNT
FOR THE YEAR ENDED 31 DECEMBER 20-4

	£
Profit for the year	60,000
Share of profits:	
Ela	20,000
Fay	20,000
Gen	20,000
	60,000

The above is a simple appropriation of profits. A more complex appropriation account (see Worked Example on page 57) deals with other accounting points which may be included in the partnership agreement.

separate capital accounts

Each partner has a separate capital account, which operates in the same way as for a sole trader. Thus the partner's capital accounts show:

- capital introduced
- share of profits/losses
- drawings

Continuing the example of Ela, Fay and Gen (above), if each partner started the year with capital of £100,000 and drawings were £10,000 for Ela and £15,000 for Fay and Gen, the capital section of their balance sheet at 31 December 20-4 appears as:

ELA, FAY AND GEN
BALANCE SHEET (EXTRACT) AS AT 31 DECEMBER 20-4

	£	£	£	£
FINANCED BY				
Capital Accounts				
	Ela	Fay	Gen	
Opening capital	100,000	100,000	100,000	
Add Profit for the year	20,000	20,000	20,000	
	120,000	120,000	120,000	
Less Drawings	10,000	15,000	15,000	
Closing capital	110,000	105,000	105,000	320,000

Note: £320,000 is the total of all partners' capital accounts at the date of the balance sheet.

The above is a simple illustration of the use of capital accounts – in practice most partnerships use both a capital account and a current account (see page 55) to record partners' contributions to the business.

PARTNERSHIP AGREEMENT

The accounting rules from the Partnership Act are often varied with the agreement of all partners by means of a partnership agreement. A partnership agreement will usually cover the following:

- division of profits and losses between partners
- partners' salaries/commission
- whether interest is to be allowed on capital, and at what rate
- whether interest is to be charged on partners' drawings, and at what rate

The money amounts involved for each of these points (where allowed by the partnership agreement) are shown in the partnership appropriation account (see Worked Example on page 57).

division of profits and losses between partners

The Partnership Act states that, in the absence of an agreement to the contrary, profits and losses are to be shared equally. A partner's share of the profits is normally taken out of the business in the form of drawings. Clearly, if one partner has contributed much more capital than the other partner(s), it would be unfair to apply this clause from the Act. Consequently, many partnerships agree to share profits and losses on a different basis – often in the same proportions as they have contributed capital. Note that, in examination questions, you will normally be told the agreed division of profits; however, if there is no mention of this, you should assume that the partners receive an equal share.

partners' salaries/commission

Although the Act says that no partner is entitled to a salary, it is quite usual in the partnership agreement for one or more partners to be paid a salary. The reason for doing this is that often in a partnership, one of the partners spends more time working in the partnership than the other(s). The agreement to pay a salary is in recognition of the work done. Note that partners' salaries are not shown as an expense in the income statement; instead they appear in the partnership appropriation account (see the example on page 57).

Many professional partnerships, such as solicitors and accountants, have junior partners who receive a partnership salary because they work full-time in the business, but have not yet contributed any capital. In a partnership, there may not be a requirement to contribute capital, unless the partnership agreement states otherwise; however, most partners will eventually do so.

As an alternative to a salary, a partner might be paid a commission on sales. As with a salary, this is not shown as an expense in the income statement, but appears in the partnership appropriation account.

interest allowed on capital

Many partnerships include a clause in their partnership agreement which allows interest to be paid on capital; the rate of interest will be stated also. This clause is used to compensate partners for the loss of use of their capital, which is not available to invest elsewhere. Often, interest is allowed on capital in partnerships where profits and losses are shared equally – it is one way of rewarding partners for different capital balances. As noted earlier, the Partnership Act does not permit interest to be paid on capital, so reference to it must be made in the partnership agreement.

When calculating interest on capital, it may be necessary to allow for part years. For example:

1 January 20-4 capital balance	£20,000
1 July 20-4 additional capital contributed	£4,000
the rate of interest allowed on capital	10% per annum
the partnership's financial year-end	31 December 20-4

Interest allowed on capital is calculated as:

1 January - 30 June £20,000 x 10% x 6 months	£1,000
1 July - 31 December £24,000 x 10% x 6 months	£1,200
Interest allowed on capital for year	£2,200

interest charged on partners' drawings

In order to discourage partners from drawing out too much money from the business early in the financial year, the partnership agreement may stipulate that interest is to be charged on partners' drawings, and at what rate. This acts as a penalty against early withdrawal when the business may be short of cash. For example:

a partner's drawings during the year	£24,000
withdrawal at the end of each quarter (31 March, 30 June, 30 September, 31 December)	£6,000
the rate of interest charged on partners' drawings	10% per annum
the partnership's financial year-end	31 December

Interest charged on this partner's drawings is calculated as:

31 March: £6,000 x 10% x 9 months	£450
30 June: £6,000 x 10% x 6 months	£300
30 September: £6,000 x 10% x 3 months	£150
Interest charged on the partners' drawings for year	£900

No interest is charged on the withdrawal on 31 December, because it is at the end of the financial year. The amount of interest charged on drawings for the year is shown in the partnership appropriation account, where it increases the profit to be shared amongst the partners.

interest paid on loans

If a partner makes a loan to the partnership, the rate of interest to be paid needs to be agreed, otherwise the rate specified in the Partnership Act 1890 applies – five per cent per annum.

Interest on loans is charged as an expense in the income statement, and is not shown in the partnership appropriation account.

Note that, where a partner lends money to the partnership, the loan account is kept entirely separate from that partner's capital account and current account.

CAPITAL ACCOUNTS AND CURRENT ACCOUNTS

As noted previously, each partner has a separate capital account to record his or her permanent contribution to the business. Often, this will suffice for partnerships where the agreement is simply to split profits and losses equally. With more complex partnership agreements, each partner usually has both a capital account and a current account. The capital account is normally **fixed**, and only alters if a permanent increase or decrease in capital contributed by the partner takes place. The current account is **fluctuating** and it is to this account that:

- share of profit is credited
- share of loss is debited
- salary/commission is credited
- interest allowed on partners' capital is credited
- drawings and goods for own use are debited
- interest charged on partners' drawings is debited

Thus, the current account is a working account, while capital account remains fixed, except for capital introduced or withdrawn, or when changes are made to the partnership (see Chapter 4). With this arrangement the fixed capital account makes interest on capital – where permitted by the partnership agreement – easy to calculate, while at the same time shows whether or not partners are maintaining their permanent capital in the business. The fluctuating current account shows whether or not partners have withdrawn more profit from the business than they are earning. However, it should be pointed out that separate capital and current accounts require more work and are, therefore, more time-consuming for the book-keeper than using the partners' capital accounts for all transactions. As to which is used will depend on the size and complexity of the partnership business.

A partner's current account has the following layout:

Dr		Partner Aye: Current Account		Cr
	£			£
Share of loss		Balance b/d		
Drawings/goods for own use		Share of profit		
Interest charged on drawings*		Salary/commission*		
Balance c/d		Interest on capital*		

* if these items are allowed by the partnership agreement

Note that the normal balance on a partner's current account is credit. However, when a partner has drawn out more than his or her share of the profits, then the balance will be debit – as shown by Ali's current account in the Worked Example which follows.

As noted earlier, any loan account in the name of a partner – used to account for money loaned by the partner to the partnership – is kept entirely separate from that partner's capital account and current account. Such a loan does not receive a share of the profits and is only entitled to receive interest at the rate stated in the partnership agreement, otherwise the rate specified in the Partnership Act 1890 applies – five per cent per annum. Such interest is charged in the income statement as an expense before any appropriation of profit is made.

WORKED EXAMPLE: APPROPRIATION OF PARTNERSHIP PROFITS

As we have seen earlier in this chapter, the appropriation section (often described as the partnership appropriation account) follows the income statement and shows how profit for the year is divided amongst the partners. This Worked Example shows a partnership salary (which is not shown in the income statement) and interest allowed on partners' capital.

situation

Ali and Bob are in partnership sharing profits and losses 60 per cent and 40 per cent respectively. Profit for the year ended 31 March 20-4 is £42,000.

At 1 April 20-3 (the start of the year), the partners have the following balances:

	Capital account £	Current account £
Ali	40,000	2,000 Cr
Bob	30,000	400 Cr

- There have been no changes to the capital accounts during the year; interest is allowed on partners' capitals at the rate of eight per cent per year.
- Bob is entitled to a salary of £16,000 per year.
- On 30 September 20-3 (half-way through the financial year), partners' drawings were made: Ali £18,000, Bob £24,000; there were no other drawings. Interest is charged on partners' drawings at the rate of ten per cent per year.

solution

The appropriation of profits will be made as follows:

ALI AND BOB, IN PARTNERSHIP		
INCOME STATEMENT APPROPRIATION ACCOUNT FOR THE YEAR ENDED 31 MARCH 20-4		
	£	£
Profit for the year		42,000
Add interest charged on partners' drawings:		
Ali (£18,000 x six months x 10%)	900	
Bob (£24,000 x six months x 10%)	1,200	
		2,100
		44,100
Less appropriation of profit:		
Salary: Bob		16,000
Interest allowed on partners' capitals:		
Ali £40,000 x 8%	3,200	
Bob £30,000 x 8%	2,400	
		5,600
		22,500
Share of remaining profit:		
Ali (60%)	13,500	
Bob (40%)	9,000	
		22,500

Note that all of the available profit – after allowing for any salary, and interest allowed on capital and charged on drawings – is shared amongst the partners, in the ratio in which they share profits and losses.

The partners' current accounts for the year are shown below. Here the layout for the partners' current accounts uses a normal 'T' account but in a side-by-side format with a column for each partner on both the debit and credit sides. As an alternative, separate current accounts can be produced for each partner.

Dr				Partners' Current Accounts			Cr
		Ali	Bob			Ali	Bob
20-3/4		£	£	20-3/4		£	£
31 Mar	Drawings	18,000	24,000	1 Apr	Balances b/d	2,000	400
31 Mar	Interest on drawings	900	1,200		Salary	–	16,000
31 Mar	Balance c/d	–	2,600	31 Mar	Interest on capital	3,200	2,400
				31 Mar	Share of profit	13,500	9,000
				31 Mar	Balance c/d	200	–
		18,900	27,800			18,900	27,800
20-4/5				2004/5			
1 Apr	Balance b/d	200	–	1 Apr	Balance b/d	–	2,600

From the current accounts we can see that Ali has drawn more out than the balance of the account; accordingly, at the end of the year, Ali has a debit balance of £200 on current account. By contrast, Bob has a credit balance of £2,600 on current account.

BALANCE SHEET

The balance sheet of a partnership must show the year end balances on each partner's capital and current account. However, the transactions that have taken place on each account can be shown in summary form – in the same way that, in a sole trader's balance sheet, profit for the year is added and drawings for the year are deducted.

The other sections of the balance sheet – non-current assets, current assets, current and non-current liabilities – are presented in the same way as for a sole trader.

The following is an example balance sheet layout for the 'financed by' section (the other sections of the balance sheet are not shown). It details the capital and current accounts of the partnership of Ali and Bob (see Worked Example above).

```
                    ALI AND BOB, IN PARTNERSHIP
              BALANCE SHEET (EXTRACT) AS AT 31 MARCH 20-4

        FINANCED BY                              £              £
        Capital Accounts
          Ali                                 40,000
          Bob                                 30,000
                                                           70,000

        Current Accounts
          Ali                                  (200)
          Bob                                  2,600
                                                            2,400
                                                           72,400
```

PARTNERSHIP FINAL ACCOUNTS FROM THE TRIAL BALANCE

The financial statements of a partnership are prepared in exactly the same way as for sole traders. The only differences to note are that partners' capital and current accounts are shown in the balance sheet. Transactions affecting the partners' current accounts – such as share of profits, partners' salaries, drawings, etc – can be shown either in the form of a double-entry 'T' account (see previous page for an example), or directly on the face of the balance sheet (see the following Worked Example). Whichever way this is done, it is the closing balances of the current accounts that are added in to the 'financed by' section of the balance sheet.

WORKED EXAMPLE: PARTNERSHIP FINAL ACCOUNTS

situation
The trial balance for the partnership of Ramjit Singh and Veta Bix, trading as Rave Music, at 31 December 20-5 is shown on the next page.

RAMJIT SINGH AND VETA BIX IN PARTNERSHIP, TRADING AS RAVE MUSIC
TRIAL BALANCE AS AT 31 DECEMBER 20-5

		Dr £	Cr £
Inventory at 1 January 20-5		20,000	
Revenue (Sales)			250,000
Purchases		120,000	
Freehold property		200,000	
Provision for depreciation: freehold property			9,000
Fixtures and fittings		20,000	
Provision for depreciation: fixtures and fittings			8,000
Wages and salaries		35,000	
Shop expenses		20,000	
Trade receivables		3,000	
Trade payables			7,000
Bank overdraft			6,000
Bank loan			80,000
Capital accounts:	Ramjit Singh		50,000
	Veta Bix		45,000
Current accounts:	Ramjit Singh		4,000
	Veta Bix		1,000
Drawings:	Ramjit Singh	24,000	
	Veta Bix	18,000	
		460,000	460,000

Notes at 31 December 20-5:
- inventory was valued at £30,000
- wages and salaries owing £1,700
- shop expenses prepaid £800
- depreciate the freehold property by £3,000, and the fixtures and fittings by 10 per cent (straight-line method)
- goods taken for own use, Ramjit £500, Veta £400
- Veta is to receive a partnership salary of £10,000
- interest is to be allowed on partners' capital accounts at 10 per cent per year
- remaining profits and losses are to be shared equally
- there is no interest charged on partners' drawings

solution

The final accounts of the partnership of Ramjit Singh and Veta Bix, trading as 'Rave Music', are shown on the next page.

RAMJIT SINGH AND VETA BIX IN PARTNERSHIP, TRADING AS 'RAVE MUSIC'
INCOME STATEMENT FOR THE YEAR ENDED 31 DECEMBER 20-5

	£	£	£
Revenue			250,000
Opening inventory		20,000	
Purchases	120,000		
Less Goods for own use	900		
		119,100	
		139,100	
Less Closing inventory		30,000	
Cost of sales			109,100
Gross profit			140,900
Less expenses:			
Wages and salaries		36,700	
Shop expenses		19,200	
Provision for depreciation:			
freehold property		3,000	
fixtures and fittings		2,000	
			60,900
Profit for the year			80,000
Less appropriation of profit:			
Salary: Veta Bix			10,000
Interest allowed on partners' capitals:			
Ramjit Singh	£50,000 x 10%	5,000	
Veta Bix	£45,000 x 10%	4,500	
			9,500
			60,500
Share of remaining profit:			
Ramjit Singh (50%)			30,250
Veta Bix (50%)			30,250
			60,500

RAMJIT SINGH AND VETA BIX IN PARTNERSHIP, TRADING AS 'RAVE MUSIC'
BALANCE SHEET AS AT 31 DECEMBER 20-5

Non-current Assets	Cost £	Provision for depreciation £	Net book value £
Freehold property	200,000	12,000	188,000
Fixtures and fittings	20,000	10,000	10,000
	220,000	22,000	198,000

Current Assets			
Inventory		30,000	
Trade receivables		3,000	
Prepayment of expenses		800	
		33,800	

Less Current Liabilities			
Trade payables	7,000		
Accrual of expenses	1,700		
Bank overdraft	6,000		
		14,700	

Net Current Assets			19,100
			217,100

Less Non-current Liabilities			
Bank loan			80,000
NET ASSETS			137,100

FINANCED BY
Capital Accounts

Ramjit Singh		50,000	
Veta Bix		45,000	
			95,000

Current Accounts	R Singh	V Bix	
Opening balance	4,000	1,000	
Add: Salary	–	10,000	
Interest on capital	5,000	4,500	
Share of profit	30,250	30,250	
	39,250	45,750	
Less: Drawings	24,000	18,000	
Goods for own use*	500	400	
Closing balance	14,750	27,350	
			42,100
			137,100

* goods for own use can be included with the amount for drawings – shown here separately so that the accounting treatment can be seen clearly.

COMMENTING ON PARTNERSHIP FINANCIAL STATEMENTS

In examination questions you will be asked to prepare different accounting aspects of partnerships, eg partners' capital and current accounts, appropriation accounts, and partnership final accounts. Many examination questions will also ask you to discuss or comment on a variety of aspects of partnerships. Topics for discussions or comment may include:

- the terms of the Partnership Act 1890, with reference to sharing profits and losses
- the merits of having a partnership agreement
- the circumstances under which partners use capital accounts only
- the arguments for and against the use of capital and current accounts (to include the meaning of debit or credit balances on current accounts)
- the distinction between a partner's loan account and capital account, and the accounting treatment of each

Some questions may also link to other parts of the A2 Accounting Unit – for example, a partnership may not keep double-entry accounts, instead using incomplete records; you might then be asked to prepare partnership final accounts from such incomplete records.

CHAPTER SUMMARY

- A partnership is formed when two or more (usually up to a maximum of twenty) people set up in business.

- The Partnership Act 1890 states certain accounting rules, principally that profits and losses must be shared equally.

- Many partnerships over-ride the accounting rules of the Act by having a partnership agreement which covers the following main points:
  - division of profits and losses between partners
  - partners' salaries/commission
  - whether interest is to be allowed on capital, and at what rate
  - whether interest is to be charged on partners' drawings, and at what rate
  - the rate of interest to be paid on loans made by partners to the partnership

- A common way to account for partners' capital is to maintain a fixed capital account for each partner. This is complemented by a fluctuating current account which is used as a working account for share of profits, drawings, etc.

The final accounts of partnerships are similar to those of sole traders, but incorporate:

- an appropriation section, as a continuation of the income statement, to show the share of profits and losses

- accounts for each partner– usually separate capital and current accounts – shown in the balance sheet

In the next chapter we continue the theme of partnerships and look at changes in partnerships, such as a change in profit-sharing ratios, admission of a new partner, and retirement of a partner.

QUESTIONS

visit
www.osbornebooks.co.uk
to take an online test

An asterisk (*) after the question number means that the answer is given at the end of this book.

3.1*   Which one of the following contravenes the provisions of the Partnership Act 1890?

(a)   no partner is entitled to a salary

(b) • profits and losses are to be shared in proportion to capital

(c)   partners are not entitled to receive interest on their capital

(d)   interest is not to be charged on partners' drawings

Answer (a) or (b) or (c) or (d)

3.2*   A partnership may choose to over-ride some or all of the accounting rules in the Partnership Act 1890 by the partners entering into a separate:

(a)   appropriation account

(b)   accounting policy

(c) ◦ partnership agreement

(d)   loan agreement

Answer (a) or (b) or (c) or (d)

3.3   Profits of a two-person partnership are £32,800 before the following are taken into account:

- interest allowed on partners' capital accounts, £1,800

- salary of one partner, £10,000

- interest on partners' drawings, £600

If the remaining profits are shared equally, how much will each partner receive?

3.4   The current account of a partner, Tara Shah, has a balance at the beginning of the financial year of £550 debit. During the year, the following transactions pass through her current account:

* interest allowed on capital, £900

* partnership salary, £10,000

* drawings, £14,000

* share of profits, £4,230

What is the balance of Tara Shah's current account at the end of the financial year?

3.5*   Lysa and Mark are in partnership and own a shop, 'Trends', which sells fashionable teenage clothes. The following figures are extracted from their accounts for the year ended 31 December 20-4:

	£	
Capital accounts at 1 January 20-4:		
Lysa	50,000	Cr
Mark	40,000	Cr
Current accounts at 1 January 20-4:		
Lysa	420	Cr
Mark	1,780	Cr
Drawings for the year:		
Lysa	13,000	
Mark	12,250	
Interest on capital for the year:		
Lysa	2,500	
Mark	2,000	
Share of profits for the year:		
Lysa	9,300	
Mark	9,300	

Notes:
* neither partner is entitled to receive a salary
* there is no interest charged on partners' drawings

You are to show the partners' capital and current accounts for the year ended 31 December 20-4.

3.6　Mike and Bernie are in partnership as 'M & B Builders'. The following figures are extracted from their accounts for the year ended 31 December 20-4:

Capital accounts at 1 January 20-4:	£	
Mike	30,000	Cr
Bernie	20,000	Cr
Current accounts at 1 January 20-4:		
Mike	1,560	Cr
Bernie	420	Dr
Drawings for the year:		
Mike	21,750	
Bernie	17,350	
Partnership salary:		
Bernie	7,500	
Interest on capital for the year:		
Mike	1,500	
Bernie	1,000	
Share of profits for the year:		
Mike	20,200	
Bernie	10,100	

Note: there is no interest charged on partners' drawings.

You are to show the partners' capital and current accounts for the year ended 31 December 20-4.

3.7*　Sigrid and Tomascz are in partnership as 'S & T Plumbers'. Their partnership agreement states:
- profits and losses are to be shared in the ratio 60:40
- interest is to be allowed on partners' capital accounts at the rate of 10% per year
- interest is to be charged on drawings
- Tomascz is to receive a partnership salary of £12,000 per year

Profit for the year ended 30 June 20-2 is £50,500. The following data is also available:

	Sigrid		Tomascz	
	£		£	
Capital accounts at 1 July 20-1	40,000		30,000	
Current accounts at 1 July 20-1	1,200	Cr	2,500	Dr
Drawings for the year	26,000		21,500	
Salary	–		12,000	
Interest on drawings	1,280		920	

You are to:

(a)   Prepare the partnership appropriation account for the year ended 30 June 20-2.

(b)   Show the partners' capital and current accounts for the year ended 30 June 20-2.

3.8* John James and Steven Hill are in partnership and own a wine shop called 'Grapes'. The following trial balance has been taken from their accounts for the year ended 31 December 20-4, after the calculation of gross profit:

	Dr £	Cr £
Capital accounts:		
James		38,000
Hill		32,000
Current accounts:		
James	3,000	
Hill		1,000
Drawings:		
James	10,000	
Hill	22,000	
Gross profit		89,000
Rent and rates	7,500	
Advertising	12,000	
Heat and light	3,500	
Wages and salaries	18,000	
Sundry expenses	4,000	
Shop fittings at cost	20,000	
*Closing inventory – balance sheet	35,000	
Bank	29,000	
Trade receivables	6,000	
Trade payables		10,000
	170,000	170,000

*   Only the closing inventory is included in the trial balance because gross profit for the year has already been calculated.

Notes at 31 December 20-4:
- depreciation is to be charged on the shop fittings at 10 per cent per year
- Steven Hill is to receive a partnership salary of £15,000 per year
- interest is to be allowed on partners' capital accounts at 10 per cent per year
- remaining profits and losses are to be shared equally
- there is no interest charged on partners' drawings

You are to:

(a) Show the partners' capital and current accounts for the year ended 31 December 20-4.

(b) Prepare the partnership final accounts for the year ended 31 December 20-4.

(c) On receiving the accounts, John James asks a question about the partners' current accounts. He wants to know why the balances brought down at the start of the year for the two partners are on opposite sides.

Write a note to John James explaining:

• what the balance on a partner's current account represents

• what a debit balance on a partner's current account means

• what a credit balance on a partner's current account means

3.9 Daniel and Freda commenced business in partnership on 1 January 2005. They had no partnership agreement and decided not to keep proper books of account.

Capital introduced by each partner on 1 January 2005 was as follows:

	£
Daniel	20,000
Freda	30,000

The following information is given at 31 December 2005, at the end of the first year of trading:

	£
Property	40,000
Vehicle	3,750
Office equipment	6,000
Inventory	2,400
Trade receivables	150
Trade payables	3,250
Cash at bank	10,950

Daniel had withdrawn £17,000 and Freda had withdrawn £23,000 for personal use during the year.

REQUIRED

(a) Calculate the partnership profit or loss for the year ended 31 December 2005. An income statement is not required.

(b) The partners have decided that, from 1 January 2006, they should maintain a double-entry system of keeping their financial records.

Evaluate the decision that the partners have reached with regard to maintaining their financial records in future.

Assessment and Qualifications Alliance (AQA), 2007 (part of question)

Tutorial note: the remaining parts of this question deal with a change in the partnership of Daniel and Freda – this topic is covered in the next chapter, where the rest of this past examination question forms question 4.10.

3.10* Clark and Pearce are in partnership selling business computer systems. The following trial balance has been taken from their accounts for the year ended 30 June 20-4, after the calculation of gross profit:

	Dr £	Cr £
Gross profit		105,000
Salaries	30,400	
Electricity	2,420	
Telephone	3,110	
Rent and rates	10,000	
Discount allowed	140	
Office expenses	10,610	
*Closing inventory	41,570	
Trade receivables and trade payables	20,000	12,190
Bad debts written off	1,200	
Provision for doubtful debts		780
Office equipment at cost	52,000	
Provision for depreciation on office equipment		20,800
Clark: Capital account		60,000
Current account		430
Drawings	20,600	
Pearce: Capital account		30,000
Current account		300
Drawings	15,700	
Bank	21,750	
	229,500	229,500

*   Only the closing inventory is included in the trial balance because gross profit for the year has been calculated already.

Notes at 30 June 20-4:
• depreciate the office equipment at 20 per cent per year, using the straight-line method
• Pearce is to receive a partnership salary of £12,000

- remaining profits and losses are shared as follows: Clark two-thirds, Pearce one-third
- there is no interest allowed on partners' capital accounts or charged on partners' drawings

You are to:

(a) Show the partners' capital and current accounts for the year.

(b) Prepare the partnership final accounts for the year ended 30 June 20-4.

3.11

Sara and Simon Penny are in partnership running a catering service called 'Class Caterers'. The following trial balance has been taken from their accounts for the year ended 31 March 20-5:

		Dr £	Cr £
Capital accounts:	Sara		10,000
	Simon		6,000
Current accounts:	Sara		560
	Simon		1,050
Drawings:	Sara	12,700	
	Simon	7,400	
Purchases		11,300	
Revenue (Sales)			44,080
Opening inventory		2,850	
Wages		8,020	
Rent and rates		4,090	
Sundry expenses		1,390	
Equipment		8,000	
Trade receivables		4,500	
Trade payables			7,200
Bank		8,640	
		68,890	68,890

Notes at 30 June 20-5:
- inventory was valued at £3,460
- sundry expenses owing, £110
- depreciation is to be charged on the equipment at 10 per cent per year

- Sara is to receive a partnership salary of £8,000
- interest is to be allowed on partners' capital accounts at 10 per cent per year
- remaining profits and losses are to be shared equally
- there is no interest charged on partners' drawings

You are to:

(a) Show the partners' capital and current accounts for the year.

(b) Prepare the partnership final accounts for the year ended 31 March 20-5.

3.12 Anne Adams and Jenny Beeson are partners in an electrical supplies shop called 'A & B Electrics'. The following trial balance has been taken from their accounts for the year ended 30 June 20-5:

		Dr	Cr
		£	£
Capital accounts:	A Adams		30,000
	J Beeson		20,000
Current accounts:	A Adams		780
	J Beeson		920
Drawings:	A Adams	16,000	
	J Beeson	10,000	
Opening inventory		26,550	
Purchases and Revenue (Sales)		175,290	250,140
Returns		1,360	850
Rent and rates		8,420	
Wages		28,700	
Vehicle expenses		2,470	
General expenses		6,210	
Vehicle at cost		12,000	
Fixtures and fittings at cost		4,000	
Provision for depreciation: vehicle			3,000
fixtures and fittings			800
Trade receivables and trade payables		6,850	14,770
Bank		22,009	
Cash		1,376	
Bad debts written off		175	
Provision for doubtful debts			150
		321,410	321,410

Notes at 30 June 20-5:

- inventory is valued at £27,750

- rates paid in advance £250

- wages owing £320

- provision for doubtful debts to be equal to 2 per cent trade receivables

- depreciation on fixtures and fittings to be provided at 10 per cent per year, using the straight line method

- depreciation on vehicles to be provided at 25 per cent per year, using the reducing balance method

- Anne Adams is to receive a partnership salary of £6,000

- remaining profits and losses are to be shared equally

- there is no interest charged on partners' drawings

You are to:

(a) Show the partners' capital and current accounts for the year.

(b) Prepare the partnership final accounts for the year ended 30 June 20-5.

3.13* Tom and Geraldine have been in partnership for a number of years as building contractors. They share profits and losses equally. The balances on their current accounts at 30 April 2006, after the preparation of their draft final accounts, were Tom £3,720 (cr) and Geraldine £1,450 (dr).

In early May 2006, the following information became available:

(1) During the financial year ended 30 April 2006, the partnership had built an office for business use. The building materials used cost £12,450 and had been included in the purchases account; the labour costs of £18,240 had been included in the wages account.

(2) No entry had been made in the accounts to record the use of materials taken from the business for work done in Geraldine's home. The materials cost £2,780.

(3) Included in Tom's drawings was a payment of £600 cash to his son for work carried out on behalf of the partnership.

(4) A piece of equipment, purchased on 1 May 2003 at a cost of £20,000, was sold on 30 April 2006 for £8,000. The only entries relating to the sale of the equipment were:

> Debit – cash £8,000
>
> Credit – sales £8,000

The equipment had been depreciated at 25% per annum using the straight-line method up to 30 April 2006.

REQUIRED

(a) Prepare a statement showing:

(i) the effect of each of items (1) to (4) on the draft profit for the year;

(ii) the change in profit for the year ended 30 April 2006.

(b) Prepare current accounts of Tom and Geraldine at 30 April 2006 to record the adjustments that may be necessary because of the four items.

(c) Evaluate the usefulness of maintaining separate capital and current accounts.

Assessment and Qualifications Alliance (AQA), 2006

3.14

Tutorial note

This question is a combination of incomplete records and partnership final accounts.

Martin and Nasser are in partnership. Their partnership agreement provides that:

- Nasser be credited with a partnership salary of £3,000 per annum
- partners be credited with interest on capital of 6% per annum
- interest on drawings be charged
- residual profits and losses be shared in the ratio of 3:2 respectively.

The partners have never kept a full set of accounting records. However, they are able to provide the following information:

Cash book summary			
	£		£
Balance 1 January 2006	2,178	Wages	63,156
Cash sales	332,467	Purchase of machine	8,800
Cash received from trade receivables	44,049	General expenses	56,676
Rent received	7,000	Payments to trade payables	195,911
Balance 31 December 2006	989	Drawings – Martin	35,660
		– Nasser	26,480
	386,683		386,683
		Balance 1 January 2007	989

Additional information

		At 1 January 2006		At 31 December 2006	
		£		£	
Fixed capital accounts:	Martin	100,000	Cr	100,000	Cr
	Nasser	70,000	Cr	70,000	Cr
Current accounts:	Martin	3,210	Cr	?	
	Nasser	1,304	Cr	?	
Machinery at valuation		147,000		145,000	
Vehicle at valuation		16,000		8,000	
Inventory		14,003		13,471	
Trade receivables		317		183	
Trade payables		4,872		5,163	
Wages accrued		612		938	
Rent receivable owing		500		–	
Rent receivable paid in advance		–		500	

During the year, an old machine that cost £10,000 was traded for £3,200 in part exchange for a new machine costing £12,000. The old machine had been depreciated by £6,000 over its lifetime.

Interest on drawings for the year amounted to: Martin   £230

Nasser   £100

REQUIRED

Prepare the following:

(a) a sales ledger control account for the year ended 31 December 2006

(b) a purchases ledger control account for the year ended 31 December 2006

(c) an income statement for the year ended 31 December 2006

(d) a partnership appropriation account for the year ended 31 December 2006

(e) partners' current accounts at 31 December 2006

Many partnerships maintain separate capital and current accounts.

REQUIRED

(f) Evaluate the extent to which a partnership is likely to benefit from this practice.

Assessment and Qualifications Alliance (AQA), 2007

4 CHANGES IN PARTNERSHIPS

In this chapter we continue our study of partnerships by looking at the principles involved and the accounting entries for:

- admission of a new partner
- retirement of a partner
- death of a partner
- changes in profit-sharing ratios
- revaluation of assets
- partnership changes when there are split years
- dissolution of a partnership, including application of the rule in *Garner v Murray*

Before we look at each of these, we need to consider the goodwill of the partnership business.

GOODWILL

The balance sheet of a partnership, like that of many businesses, rarely indicates the true 'going concern' value of the business: usually the recorded figures underestimate the worth of a business. There are two main reasons for this:

- **Prudence** – if there is any doubt about the value of assets, they are stated at the lowest possible figure.
- **Goodwill** – a going concern business will often have a value of goodwill, because of various factors, such as the trade that has been built up, the reputation of the business, the location of the business, the skill of the workforce, and the success at developing new products.

definition of goodwill

Goodwill is an intangible non-current asset without physical form. It is defined formally in accounting terms as:

the difference between the value of a business as a whole, and the net value of its separate assets and liabilities.

For example, an existing business is bought for £500,000, with the separate assets and liabilities being worth £450,000 net; goodwill is, therefore, £50,000.

Thus goodwill has a value as an intangible non-current asset to the owner or owners of a going concern business, whether or not it is recorded on the balance sheet. As you will see in the sections which follow, a valuation has to be placed on goodwill when changes take place in a partnership.

valuation of goodwill

The valuation of goodwill is always subject to negotiation between the people concerned if, for instance, a partnership business is to be sold. It is, most commonly, based on the profits of the business – eg the average profit over the last, say, three years and multiplied by an agreed figure, perhaps six times.

We will now see how goodwill is created when changes are made to partnerships, such as the admission of a new partner or retirement of an existing partner. For these changes, a value for goodwill is agreed and this amount is temporarily debited to goodwill account, and credited to the partners' capital accounts in their profit-sharing ratio. After the change in the partnership, it is usual practice for the goodwill to be written off – the partners' capital accounts are debited and goodwill account is credited. Thus a 'nil' balance remains on goodwill account and, therefore, it is not recorded on the partnership balance sheet. This follows the prudence concept, and is the method commonly followed when changes are made to partnerships.

ADMISSION OF A NEW PARTNER

A new partner – who can only be admitted with the consent of all existing partners – is normally charged a premium for goodwill. This is because the new partner will start to share in the profits of the business immediately and will benefit from the goodwill established by the existing partners. If the business was to be sold shortly after the admission of a new partner, a price will again be agreed for goodwill and this will be shared amongst all the partners (including the new partner).

To make allowance for this benefit it is necessary to make book-keeping adjustments in the partners' capital accounts. The most common way of doing this is to use a goodwill account which is opened by the old partners with the agreed valuation of goodwill and, immediately after the admission of the new partner, is closed by transfer to the partners' capital accounts, including that of the new partner.

The procedures on admission of a new partner are:

- **agree a valuation for goodwill**
- **old partners: goodwill created**
  - debit goodwill account with the amount of goodwill
  - credit partners' capital accounts (in their old profit-sharing ratio) with the amount of goodwill

- **old partners + new partner: goodwill written off**
  - debit partners' capital accounts (in their new profit-sharing ratio) with the amount of goodwill
  - credit goodwill account with the amount of goodwill

The effect of this is to charge the new partner with a premium for goodwill.

WORKED EXAMPLE: ADMISSION OF A NEW PARTNER

situation

Al and Ben are in partnership sharing profits and losses equally. Their balance sheet as at 31 December 20-4 is as follows:

BALANCE SHEET OF AL AND BEN AS AT 31 DECEMBER 20-4	
	£
Net assets	80,000
Capital accounts:	
Al	45,000
Ben	35,000
	80,000

On 1 January 20-5 the partners agree to admit Col into the partnership, with a new profit-sharing ratio of Al (2), Ben (2) and Col (1). Goodwill has been agreed at a valuation of £25,000. Col will bring £20,000 of cash into the business as his capital, part of which represents a premium for goodwill.

solution

The accounting procedures on the admission of Col into the partnership are as follows:

- goodwill has been valued at £25,000
- old partners: goodwill created
  - debit goodwill account   £25,000
  - credit capital accounts (in their old profit-sharing ratio)

    Al   £12,500

    Ben   £12,500
- old partners + new partner: goodwill written off
  - debit capital accounts (in their new profit-sharing ratio)

    Al   £10,000

    Ben   £10,000

    Col   £5,000
  - credit goodwill account   £25,000

The capital accounts of the partners, after the above transactions have been recorded, appear as:

Dr				**Partners' Capital Accounts**				Cr
	Al	Ben	Col		Al	Ben	Col
	£	£	£		£	£	£
Goodwill written off	10,000	10,000	5,000	Balances b/d	45,000	35,000	-
Balances c/d	47,500	37,500	15,000	Goodwill created	12,500	12,500	-
				Bank	-	-	20,000
	57,500	47,500	20,000		57,500	47,500	20,000
				Balances b/d	47,500	37,500	15,000

The balance sheet, following the admission of Col, appears as:

BALANCE SHEET OF AL, BEN AND COL AS AT 1 JANUARY 20-5

		£
Net assets (£80,000 + £20,000)		100,000
Capital accounts:		
Al	(£45,000 + £12,500 - £10,000)	47,500
Ben	(£35,000 + £12,500 - £10,000)	37,500
Col	(£20,000 - £5,000)	15,000
		100,000

In this way, the new partner has paid the existing partners a premium of £5,000 for a one-fifth share of the profits of a business with a goodwill value of £25,000.

Although a goodwill account has been used, it has been fully utilised with adjusting entries made in the capital accounts of the partners, as follows:

Dr		**Goodwill Account**			Cr
		£			£
Capital accounts:			Capital accounts:		
Al	goodwill	12,500	Al	goodwill	10,000
Ben	created	12,500	Ben	written off	10,000
			Col		5,000
		25,000			25,000

RETIREMENT OF A PARTNER

When a partner retires it is necessary to calculate how much is due to the partner in respect of capital and profits. The partnership agreement normally details the procedures to be followed when a partner retires. The most common procedure requires goodwill to be valued and this operates in a similar way to the admission of a new partner, as follows:

- **agree a valuation for goodwill**
- **old partners: goodwill created**
  - debit goodwill account with the amount of goodwill
  - credit partners' capital accounts (in their old profit-sharing ratio) with the amount of goodwill
- **remaining partners: goodwill written off**
  - debit partners' capital accounts (in their new profit-sharing ratio) with the amount of goodwill
  - credit goodwill account with the amount of goodwill

The effect of this is to credit the retiring partner with the amount of the goodwill built up whilst he or she was a partner. This amount, plus the retiring partner's capital and current account balances can then be paid out of the partnership bank account. (If there is insufficient money for this, it is quite usual for a retiring partner to leave some of the capital in the business as a loan, which is repaid over a period of time.)

As well as agreeing an amount for goodwill, the retirement of a partner often includes a revaluation of assets – see page 84. Such changes – either upwards or downwards – in the value of assets are recorded in the accounts by using a revaluation account.

WORKED EXAMPLE: RETIREMENT OF A PARTNER

situation

Jane, Kay and Lil are in partnership sharing profit and losses in the ratio of 2:2:1 respectively. Partner Jane decides to retire on 31 December 20-4 when the partnership balance sheet is as follows:

BALANCE SHEET OF JANE, KAY AND LIL AS AT 31 DECEMBER 20-4	
	£
Net assets	100,000
Capital accounts:	
Jane	35,000
Kay	45,000
Lil	20,000
	100,000

Goodwill is agreed at a valuation of £30,000. Kay and Lil are to continue in partnership and will share profits and losses in the ratio of 2:1 respectively. Jane agrees to leave £20,000 of the amount due to her as a loan to the new partnership.

solution

The accounting procedures on the retirement of Jane from the partnership are as follows:

- goodwill has been valued at £30,000
- old partners: goodwill created
  - debit goodwill account   £30,000
  - credit capital accounts (in their old profit-sharing ratio of 2:2:1)

    Jane   £12,000

    Kay   £12,000

    Lil   £6,000

- remaining partners: goodwill written off
  - debit capital accounts (in their new profit-sharing ratio of 2:1)

    Kay   £20,000

    Lil   £10,000

  - credit goodwill account   £30,000

The capital accounts of the partners, after the above transactions have been recorded, appear as:

Dr				Partners' Capital Accounts				Cr
	Jane	Kay	Lil		Jane	Kay	Lil
	£	£	£		£	£	£
Goodwill written off	–	20,000	10,000	Balances b/d	35,000	45,000	20,000
Loan account	20,000			Goodwill created	12,000	12,000	6,000
Bank	27,000						
Balances c/d	–	37,000	16,000				
	47,000	57,000	26,000		47,000	57,000	26,000
				Balances b/d	–	37,000	16,000

Note: After recording goodwill, the balance of Jane's capital account is £47,000 (ie £35,000 + £12,000, being her share of the goodwill). Of this, £20,000 will be retained in the business as a loan, and £27,000 will be paid to her from the partnership bank account.

The balance sheet, after the retirement of Jane, appears as follows (see next page):

```
            BALANCE SHEET OF KAY AND LIL AS AT 1 JANUARY 20-5
                                 £
   Net assets (£100,000 – £27,000 paid to Jane)             73,000
   Less Loan account of Jane                                20,000
                                                            53,000


   Capital accounts:
          Kay      (£45,000 + £12,000 – £20,000)            37,000
          Lil      (£20,000 + £6,000 – £10,000)             16,000
                                                            53,000
```

The effect of this is that the remaining partners have bought out Jane's £12,000 share of the goodwill of the business, ie it has cost Kay £8,000, and Lil £4,000. If the business was to be sold later, Kay and Lil would share the goodwill obtained from the sale in their new profit-sharing ratio.

DEATH OF A PARTNER

The accounting procedures on the death of a partner are very similar to those for a partner's retirement. The only difference is that the amount due to the deceased partner is placed in an account called 'Executors (or Administrators) of X deceased' pending payment.

CHANGES IN PROFIT-SHARING RATIOS

It may be necessary, from time-to-time, to change the profit-sharing ratios of partners. A partner's share of profits might be increased because of an increase in capital in relation to the other partners, or because of a more active role in running the business. Equally, a share of profits may be decreased if a partner withdraws capital or spends less time in the business. Clearly, the agreement of all partners is needed to make changes, and the guidance of the partnership agreement should be followed.

Generally, a change in profit-sharing ratios involves establishing a figure for goodwill, even if the partnership is to continue with the same partners; this is to establish how much goodwill was built up while they shared profits in their old ratios. Each partner will, therefore, receive a value for the goodwill based on the old profit-sharing ratio.

WORKED EXAMPLE: CHANGES IN PROFIT-SHARING RATIOS

situation

Des and Eve are in partnership sharing profits and losses equally. The balance sheet at 31 December 20-4 is as follows:

BALANCE SHEET OF DES AND EVE AS AT 31 DECEMBER 20-4	
	£
Net assets	60,000
Capital accounts:	
Des	35,000
Eve	25,000
	60,000

The partners agree that, as from 1 January 20-5, Des will take a two-thirds share of the profits and losses, with Eve taking one-third. It is agreed that goodwill shall be valued at £30,000.

solution

The accounting procedures on the change in the profit-sharing ratio are as follows:

- goodwill has been valued at £30,000
- old profit-sharing ratio: goodwill created
  - debit goodwill account   £30,000
  - credit capital accounts (in their old profit-sharing ratio of 1:1)

    Des   £15,000

    Eve   £15,000
- new profit-sharing ratio: goodwill written off
  - debit capital accounts (in their new profit-sharing ratio of 2:1)

    Des   £20,000

    Eve   £10,000
  - credit goodwill account   £30,000

The capital accounts of the partners, after the above transactions have been recorded, appear as:

Dr			Partners' Capital Accounts		Cr
	Des	Eve		Des	Eve
	£	£		£	£
Goodwill written off	20,000	10,000	Balances b/d	35,000	25,000
Balances c/d	30,000	30,000	Goodwill created	15,000	15,000
	50,000	40,000		50,000	40,000
			Balances b/d	30,000	30,000

The balance sheet at 1 January 20-5 appears as:

BALANCE SHEET OF DES AND EVE AS AT 1 JANUARY 20-5	
	£
Net assets	60,000
Capital accounts:	
Des (£35,000 + £15,000 – £20,000)	30,000
Eve (£25,000 + £15,000 – £10,000)	30,000
	60,000

The effect is that Des has 'paid' Eve £5,000 to increase his share of the profits from half to two-thirds. This may seem unfair but neither partner is worse off in the event of the business being sold, assuming that the business is sold for £90,000 (£60,000 assets + £30,000 goodwill). Before the change in the profit-sharing ratio they would have received:

Des £35,000 capital + £15,000 half-share of goodwill = £50,000

Eve £25,000 capital + £15,000 half-share of goodwill = £40,000

After the change, they will receive:

Des £30,000 capital + £20,000 two-thirds share of goodwill = £50,000

Eve £30,000 capital + £10,000 one-third share of goodwill = £40,000

As far as the realisation value of the business is concerned, the position remains unchanged: it is only the profit-sharing ratios that will be different as from 1 January 20-5. Also, any increase in goodwill above the £30,000 figure will be shared in the new ratio.

REVALUATION OF ASSETS

So far in this chapter we have looked at the adjustments made for goodwill in various changes made to partnerships. Goodwill, however, reflects only one aspect of a partner's interest in the business. For example, some of the assets may have appreciated in value, but adjustments may not have been made in the accounts; other assets may have fallen in value, while provisions for depreciation and/or doubtful debts may have been too much or too little. With a change in the partnership, a revaluation account may be needed to correct any discrepancies in values. The accounting procedure is:

* **increase in the value of an asset**
  - debit asset account with the amount of the increase
  - credit revaluation account with the amount of the increase

- **reduction in the value of an asset**
  - debit revaluation account with the amount of the reduction
  - credit asset account with the amount of the reduction
- **increase in provision for depreciation/doubtful debts**
  - debit revaluation account with the amount of the increase
  - credit provision account with the amount of the increase
- **reduction in provision for depreciation/bad debts**
  - debit provision account with the amount of the reduction
  - credit revaluation account the amount of the reduction

After these adjustments have been recorded in the books of account, the balance of the revaluation account is divided among the partners in their profit-sharing ratios.

WORKED EXAMPLE: REVALUATION OF ASSETS

situation

Matt, Nia and Olly are in partnership sharing profits and losses equally. On 31 December 20-1 their balance sheet is as follows:

BALANCE SHEET OF MATT, NIA AND OLLY AS AT 31 DECEMBER 20-1		
	£	£
Non-current Assets		
Property (net book value)		100,000
Machinery (net book value)		40,000
		140,000
Current Assets		
Inventory	30,000	
Trade receivables	20,000	
Bank	5,000	
	55,000	
Less Current Liabilities		
Trade payables	25,000	
Net Current Assets		30,000
NET ASSETS		170,000
FINANCED BY		
Capital accounts		
Matt		60,000
Nia		60,000
Olly		50,000
		170,000

Olly decides to retire at 31 December 20-1; Matt and Nia are to continue the partnership and will share profits and losses equally. The following valuations are agreed:

Goodwill	£30,000
Property	£150,000
Machinery	£30,000
Inventory	£21,000

A provision for doubtful debts equal to five per cent of trade receivables is to be made.

Olly agrees that the monies owing on retirement are to be retained in the business as a long-term loan.

Show revaluation account, goodwill account and the adjusted balance sheet at 1 January 20-2.

solution

Dr		**Revaluation Account**		Cr
	£			£
Machinery	10,000	Property		50,000
Inventory	9,000			
Provision for doubtful debts	1,000			
Capital accounts:				
Matt (one-third)	10,000			
Nia (one-third)	10,000			
Olly (one-third)	10,000			
	50,000			50,000

Dr			**Goodwill Account**			Cr
		£				£
Capital accounts:			Capital accounts:			
Matt (one-third)	goodwill	10,000	Matt (one-half)	goodwill		15,000
Nia (one-third)	created	10,000	Nia (one-half)	written off		15,000
Olly (one-third)		10,000				
		30,000				30,000

Note: goodwill created is credited to the partners' capital accounts, and goodwill written off is debited – in this way goodwill will not be shown on the balance sheet.

```
┌─────────────────────────────────────────────────────────────────────┐
│           BALANCE SHEET OF MATT AND NIA AS AT 1 JANUARY 20-2          │
│                                              £              £         │
│  Non-current Assets                                                   │
│  Property (revaluation)                                   150,000     │
│  Machinery (revaluation)                                   30,000     │
│                                                           180,000     │
│                                                                       │
│  Current Assets                                                       │
│  Inventory                                   21,000                   │
│  Trade receivables              20,000                                │
│  Less provision for doubtful debts 1,000                              │
│                                              19,000                   │
│  Bank                                         5,000                   │
│                                              45,000                   │
│  Less Current Liabilities                                             │
│  Trade payables                              25,000                   │
│  Net Current Assets                                        20,000     │
│                                                           200,000     │
│                                                                       │
│  Less Non-current Liabilities                                         │
│  Loan account of Olly (£50,000 + £10,000 + £10,000)        70,000     │
│  NET ASSETS                                               130,000     │
│                                                                       │
│  FINANCED BY                                                          │
│  Capital accounts                                                     │
│  Matt   (£60,000 + £10,000 + £10,000 − £15,000)            65,000     │
│  Nia    (£60,000 + £10,000 + £10,000 − £15,000)            65,000     │
│                                                           130,000     │
└─────────────────────────────────────────────────────────────────────┘
```

PARTNERSHIP CHANGES: SPLIT YEARS

Any of the changes in partnerships that we have looked at so far in this chapter may occur during the course of an accounting year, rather than at the end of it.

For example, part-way through the year:

- the partners might decide to admit a new partner
- a partner might retire, or die
- the partners might decide to change their profit-sharing ratios

To avoid having to prepare final accounts at the date of the change, it is usual to continue the accounts until the normal year end. Then, when profit for the year has been calculated, it is necessary to apportion the profit between the two parts of the financial year, ie to split the year into the period before the change, and the period after the change. This is often done by assuming that the profit for the year has been earned at an equal rate throughout the year.

The apportionment is done by dividing the appropriation account between the two time periods.

WORKED EXAMPLE: PARTNERSHIP SPLIT YEARS

situation

Raj and Sam are in partnership; their partnership agreement states:

- interest is allowed on partners' capital accounts at the rate of ten per cent per annum
- Sam receives a partnership salary of £18,000 per annum
- the balance of partnership profits and losses are shared between Raj and Sam in the ratio 2:1 respectively

At the beginning of the financial year, on 1 January 20-4, the balances of the partners' capital accounts were:

Raj   £70,000

Sam   £50,000

During the year ended 31 December 20-4, the profit of the partnership was £50,500 before appropriations. The profit had accrued evenly throughout the year.

On 1 October 20-4, Raj and Sam admitted Tom as a partner. Tom introduced £40,000 of cash into the business as his capital.

The partnership agreement was amended on 1 October 20-4 as follows:

- interest is allowed on partners' capital accounts at the rate of ten per cent per annum
- Sam and Tom are each to receive a partnership salary of £12,000 per annum
- the balance of partnership profits and losses is to be shared between Raj, Sam and Tom in the ratio of 2:2:1 respectively

Note: no accounting entries for goodwill are to be recorded.

solution

The income statement appropriation account of the partnership for the year is shown on the next page.

RAJ, SAM AND TOM IN PARTNERSHIP
INCOME STATEMENT APPROPRIATION ACCOUNT
FOR THE YEAR ENDED 31 DECEMBER 20-4

		9 months to 30 September	3 months to 31 December	Total for year
		£	£	£
Profit for the year		37,875	12,625	50,500
Less appropriation of profit:				
Salaries:				
Sam	£18,000 pa x 9 months	13,500	–	
	£12,000 pa x 3 months		3,000	16,500
Tom	£12,000 pa x 3 months		3,000	3,000
Interest on partners' capitals:				
Raj	£70,000 @ 10% pa x 9 months	5,250	–	
	£70,000 @ 10% pa x 3 months	–	1,750	7,000
Sam	£50,000 @ 10% pa x 9 months	3,750	–	
	£50,000 @ 10% pa x 3 months	–	1,250	5,000
Tom	£40,000 @ 10% pa x 3 months	–	1,000	1,000
		*15,375	**2,625	18,000
Share of remaining profit:				
Raj		(2/3) 10,250	(2/5) 1,050	11,300
Sam		(1/3) 5,125	(2/5) 1,050	6,175
Tom		–	(1/5) 525	525
		15,375	2,625	18,000

*   Raj and Sam shared profits 2:1 respectively
** Raj, Sam and Tom shared profits 2:2:1 respectively

DISSOLUTION OF A PARTNERSHIP

There are various reasons why a partnership may come to an end:

- a partnership may be formed for a fixed term or for a specific purpose and, at the end of that term or when that purpose has been achieved, it is dissolved
- a partnership might be dissolved as a result of bankruptcy, or because a partner retires or dies and no new partners can be found to keep the firm going
- sales may fall due to changes in technology and product obsolescence, with the partners not feeling it is worthwhile to seek out and develop new products
- at the other end of the scale, the business might expand to such an extent that, in order to acquire extra capital needed for growth, the partnership may be dissolved and a limited company formed to take over its assets and liabilities

Whatever the reason for dissolving the partnership, the accounts have to be closed. A realisation (or dissolution) account is used to record the closing transactions, and this account shows the net gain or loss that is available for distribution among the partners. The Partnership Act 1890 requires that monies realised from the sale of assets are to be applied in the following order:

- in settlement of the firm's debts, other than those to partners
- in repayment of partners' loans
- in settlement of partners' capital and current accounts

steps to close the books of a partnership

- Asset accounts (except for cash and bank) are closed by transfer to realisation account:
    - debit realisation (or dissolution) account
    - credit asset accounts
- As assets are sold, the proceeds are placed to cash/bank account, and the sum recorded in realisation account:
    - debit cash/bank account
    - credit realisation account
- If a partner takes over any assets, the value is agreed and the amount is deducted from the partner's capital account and transferred to realisation account:
    - debit partner's capital account
    - credit realisation account
- As expenses of realisation are incurred, they are paid from cash/bank account and entered in realisation account:
    - debit realisation account
    - credit cash/bank account

- Trade payables are paid off:
  - debit trade payables' accounts
  - credit cash/bank account
- The balance of realisation account, after all assets have been sold and all trade payables have been paid, represents the profit or loss on realisation, and is transferred to the partners' capital accounts in the proportion in which profits and losses are shared. If a profit has been made, the transactions are:
  - debit realisation account
  - credit partners' capital accounts

  Where a loss has been made, the entries are reversed
- Partners' loans (if any) are repaid:
  - debit partners' loan accounts
  - credit cash/bank account
- Partners' current accounts are transferred to capital accounts:
  - debit partners' current accounts
  - credit partners' capital accounts

  If a partner has a debit balance on current account, the entries will be reversed
- If any partner now has a debit balance on capital account, he or she must introduce cash to clear the balance:
  - debit cash/bank account
  - credit partner's capital account

  Note that if a partner is unable to settle his or her debt because of insolvency, and the partnership agreement does not cover such circumstances, then the rule in *Garner v Murray* (see page 93) applies.
- The remaining cash and bank balances are used to repay the credit balances on partners' capital accounts:
  - debit partners' capital accounts
  - credit cash/bank account

WORKED EXAMPLE: DISSOLUTION OF A PARTNERSHIP

situation

Dan, Eve and Fay are in partnership, sharing profits and losses equally. As a result of falling sales they decide to dissolve the partnership as from 31 December 20-2. The balance sheet at that date is shown on the next page:

BALANCE SHEET OF DAN, EVE AND FAY AS AT 31 DECEMBER 20-2

	£	£	£
Non-current Assets			
Machinery (net book value)			15,000
Delivery van (net book value)			5,000
			20,000
Current Assets			
Inventory		12,000	
Trade receivables		10,000	
Bank		3,000	
		25,000	
Less Current Liabilities			
Trade payables		8,000	
Net Current Assets			17,000
NET ASSETS			37,000
FINANCED BY			
Capital accounts			
Dan			13,000
Eve			12,000
Fay			12,000
			37,000

The sale proceeds of the assets are machinery £12,000, inventory £8,000, trade receivables £9,000. Dan is to take over the delivery van at an agreed valuation of £3,000. The expenses of realisation amount to £2,000.

Show the realisation account, partners' capital accounts and bank account to record the dissolution of the partnership.

solution

Dr		**Realisation Account**	Cr
	£		£
Machinery	15,000	Bank: machinery	12,000
Delivery van	5,000	Bank: inventory	8,000
Inventory	12,000	Bank: trade receivables	9,000
Trade receivables	10,000	Dan's capital account: van	3,000
Bank: realisation expenses	2,000	Loss on realisation:	
		Dan (one-third)	4,000
		Eve (one-third)	4,000
		Fay (one-third)	4,000
	44,000		44,000

Dr				**Partners' Capital Accounts**				Cr
	Dan	Eve	Fay		Dan	Eve	Fay	
	£	£	£		£	£	£	
Realisation account:				Balances b/d	13,000	12,000	12,000	
delivery van	3,000	-	-					
Realisation account:								
loss	4,000	4,000	4,000					
Bank	6,000	8,000	8,000					
	13,000	12,000	12,000		13,000	12,000	12,000	

Dr		**Bank Account**		Cr
	£			£
Balance b/d	3,000	Realisation account: expenses		2,000
Machinery	12,000	Trade payables		8,000
Inventory	8,000	Capital accounts:		
Trade receivables	9,000	Dan		6,000
		Eve		8,000
		Fay		8,000
	32,000			32,000

As can be seen from the above accounts, the assets have been realised, the liabilities paid, and the balances due to the partners have been settled; the partnership has been dissolved.

THE RULE IN *GARNER V MURRAY*

When a partnership is dissolved, any partner with a debit balance remaining on capital account must pay in monies from private funds to clear the balance. However, if such a partner is unable to settle his or her debt because of insolvency, then the other partners must share the loss in the ratio of their last agreed capital balances, ie the balances of their capital accounts before the dissolution began.

This rule was established in the legal case of *Garner v Murray* (1904) and is a departure from other changes to partnerships where the ratio in which profits or losses are shared is used.

situation

Una, Viv and Wes were in partnership, sharing profits and losses in the ratios 2:2:1 respectively. The partnership has been dissolved and, after realisation of all assets, their balance sheet is as follows:

BALANCE SHEET OF UNA, VIV AND WES AS AT 30 JUNE 20-9

	£
Bank	55,000
Capital accounts:	
Una	35,000
Viv	25,000
Wes	(5,000)
	55,000

In the previous balance sheet, before the dissolution began, their capital account balances were: Una £60,000, Viv £40,000 and Wes £10,000.

Wes is insolvent and unable to pay any of the debt to the partnership.

solution

As Wes cannot pay any of the debt to the partnership, it must be shared between Una and Viv, the solvent partners, in the ratio of their last agreed capitals.

- Una will have to pay: $\dfrac{£60,000}{£60,000 + £40,000}$ x £5,000 = £3,000

- Viv will have to pay: $\dfrac{£40,000}{£60,000 + £40,000}$ x £5,000 = £2,000

The partners' capital accounts record the transactions to close the partnership books of account as follows:

Dr	Partners' Capital Accounts							Cr
	Una	Viv	Wes		Una	Viv	Wes
	£	£	£		£	£	£
Balance b/d	–	–	5,000	Balances b/d	35,000	25,000	–
Wes	3,000	2,000	–	Una			3,000
Bank	32,000	23,000	–	Viv			2,000
	35,000	25,000	5,000		35,000	25,000	5,000

The amounts paid to Una and Viv from the bank are £32,000 and £23,000 = £55,000, which is the amount of the bank balance shown on the partnership balance sheet.

CHAPTER SUMMARY

- Goodwill is an intangible non-current asset.

- With partnerships, goodwill is usually valued for transactions involving changes in the structure of the business to cover:
  - admission of a new partner
  - retirement of a partner
  - death of a partner
  - changes in profit-sharing ratios

  A goodwill account is created just before the change, and then written off immediately after the change, ie it does not appear on the partnership balance sheet.

- When partnership changes take place part-way through the financial year, it is necessary to apportion the profit between the two parts of the financial year, usually by assuming that the profit has been earned at a uniform rate throughout the year.

- A revaluation account is used whenever assets are revalued prior to making changes to the partnership.

- When a partnership is dissolved, a realisation account is used to record the sale proceeds of assets, and to calculate any profit or loss on realisation due to the partners.

- The rule in *Garner v Murray* is followed when an insolvent partner is unable to pay in monies from private funds to clear a debit balance on his or her capital account.

In the next chapter we turn our attention to the published accounts of limited companies. Such accounts must be prepared in accordance with the Companies Acts and with accounting standards.

QUESTIONS

visit
www.osbornebooks.co.uk
to take an online test

An asterisk (*) after the question number means that the answer is given at the end of this book.

4.1   (a)   Explain the concept of goodwill in partnership accounting.

       (b)   Using figures of your choice, demonstrate the accounting procedures that must be undertaken in order to admit a new partner to the business where goodwill is valued and then eliminated from the books of account.

4.2* Where changes in partnerships take place, a goodwill account is opened, usually temporarily. After the change has taken place, this goodwill account is usually written off. This follows the accounting concept of:

(a) prudence

(b) accruals

(c) going concern

(d) consistency

Answer (a) or (b) or (c) or (d)

4.3* Andrew and Barry are in partnership sharing profits equally. Colin is admitted to the partnership and the profit sharing ratios now become Andrew (2), Barry (2) and Colin (1). Goodwill at the time of Colin joining is valued at £50,000. What will be the goodwill adjustments to Andrew's capital account?

(a) debit £25,000, credit £25,000

(b) debit £20,000, credit £25,000

(c) debit £20,000, credit £20,000

(d) debit £25,000, credit £20,000

Answer (a) or (b) or (c) or (d)

4.4* Jim and Maisie are in partnership sharing profits and losses in the ratio 3:2 respectively. At 31 December 20-4 the balances of their capital accounts are £60,000 and £40,000 respectively. Current accounts are not used by the partnership.

On 1 January 20-5, Matt is admitted into the partnership, with a new profit-sharing ratio of Jim (3), Maisie (2) and Matt (1). Goodwill has been agreed at a valuation of £48,000. Matt will bring £28,000 of cash into the business as his capital and premium for goodwill. Goodwill is to be eliminated from the accounts.

For the year ended 31 December 20-5, the partnership profits amount to £60,000, and the partners' drawings were:

	£
Jim	12,000
Maisie	12,000
Matt	8,000

You are to show the partners' capital accounts for the period from 31 December 20-4 to 1 January 20-6.

4.5   Reena, Sam and Tamara are in partnership sharing profits in the ratio 4:2:2 respectively. Sam is to retire on 31 August 20-4 and is to be paid the amount due to him by cheque.

The balance sheet drawn up immediately before Sam's retirement was as follows:

	£
Non-current assets	50,000
Current assets	10,000
Bank	25,000
	85,000
Trade payables	(10,000)
	75,000
Capital Accounts:	
Reena	33,000
Sam	12,000
Tamara	30,000
	75,000

Goodwill is to be valued at £16,000 and non-current assets are to be revalued at £74,000. No goodwill is to remain in the accounts after Sam's retirement.

In the new partnership Reena and Tamara are to share profits equally.

Note that current accounts are not used by the partnership.

You are to:

(a)   prepare the revaluation account, goodwill account and partners' capital accounts to show the amount to be paid to Sam upon retirement

(b)   show the balance sheet immediately after Sam's retirement from the partnership

4.6*   Mei, Janet and Michael have been in partnership for a number of years, sharing profits and losses in the ratio 3:2:1 respectively.

The summarised partnership balance sheet at 30 September 2005 is shown below.

	£	£
Non-current assets		60,000
Bank	1,000	
Other current assets	28,000	
	29,000	
Current liabilities	24,000	5,000
		65,000
Capital accounts: Mei		40,000
Janet		20,000
Michael		5,000
		65,000

Janet retired from the partnership at close of business on 30 September 2005. Mei and Michael continued in partnership; they shared profits in the ratio 2:1 respectively. The three partners agreed that the following asset valuations applied at 30 September 2005.

	£
Non-current assets	130,000
Goodwill	75,000
Current assets (excluding bank)	27,000

It was further agreed that goodwill would not appear in the books of account. Mei and Michael were unsure how any debt owed to Janet should be settled. In the short term, the amount was transferred to a temporary loan account.

REQUIRED

Prepare the three partners' capital accounts at 30 September 2005, showing the effects of Janet's retirement.

Assessment and Qualifications Alliance (AQA), 2007 (part of question)

4.7 Ibrahim, Joan and Kelly are in partnership; they share profits and losses in the ratio 3:2:1 respectively. The partnership balance sheet at 28 February 2007 is shown below.

Balance sheet at 28 February 2007			
	£	£	£
Non-current assets at net book value			123,000
Current assets			
Inventory		12,560	
Trade receivables		7,890	
		20,450	
Current liabilities			
Trade payables	6,750		
Bank overdraft	4,590	11,340	9,110
			132,110
Loan – Joan			15,000
			117,110
Capital accounts			
Ibrahim			45,000
Joan			30,000
Kelly			35,000
			110,000
Current accounts			
Ibrahim		3,278	
Joan		(1,532)	
Kelly		5,364	7,110
			117,110

The partners had been in dispute for the past year about the direction the business should take. As a result, Joan retired from the partnership at the close of business on 28 February 2007 taking all monies due to her.

The partners agreed the non-current assets be valued at £120,000 and that goodwill be valued at £75,000. Ibrahim and Kelly are to continue in the partnership sharing profits and losses in the ratio 3:2 respectively. They further agreed that goodwill should not be shown in future balance sheets.

REQUIRED

(a) Prepare detailed partners' capital accounts at the close of business on 28 February 2007.

(b) Calculate the balance of the new partnership bank account on 1 March 2007.

Assessment and Qualifications Alliance (AQA), Specimen Paper for 2010 (part of question)

4.8*   Dave and Elsa are in partnership sharing profits and losses equally. Their balance sheet at 30 September 20-4 is as follows:

BALANCE SHEET OF DAVE AND ELSA AS AT 30 SEPTEMBER 20-4	
	£
Net assets	130,000
Capital accounts:	
Dave	80,000
Elsa	50,000
	130,000

The partners agree that, as from 1 October 20-4, Dave will take a two-thirds share of the profits and losses, with Elsa taking one-third. It is agreed that goodwill should be valued at £45,000. No goodwill is to remain in the accounts following the change.

Note that current accounts are not used by the partnership.

You are to show:

(a) the partners' capital accounts to record the change in the profit-sharing ratio

(b) the balance sheet of Dave and Elsa after the change in the profit-sharing ratio

4.9   Jean and David are in partnership. Profit for the year ended 31 December 20-4 is £32,700 before appropriation of profit. Their capital account balances at 31 December 20-4 are Jean £10,000, David £12,000. Their partnership agreement allows for the following:

• partnership salaries
  - Jean £12,000
  - David £10,000

- interest is allowed on capital at 5 per cent per year on the balance at the year end
- profit share, effective until 30 June 20-4
  - Jean two-thirds
  - David one-third
- profit share, effective from 1 July 20-4
  - Jean one-half
  - David one-half

Notes:

- no accounting entries for goodwill are to be recorded
- profit had accrued evenly throughout the year
- drawings for the year were: Jean £18,600, David £14,200

You are to:

(a) prepare the income statement appropriation account for the partnership of Jean and David for the year ended 31 December 20-4

(b) update the partners' current accounts for the year ended 31 December 20-4, showing clearly the balances carried down

Dr		Jean	David	20-4		Jean	David
20-4		£	£			£	£
1 Jan	Balance b/d	–	1,250	1 Jan	Balance b/d	2,400	–

Partners' Current Accounts — Cr

4.10 *Tutorial note:* parts (a) and (b) of this question have been seen already as question 3.9.

Daniel and Freda commenced business in partnership on 1 January 2005. They had no partnership agreement.

During the early part of 2006, the partners thought that the business was doing so well that the time had come to expand. In order to finance the expansion, Helen was admitted as a partner with effect from 1 July 2006. The partners drew up a written agreement to take effect from 1 July 2006. The agreement provided that:

(1)   Helen be credited with a partnership salary of £5,000 per annum;

(2)   partners be credited with interest on capital at 6% per annum;

(3)   residual profits and losses be shared in the ratios Daniel one-half; Freda one-third; Helen one-sixth;

(4)   partners be charged interest on drawings.

The agreement further provided that the partners would maintain separate capital and current accounts.

At 30 June 2006, the partnership balance sheet was as follows:

	£	£
Non-current assets		
Property		40,000
Vehicle		3,125
Office equipment		5,700
		48,825
Current assets		
Inventory	3,200	
Trade receivables	1,985	
Bank balance	3,170	
	8,355	
Current liabilities		
Trade payables	4,180	4,175
		53,000
Capital accounts – Daniel		25,000
– Freda		28,000
		53,000

When Helen was admitted to the partnership, it was agreed that certain assets would be valued at the following amounts:

	£
Non-current assets	100,000
Inventory	2,600
Trade receivables	1,410
Goodwill	60,000

It was further agreed that goodwill would not appear in the business books of account.

Helen agreed to introduce £50,000 cash as capital.

REQUIRED

(c)   Prepare the partners' capital accounts as they would appear on 1 July 2006, immediately after Helen was admitted as a partner

The profit for the year ended 31 December 2006 was £90,000. The profit had accrued evenly throughout the year.

The drawings and interest on drawings for the year for each partner are given below.

	Daniel	Freda	Helen
	£	£	£
Drawings	41,000	35,000	12,000
Interest charged on drawings	250	80	160

REQUIRED

(d) Prepare income statement appropriation account for the year ended 31 December 2006.

(e) Prepare partners' current accounts for the year ended 31 December 2006.

(f) Evaluate the decision to keep separate capital and current accounts.

Assessment and Qualifications Alliance (AQA), 2007 (part of question)

4.11* Henry and Jenny are in partnership sharing profits and losses in a 3:2 ratio. Their balance sheet at 31 December 20-8 is as follows:

BALANCE SHEET OF HENRY AND JENNY AS AT 31 DECEMBER 20-8		
Non-current Assets	£	£
Property (net book value)		150,000
Vehicles (net book value)		30,000
		180,000
Current Assets		
Inventory	20,000	
Trade receivables	25,000	
Bank	3,000	
	48,000	
Less Current Liabilities		
Trade payables	28,000	
Net Current Assets		20,000
NET ASSETS		200,000
FINANCED BY		
Capital accounts		
Henry		100,000
Jenny		90,000
		190,000
Current accounts		
Henry	8,500	
Jenny	1,500	
		10,000
		200,000

On 1 January 20-9 the partners decide to admit Kylie into the partnership. On this date:

- goodwill was valued at £40,000
- the property was valued at £180,000
- the inventory valuation includes £3,000 of inventory which is obsolete and should be written off
- an amount of £2,000, owed by a trade receivable, is considered to be irrecoverable, and the balance was written off

The new partnership agreement states that Henry, Jenny and Kylie are to share profits and losses in a 2:2:1 ratio.

Kylie will pay £50,000 into the business by cheque as her capital, part of which represents a premium for goodwill.

You are to prepare the following:

- the revaluation account for Henry and Jenny in partnership
- the goodwill account for the partnership
- partners' capital accounts
- the balance sheet at 1 January 20-9 for Henry, Jenny and Kylie in partnership

4.12* The following is the summarised balance sheet of Amy, Briony, Clarissa and Daljit who share profits and losses in the ratio of 4:3:2:1 respectively:

BALANCE SHEET AS AT 30 JUNE 20-5		
Non-current Assets	£	£
Property (net book value)	100,000	
Plant and equipment (net book value)	30,000	
Vehicles (net book value)	20,000	
		150,000
Current Assets		
Inventory	25,000	
Trade receivables	20,000	
Bank	5,000	
	50,000	
Less Current Liabilities		
Trade payables	25,000	
Net Current Assets		25,000
NET ASSETS		175,000
FINANCED BY		
Capital accounts		
Amy	60,000	
Briony	50,000	
Clarissa	40,000	
Daljit	25,000	
		175,000

The partners decide to dissolve the business as from 30 June 20-5. The following are the proceeds of sale:

- the property realised £160,000; the plant and equipment was sold at auction for £26,000

- the vehicles were sold to a garage for £18,000

- the inventory and trade receivables collectively realised £38,000; trade payables after discounts were settled for £23,000

- the costs of realisation and the auction amounted to £4,000 which was paid for by cheque

REQUIRED

Draft the closing entries in the partnership books of account.

4.13* (a) When a partnership is dissolved, explain how any remaining debit balances on partners' capital accounts are to be cleared.

(b) Keith, Liz and Mina were in partnership, sharing profits and losses in the ratios 3:2:1 respectively. The partnership has been dissolved and, after realisation of all assets their balance sheet is as follows:

BALANCE SHEET OF KEITH, LIZ AND MINA AS AT 30 JUNE 20-2	
	£
Bank	50,000
Capital Accounts:	
Keith	55,000
Liz	(15,000)
Mina	10,000
	50,000

In the previous balance sheet, before the dissolution began, their capital account balances were: Keith £80,000, Liz £50,000 and Mina £20,000.

Liz is insolvent and unable to pay any of the debt to the partnership.

You are to calculate how Liz's deficiency is to be shared out among the solvent partners and show the partners' capital accounts to close the partnership books of account.

4.14   Ali, Bambi and Charlie have been in partnership for many years. They share profits and losses in the ratio 3:2:1 respectively. After a number of years of poor results, they agree to dissolve the partnership on 31 December 2006.

The partnership balance sheet at 31 December 2006 is shown below.

ALI, BAMBI AND CHARLIE
BALANCE SHEET AT 31 DECEMBER 2006

		£	£
All assets (other than bank)			82,020
Bank balance			700
Liabilities			(23,420)
			59,300
Capital accounts – Ali		40,000	
Bambi		10,000	
Charlie		10,000	
			60,000
Current accounts – Ali		1,700	
Bambi		(4,700)	
Charlie		2,300	
			(700)
			59,300

Daphne agreed to purchase the business for £40,000 cash.

All assets and liabilities, other than the bank balance, were taken over by Daphne.

The dissolution took place and was completed on 1 January 2007.

Bambi was unable to meet any liability to the partnership out of his personal funds.

REQUIRED

(a)   Calculate the profit or loss on dissolution.

(b)   Prepare detailed capital accounts to close the partnership books of account.

Assessment and Qualifications Alliance (AQA), 2007

5 PUBLISHED ACCOUNTS OF LIMITED COMPANIES

In this chapter we look at:

- the purpose and components of limited company financial statements
- the format of published accounts
- interpretation of the auditors' report
- the accounting policies followed by a particular company
- the different user groups of the corporate report

The chapter includes extracts from the annual report and accounts of Tesco PLC. To help with your studies you should obtain a set of published accounts from a public limited company that is of interest to you.

INTRODUCTION TO PUBLISHED ACCOUNTS

The preparation of the published financial statements of limited companies is a natural progression from the final accounts of sole traders and partnerships. The layouts of published accounts are similar; however, some of the terminology is different and is fully explained in the chapter.

The major development to note is that we will be applying international accounting standards (IAS) which, together with the Companies Acts, form the regulatory framework within which company financial statements must be prepared. For the chapters which follow for this Unit 3 of A2 Accounting we will be referring to several international accounting standards. In particular, in this chapter, we use IAS 1, *Presentation of financial statements*, to study the form and content of limited company published accounts.

Tutorial note:

For the AQA A2 Accounting examination you should understand the contents of the published accounts of a limited company and be able to contrast these with internal final accounts. However, you will not be expected to prepare income statements or balance sheets in a form suitable for publication, or notes to the assets – other than schedules of non-current assets – or have a detailed knowledge of formats.

TERMS USED IN LIMITED COMPANY ACCOUNTS

The accounting terminology used in limited company financial statements follows the terms used in international accounting standards (IAS). This is shown in the left-hand column of the table below. Other terms which are sometimes used in sole trader and partnership financial statements are shown in the right-hand column. In this book we use IAS terminology throughout as this is the practice in the published financial statements of all larger limited companies. Note though that AQA assessments for the time being continue to use the term 'balance sheet'.

Accounting terminology

IAS terms	Other terms
Income statement	*Profit and loss account*
Revenue	Sales
Finance costs	Interest payable
Profit for year	Net profit
Statement of financial position	*Balance sheet*
Non-current assets	Fixed assets
Investment property	Investments, land and buildings
Inventory	Stock
Trade receivables	Trade debtors
Other receivables	Accruals
Cash and cash equivalents	Bank and cash
Trade payables	Trade creditors
Other payables	Accruals
Non-current liabilities	Long-term liabilities
Equity	Capital and reserves
Retained earnings	Profit and loss balance

PUBLISHED ACCOUNTS

All limited companies have shareholders. Each shareholder owns a part of the company and, although they do not take part in the day-to-day running of the company (unless they are also directors), they are entitled to know the financial results of the company.

Every limited company, whether public or private, is required by law to produce financial statements each year, which are also available for anyone to inspect if they so wish. We need to distinguish between the **statutory accounts** and the **annual report and accounts**. The **statutory accounts** are those which are required to be produced under company law, and a copy of these is filed with the Registrar of Companies. Note that public companies must file their accounts within six months of the end of their financial year.

The **annual report and accounts** is available to every shareholder and contains the main elements of published accounts:

*   income statement (also known as a 'statement of comprehensive income')
*   balance sheet
*   cash flow statement
*   statement of changes in equity
*   notes to the financial statements, including a statement of the company's accounting policies
*   directors' report
*   auditors' report

The annual report and accounts – often referred to as the corporate report – of large well-known companies are often presented in the form of a glossy booklet, well illustrated with photographs and diagrammatic presentations. Some companies, by agreement with individual shareholders, issue a simpler form of annual review, including a **summary financial statement**, the full report and accounts being available on request.

Companies often include the report and accounts on their websites, where they are readily accessible.

RESPONSIBILITIES OF DIRECTORS

The directors of a limited company are elected by the shareholders to manage the company on their behalf. The directors are put in a position of trust by the shareholders to be responsible for the stewardship of the company's accounting information.

Directors have a general duty under the Companies Act 2006 to:

*   act within their powers (normally derived from the company's constitution, eg the Articles of Association)
*   promote the success of the company

- exercise independent judgement
- exercise reasonable care, skill and diligence
- avoid conflicts of interest
- not accept benefits from third parties
- disclose an interest in any proposed transactions involving the company

The directors are responsible for ensuring that the provisions of the Companies Acts 1985 and 2006 which relate to accounting records and statements are followed. The main provisions of the Acts are that:

- a company's accounting records must:
  - show and explain the company's transactions
  - disclose with reasonable accuracy at any time the financial position of the company
  - enable the directors to ensure that the company's income statement and balance sheet give a true and fair view of the company's financial position

  Note:
  - 'true' means that if any of the financial statements states that a transaction has taken place then, in reality, it has taken place; likewise, if an asset is shown on a balance sheet, then the asset actually exists
  - 'fair' implies that transactions and assets are shown using generally accepted accounting rules and principles

- a company's accounting records must contain:
  - day-to-day entries of money received and paid, together with details of the transactions
  - a record of the company's assets and liabilities
  - details of inventories held at the end of the year

- a company's financial statements must be prepared in accordance with the Companies Acts and with either UK accounting standards or international accounting standards (note that, for AQA A2 Accounting, we shall study only accounts which comply with IASs); additionally, companies listed on the stock exchange must comply with the regulations of the stock exchange.

  Note that the directors are responsible for preparing the financial statements, which are then audited by external auditors, appointed by the shareholders of the company (see page 125).

- the directors must report annually to the shareholders on the way that they have run the company on behalf of the shareholders

Every company director has a responsibility to ensure that the statutory accounts are produced and filed with the Registrar of Companies, where they are available for public inspection. The annual accounts must be approved by the company's board of directors and the copy of the balance sheet filed with the Registrar of Companies must be signed by one of the directors on behalf of the board. The directors must prepare a directors' report (see page 124) – this must be approved by the board and the copy to be filed with the Registrar of Companies must be signed on behalf of the board by a director (or the company secretary).

The statutory accounts must be laid before the company at the annual general meeting, and they must be circulated beforehand to shareholders, debenture holders and any other persons entitled to attend the meeting.

The statutory accounts are normally included in the corporate report (see page 129), together with a range of other financial and general information about the company.

A statement of directors' responsibilities for the Tesco group of companies is shown below. Note that the reference to international financial reporting standards (IFRS) also encompasses international accounting standards (IAS) – see Chapter 7.

Statement of Directors' responsibilities

The Directors are required by the Companies Act 2006 to prepare financial statements for each financial year which give a true and fair view of the state of affairs of the Group and the Company as at the end of the financial year and of the profit or loss of the Group for the financial year. Under that law the Directors are required to prepare the Group financial statements in accordance with International Financial Reporting Standards ('IFRS') as endorsed by the European Union ('EU') and have elected to prepare the Company financial statements in accordance with UK Accounting Standards.

In preparing the Group and Company financial statements, the Directors are required to:

- select suitable accounting policies and then apply them consistently;
- make reasonable and prudent judgements and estimates;
- for the Group financial statements, state whether they have been prepared in accordance with IFRS, as endorsed by the EU;
- for the Company financial statements state whether applicable UK Accounting Standards have been followed; and
- prepare the financial statements on the going concern basis, unless it is inappropriate to presume that the Group and the Company will continue in business.

The Directors confirm that they have complied with the above requirements in preparing the financial statements.

The Directors are responsible for keeping proper accounting records, which disclose with reasonable accuracy at any time the financial position of the Group and the Company and which enable them to ensure that the financial statements and the Directors' Remuneration Report comply with the Companies Act 2006 and, as regards the Group financial statements, Article 4 of the IAS Regulation.

The Business Review contained within this document includes a fair review of the business and important events impacting it, as well as a description of the principal risks and uncertainties faced by the business.

The Directors are responsible for the maintenance and integrity of the Annual Review and Summary Financial Statement and Annual Report and Financial Statements published on the Group's corporate website. Legislation in the UK concerning the preparation and dissemination of financial statements may differ from legislation in other jurisdictions.

The Directors have general responsibility for taking such steps as are reasonably open to them to safeguard the assets of the Group and of the Company and to prevent and detect fraud and other irregularities.

Statement of directors' responsibilities for the Tesco group of companies

IAS 1 – PRESENTATION OF FINANCIAL STATEMENTS

The objective of this international accounting standard is to set out how financial statements should be presented to ensure comparability with previous accounting periods and with other companies. The standard states that the purpose of financial statements is to *'provide information about the financial position, financial performance and cash flows of an entity that is useful to a wide range of users in making economic decisions'*.

Note the following from the definition:

- *financial position* – is reported through the balance sheet
- *financial performance* – is reported through the income statement
- *cash flows* – are reported through the cash flow statement (see Chapter 6)
- *entity* – an organisation, such as a limited company
- *wide range of users* – financial statements are used by a member of user groups
- *economic decisions* – information from financial statements is used to help in making decisions about investment in the company

components of financial statements

IAS 1 states that a complete set of financial statements comprises:

- income statement (also known as a 'statement of comprehensive income')
- statement of financial position (balance sheet)
- statement of changes in equity
- statement of cash flows (cash flow statement)
- accounting policies and explanatory notes

accounting concepts

IAS 1 requires that companies comply with a number of accounting concepts as follows:

- *going concern* – financial statements are prepared on the basis that the company will continue to operate in the foreseeable future
- *accruals* – financial statements are prepared on the basis that income and expenses occurring in the same accounting period are matched
- *consistency* – presentation and classification of information shown in financial statements from one period to the next should remain the same
- *materiality* – some items of expenditure are so low in value that to record them separately would be inappropriate; this allows aggregation of similar items rather than showing them separately in the financial statements, eg in the classification of assets as non-current or current

There are a number of further accounting concepts which continue to be used when preparing financial statements; these continue to provide the 'bedrock' of accounting:

- *prudence* – financial statements should take a conservative approach where there is any doubt in the reporting of profits or the valuation of assets

- *business entity* – financial statements should not include the personal expenses or income, or record personal assets and liabilities, for any of the people involved in owning or running the company

- *money measurement* – only transactions which can be measured in money terms can be included in financial records or financial statements

- *realisation* – all financial transactions are recorded when legal title passes between buyer and seller, which may not be at the same time as payment is made

- *historical cost* – all financial transactions are recorded using the actual cost of purchase

- *duality* – every accounting transaction has a dual aspect, one aspect considers the assets of the company, the other considers any claims against the assets

other considerations

As well as complying with accounting concepts, IAS 1 gives two other considerations that must be taken into account when preparing company financial statements:

- *offsetting* – generally it is not permitted to set-off assets and liabilities, and income and expenses against each other in order to show a net figure, eg cash at bank is not to be netted off against a bank overdraft

- *comparative information* – it is a requirement to show the figures from previous time periods in the financial statements in order to help users of the statements

structure and content – general principles

IAS 1 sets out the detailed disclosures to be shown on the face of the income statement, balance sheet, and statement of changes in equity. We shall be covering these later in this chapter.

There are some general principles that the international accounting standard requires.

- the financial statements are clearly shown separately from other information shown in the corporate report

- the name of the company is shown

- the period covered by the financial statements is shown, eg for the year ended 31 December 2009

- the currency of the financial statements is indicated, eg £ Sterling, Euros

- the level of rounding for money amounts is stated, eg thousands, millions

Generally, financial statements are to be prepared at least annually. However, if the reporting period changes, the financial statements will be prepared for longer or shorter than a year. In these circumstances the company must disclose the reason for the change and give a warning that figures may not be comparable with those of previous periods.

INCOME STATEMENT

> **Tutorial note:**
>
> An example of an income statement which complies with IAS 1 is shown in the diagram on pages 114 and 115. Explanations are set out on the left-hand page.

The published income statement does not have to detail every single overhead or expense incurred by the company – to do so would be to disclose important management information to competitors. Instead, the main items are summarised; however, IAS 1 requires that certain items must be detailed on the face of the income statement, including:

- revenue
- finance costs
- tax expense

Note that further detail may be needed to give information relevant to an understanding of financial performance.

The income statement concludes by showing the profit or loss for the period attributable to equity holders.

Expenses must be analysed either by nature (raw materials, employee costs, depreciation, etc) or by function (cost of sales, distribution expenses, sales and marketing expenses, administrative expenses, etc) – depending on which provides the more reliable and relevant information. The analysis by nature is often appropriate for manufacturing companies, while the analysis by function is commonly used by trading companies. The example income statement on page 115 shows an analysis by function.

Much of the detail shown in the income statement is summarised. For example:

- distribution expenses include warehouse costs, post and packing, delivery drivers' wages, running costs of delivery vehicles, depreciation of delivery vehicles, etc
- sales and marketing expenses include advertising costs, the salaries of sales people, the running costs of sales people's cars, the cost of sales promotions, etc
- administrative expenses include office costs, rent and rates, heating and lighting, depreciation of office equipment, etc.

A recent income statement for the Tesco group of companies is shown on page 116. This gives the consolidated (or group) income statement, together with the figures for the previous year.

The **overheads** of a limited company are usually split between the expenses of distribution, sales and marketing, and administration.

The company has recorded a **profit from operations** of £49,000, before deduction of finance costs (such as debenture interest, bank and loan interest).

Tax, the corporation tax that a company has to pay, based on its profits, is shown. We shall not be studying the calculations for corporation tax in this book. It is, however, important to see how the tax is recorded in the financial statements.

The company has recorded a **profit for the year**, ie after deducting finance costs and tax, of £28,000. This amount is taken to the statement of changes in equity.

The **statement of changes in equity**, of which an extract is shown here, demonstrates how profit for the year is added to the brought forward balance of retained earnings (a revenue reserve), while dividends paid during the year are deducted. The resultant balance of retained earnings at the end of the year is shown in the balance sheet in the equity section.
Also included in the statement of changes in equity would be other items such as a new issue of shares and the unrealised profits from, for example, an upwards revaluation of property.

ORION PLC

INCOME STATEMENT FOR THE YEAR ENDED 31 DECEMBER 20-6

	£	£
Revenue		725,000
Opening inventories	45,000	
Purchases	<u>381,000</u>	
	426,000	
Less Closing inventories	<u>50,000</u>	
Cost of sales		<u>(376,000)</u>
Gross profit		349,000
Overheads:		
Distribution expenses	(75,000)	
Sales and marketing expenses	(100,000)	
Administrative expenses	<u>(125,000)</u>	
		<u>(300,000)</u>
Profit/(loss) from operations		49,000
Finance costs		<u>(6,000)</u>
Profit/(loss) before tax		43,000
Tax		<u>(15,000)</u>
Profit/(loss) for the year attributable to equity holders		<u>28,000</u>

STATEMENT OF CHANGES IN EQUITY (EXTRACT)

Retained earnings

Balance at 1 January 20-6	41,000
Profit for the year	<u>28,000</u>
	69,000
Dividends paid	<u>(20,000)</u>
Balance at 31 December 20-6	<u>49,000</u>

Group income statement

Year ended 25 February 2012	notes	52 weeks 2012 £m	52 weeks 2011* £m
Continuing operations			
Revenue	2	64,539	60,455
Cost of sales		(59,278)	(55,330)
Gross profit		5,261	5,125
Administrative expenses		(1,652)	(1,640)
Profits/losses arising on property-related items		376	432
Operating profit		3,985	3,917
Share of post-tax profits of joint ventures and associates	13	91	57
Finance income	5	176	150
Finance costs	5	(417)	(483)
Profit before tax	3	3,835	3,641
Taxation	6	(879)	(864)
Profit for the year from continuing operations		2,956	2,777
Discontinued operations			
Loss for the year from discontinued operations	7	(142)	(106)
Profit for the year		2,814	2,671
Attributable to:			
Owners of the parent		2,806	2,655
Non-controlling interests		8	16
		2,814	2,671
Earnings per share from continuing and discontinued operations			
Basic	9	34.98p	33.10p
Diluted	9	34.88p	32.94p
Earnings per share from continuing operations			
Basic	9	36.75p	34.43p
Diluted	9	36.64p	34.25p

Non-GAAP measure: underlying profit before tax	notes	52 weeks 2012 £m	52 weeks 2011* £m
Profit before tax from continuing operations		3,835	3,641
Adjustments for:			
IAS 32 and IAS 39 'Financial Instruments' – fair value remeasurements	1/5	(44)	(19)
IAS 19 'Employee Benefits' – non-cash Group Income Statement charge for pensions	1	17	113
IAS 17 'Leases' – impact of annual uplifts in rent and rent-free periods	1	38	48
IFRS 3 'Business Combinations' – intangible asset amortisation charges and costs arising from acquisitions	1	22	42
IFRIC 13 'Customer Loyalty Programmes' – fair value of awards	1	17	8
Restructuring and other one-off costs	1	30	20
Underlying profit before tax from continuing operations	1	3,915	3,853

* See Note 1 Accounting policies for details of reclassifications.

The notes on pages 95 to 141 form part of these financial statements.

Income statement for the Tesco group of companies

(note that, for comparison, figures for both the current year and last year are shown)

STATEMENT OF CHANGES IN EQUITY

IAS 1 requires that a statement of changes in equity is one of the year-end financial statements. As its name implies, it shows the changes that have taken place to the shareholders' stake in the company – not only the *realised* profit or loss from the income statement, but also *unrealised* profits (such as the gain on the upwards revaluation of property) which are taken directly to reserves.

Note that IAS 1 requires information to be given, either on the face of the statement of changes in equity, or in the notes to the financial statements, on:

- details of transactions with shareholders, showing dividends paid to shareholders
- opening and closing balances of retained earnings and changes during the period
- opening and closing balances of each reserve and changes during the period

BALANCE SHEET

> **Tutorial note:**
>
> An example of a balance sheet which complies with IAS 1 is shown in the diagram on pages 120 to 121. Explanations are set out on the left-hand page.
>
> IAS 1 does not set out a required format for balance sheets: assets can be presented first, then liabilities and equity; or, in a version common in the UK, non-current assets can be followed by net current assets (current assets minus current liabilities), then non-current liabilities, all balanced against equity. This latter layout is shown in the example balance sheet (with specimen figures).

IAS 1 specifies the items to be shown on the face of the balance sheet as a minimum. The Standard does not, however, state the order in which the items are to be presented.

The items to be shown on the face of the balance sheet include:

- property, plant and equipment
- investment property
- intangible assets
- inventories
- trade and other receivables
- cash and cash equivalents
- trade and other payables
- tax liabilities
- issued capital and reserves

In their balance sheets, IAS 1 requires most companies to separate out current and non-current assets and liabilities:

Current assets are

- cash or cash equivalent
- those to be realised, sold or used within the normal operating cycle
- assets held for trading and expected to be realised within twelve months

Examples of current assets are trade receivables, inventories, and cash and cash equivalents.

All other assets are non-current.

Current liabilities are:

- those expected to be settled within the normal operating cycle
- liabilities held for trading and expected to be settled within twelve months
- where the company does not have the right to defer payment beyond twelve months

Examples of current liabilities are trade payables, tax liabilities and bank overdraft.

All other liabilities are non-current.

Further detail can be given about balance sheet items – either on the face of the balance sheet or in the notes. Examples include:

- property, plant and equipment may be shown by different classes – such as property, machinery, motor vehicles, office equipment, etc
- receivables may be split into amounts due from trade customers, prepayments, etc
- inventories can be sub-classified into raw materials, work-in-progress, finished goods, etc
- share capital and reserves can be shown by the various classes of shares and reserves

In particular, IAS 1 requires the following disclosures about share capital (either on the face of the balance sheet or in the notes):

- the number of shares authorised
- the number of shares issued and fully paid, and issued but not fully paid
- the par (or nominal) value

A recent balance sheet for the Tesco group of companies is shown on page 119. This gives the consolidated (or group) balance sheet, together with the figures for the previous year.

Group balance sheet

	notes	25 February 2012 £m	26 February 2011* £m
Non-current assets			
Goodwill and other intangible assets	10	4,618	4,338
Property, plant and equipment	11	25,710	24,398
Investment property	12	1,991	1,863
Investments in joint ventures and associates	13	423	316
Other investments	14	1,526	938
Loans and advances to customers	17	1,901	2,127
Derivative financial instruments	21	1,726	1,139
Deferred tax assets	6	23	48
		37,918	35,167
Current assets			
Inventories	15	3,598	3,162
Trade and other receivables	16	2,657	2,330
Loans and advances to customers	17	2,502	2,514
Derivative financial instruments	21	41	148
Current tax assets		7	4
Short-term investments		1,243	1,022
Cash and cash equivalents	18	2,305	2,428
		12,353	11,608
Assets of the disposal group and non-current assets classified as held for sale	7	510	431
		12,863	12,039
Current liabilities			
Trade and other payables	19	(11,234)	(10,484)
Financial liabilities:			
Borrowings	20	(1,838)	(1,386)
Derivative financial instruments and other liabilities	21	(128)	(255)
Customer deposits and deposits by banks	23	(5,465)	(5,110)
Current tax liabilities		(416)	(432)
Provisions	24	(99)	(64)
		(19,180)	(17,731)
Liabilities of the disposal group classified as held for sale	7	(69)	–
Net current liabilities		(6,386)	(5,692)
Non-current liabilities			
Financial liabilities:			
Borrowings	20	(9,911)	(9,689)
Derivative financial instruments and other liabilities	21	(688)	(600)
Post-employment benefit obligations	26	(1,872)	(1,356)
Deferred tax liabilities	6	(1,160)	(1,094)
Provisions	24	(100)	(113)
		(13,731)	(12,852)
Net assets		17,801	16,623
Equity			
Share capital	27	402	402
Share premium		4,964	4,896
Other reserves		40	40
Retained earnings		12,369	11,197
Equity attributable to owners of the parent		17,775	16,535
Non-controlling interests		26	88
Total equity		17,801	16,623

* See Note 1 Accounting policies for details of reclassifications.

The notes on pages 95 to 141 form part of these financial statements.

Philip Clarke
Laurie McIlwee

Directors
The financial statements on pages 90 to 141 were authorised for issue by the Directors on 4 May 2012 and are subject to the approval of the shareholders at the Annual General Meeting on 29 June 2012.

Balance sheet for the Tesco group of companies

The **non-current assets** section of a limited company balance sheet usually distinguishes between:

intangible non-current assets, which do not have material substance but belong to the company and have value, eg goodwill (the amount paid for the reputation and connections of a business that has been taken over), patents and trademarks; the intangible non-current assets are amortised (depreciated) and/or are subject to impairment reviews.

property, plant and equipment, which are tangible (ie have material substance) non-current assets and are depreciated over their useful lives and may be subject to impairment reviews.

As well as the usual **current liabilities**, for limited companies, this section also contains the amount of tax to be paid within the next twelve months.

Non-current liabilities are those liabilities that are due to be repaid more than twelve months from the date of the balance sheet, eg loans and debentures.

Authorised share capital is included on the balance sheet 'for information', but is not added into the balance sheet total, as it may not be the same amount as the issued share capital. It can also be disclosed as a note to the accounts.

Issued share capital shows the shares that have been issued. In this balance sheet, the shares are described as being fully paid, meaning that the company has received the full amount of the value of each share from the shareholders. Sometimes shares will be partly paid, eg ordinary shares of £1, but 75p paid. This means that the company can make a call on the shareholders to pay the extra 25p to make the shares fully paid.

Capital reserves are created as a result of non-trading profit and cannot be distributed as dividends.

Revenue reserves are retained earnings from the statement of changes in equity and can be distributed as dividends.

Total equity is the stake of the ordinary shareholders in the company. It comprises share capital, plus capital and revenue reserves.

ORION PLC

BALANCE SHEET AS AT 31 DECEMBER 20-6

Non-current Assets	Valuation	Cost	Aggregate Depreciation	Net
	£	£	£	£
Intangible				
Goodwill		50,000	20,000	30,000
Property, plant and equipment				
Freehold property	280,000		40,000	240,000
Machinery		230,000	100,000	130,000
Fixtures and fittings		100,000	25,000	75,000
	280,000	380,000	185,000	475,000

Current Assets		
Inventories		50,000
Trade receivables		38,000
Cash and cash equivalents		21,000
		109,000
Total assets 475,000 + 109,000		**584,000**

Current Liabilities		
Trade payables		(30,000)
Tax liabilities		(15,000)
		(45,000)
Net Current Assets		64,000
		539,000

Non-current Liabilities		
7% debentures (repayable in 20-9)		(60,000)
Total liabilities 45,000 + 60,000		**105,000**
Net Assets		*479,000

EQUITY		
Authorised Share Capital		
600,000 ordinary shares of £1 each		600,000
Issued Share Capital		
400,000 ordinary shares of £1 each, fully paid		400,000
Capital Reserves		
Share premium	10,000	
Revaluation reserve	20,000	
		30,000
Revenue Reserve		
Retained earnings		49,000
TOTAL EQUITY		479,000

* **Note:** The amounts shown for total assets and total liabilities (arrowed and shaded above) are *for information only* – they are not themselves added or deducted in the balance sheet. They confirm the accounting equation of assets minus liabilities equals equity, here £584,000 – £105,000 = £479,000.

SCHEDULE OF NON-CURRENT ASSETS

In the AQA A2 Accounting examination, you may be required to prepare a schedule of non-current assets. The two Worked Examples which follow are similar to the type of questions you may be asked to answer in the examination.

WORKED EXAMPLE 1: SCHEDULE OF NON-CURRENT ASSETS

situation

The directors of Durning plc provide the following balance sheet extracts:

	31 December 20-8	31 December 20-9
Non-current Assets	£000	£000
Property, plant and equipment	5,091	4,579

Additional information:

* In the year to 31 December 20-9, property, plant and equipment, which had originally cost £1,352,000, was sold. The depreciation charge on these non-current assets up to 31 December 20-9 was £480,000. The loss on disposal was £122,000.

* In the year to 31 December 20-9, new property, plant and equipment was purchased at a cost of £845,000.

The directors of Durning plc ask you to prepare the detailed note for the published accounts for the year to 31 December 20-9 which shows the movements in property, plant and equipment.

solution

For the purposes of the balance sheet note you should ignore any profit or loss on sale – this will have been shown in the income statement. The note can be set out either vertically or horizontally – both versions are shown below.

Non-current Assets	£000
Property, plant and equipment	
Net book value at start of year	5,091
Additions at cost	845
Disposals during year (£1,352 – £480)	(872)
Depreciation for year	*(485)
Net book value at end of year	4,579
*note that depreciation for the year is calculated as a 'missing figure'	

	Net book value at start	Additions at cost	Disposals during year	Depreciation for year	Net book value at end
Non-current Assets	£000	£000	£000	£000	£000
Property, plant and equipment	5,091	845	(872)	(485)	4,579

WORKED EXAMPLE 2: SCHEDULE OF NON-CURRENT ASSETS

situation

The directors of Goodwin plc provide the following balance sheet extracts at 30 June 20-3:

	Cost	Depreciation	NBV
	£	£	£
Property plant and equipment:			
Land and buildings	200,000	55,000	145,000
Plant and machinery	75,000	35,800	39,200
Fixtures and fittings	50,000	12,400	37,600
	325,000	103,200	221,800

During the year ended 30 June 20-4, the following transactions took place:

• Land and buildings were revalued at £260,000 on 1 July 20-3

• Plant and machinery was purchased at a cost of £25,000

• Fixtures and fittings purchased on 1 July 20-1 for £10,000 were sold during the year for £6,000

• Fixtures and fittings were purchased at a cost of £15,000

Goodwin plc's depreciation policy is as follows:

• Land and buildings are depreciated using the straight-line method at 2% per annum

• Plant and machinery is depreciated using the reducing balance method at 25% per annum

• Fixtures and fittings are depreciated at 15% per annum on cost

• All non-current assets are depreciated for a whole year in the year of purchase but are not depreciated during the year of disposal

The directors of Goodwin plc ask you to prepare a schedule of non-current assets at 30 June 20-4 (a total column is not required).

solution

SCHEDULE OF NON-CURRENT ASSETS AT 30 JUNE 20-4
PROPERTY PLANT AND EQUIPMENT

	Land and buildings £	Plant and machinery £	Fixtures and fittings £
Cost			
As at 1 July 20-3	200,000	75,000	50,000
Additions at cost		25,000	15,000
Disposals			(10,000)
Revaluation	60,000		
As at 30 June 20-4	260,000	100,000	55,000
Depreciation			
As at 1 July 20-3	55,000	35,800	12,400
Charge for the year	5,200	16,050	8,250
Eliminated on disposal			(3,000)
Eliminated on revaluation	(55,000)		
As at 30 June 20-4	5,200	51,850	17,650
Net book value at 30 June 20-4	254,800	48,150	37,350

workings

- Land and buildings depreciation charge:

  260,000 x 2% = 5,200

- Plant and machinery depreciation charge:

  (39,200 + 25,000) x 25% = 16,050

- Fixtures and fittings depreciation charge:

  (50,000 - 10,000 + 15,000) x 15% = 8,250

- Fixtures and fittings eliminated depreciation:

  (10,000 x 15%) x 2 years = 3,000

DEALING WITH DIVIDENDS IN THE FINANCIAL STATEMENTS

Dividends are distributions to the shareholders, who own the company, as a return on their investment. Many companies pay dividends twice a year – an *interim dividend*, which is usually paid just over halfway through the financial year, and a *final dividend* which is paid early in the next financial year. The interim dividend is based on the profits reported by the company during the first half of the year, while the final dividend is based on the profits reported for the full year. The final dividend is proposed by the directors but has to be approved by shareholders at the Annual General Meeting (AGM) of the company. Thus the financial calendar for a company with a financial year end of 31 December 2009 might take the following form:

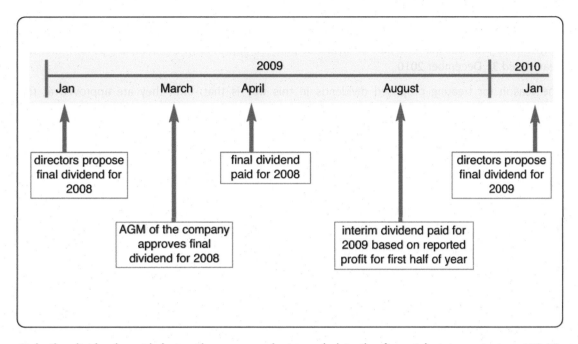

Only the dividends paid during the year can be recorded in the financial statements (see IAS 10, *Events after the Reporting Period*, page 191). In the above example, the dividends paid in April 2009 (final dividend for the previous year) and August 2009 (interim dividend for the current year) are recorded in the financial statements for the year ended 31 December 2009. The proposed final dividend for the year ended 31 December 2009 is disclosed as a note to the accounts, stating that it is subject to approval by the shareholders at the company's Annual General Meeting. An example of a note to the published accounts for dividends is as follows:

DIVIDENDS
note for published accounts for the year ended 31 December 2009

	£000
Amounts recognised as distributions to equity holders during the year:	
• *Final dividend* for the year ended 31 December 2008 of 7.5p per share	375
• *Interim dividend* for the year ended 31 December 2009 of 5p per share	250
	625
Proposed final dividend for the year ended 31 December 2009 of 10p per share	500

The proposed final dividend is subject to approval by shareholders at the Annual General Meeting and has not been included as a liability in these financial statements

---

The amount of £625,000 will be shown as part of the Statement of Changes in Equity, and will also be recorded in the cash flow statement (see Chapter 6). The proposed final dividend is shown as a note only for this year, but will form part of dividends paid – if approved at the company's AGM – for the year ended 31 December 2010.

The reason for treating proposed dividends in this way is that, until they are approved at the company's AGM, they are not liabilities of the company and should not, therefore, be shown in the financial statements.

DIRECTORS' REPORT

The directors' report, which forms part of the published accounts, contains details of the following:
- the principal activities of the company
- a review of the activities of the company over the past year
- likely developments that will affect the company in the future, including research and development activity
- directors' names and their shareholdings in the company
- proposed dividends
- any significant differences between the book value and market value of property
- political and charitable contributions
- actions taken on employee involvement and consultation
- the company's policies on:
  - employment of disabled people
  - health and safety at work of employees
  - payment of suppliers

CASH FLOW STATEMENTS

International accounting standard number 7 (IAS 7) requires that limited companies must include, as part of their accounts, a cash flow statement, which we will look at in detail in Chapter 6. Such a statement shows an overall view of money flowing in and out during an accounting period. It links profit with changes in assets and liabilities and the effect on the cash of the company.

AUDITORS' REPORT

The directors are responsible for preparing the company's published accounts. The accounts must then – for larger companies – be audited by external auditors appointed by the shareholders to check them. The auditors' report, which is printed in the published accounts, is the culmination of their work. The three main sections of the auditors' report are:

- **respective responsibilities of directors and auditors** – the auditors' report states that directors are responsible for preparing the accounts, while the auditors are responsible for forming an opinion on the accounts

- **basis of audit opinion** – the way in which the audit was conducted, other assessments, and the way in which the audit was planned and performed

- **opinion** – the auditors' view of the company's accounts

The opinion is 'unqualified' if the auditors are of the opinion that:

- the financial statements have been prepared properly, and

- they give a true and fair view of the company's affairs in accordance with company law and international financial reporting standards (IFRS)*, as adopted by the European Union, and

- the information given in the directors' report is consistent with the financial statements

  * reference to IFRS also encompasses international accounting standards (IAS) – the difference between these is explained in Chapter 7.

Note that the auditors' report may be 'qualified' if the auditors feel that certain parts of the financial statements have not been dealt with correctly and that this is important enough to be brought to the attention of the Registrar of Companies and other users of the accounts, such as investors or suppliers.

Note that small private companies are exempt from audit requirements.

ACCOUNTING POLICIES

Accounting policies are the specific accounting methods selected by the directors and followed by the company, such as the method of depreciation. IAS 1 requires companies to include details of the accounting policies used. In selecting and applying accounting policies:

- where an accounting policy is given in an international accounting standard (IAS and IFRS) then that policy must apply

- where there is no standard then managers of a company must use their judgement to provide information that is relevant and reliable

Once adopted by a company, accounting policies are to be applied consistently for similar transactions – unless an accounting standard allows differing policies to be applied to categories of items. Changes of accounting policies can only occur:

- if the change is required by an accounting standard; or

- if the change results in the financial statements providing reliable and more relevant information

When there are changes in accounting policies, they are to be applied retrospectively. Any changes require the figure for equity and other figures from the income statement and balance sheet to be altered for previous financial statements.

Accounting policies are important to the user of published accounts as they enable the user to:

* understand the accounts
* rely on the accounts as being free from bias
* make comparison with different companies
* make reliable decisions based on the information given

NOTES TO THE FINANCIAL STATEMENTS

IAS 1 requires notes to the financial statements. These notes provide detailed information regarding:

* the basis of preparation used in the financial statements and the specific accounting policies used
* information required by international accounting standards that is not already included in the financial statements
* any additional information that is relevant to the understanding of the financial statements

PUBLISHED ACCOUNTS AND INTERNAL USE ACCOUNTS

It is the regulatory framework of accounting – comprising the Companies Acts and international accounting standards – that sets out the requirements for published accounts. The regulatory framework details the financial statements that are to be produced, together with their content. The objective is to ensure that 'standard' sets of published accounts are produced – for example, income statements are in the same format, balance sheets use the same headings, notes to the accounts give the same level of information. All this enables the published accounts of two or more companies – even if they are from different sorts of business – to be compared. At the same time, published accounts are audited by external auditors who give their opinion on the company's accounts.

By contrast, internal use company accounts are not subject to regulation and do not need to be audited. As their name suggests, they are for the internal use of the company's directors and managers. This means that they can be presented in a form that suits the users – both in the format of the financial statements and also the level of detail provided. Often internal use accounts provide additional figures for sales and costs which are useful within the company, but would disclose too much information to rivals if it were included in the published accounts.

Whilst published accounts must be produced each year, internal use accounts can be prepared as often as the company wishes.

limitations of published accounts

- published accounts are produced annually – the fortunes of a company could change quite considerably within such a time period

- public companies must file their statutory accounts with the Registrar of Companies within six months of the financial year end – this means that, by the time the information is available to users of accounts, the accounts are out-of-date

- the regulatory framework for accounting details the requirements for published accounts – invariably companies will not disclose additional information

- published accounts report on what has gone on in the past and give little indication of what will happen in the future – eg changing markets or the state of the economy which could impact on the performance of the business in the future

- published accounts cannot record aspects of the company which will affect future performance – eg quality of management, motivation of the workforce, product life cycles, environmental input, ethical considerations

THE CORPORATE REPORT: USER GROUPS

A number of people are interested in reading the annual report and accounts – the corporate report – of a company, especially those of large public limited companies. These user groups include actual or potential:
- shareholders
- loan stock holders/debenture holders
- trade payables
- managers and employees

Each of these user groups is interested in different aspects, as summarised in the diagram on the next page.

There are a number of other user groups interested more generally in the report and accounts of companies. Examples include:
- the Government and government agencies – interested in the tax and VAT due
- the public – interested in the contribution of the company to the economy
- stock market analysts – interested in the investment potential within the company, and whether the company's share can be recommended to their investor clients
- pressure groups, such as environmentalists – interested in the company's stance on social and environmental issues

the Corporate Report: user groups		
Who is interested?	**What are they interested in?**	**Why are they interested?**
Shareholders	• Dividends • Profits	• To see how much cash they are receiving in dividends from their investment and to enable comparison with previous years/other investments • To see how much profit is being retained by the company for investment, and to assess the future prospects of the company in terms of long-term profitability and the security of their investment
Loan stock holders, debenture holders	• Total loans • Interest paid • Profits	• To check if there are other lenders who need to be repaid, so reducing the ability of the company to repay its lending • To ensure that interest is paid to date • To see how much profit is being made in order to assess the likelihood of receiving interest payments and loan repayments
Trade payables	• Current assets, net current assets • Profits	• To assess whether the current assets/net current assets provide sufficient liquidity (ie the stability of the company on a short-term basis) for the company to pay its trade payables as they fall due • To see how much profit is being made in order to assess the ability to pay trade payables; to see if the company is expanding, so creating an increased level of purchases from its suppliers; to make comparison of profits with previous years
Managers and employees	• Profits • Net assets	• To assess whether the company is making profits to be able to afford pay rises; to make comparison of profits with previous years • To consider the net assets of the company, which show its financial strength and indicate its ability to continue in business, so assuring future employment prospects

CHAPTER SUMMARY

○ The annual report and accounts, or corporate report, is available to every shareholder of a company. It includes the financial statements and the directors' report and auditors' report.

○ The directors are responsible for ensuring that the company keeps accounting records and that financial statements are prepared.

○ IAS 1, *Presentation of Financial Statements*, sets out how financial statements should be prepared to ensure comparability. It states that a complete set of financial statements comprises:
  • income statement (also known as a 'statement of comprehensive income')
  • statement of financial position (balance sheet)
  • statement of changes in equity
  • statement of cash flows (cash flow statement)
  • accounting policies and explanatory notes

○ IAS 1 requires compliance with a number of accounting concepts and other considerations:
  • going concern
  • accruals
  • consistency
  • materiality
  • offsetting
  • comparative information

○ For larger companies, external auditors report to the shareholders and give their opinion on the company's financial statements as to whether they give a true and fair view of the financial position of the company.

○ The directors establish the accounting policies, which are the specific accounting methods to be followed by the company.

○ User groups interested in the corporate report of companies include actual or potential:
  • shareholders
  • loan stock holders/debenture holders
  • trade payables
  • employees

The next chapter focuses on the cash flow statement – this uses information from the income statement and balance sheet to show the effect on the cash of the business.

QUESTIONS

visit
www.osbornebooks.co.uk
to take an online test

An asterisk (*) after the question number means that the answer is given at the end of this book.

5.1   Explain what is contained within the annual report and accounts – or corporate report – of a public limited company.

5.2*   Outline the benefits to a company's shareholders of the statement of changes in equity.

5.3   What are the responsibilities of the directors of a limited company in respect of accounting records and financial statements?

5.4*   One of the responsibilities of the directors is to ensure that the company's income statement and balance sheet give a true and fair view of the company's financial position.

Explain what is meant by the words 'true' and 'fair'.

5.5*   List four items that have to be included in a directors' report.

5.6   The directors of Presingold plc, a recently-formed trading company, seek your guidance on the following issues:

(a)   What items do we have to show on the face of the income statement?

(b)   How should we analyse our expenses for the income statement?

5.7   Select a public limited company of your choice and obtain the latest set of published accounts. (Write to the company asking for a set or look on the company's website.)

Read the report and accounts and, from the financial statements, extract the following information for the current and previous year (if there is a choice of figures, use those from the consolidated accounts):

income statement
*   revenue
*   profit or loss from operations
*   profit or loss attributable to equity holders

balance sheet
*   total of non-current assets
*   total of current assets
*   total of current liabilities
*   total of non-current liabilities
*   total equity

cash flow statement (see also Chapter 6)
- cash flow from operating activities
- cash flow from investing activities
- cash flow from financing activities
- net increase or decrease in cash

auditors' report (current year only)
- does it state that the financial statements show a 'true and fair view'?
- are there any 'qualifications' to the report

accounting policies (current year only)
- state two accounting policies followed by the plc

You are to compile a short report – from the point of view of a private investor – which contains:

- an introduction to the selected plc; its structure, size, products, position in its own industry
- the information extracted from the published accounts
- a portfolio of your observations from the report and accounts, eg
  - is the company expanding/declining/remaining static?
  - have the shareholders received higher/lower dividends?

5.8* (a) Define the following terms used in published accounts, giving an example for each:

(i) intangible non-current assets

(ii) current assets

(iii) current liabilities

(b) Published accounts also include a directors' report and an auditors' report.

(i) Identify **three** areas you would expect the directors' report to cover.

(ii) What is the difference between the duties of directors and auditors with regard to the published accounts?

5.9   The following is an extract from the balance sheet of Chiverton plc as at 30 September 20-9:

	£000	£000
EQUITY		
Issued Share Capital		
Ordinary shares of £1 each		500
Capital Reserves		
Share premium	100	
Revaluation reserve	200	
		300
Revenue Reserve		
Retained earnings		175
TOTAL EQUITY		975

REQUIRED

(a)   Explain the meaning of the following:

  •   share premium

  •   revaluation reserve

(b)   One of the directors of Chiverton plc asks if £100,000 of the retained earnings can be used to build a new warehouse for the company. How would you reply?

(c)   What is the difference between 'equity' and 'non-current liabilities'.

Tutorial note

Parts (a) and (b) of this question will have been studied in AS Accounting.

5.10 The directors of Verfico plc provide the following balance sheet extracts.

	At 31 December 2007	At 31 December 2008
	£000	£000
Assets		
Non-current assets		
Property, plant and equipment	4,217	4,301

Additional information

(1) During the year ended 31 December 2008, property, plant and equipment which had originally cost £1,634,000 was sold. The depreciation charge on these non-current assets up to 31 December 2008 was £920,000.

The loss on disposal amounted to £294,000.

(2) During the year ended 31 December 2008, additions to property, plant and equipment cost £930,000.

REQUIRED

Prepare a detailed note to the accounts showing movements in property, plant and equipment during the year ended 31 December 2008.

Assessment and Qualifications Alliance (AQA), Additional Specimen Questions

5.11* The directors of Perran plc provide the following balance sheet extracts:

	31 December 20-1	31 December 20-2
	£000	£000
Non-current assets		
Property, plant and equipment	3,832	3,584

Additional information

• In the year to 31 December 20-2, property, plant and equipment, which had originally cost £1,076,000 was sold. The depreciation charge on these non-current assets up to 31 December 20-2 was £695,000. The loss on disposal was £54,000.

• In the year to 31 December 20-2, new property, plant and equipment was purchased at a cost of £722,000.

REQUIRED

Prepare the detailed note for the published accounts for the year to 31 December 20-2 which shows the movements in property, plant and equipment during the year.

5.12 The directors of Zelah plc provide the following balance sheet extracts:

	30 June 20-4	30 June 20-5
	£000	£000
Non-current assets		
Property, plant and equipment	8,074	7,647

Additional information

- In the year to 30 June 20-5, property, plant and equipment, which had originally cost £2,168,000 was sold. The depreciation charge on these non-current assets up to 30 June 20-5 was £970,000. The profit on disposal was £85,000.

- In the year to 30 June 20-5, new property, plant and equipment was purchased at a cost of £1,175,000.

REQUIRED

Prepare the detailed note for the published accounts of Zelah plc for the year to 30 June 20-5 which shows the movements in property, plant and equipment during the year.

5.13* Four groups of users of published accounts are:
- shareholders
- loan stock holders
- trade payables
- employees

For each user group:

(i)   state two items from the final accounts which would be of particular interest to them

(ii) give reasons for your choice

5.14   The Chairman's statement in the accounts of Chapelporth plc contains the following:

> "I am pleased to report that the profit from operations for the year to 30 November 20-6 was £68 million. These good results were achieved despite higher overheads. After finance costs of £15 million the profit before tax of £53 million was 12 per cent up on the same period in 20-5. Future investment will be concentrated on those areas offering the highest returns and the greatest growth prospects."

This reported profit will please the groups of users of financial statements but for different reasons.

REQUIRED

Explain why the following groups will be pleased with the increase in the profits of Chapelporth plc.

(a)   Shareholders

(b)   Loan stock holders

(c)   Employees

Tutorial note

The next two questions each require the preparation of a published income statement (including a statement of the change in retained earnings) and balance sheet. These questions are included for practice purposes to help with your understanding of the content of published accounts. Note that, in the AQA A2 Accounting examination, you will not be expected to prepare income statements or balance sheets in a form suitable for publication.

5.15* The following trial balance has been extracted from the books of account of Crantock plc as at 31 March 20-2.

	£000	£000
Administrative expenses	240	
Share capital (£1 ordinary shares)		700
Trade receivables	525	
Cash and cash equivalents	75	
Share premium		200
Distribution expenses	500	
Plant and machinery at cost	1,600	
Aggregate depreciation on plant and machinery		500
Retained earnings at 1 April 20-1		350
Purchases	1,200	
Inventories at 1 April 20-1	160	
Trade payables		395
Revenue		2,295
Dividends paid	140	
	4,440	4,440

Additional information

- Inventories at 31 March 20-2 were valued at £180,000.
- The tax charge based on the profits for the year is £65,000.

Note that depreciation has already been provided for in the list of balances above and allocated to distribution expenses and administrative expenses accordingly.

REQUIRED

As far as the information permits, prepare the company's published income statement (including a statement of the change in retained earnings) for the year ended 31 March 20-2 and a balance sheet as at that date.

5.16 The following list of balances was extracted from the books of Mithian plc on 31 December 20-2:

	£
Revenue	2,640,300
Administrative expenses	220,180
Distribution expenses	216,320
Interest paid on loan stock	20,000
Dividends paid	20,000
Share premium	40,000
Purchases	2,089,600
Inventories at 1 January 20-2	318,500
Cash and cash equivalents	20,640
Trade receivables	415,800
Bad debts	8,900
Trade payables	428,250
10% Loan stock	200,000
Office equipment	110,060
Aggregate depreciation on office equipment	48,200
Vehicles	235,000
Aggregate depreciation on vehicles	55,000
Share capital (£1 ordinary shares)	200,000
Retained earnings at 1 January 20-2	63,250

Notes:

- Inventories at 31 December 20-2 were valued at £340,600.

- Provide for tax of £30,000 which is payable on 1 October 20-3.

- Depreciation has already been provided for in the list of balances above and allocated to distribution expenses and administrative expenses accordingly.

REQUIRED

As far as the information permits, prepare the company's published income statement (including a statement of the change in retained earnings) for the year ended 31 December 20-2 and a balance sheet as at that date.

6 CASH FLOW STATEMENTS

The cash flow statement links profit from the income statement with changes in assets and liabilities in the balance sheet, and shows the effect on the cash flows of the company over a period of time.

In this chapter we will cover:

- an appreciation of the need for a cash flow statement
- the layout of a cash flow statement
- the cash flows for the sections of the statement
- assessing the cash flow statements
- users of the cash flow statement

In the layouts of cash flow statements in this chapter, we follow what is termed the 'indirect method' from International Accounting Standard No 7, *Statement of Cash Flows*.

Tutorial note

For the AQA A2 Accounting examination you could be asked to prepare a cash flow statement from information given in balance sheets prepared at the end of two consecutive years. A shorter question could ask you to prepare 'a reconciliation of profit from operations to net cash flow from operating activities'.

WHAT ARE CASH FLOWS?

By using the term 'cash' accountants don't just mean cash in the form of banknotes and coins; instead they mean money in a wider sense – cash, money in the bank, bank overdraft, together with any money on deposit which can be withdrawn on demand. Collectively these 'cash' items are referred to in published balance sheets as 'cash and cash equivalents' – as we have seen in the previous chapter.

Cash flows are receipts and payments of money flowing in and out of a business during an accounting period.

With most transactions it is easy to identify the cash flow and we will soon see how they fit into the cash flow statement. For example:

- cash purchase of goods, paid for by cheque – here there is a cash outflow (note that the term 'cash purchase' means that the buyer is paying for the goods immediately)
- purchase of a new non-current asset, paying by cheque – clearly this is another cash outflow (as we will see later, we need to note that this is for the purchase of non-current assets)
- raising a loan by issuing debentures, receiving a cheque – this is a cash inflow for a loan raised
- paying dividends by cheque – a cash outflow (which is paid to the shareholders)

It is important to note that some transactions do not have an effect on cash, for example:

- selling goods on credit – this is a 'non-cash' transaction, with the money being received at a later date (but note that the profit on the goods sold will be taken immediately – based on the realisation concept)
- allowing for depreciation of non-current assets – this is a non-cash transaction (because the fall in value of non-current assets does not directly affect the cash of a business, eg a car depreciating over time, does not cause a cash outflow)

FUNCTION OF THE CASH FLOW STATEMENT

IAS 7, *Statement of Cash Flows*, requires that a cash flow statement - or statement of cash flows - is included as part of a company's financial statements. It complements the income statement and balance sheet as follows:

- the income statement reports on the financial performance of the company
- the balance sheet reports on the financial position of the company
- the cash flow statement focuses on cash inflows and cash outflows, and reports on changes in the financial position of the company

These three financial statements together provide users of published accounts with much of the information they need to understand the financial performance of the company.

A cash flow statement uses information from the accounting records (including income statement and balance sheet) to show an overall view of money flowing in and out of a business during an accounting period.

Such a statement explains to the shareholders why, after a year of good profits for example, there is a reduced balance at the bank or a larger bank overdraft at the year end than there was at the beginning of the year. The cash flow statement concentrates on the liquidity of the business: it is often a lack of cash (a lack of liquidity) that causes most businesses to fail. Cash is often described as the 'life blood' of a business.

To show why cash flow statements are important, look at the following figures taken from last year's accounts of a company:

	£
Bank balance at the start of the year	20,000
Bank balance at the end of the year	10,000 overdrawn
Profit for year	7,500

What has caused the change in the bank – an outflow of cash of £30,000 (from £20,000 in the bank to £10,000 overdraft)? A cash flow statement is needed to explain why, after a profit of £7,500, there has been a fall in the bank balance during the year.

The importance of the cash flow statement is such that all but small limited companies have to include the statement as a part of their published accounts. For smaller companies, the information the statement contains is of considerable interest to the directors and to a lender, such as a bank.

The diagram which follows shows the links between the three financial statements and the place of the cash flow statement:

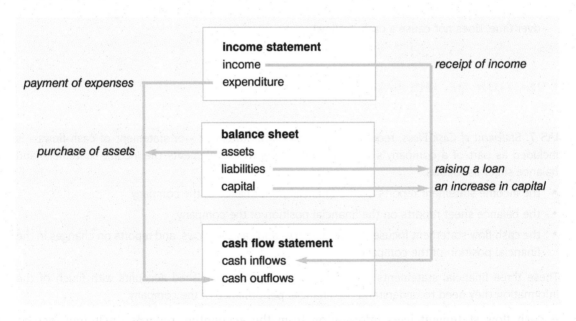

FORMAT OF THE CASH FLOW STATEMENT

IAS 7, *Statement of Cash Flows*, provides the format for cash flow statements, divided into three sections:
* **Operating activities** – the main revenue-producing activities of the business, together with the payment of interest and tax
* **Investing activities** – the acquisition and disposal of non-current assets, and other investments
* **Financing activities** – receipts from the issue of new shares, payments to repay shares, changes in long-term borrowings, and dividends paid

The cash flows for the year affecting each of these areas of business activity are shown in the statement.

At the bottom of the cash flow statement is shown the net increase in cash and cash equivalents for the period, together with the cash and cash equivalents, both at the beginning and at the end of the period. (You will remember that cash and cash equivalents is the IAS term for cash at bank and in hand.)

The diagram on page 145 shows the main cash flows (inflows and outflows of cash and cash equivalents) under each heading, and indicates the content of the cash flow statement. The first section – operating activities – needs a word of further explanation, particularly as it is the main source of cash flow for most companies.

operating activities

The cash flow from operating activities is calculated by using figures from the income statement and balance sheet as follows:

	profit from operations (profit, before deduction of tax and interest)
add	depreciation charge for the year
add	loss on sale of non-current assets (or *deduct* gain on sale of non-current assets) – see page 152
add	decrease in inventories (or *deduct* increase in inventories)
add	decrease in trade receivables (or *deduct* increase in trade receivables)
add	increase in trade payables (or *deduct* decrease in trade payables)
equals	**cash (used in)/from operations**
deduct	interest paid in the year
deduct	tax paid on income in the year (eg corporation tax)
equals	**net cash (used in)/from operating activities**

Notes:

• Depreciation is added to profit because depreciation is a non-cash expense, that is, no money is paid out by the company in respect of depreciation charged to the income statement.

• Cash flows relating to the purchase and sale of non-current assets are shown in the investing activities section – see diagram on page 145.

The Worked Example which follows shows how the cash from operations is calculated.

WORKED EXAMPLE: CASH FROM OPERATIONS

situation

You are helping the accountant of Chatsala Limited to prepare the company's cash flow statement for the year ended 30 April 20-8. The following information is available to you:

	£
Profit before tax (after deducting interest paid of £2,500)	137,200
Depreciation of non-current assets for the year	15,000
Decrease in inventories during the year	3,500
Increase in trade receivables during the year	5,000
Increase in trade payables during the year	4,000

The accountant asks you to calculate the cash from operations.

solution

Profit from operations is calculated by adding back interest paid to the profit before tax, ie £2,500 + £137,200 = £139,700 profit from operations. This is because profit from operations is profit before interest paid is deducted:

	£	
Profit from operations	139,700	
Less interest paid	2,500	add back interest paid
Profit before tax	137,200	

The cash from operations is now calculated:

	£
Profit from operations	139,700
Depreciation for year	15,000
Decrease in inventories	3,500
Increase in trade receivables	(5,000)
Increase in trade payables	4,000
Cash from operations	157,200

Note that:

* depreciation is a non-cash expense, so it is added back to profit
* a decrease in inventories is a cash inflow – because inventories are being sold for cash – and is added to profit
* an increase in trade receivables is a cash outflow – because the company is financing additional receivables – and is deducted from profit
* an increase in trade payables is a cash inflow – because the company has increased the amount it owes – and is added to profit

LAYOUT OF A CASH FLOW STATEMENT

IAS 7 requires that companies prepare a cash flow statement in the format described in the standard – see the example on the next page (with specimen figures included) and the explanatory notes on page 147.

CONTENTS OF A CASH FLOW STATEMENT

Operating activities

- Profit from operations (ie profit, before deduction of tax and interest)

- Depreciation charge for the year (see page 152 for treatment of a gain or a loss on sale of non-current assets)

- Changes in inventories, trade receivables and trade payables

- Less interest paid

- Less taxes paid on income (eg corporation tax)

Investing activities

- Inflows: sale proceeds from property, plant and equipment, intangibles, and other long-term (non-current) assets

- Outflows: purchase cost of property, plant and equipment, intangibles, and other long-term (non-current) assets

- Interest received

- Dividends received

Financing activities

- Inflows: receipts from increase in share capital (note: no cash inflow from a bonus issue of shares), raising/increase of loans

- Outflows: repayment of share capital and loans

- Dividends paid

ORION PLC
CASH FLOW STATEMENT FOR THE YEAR ENDED 31 DECEMBER 20-6

	£	£
Net cash (used in)/from operating activities		52,000
Cash flows from investing activities		
Purchase of non-current assets	(125,000)	
Proceeds from sale of non-current assets	15,000	
Interest received	10,000	
Dividends received	–	
Net cash (used in)/from investing activities		(100,000)
Cash flows from financing activities		
Proceeds from issue of share capital	100,000	
Repayment of share capital	(–)	
Proceeds from long-term borrowings	–	
Repayment of long-term borrowings	(40,000)	
Dividends paid (note: amount paid during year)	(20,000)	
Net cash (used in)/from financing activities		40,000
Net increase/(decrease) in cash and cash equivalents		(8,000)
Cash and cash equivalents at beginning of year		29,000
Cash and cash equivalents at end of year		21,000

RECONCILIATION OF PROFIT FROM OPERATIONS TO NET CASH FLOW FROM OPERATING ACTIVITIES

	£
Profit from operations (note: before tax and interest)	49,000
Adjustments for:	
Depreciation for year	10,000
Decrease in inventories	2,000
Increase in trade receivables	(5,000)
Increase in trade payables	7,000
Cash (used in)/from operations	63,000
Interest paid (note: amount paid during year)	(5,000)
Income taxes paid (note: amount paid during year)	(6,000)
Net cash (used in)/from operating activities	52,000

Notes on the cash flow statement of Orion PLC:

- The separate amounts shown for each section can, if preferred, be detailed in a note to the cash flow statement. The operating activities section is invariably set out in detail as a note below the cash flow statement, with just the figure for net cash from operating activities (see example opposite) being shown on the statement – see grey line. (Tutorial note: some examination questions ask only for this section to be completed.)

- Money amounts shown in brackets indicate a deduction or, where the figure is a sub-total, a negative figure.

- The changes in the main working capital items of inventories, trade receivables and trade payables have an effect on cash balances. For example, a decrease in inventory increases cash, while an increase in receivables reduces cash.

- The cash flow statement concludes with a figure for the net increase or decrease in cash and cash equivalents for the year. This is calculated from the subtotals of each of the three sections of the statement. Added to this is the amount of cash and cash equivalents at the beginning of the year. Thus the final figure of the statement is that of cash and cash equivalents at the end of the year.

WORKED EXAMPLE: PREPARING A CASH FLOW STATEMENT

situation

The balance sheets of Newtown Trading Company PLC for 20-5 and 20-6 are shown on the next page. Prepare a cash flow statement for the year ended 31 December 20-6 and assess the main points highlighted by the statement. Note the following points:

- Extract from the income statement for 20-6:

	£
Profit from operations	9,400
Interest paid	(400)
Profit before tax	9,000
Tax	(1,500)
Profit for the year	7,500

- Dividends of £2,000 were paid in 20-6.
- During 20-6 the property was revalued at £125,000.

Tutorial note

When preparing a cash flow statement from financial statements, take a moment or two to establish which is the earlier year and which is the later year. In this Worked Example they are set out from left to right, ie 20-5 followed by 20-6. In some questions, the later year is shown first, ie 20-6 followed by 20-5.

NEWTOWN TRADING COMPANY PLC

BALANCE SHEETS AS AT 31 DECEMBER

	20-5			20-6		
	£	£	£	£	£	£
	Cost	Aggregate depreciation	Net book value	Cost or revaluation	Aggregate depreciation	Net book value
Non-current Assets						
Property	75,000	–	75,000	125,000	–	125,000
Plant and equipment	22,200	6,200	16,000	39,000	8,900	30,100
	97,200	6,200	91,000	164,000	8,900	155,100
Current Assets						
Inventories		7,000			11,000	
Trade receivables		5,000			3,700	
Cash and cash equivalents		1,000			500	
		13,000			15,200	
Current Liabilities						
Trade payables		(5,500)			(6,800)	
Tax liabilities		(1,000)			(1,500)	
		(6,500)			(8,300)	
Net Current Assets			6,500			6,900
			97,500			162,000
Non-Current Liabilities						
Debentures			(5,000)			(3,000)
NET ASSETS			92,500			159,000
EQUITY						
Ordinary share capital			80,000			90,000
Share premium			1,500			2,500
Revaluation reserve			–			50,000
Retained earnings			11,000			16,500
TOTAL EQUITY			92,500			159,000

solution

NEWTOWN TRADING COMPANY PLC
CASH FLOW STATEMENT FOR THE YEAR ENDED 31 DECEMBER 20-6

	£	£
Net cash (used in)/ from operating activities (see below)		9,300
Cash flows from investing activities		
Purchase of non-current assets (plant and equipment)	(16,800)	
Net cash (used in)/ from investing activities		(16,800)
Cash flows from financing activities		
Issue of ordinary shares at a premium		
ie £10,000 + £1,000 =	11,000	
Repayment of debentures	(2,000)	
Dividends paid	(2,000)	
Net cash (used in)/ from financing activities		7,000
Net increase/(decrease) in cash and cash equivalents		(500)
Cash and cash equivalents at beginning of year		1,000
Cash and cash equivalents at end of year		500

RECONCILIATION OF PROFIT FROM OPERATIONS
TO NET CASH FLOW FROM OPERATING ACTIVITIES

	£
Profit from operations (before tax and interest)	9,400
Adjustments for:	
Depreciation for year	2,700
Increase in inventories	(4,000)
Decrease in trade receivables	1,300
Increase in trade payables	1,300
Cash (used in)/from operations	10,700
Interest paid	(400)
Income taxes paid	(1,000)
Net cash (used in)/ from operating activities	9,300

Notes on the cash flow statement

- Depreciation is £2,700, ie £8,900 for 20-6 minus £6,200 for 20-5.

- The liability for tax – which is a current liability of £1,000 at 31 December 20-5 – is paid in 20-6. Likewise, the current liability for tax of £1,500 at 31 December 20-6 will be paid in 20-7 (and will appear in that year's cash flow statement).

- The dividend is the amount *paid* during 20-6, ie £2,000.

- The cash raised from the issue of ordinary shares is £11,000, ie an increase in shares of £10,000 (£90,000 for 20-6 minus £80,000 for 20-5) plus an increase in share premium (£2,500 for 20-6 minus £1,500 for 20-5).

- The revaluation of the property (increase in the value of the non-current asset, and revaluation reserve recorded in the equity section) does not feature in the cash flow statement because it is a non-cash transaction.

Assessing the cash flow statement

The following points are highlighted by the cash flow statement:

- cash generated from operations is £10,700 (this is before interest and tax is paid for the year)

- net cash from operating activities is £9,300

- a purchase of plant and equipment of £16,800 has been made, financed partly by operating activities, and partly by an issue of shares at a premium

- the net cash from financing is £7,000, which has provided some of the money for the purchase of plant and equipment

- the bank balance during the year has fallen by £500, ie from £1,000 to £500

In conclusion, the picture shown by the cash flow statement is that of a business which is generating cash from its operating activities and raising cash from its financing activities in order to build for the future.

an example of a published cash flow statement

The cash flow statement for the Tesco group of companies is shown on the next page.

Group cash flow statement

Year ended 25 February 2012	notes	52 weeks 2012 £m	52 weeks 2011* £m
Cash flows from operating activities			
Cash generated from operations	29	5,688	5,613
Interest paid		(531)	(614)
Corporation tax paid		(749)	(760)
Net cash generated from operating activities		4,408	4,239
Cash flows from investing activities			
Acquisition of subsidiaries, net of cash acquired		(65)	(89)
Proceeds from sale of property, plant and equipment, investment property and non-current assets classified as held for sale		1,141	1,906
Purchase of property, plant and equipment and investment property		(3,374)	(3,178)
Proceeds from sale of intangible assets		–	3
Purchase of intangible assets		(334)	(373)
Net decrease/(increase) in loans to joint ventures		122	(194)
Investments in joint ventures and associates		(49)	(174)
Investments in short-term and other investments		(1,972)	(683)
Proceeds from sale of short-term and other investments		1,205	719
Dividends received from joint ventures and associates		40	62
Interest received		103	128
Net cash used in investing activities		(3,183)	(1,873)
Cash flows from financing activities			
Proceeds from issue of ordinary share capital		69	98
Increase in borrowings		2,905	2,217
Repayment of borrowings		(2,720)	(4,153)
Repayment of obligations under finance leases		(45)	(42)
Purchase of non-controlling interests		(89)	–
Dividends paid to equity owners		(1,180)	(1,081)
Dividends paid to non-controlling interests		(3)	(2)
Own shares purchased		(303)	(31)
Net cash used in financing activities		(1,366)	(2,994)
Net decrease in cash and cash equivalents		(141)	(628)
Cash and cash equivalents at beginning of the year		2,428	3,102
Effect of foreign exchange rate changes		24	(46)
Cash and cash equivalents including cash held in disposal group at the end of the year		2,311	2,428
Cash held in disposal group		(6)	–
Cash and cash equivalents at the end of the year	18	2,305	2,428

Reconciliation of net cash flow to movement in net debt note

Year ended 25 February 2012	note	52 weeks 2012 £m	52 weeks 2011* £m
Net decrease in cash and cash equivalents		(141)	(628)
Elimination of net decrease/(increase) in Tesco Bank cash and cash equivalents		126	(219)
Investment in Tesco Bank		(112)	(446)
Debt acquired on acquisition		(98)	(17)
Net cash outflow to repay Retail debt and lease financing		262	2,870
Dividend received from Tesco Bank		100	150
Increase/(decrease) in Retail short-term investments		221	(292)
(Decrease)/increase in Retail joint venture loan receivables		(122)	159
Other non-cash movements		(330)	(480)
Elimination of other Tesco Bank non-cash movements		46	42
(Increase)/decrease in net debt for the year		(48)	1,139
Opening net debt	30	(6,790)	(7,929)
Closing net debt	30	(6,838)	(6,790)

NB. The reconciliation of net cash flow to movement in net debt note is not a primary statement and does not form part of the cash flow statement but forms part of the notes to the financial statements.

* See Note 1 Accounting policies for details of reclassifications.

The notes on pages 95 to 141 form part of these financial statements.

94 Tesco PLC Annual Report and Financial Statements 2012

Cash flow statement for the Tesco group of companies

GAIN OR LOSS ON DISPOSAL OF NON-CURRENT ASSETS

When a company sells non-current assets it is most unlikely that the resultant sale proceeds will equal the net book value (cost/revaluation less accumulated depreciation). The accounting solution is to transfer any small gain or loss on sale – non-cash items – to the income statement. However, such a gain or loss on sale must be handled with care when preparing a cash flow statement because, in such a statement we have to adjust for non-cash items when calculating the net cash from operating activities; at the same time we must separately identify the amount of the sale proceeds of non-current assets in the investing activities section.

WORKED EXAMPLE:
GAIN OR LOSS ON DISPOSAL OF NON-CURRENT ASSETS

situation

H & J Wells Limited is an electrical contractor. For the year ended 30 June 20-2 its income statement is as follows:

			£	£
Gross profit				37,500
Overheads:				
General expenses			(23,000)	
Provision for depreciation:	plant		(2,000)	
	equipment		(3,000)	
				(28,000)
Profit from operations				9,500

gain on sale

During the course of the year the company has sold the following non-current asset; the effects of the sale transaction have not yet been recorded in the income statement:

		£
Plant:	cost price	1,000
	depreciation to date	(750)
	net book value	250
	sale proceeds	350

As the plant has been sold for £100 more than book value, this sum is shown in the income statement, as follows:

	£	£
Gross profit		37,500
Gain on sale of non-current assets		100
		37,600
Overheads:		
General expenses	(23,000)	
Provision for depreciation: plant	(2,000)	
equipment	(3,000)	
		(28,000)
Profit from operations		9,600

The cash flow statement, based on the amended income statement, will include the following figures:

CASHFLOW STATEMENT (EXTRACT) OF H & J WELLS LIMITED
FOR THE YEAR ENDED 30 JUNE 20-2

	£	£
Cash flows from operating activities		
Profit from operations	9,600	
Adjustments for:		
Depreciation for year	5,000	
Gain on sale of non-current assets	(100)	
(Increase)/decrease in inventories	. . .	
(Increase)/decrease in trade receivables	. . .	
Increase/(decrease) in trade payables	____	. . .
Net cash (used in)/from operating activities		14,500
Cash flows from investing activities		
Purchase of non-current assets	(. . .)	
Proceeds from sale of non-current assets	350	
Net cash (used in)/from investing activities		350

Note that the gain on sale of non-current assets is deducted in the operating activities section because it is non-cash income. (Only the sections of the cash flow statement affected by the sale are shown above.)

loss on sale

If the plant in the Worked Example had been sold for £150, this would have given a 'loss on sale' of £100. This amount would be debited to the income statement, to give an amended profit from operations of £9,400. The effect on the cash flow statement would be twofold:

1 In the operating activities section, loss on sale of non-current assets of £100 would be added; the net cash from operating activities remains at £14,500 (which proves that both gain and loss on sale of non-current assets are items which do not affect cash)

2 In the investing activities section, proceeds from sale of non-current assets would be £150

summary: gain or a loss on sale of non-current assets

The rule for dealing with a gain or a loss on sale of non-current assets in cash flow statements is:

• add the amount of the loss on sale, or deduct the amount of the gain on sale, to or from the profit from operations when calculating the net cash from operating activities

• show the total sale proceeds, ie the amount of the cheque received, as proceeds from sale of non-current assets in the investing activities section

The Worked Example of Retail News PLC (see below) incorporates calculations for both a gain and a loss on sale of non-current assets.

REVALUATION OF NON-CURRENT ASSETS

From time-to-time some non-current assets are revalued upwards and the amount of the revaluation is recorded in the balance sheet. The most common asset to be treated in this way is property. The value of the non-current asset is increased and the amount of the revaluation is placed to a revaluation reserve in the equity section of the balance sheet where it increases the value of the shareholders' investment in the company. As a revaluation is purely a 'book' adjustment, ie no cash has changed hands, it does not feature in a cash flow statement – see the Worked Example of Newtown Trading Company PLC on pages 147 to 150.

WORKED EXAMPLE: PREPARING THE CASH FLOW STATEMENTS

Tutorial note

This is quite a complex example of cash flow statements which incorporates a number of points:

• gain on sale of non-current assets
• loss on sale of non-current assets
• issue of shares at a premium

As there are two years' cash flow statements to produce, you should work through the Worked Example seeing how the figures have been prepared for the first year (year ended 20-5); then attempt the second year (year ended 20-6) yourself, checking against the Worked Example.

situation

Martin Jackson is a shareholder in Retail News PLC, a company that operates a chain of newsagent shops. Martin comments that, whilst the company is making reasonable profits, the bank balance has fallen quite considerably. He gives you the following information for Retail News PLC:

RETAIL NEWS PLC
BALANCE SHEET AS AT 31 DECEMBER

	20-4		20-5		20-6	
	£000	£000	£000	£000	£000	£000
Non-current Assets at cost		274		298		324
Depreciation		(74)		(98)		(118)
		200		200		206
Current Assets						
Inventories	50		74		85	
Trade receivables	80		120		150	
Cash and cash equivalents	10		–		–	
	140		194		235	
Current Liabilities						
Trade payables	(72)		(89)		(95)	
Bank overdraft	–		(15)		(46)	
Tax liabilities	(4)		(5)		(8)	
	(76)		(109)		(149)	
Net Current Assets		64		85		86
NET ASSETS		264		285		292
EQUITY						
Ordinary share capital		200		210		210
Share premium		–		5		5
Retained earnings		64		70		77
TOTAL EQUITY		264		285		292

INCOME STATEMENT (EXTRACTS) FOR THE YEAR ENDED 31 DECEMBER

	20-4	20-5	20-6
	£000	£000	£000
Profit from operations	25	31	50
Interest paid	–	(3)	(15)
Profit before tax	25	28	35
Tax	(5)	(7)	(10)
Profit for the year	20	21	25

Notes

- Dividends paid were: £15,000 in 20-5, and £18,000 in 20-6.

- Tax paid was: £6,000 in 20-5 and £7,000 in 20-6.

- During the year to 31 December 20-5, non-current assets were sold for £30,000, the cost of the assets sold was £40,000 and depreciation was £20,000.

- During the year to 31 December 20-6, non-current assets with an original cost of £35,000 were sold at a loss on sale of £5,000 below net book value; the depreciation on these assets sold had amounted to £15,000.

REQUIRED: **Prepare a cash flow statement for the years ended 20-5 and 20-6.**

solution

RETAIL NEWS PLC
CASH FLOW STATEMENT FOR THE YEAR ENDED 31 DECEMBER

	20-5		20-6	
	£000	£000	£000	£000
	£	£	£	£
Net cash (used in)/from operating activities (see below)		9		33
Cash flows from investing activities				
Purchase of non-current assets (see below)	(64)		(61)	
Proceeds from sale of non-current assets	30		15	
Net cash (used in)/from investing activities		(34)		(46)
Cash flows from financing activities				
Proceeds from issue of share capital at a premium				
(see below)	15		–	
Dividends paid	(15)		(18)	
Net cash (used in)/from financing activities		–		(18)
Net increase/(decrease) in cash and cash equivalents		(25)		(31)
Cash and cash equivalents at beginning of year		10		(15)
Cash and cash equivalents at end of year		(15)		(46)

RECONCILIATION OF PROFIT FROM OPERATIONS TO NET CASH FLOW FROM OPERATING ACTIVITIES		
	20-5	20-6
	£000	£000
Profit from operations	31	50
Adjustments for:		
Depreciation for year	44	35
(Gain)/loss on sale of non-current assets (see below)	(10)	5
Increase in inventories	(24)	(11)
Increase in trade receivables	(40)	(30)
Increase in trade payables	17	6
Cash (used in)/from operations	18	55
Interest paid	(3)	(15)
Income taxes paid	(6)	(7)
Net cash (used in)/from operating activities	9	33

POINTS TO NOTE FROM THE CASH FLOW STATEMENT:

■ Depreciation for year

	20-5	20-6
	£000	£000
Depreciation at start of year*	74	98
Depreciation on asset sold	(20)	(15)
	54	83
Depreciation at end of year*	98	118
Depreciation for year	44	35

* figures taken from balance sheet

■ Gain/(loss) on sale of non-current assets

	20-5	20-6
	£000	£000
Cost price of assets sold	40	35
Depreciation to date	(20)	(15)
Net book value	20	20
Proceeds from sale	30	**15
Gain/(loss) on sale of non-current assets	10	(5)

** Proceeds from sale at £5,000 below net book value

Note that the gain on sale is *deducted from*, and loss on sale is *added to*, profit from operations because they are non-cash income; the proceeds from sale are shown in the investing activities section.

■ **Payments to acquire non-current assets**

	20-5	20-6
Non-current assets at cost at start of year	274	298
Cost price of asset sold	(40)	(35)
	234	263
Non-current assets at cost at end of year	298	324
Purchase of non-current assets	64	61

■ **Dividends and tax paid**

From the information given, the amount of dividends and tax paid were:

20-5   dividends: £15,000; tax £6,000

20-6   dividends: £18,000; tax £7,000

These amounts are shown in the relevant year's cash flow statement.

■ **Issue of ordinary shares at a premium**

	20-5
Ordinary share capital at start of year	200
Share premium at start of year	—
	200
Ordinary share capital at end of year	210
Share premium at end of year	5
	215
Issue of ordinary shares at a premium	15

ASSESSING THE CASH FLOW STATEMENT

The points highlighted by the cash flow statements of Retail News PLC for 20-5 and 20-6 are:

*   a good cash flow generated from operations in both years – well above the amounts paid for tax and dividends

*   inventories, trade receivables and trade payables have increased each year – in particular the receivables have increased significantly

*   interest paid in 20-6 is high because of the increasing bank overdraft (and will, most probably, be even higher in 20-7)

*   new non-current assets have been bought each year – £64,000 in 20-5 and £61,000 in 20-6; apart from a share issue of £15,000 in 20-5, these have been financed through the bank account

The company appears to be expanding quite rapidly, with large increases in non-current assets and the net current asset items. As most of this expansion has been financed through the bank (apart from the share issue of £15,000 in 20-5), there is much pressure on the bank account. It would be better to obtain long-term finance – either a loan or a new issue of shares – rather than using the bank overdraft.

ASSESSING CASH FLOW STATEMENTS

The cash flow statement is important because it identifies the sources of cash flowing into the company and shows how they have been used. To get an overall view of the company, we need to assess the statement in conjunction with the other main financial statements – income statement and balance sheet – and also in the context of the previous year's statements.

You could be asked to assess a cash flow statement in the examination. The following points should be borne in mind:

• Like the other financial statements, the cash flow statement uses the money measurement concept. This means that only items which can be recorded in money terms can be included; also we must be aware of the effect of inflation if comparing one year with the next.

• Look for positive cash flows from the operating activities section. In particular, look at the subtotal 'cash (used in)/from operations' – this shows the cash from revenue-producing activities before the payment of interest and tax.

• Make a comparison between the amount of profit and the amount of cash generated from operations. Identify the reasons for major differences between these figures – look at the changes in the net current asset items of inventories, trade receivables and trade payables, and put them into context. For example, it would be a warning sign if there were large increases in these items in a company with falling profits, and such a trend would put a strain on the liquidity of the business. Also consider the company's policies on collecting trade receivables (and potential for bad debts), payment to trade payables (is the company paying too quickly?) and control of inventories (are surpluses building up?).

• Look at the figure for 'net cash (used in)/from operating activities', ie the cash from operations after interest and tax have been paid. If it is a positive figure, it shows that the company has been able to meet its interest and tax obligations to loan providers and the tax authorities.

• The investing activities section of the statement shows the amount of investment made during the year (eg the purchase of non-current assets). In general there should be a link between the cost of the investment and an increase in loans and/or share capital – it isn't usual to finance non-current assets from short-term sources, such as a bank overdraft.

• In the financing activities section of the statement, where there has been an increase in loans and/or share capital, look to see how the money has been used. Was it to buy non-current assets, or to finance inventories and trade receivables, or other purposes?

• Look at the amount of dividends paid – this is an outflow of cash that will directly affect the change in the bank balance. As a quick test, the amount of net cash from operating activities should, in theory, be sufficient to cover dividends paid; if it doesn't, then it is likely that the level of dividends will have to be reduced in future years.

• The cash flow statement, as a whole, links profit with changes in cash. Both of these are important: without profits the company cannot generate cash (unless it sells non-current assets), and without cash it cannot pay bills as they fall due.

Users of Cash Flow Statements

As cash flow statements are included in the published accounts of all but smaller companies, they are widely available to be read by a number of interested user groups.

shareholders

Shareholders will read the statement because:

- it demonstrates the ability of the company to generate cash from operating activities
- it shows the liquidity of the business
- it identifies the sources of cash and shows how they have been used over the year
- it shows the investment of the company in non-current assets, which should flow through into increasing profits and share price
- it shows the amount of dividends paid to shareholders

loan stock holders/debenture holders

The cash flow statement shows:

- the cash available at the year end, thus demonstrating the security of loan stock and debentures
- the financing activities section shows additional loans raised, or repayment of lending
- interest paid to lenders, in the operating activities section

trade payables

Trade payables will be interested in the cash flow statement because:

- it shows the liquidity of the company and, therefore, the likelihood of being paid for the goods or services they have supplied
- it shows the cash available at the year end for future development which should lead to suppliers doing more business with the company
- it shows whether the company is financing itself through lending (which is usually repaid ahead of trade payables in the event of the company 'going bust') or through shareholders (which rank after trade payables)
- as it shows flows of cash, it is considered to be the most objective of the three main financial statements – thus it gives a good picture of the state of the company's finances

managers and employees

The cash flow statement is useful because:

- it highlights further information on the state of the company's finances that is not readily available from the income statement and balance sheet
- it identifies the sources of cash and shows how they have been used over the year

- it shows the cash available at the year end for future development of the company and, therefore, security of employment
- it may help managers with decision-making and development of the company
- a surplus of cash for the year may indicate to employees that the company can afford pay increases

other users

Other user groups include potential investors, stock market analysts, the bank, customers and the public.

CHAPTER SUMMARY

- The objective of a cash flow statement is to show an overall view of money flowing in and out of a company during an accounting period.

- IAS 7, *Statement of Cash Flows*, is the accounting standard that sets out the requirements of cash flow statements.

- A cash flow statement is divided into three sections:
  1 operating activities – the main revenue-producing activities of the business, together with the payment of interest and tax
  2 investing activities – the acquisition and disposal of non-current assets, and some other investments
  3 financing activities – receipts from the issue of new shares, payments to cover the repayment of shares, changes in long-term borrowings

- **Cash from operations** is profit from operations (ie before deduction of tax and interest), add depreciation for the year, add loss (or deduct gain) on sale of non-current assets, deduct investment income, together with changes in inventories, trade receivables and payables.

- **Net cash from operating activities** is cash generated from operations (see above), deduct interest paid in period, deduct taxes paid on income in period.

- **Investing activities** are the cost of purchase and/or proceeds of sale of non-current assets; dividends received; interest received.

- **Financial activities** are the issue or repayment of share capital and/or long-term borrowings; dividends paid.

● Larger limited companies are required to include a cash flow statement as a part of their financial statements. They are also useful statements for smaller limited companies.

● User groups include:

- shareholders

- loan stock holders/debenture holders

- trade payables

- managers and employees

The next chapter focuses on further international accounting standards which impact on the published financial statements of limited companies.

QUESTIONS

visit
www.osbornebooks.co.uk
to take an online test

An asterisk (*) after the question number means that the answer is given at the end of this book.

6.1* Complete the following table to show the effect on cash – inflow, outflow, or no effect – of the transactions.

The first item has been completed as an example.

Transaction		Inflow of cash	Outflow of cash	No effect on cash
	Cash sales	✓		
(a)	Cash purchases			
(b)	Sold goods on credit			
(c)	Bought goods on credit			
(d)	Bought a non-current asset, paying by cheque			
(e)	A trade receivable pays by cheque			
(f)	Paid expenses in cash			
(g)	Paid a trade payable by cheque			

6.2 Explain why depreciation is added back to the profit from operations in the operating activities section of a cash flow statement.

6.3 Raven Limited has a profit from operations of £30,000 for 20-5, and there were the following movements in the year:

	£
depreciation charge	10,000
increase in inventories	5,000
decrease in trade receivables	4,000
increase in trade payables	6,000

Calculate the cash flow from operations for the year.

6.4 Meadow Limited has a loss from operations of £10,000 for 20-6, and there were the following movements in the year:

	£
depreciation charge	8,000
decrease in inventories	4,000
increase in trade receivables	5,000
decrease in trade payables	3,000

Calculate the cash flow from operations for the year.

6.5 Explain five points that you would look for when assessing the cash flow statement of a company.

6.6* (a) The cash flow statement is an integral part of the published accounts. What information will this provide for shareholders?

(b) Name two other financial statements which published accounts must contain.

Assessment and Qualifications Alliance (AQA), 2001

6.7 Set out below are figures extracted from the published cash flow statement of the Tesco group of companies.

group cash flow statement
52 weeks ended 23 February 2008

	2008 £m	2007 £m
Cash flows from operating activities		
Cash generated from operations	**4,099**	3,532
Interest paid	**(410)**	(376)
Corporation tax paid	**(346)**	(545)
Net cash from operating activities	**3,343**	2,611
Cash flows from investing activities		
Acquisition of subsidiaries, net of cash acquired	**(169)**	(325)
Proceeds from sale of subsidiary, net of cash disposed	–	22
Proceeds from sale of joint ventures and associates	–	41
Purchase of property, plant and equipment and investment property	**(3,442)**	(2,852)
Proceeds from sale of property, plant and equipment	**1,056**	809
Purchase of intangible assets	**(158)**	(174)
Increase in loans to joint ventures	**(36)**	(21)
Invested in joint ventures and associates	**(61)**	(49)
Invested in short-term investments	**(360)**	–
Dividends received	**88**	124
Interest received	**128**	82
Net cash used in investing activities	**(2,954)**	(2,343)

REQUIRED

(a) Explain the following terms:

(i) cash generated from operations

(ii) net cash from operating activities

(iii) net cash used in investing activities

(b) Explain the value of the information contained in a cash flow statement to:

(i) managers

(ii) shareholders

(iii) debenture holders

6.8* The following extract is taken from the cash flow statement of Durning Limited for the year ended 31 December 20-8. It gives the reconciliation of profit from operations to cash flow from operations.

	£
Profit from operations	71,250
Depreciation	6,500
Increase in inventories	(7,500)
Increase in trade receivables	(6,000)
Increase in trade payables	2,400
Cash from operations	66,650

(a) Explain the terms:

   (i) profit from operations

   (ii) cash from operations

(b) Explain why the following adjustments have been made to profit from operations:

   (i) depreciation – added

   (ii) increase in inventories – subtracted

   (iii) increase in trade receivables – subtracted

   (iv) increase in trade payables – added

6.9* What are the advantages to a company in producing a cash flow statement? Who will be the users of the cash flow statement and what will be their interest in it?

6.10 The Financial Accountant of Adagio plc is in the process of drafting the final accounts for the year ended 30 April 2004. She has provided the following information for the preparation of a cash flow statement:

	£000
Decrease in trade payables	1,787
Decrease in trade receivables	986
Decrease in inventories	48
Depreciation	3,490
Dividends paid	299
Loss on the disposal of non-current assets	58
Loss from operations for year	2,127
Purchase of non-current assets	1,795
Receipts from sale of non-current assets	818
Tax paid	278

REQUIRED

(a)   Prepare a 'reconciliation of profit from operations to the cash inflow/outflow from operating activities'.

(b)   Prepare a draft cash flow statement in accordance with IAS 7.

(c)   Explain to what extent a cash flow statement is essential in judging the financial performance of a company.

Assessment and Qualifications Alliance (AQA), 2004 –
amended in accordance with IAS 7

6.11   The directors of Halls-Krosby plc have produced a draft cash flow statement for the year ended 31 March 2007. The following is an extract from that cash flow statement.

Reconciliation of operating profit to net cash inflow from operating activities		
	£000	£000
Operating profit		573
Depreciation – property, plant, equipment		(206)
Loss on disposal of machinery		(18)
Receipts from sale of machinery		38
Increase in inventory		(230)
Increase in trade receivables		(62)
Decrease in trade payables		(46)
Dividends paid – preference shares	(24)	
ordinary shares	(66)	(90)
Receipt from share premium on issue of ordinary shares		950
Net cash inflow from operating activities		909

REQUIRED

(a)   Prepare a corrected reconciliation of operating profit to net cash inflow from operating activities.

(b)   Explain **three** of the changes made to the original reconciliation statement.

Assessment and Qualifications Alliance (AQA), Specimen Paper for 2010 (part of question)

6.12*   The book-keeper of Hall Plc has asked for your assistance in producing a cash flow statement for the company for the year ended 30 September 20-5 in accordance with IAS 7.

She has derived the information which is required to be included in the cash flow statement, but is not sure of the format in which it should be presented. The information is set out below:

	£000
Profit from operations (before interest and tax)	24
Depreciation charge for the year	318
Proceeds from sale of non-current assets	132
Issue of shares for cash	150
Cash received from new loan	200
Purchase of non-current assets for cash	358
Interest paid	218
Tax paid	75
Dividends paid	280
Increase in inventories	251
Increase in trade receivables	152
Increase in trade payables	165
Cash and cash equivalents at 1 October 20-4	395
Cash and cash equivalents at 30 September 20-5	50

REQUIRED

Using the information provided by the book-keeper, prepare a cash flow statement for Hall Plc for the year ended 30 September 20-5 in accordance with the requirements of IAS 7.

6.13*   Pancholi Plc's income statement for the year ended 31 December 20-3 and balance sheets for 20-2 and 20-3 were as follows:

Income Statement for the year ended 31 December 20-3

	£000	£000
Revenue		652
Cost of sales		(349)
GROSS PROFIT		303
Wages and salaries	(107)	
Depreciation charges	(30)	
Administrative expenses	(62)	(199)
PROFIT FROM OPERATIONS		104
Interest paid		(5)
PROFIT BEFORE TAX		99
Tax		(22)
PROFIT AFTER TAX		77

Balance Sheet as at 31 December

	20-3		20-2	
	£000	£000	£000	£000
NON-CURRENT ASSETS		570		600
CURRENT ASSETS				
Inventories	203		175	
Trade receivables	141		127	
Cash and cash equivalents	6			
	350		302	
CURRENT LIABILITIES				
Trade payables	(142)		(118)	
Tax liabilities	(22)		(19)	
Bank overdraft	–		(16)	
	(164)		(153)	
NET CURRENT ASSETS		186		149
		756		749
NON-CURRENT LIABILITIES				
Loans and debentures		–		(50)
NET ASSETS		756		699
EQUITY				
Share capital		300		300
Share premium		60		60
Retained earnings		396		339
TOTAL EQUITY		756		699

Notes to the accounts:
* Dividends of £20,000 were paid in 20-3.
* During the year there were no purchases or sales of non-current assets.

REQUIRED

(a) Prepare a cash flow statement for Pancholi Plc for the year ended 31 December 20-3 in accordance with the requirements of IAS 7.

(b) Assess the cash flow statement of Pancholi Plc from the point of view of the company's shareholders.

6.14* Sheehan Plc's abridged income statement for the year ended 31 October 20-3 and balance sheets for 20-2 and 20-3 were as follows:

Income Statement for the year ended 31 October 20-3

	£000
PROFIT FROM OPERATIONS	2,520
Interest paid	(168)
Profit before tax	2,352
Tax	(750)
Profit after tax	1,602

Balance Sheet as at 31 October

	20-3		20-2	
	£000	£000	£000	£000
NON-CURRENT ASSETS				
At cost	9,000		8,400	
Depreciation to date	(1,800)	7,200	(1,500)	6,900
CURRENT ASSETS				
Inventories	84		69	
Trade receivables	255		270	
Cash and cash equivalents	48		30	
	387		369	
CURRENT LIABILITIES				
Trade payables	(108)		(81)	
Tax liabilities	(291)		(285)	
	(399)		(366)	
NET CURRENT ASSETS (LIABILITIES)		(12)		3
		7,188		6,903
NON-CURRENT LIABILITIES				
Loans		(600)		(2,400)
NET ASSETS		6,588		4,503
EQUITY				
Share capital		3,000		2,550
Share premium		177		–
Retained earnings		3,411		1,953
TOTAL EQUITY		6,588		4,503

Additional Information:

- Dividends of £144,000 were paid in 20-3; tax of £744,000 was paid in 20-3.
- During the year the company sold a non-current asset for £8,000 cash. The asset had originally cost £29,000 and had been depreciated by £18,000 at the time of sale.

Required

(a) Prepare a statement to show the reconciliation of profit from operations to net cash flow from operating activities for the year ended 31 October 20-3.

(b) Prepare a cash flow statement for the year ended 31 October 20-3 in accordance with the requirements of IAS 7.

6.15 You have been given the following information about Kalsi Plc for the year ending 31 March 20-5:

Income Statement for the year ended 31 March 20-5

	£000	£000
Revenue		2,500
Opening inventories	200	
Purchases	1,500	
Less Closing inventories	210	
Cost of sales		(1,490)
GROSS PROFIT		1,010
Depreciation		(275)
Other expenses		(500)
Gain on sale of fixed asset		2
PROFIT FROM OPERATIONS		237
Interest paid		(20)
PROFIT BEFORE TAX		217
Tax		(25)
PROFIT AFTER TAX		192

Balance Sheet as at 31 March

	20-5		20-4	
	£000	£000	£000	£000
NON-CURRENT ASSETS		330		500
CURRENT ASSETS				
Inventories	210		200	
Trade receivables	390		250	
Cash and cash equivalents	–		10	
	600		460	
CURRENT LIABILITIES				
Trade payables	(150)		(160)	
Tax liabilities	(25)		(21)	
Bank overdraft	(199)		–	
	(374)		(181)	
NET CURRENT ASSETS		226		279
		556		779
NON-CURRENT LIABILITIES				
Debentures		–		(500)
Long-term loan		(200)		(100)
NET ASSETS		356		179
EQUITY				
Share capital		40		25
Retained earnings		316		154
TOTAL EQUITY		356		179

Additional information

- Dividends of £30,000 were paid in 20-5.
- In May 20-4 a non-current asset was sold which originally cost £10,000 and was purchased in July 20-2. In June 20-4 a new asset was bought for £110,000. Non-current assets are depreciated at 25 per cent of cost. The policy is to charge a full year's depreciation in the year of purchase and none in the year of sale.
- During the year, the debentures were redeemed.
- During the year, 15,000 new ordinary £1 shares were issued at par.

REQUIRED

(a) Prepare a statement to show the reconciliation of profit from operations to net cash flow from operating activities for the year to 31 March 20-5.

(b) Prepare a cash flow statement for the year to 31 March 20-5 in accordance with the requirements of IAS 7.

(c) Assess the cash flow statement of Kalsi Plc from the point of view of the company's shareholders.

7 ACCOUNTING STANDARDS

In this chapter we focus on the regulatory framework of accounting, which forms the 'rules' of preparing and presenting financial statements. The regulatory framework – which comprises accounting standards and company law – has developed over the last forty years.

In AQA A2 Accounting we use international accounting standards and look at the impact they have on the way assets, liabilities and income are accounted for in the income statements and balance sheets of limited companies.

The reasons for using international accounting standards include:

● providing a framework – the 'rules' – for preparing financial statements

● ensuring that accountants follow the same set of rules

● reducing the number of different accounting treatments

The benefits include:

● standardising financial statements internationally

● reducing the variations of accounting treatments

● allowing users of financial statements to make inter-firm comparisons

THE REGULATORY FRAMEWORK OF ACCOUNTING

The regulatory framework forms the 'rules' of accounting. When preparing and presenting financial statements for limited companies, accountants follow the same set of rules – thus enabling comparisons to be made between the financial results of different companies.

The regulatory framework comprises:

• accounting standards

• company law

Since 2005 the European Union (EU) has required all companies listed on a stock exchange to prepare their financial statements in accordance with international accounting standards. Furthermore, member states of the EU have the option of extending this regulation to apply to companies – private and public, including those not listed on a stock exchange.

The following diagram explains the development of the regulatory framework in the UK over the last forty years.

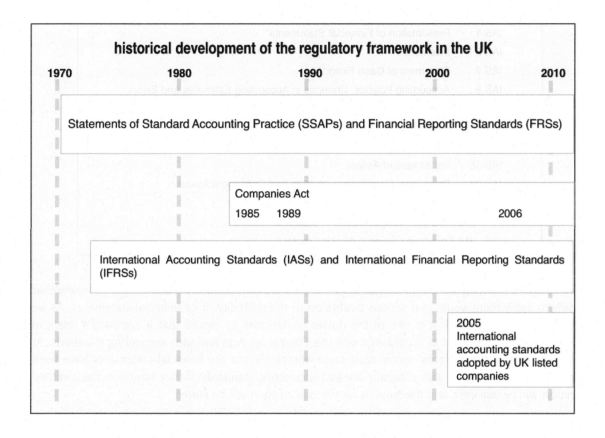

accounting standards

Over the last forty years, a number of accounting standards have been produced to provide a framework for accounting and to reduce the variety of accounting treatments which companies may use in their financial statements.

Statements of Standard Accounting Practice (SSAPs) and **Financial Reporting Standards (FRSs),** which are issued by the Financial Reporting Council, are the UK domestic accounting standards. They apply to company accounts which are not required to use international accounting standards. Note that the older standards are SSAPs – they are being replaced by FRSs.

International accounting standards – in the form of **International Accounting Standards (IASs)** and **International Financial Reporting Standards (IFRSs)** – have been developed by the International Accounting Standards Board (formerly the International Accounting Standards Committee) since 1973 with the aim of harmonising international financial reporting. Since 2005, all EU listed companies have been required to prepare their accounts in accordance with international accounting standards. It seems that it will be only a matter of time before these standards become mandatory for all UK companies.

In AQA A2 Accounting we will study a number of international accounting standards, as follows:

IAS 1	Presentation of Financial Statements*
IAS 2	Inventories
IAS 7	Statement of Cash Flows**
IAS 8	Accounting Policies, Changes in Accounting Estimates and Errors
IAS 10	Events after the Reporting Period
IAS 16	Property, Plant and Equipment
IAS 18	Revenue
IAS 36	Impairment of Assets
IAS 37	Provisions, Contingent Liabilities and Contingent Assets
IAS 38	Intangible Assets
*	IAS 1 has been covered in detail in Chapter 5
**	IAS 7 has been covered in detail in Chapter 6

Although accounting standards are not laws – ie they are non-statutory – any limited company that fails to apply them would cast serious doubts on to the reliability of its financial statements. As we have seen in Chapter 5, it is one of the duties of directors to ensure that a company's financial statements are prepared in accordance with the Companies Acts and with accounting standards. At the same time, the auditors' report must state whether or not the financial statements have been prepared in accordance with company law and accounting standards: if they have not, the auditors' report will be qualified, and the reasons for the qualification will be stated.

summary

The **reasons** for using international accounting standards are:

- to provide a framework for preparing and presenting financial statements – the 'rules' of accounting
- to ensure that accountants follow the same set of rules
- to reduce the number of different accounting treatments and so make 'window dressing' – the practice of manipulating figures to make things look better than they really are – more difficult
- to meet with the duty of the directors to ensure that financial statements comply with accounting standards
- to meet with the auditors' report requirement to state that the financial statements have been prepared in accordance with accounting standards

The **benefits** of international accounting standards are:

- to standardise financial statements internationally – thus a company operating in several countries knows that the same accounting rules have been applied to all parts of its business
- to reduce the variations of accounting treatments used in financial statements – thus making 'window dressing' the accounts more difficult
- to allow users of financial statements to make inter-firm comparisons in the knowledge that all the financial statements have been prepared using the same standards

A current list of all international accounting standards is available on the International Accounting Standards Board's website – www.iasb.org.uk – where you will be able to keep up-to-date with developments. Note that IASs are the older standards, which are being replaced with IFRSs – the collective term for both is 'international accounting standards'.

company law

Limited companies are regulated by the Companies Acts of 1985, 1989 and 2006. In particular, the Acts require that company financial statements must state that they have been prepared in accordance with applicable accounting standards and, if there have been any material departures, must give details and the reasons for such departures.

ACCOUNTING POLICIES

In Chapter 5 we have already studied the published accounts of limited companies and, in particular, the requirements of IAS 1, *Presentation of Financial Statements*. IAS 1 requires that companies comply with a number of accounting concepts and the accounting standard includes the following:

- going concern
- accruals
- consistency
- materiality

Please refer back to Chapter 5, page 111, to review these concepts in more detail.

IAS 8 – Accounting Policies, Changes in Accounting Estimates and Errors

This accounting standard defines accounting policies as '*the specific principles, bases, conventions, rules and practices applied by an entity* [eg a company] *in preparing and presenting financial statements.*' Included in the definition are accounting principles and accounting bases:

- accounting principles are the broad concepts that are applied in the preparation of financial statements, eg going concern, accruals, consistency
- accounting bases are the methods used for applying accounting principles to financial statements, which are intended to reduce subjectivity by identifying the acceptable methods, eg the use of historic cost or revaluation to value assets

Accounting policies are the specific accounting bases selected by the directors and followed by a company, such as the method of depreciation.

Once adopted by a company, accounting policies are applied consistently for similar transactions – unless an accounting standard allows differing policies to be applied to categories of items. Changes of accounting policies can only occur:

- if the change is required by an accounting standard; or
- if the change results in the financial statements providing reliable and more relevant information

Any changes in accounting policies require the figure for equity and other figures from the income statement and balance sheet to be altered for previous financial statements so that comparisons can be made.

IAS 8 also deals with the effect of errors on the financial statements. It defines errors as '*omissions from, and misstatements in, the entity's financial statements for one or more prior periods arising from a failure to use, or misuse of, reliable information that*:

- *was available when financial statements for those periods were authorised for issue; and*
- *could reasonably be expected to have been obtained and taken into account in the preparation and presentation of those financial statements.*'

Note that such errors can result from mathematical mistakes, mistakes in applying accounting policies, oversights or misinterpretations of facts, and fraud.

A company must correct material errors that occurred in previous accounting periods in the next set of financial statements by restating and comparing the incorrect information along with the correct information.

ACCOUNTING FOR ASSETS

In this section we examine the accounting treatment of assets – non-current and current – as specified by the international accounting standards. The diagram which follows shows the questions to be asked when dealing with assets:

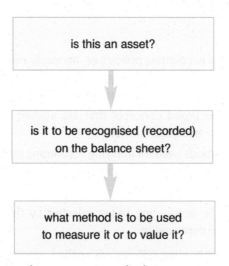

An asset is defined by international accounting standards as: '*a resource controlled by the entity as a result of past events and from which future economic benefits are expected to flow to the entity.*'

The definition refers to a resource being *controlled* (and not necessarily owned). Thus a company which leases an asset – such as a machine – from a leasing company may well recognise the asset on its balance sheet, even though it is not the legal owner. Note that there is also the requirement for the asset to generate future economic benefits for the company.

In order to be recognised (ie recorded) on the balance sheet, assets must be capable of being measured in money terms at either their historic cost or a revaluation.

Once an asset is recorded on the balance sheet, there is then the question of how it is to be subsequently measured in money terms – for example, at cost less depreciation, or revaluation. The international accounting standards which follow set out the criteria of different classes of assets: *Property, Plant and Equipment* (IAS 16), *Intangible Assets* (IAS 38) and *Inventories* (IAS 2), together with *Impairment of Assets* (IAS 36).

IAS 16 – PROPERTY, PLANT AND EQUIPMENT

The purpose of this standard is to set out the accounting treatment for property, plant and equipment (PPE). These are non-current tangible assets such as land and buildings, machinery, office equipment, shop fittings and vehicles.

The key features covered by the standard are the recognition of the assets, the measurement of assets and the depreciation charges to be recognised in relation to them.

definitions

Property, plant and equipment are tangible assets held for use in the production or supply of goods and services, which are expected to be used for more than one accounting period.

Depreciation is the systematic allocation of the depreciable amount of an asset over its useful life.

Depreciable amount is the cost or valuation of the asset, less any residual value.

Useful life is the length of time, or the number of units of production, for which an asset is expected to be used.

Residual value is the net amount the business expects to obtain for an asset at the end of its useful life after deducting the expected costs of disposal.

Fair value is the amount for which an asset could be exchanged between knowledgeable, willing parties in an arm's length transaction.

Carrying amount is the amount at which an asset is recognised in the balance sheet, after deducting any accumulated depreciation or impairment losses.

recognition

An item of property, plant and equipment is to be recognised as an asset when

– it is probable that *future economic benefits* will flow to the business; and

– the cost of the asset can be *measured reliably*

measurement of property, plant and equipment

Initially PPE are measured (recorded) at cost in the balance sheet.

Cost includes the purchase price, together with any import duties, any costs attributable to make the asset fit for use at the intended location, and any estimated costs of dismantling and removing the asset at the end of its life.

After acquisition of PPE a company must choose either the cost method or the revaluation method as its accounting policy – which is then applied to an entire class of PPE. The two methods are defined as follows:

- Cost – the tangible asset is shown in the balance sheet at cost less accumulated depreciation and impairment losses (see IAS 36, *Impairment of Assets*, page 183).

- Revaluation – the tangible asset is shown in the balance sheet at a revalued amount, being its fair value* less subsequent depreciation and impairment losses; revaluations are to be made regularly to ensure that the revalued amount does not differ materially from its fair value at the balance sheet date.

  * fair value is defined on the previous page; its use is subject to the fair value being able to be measured reliably

When an item of PPE is revalued, the entire class of assets to which it belongs must be revalued. Note that classes are groups of similar assets, for example land, buildings, machinery, vehicles, fixtures and fittings, office equipment, etc. Revaluations are dealt with as follows:

- any increase in value is credited directly to a *revaluation surplus* in the equity section of the balance sheet

- any reduction in value is shown as an expense in the income statement (although any reduction which reverses an earlier increase in value for the same asset is debited to the revaluation surplus)

depreciation

Depreciation is to be charged on all non-current assets with the exception of freehold land, which is shown at cost (but leasehold land will be depreciated). Note that land and buildings are separated out and accounted for separately – the land is not depreciated, but buildings have a limited useful life and are depreciated.

Depreciation methods include the straight-line and the diminishing (reducing) balance methods – you will be familiar with these from your studies at AS Level. Key features of these are:

- straight-line depreciation results in a constant depreciation charge over the asset's useful life

- diminishing (reducing) balance depreciation results in a decreasing depreciation charge over the useful life (ie the depreciation in the early years is greater than in later years)

A company chooses the depreciation method which best reflects the way in which the asset's economic benefits are consumed. The depreciation method used should be reviewed at least annually in order to consider if the method used is still the most appropriate one.

WORKED EXAMPLE: CALCULATING DEPRECIATION

situation

You are an accounts assistant at Brocken Limited, an engineering company. The company has recently bought a new computer-controlled cutting machine for use in the factory. You have been asked by the finance director to prepare depreciation calculations, based on the following information:

CUTTING MACHINE	
Cost price on 1 January 20-6	£20,000
Estimated life	4 years
Estimated residual value at end of four years	£4,000

The finance director wants you to compare the straight-line method and the diminishing (reducing) balance methods of depreciation, and to prepare a table for each method showing the amount of depreciation expense per year recognised in the income statement, and the net book value of the asset for the balance sheet.

solution

straight-line depreciation

With this method, a fixed percentage is written off the original cost of the asset each year. For this machine, twenty-five per cent of the depreciable amount will be written off each year by the straight-line method.

The method of calculating straight-line depreciation, taking into account the asset's estimated residual value at the end of its useful life, is:

$$\frac{\text{cost of asset – estimated residual (scrap or salvage) value}}{\text{number of years' expected use of asset}}$$

The machine is expected to have a residual value of £4,000, so the depreciation amount will be:

$$\frac{£20,000 – £4,000}{4 \text{ years}} = £4,000 \text{ per year}$$

diminishing (reducing) balance depreciation

With this method, a fixed percentage is written off the diminished balance each year. The diminished (reduced) balance is cost of the asset less depreciation to date. The machine is to be depreciated by 33.3% (one-third) each year, using the diminishing balance method (see calculations). The depreciation amounts for the four years of ownership are:

	£
Original cost of machine	20,000
20-6 depreciation: 33.3% of £20,000	<u>6,667</u>
Value at end of 20-6	13,333
20-7 depreciation: 33.3% of £13,333	<u>4,444</u>
Value at end of 20-7	8,889
20-8 depreciation: 33.3% of £8,889	<u>2,963</u>
Value at end of 20-8	5,926
20-9 depreciation: 33.3% of £5,926	<u>1,926</u>
Residual value at end of 20-9	4,000

Note that the figures have been rounded to the nearest £, and depreciation for 20-9 has been adjusted by approximately £50 to leave a residual value of £4,000.

Although you will not need to use it in your examination, you may be interested in the formula to calculate the percentage of reducing balance depreciation:

$$r = 1 - \sqrt[n]{\frac{s}{c}}$$

In this formula:

r	=	percentage rate of depreciation
n	=	number of years
s	=	residual value
c	=	cost of asset

For the machine above, the 33.3% is calculated as:

$$r = 1 - \sqrt[4]{\frac{4,000}{20,000}}$$

$$r = 1 - \sqrt[4]{0.2} \quad \text{(to find the fourth root press the square root key on the calculator twice)}$$

$$r = 1 - 0.669$$

$$r = 0.331 \text{ or } 33.1\% \text{ (which is close to the 33.3\% used above)}$$

depreciation methods compared

straight-line depreciation				
	1	2	3	4
Year	Original cost	Depreciation for year	Aggregate depreciation	Net book value (ie column 1-3)
	£	£	£	£
20-6	20,000	4,000	4,000	16,000
20-7	20,000	4,000	8,000	12,000
20-8	20,000	4,000	12,000	8,000
20-9	20,000	4,000	16,000	4,000

Note: Net book value is cost, less aggregate depreciation, ie column 1, less column 3.

These calculations will be used in the financial statements as follows: taking 20-7 as an example, the income statement will recognise £4,000 (column 2) as an expense, while the balance sheet will show £12,000 (column 4) as the net book value (carrying amount).

diminishing balance depreciation				
	1	2	3	4
Year	Original cost	Depreciation for year	Aggregate depreciation	Net book value (ie column 1-3)
	£	£	£	£
20-6	20,000	6,667	6,667	13,333
20-7	20,000	4,444	11,111	8,889
20-8	20,000	2,963	14,074	5,926
20-9	20,000	1,926	16,000	4,000

COMPARISON OF DEPRECIATION METHODS			
METHOD	**depreciation amount**	**depreciation rate**	**suitability**
straight-line	same money amount each year	lower depreciation percentage required to achieve same residual value	best used for non-current assets likely to be kept for the whole of their useful lives, eg machines, office equipment
diminishing balance	different money amounts each year: more than straight-line in early years, less in later years	higher depreciation percentage required to achieve same residual value – but can never reach nil value	best used for non-current assets which depreciate more in early years and which are not kept for whole of useful lives, eg vehicles

Note: Whichever of these two depreciation methods is selected, the total profits of the company over the life of the asset will be the same. The methods will cause the profit for individual years to be different but, overall, the same total depreciation is recognised as an expense in the income statement. IAS 16 requires that the depreciable amount (cost less residual value) of an asset is to be allocated on a systematic basis over its useful life. As depreciation is 'non-cash' there is no effect on the bank balance.

IAS 38 – INTANGIBLE ASSETS

The purpose of this standard is to set out the accounting treatment of expenditure on intangible assets.

The key features covered by the standard are the definition and recognition of intangible assets and the measurement of intangible assets. Note that IAS 38 does not cover the intangible asset of goodwill – this is dealt with under a different international accounting standard, which is not studied for AQA A2 Accounting.

definition

An intangible asset is defined as '*an identifiable non-monetary asset without physical substance*'. An asset is a resource:

– controlled by a business as a result of past events (eg a purchase transaction), and

– from which future economic benefits (eg cash inflows) are expected to flow to the business

Examples of intangible assets include patents, copyrights, customer lists, licences and marketing rights.

The definition sets out the three key elements of an intangible asset as being:

- *identifiability* – the asset is either separate from the business so that it is capable of being sold or transferred, or it arises from contractual rights

- *control* – the business has the power to obtain future economic benefits from the asset

- *future economic benefits* – include revenue from the sale of products or services, cost savings, or other benefits

recognition

Intangible assets come about from two main sources: either they are purchased, or they are internally generated (ie created within the business). In both cases the intangible asset is recognised initially in the financial statements at cost price when:

– it is probable that the expected future economic benefits that are attributable to the asset will flow to the business; and

– the cost of the asset can be measured reliably

Important note: internally generated goodwill must never be recognised as an asset and recorded in the financial statements.

measurement of intangible assets

Initially, intangible assets are recorded at cost in the balance sheet. However, after acquisition, a company can choose either the cost model or the revaluation model – in the same way as for property, plant and equipment – as follows:

- **Cost** – the intangible asset is shown in the balance sheet at cost less accumulated amortisation (depreciation) and impairment losses.

- **Revaluation** – the intangible asset is shown in the balance sheet at a revalued amount, being its fair value (see page 177) less subsequent amortisation and impairment losses.

Like tangible assets, intangible assets are amortised (depreciated) – usually using the straight-line method.

IAS 36 – IMPAIRMENT OF ASSETS

The purpose of this standard is to set out the accounting treatment to ensure that assets are shown in the balance sheet at no more than their value, or recoverable amount. If the recoverable amount of an asset is less than its carrying amount, then the carrying value is to be reduced. This is an impairment loss, which is recognised as an expense in the income statement.

The key features covered by the standard are the definition of impairment, indicators of impairment, the impairment review, and the recognition of impairment losses.

definitions

Carrying amount is the amount at which an asset is recognised after deducting any accumulated depreciation/amortisation and accumulated impairment losses (ie the amount of an asset's net book value).

Depreciation (Amortisation) is the systematic allocation of the depreciable amount of an asset over its useful life.

Note: the term 'amortisation' is customarily used in relation to intangible assets instead of 'depreciation' – however, the two terms have the same meaning.

Depreciable amount is the cost of an asset less its residual value.

Impairment loss is the amount by which the carrying amount of an asset exceeds its recoverable amount.

Fair value, less costs to sell is the amount at which an asset could be sold for, less any selling costs.

Recoverable amount of an asset is the higher of its

- fair value, less any costs that would be incurred were it to be sold

- its value in use

Useful life is either

- the period of time over which an asset is expected to be used; or

- the number of production units expected to be obtained from the asset

Value in use is the present value of the future cash flows from an asset's continued use, including cash from its final sale

scope of the standard

IAS 36 applies to most non-current assets, such as land and buildings, plant and machinery, vehicles, goodwill. Assets need to be reviewed at each balance sheet date to judge whether there is any evidence of impairment. Impairment occurs when the recoverable amount is less than the asset's carrying amount. If there is an impairment loss, the asset is shown in the balance sheet at its recoverable amount and the impairment loss is shown in the income statement as a loss.

indicators of impairment

IAS 36 gives a number of external and internal indicators of impairment, of which the following are some examples:

External sources

- a significant fall in the asset's market value
- adverse effects on the business caused by technology,' markets, the economy, laws
- increases in interest rates

Internal sources

- obsolescence or physical damage to the asset
- adverse effects on the asset of a significant reorganisation within the business

the impairment review

An impairment review involves comparing the asset's carrying amount with the recoverable amount. The three steps are as follows:

STEP 1   What is the asset's carrying amount (net book value, ie cost/revaluation less depreciation/amortisation to date)?

STEP 2   What is the asset's recoverable amount? See the diagram below.

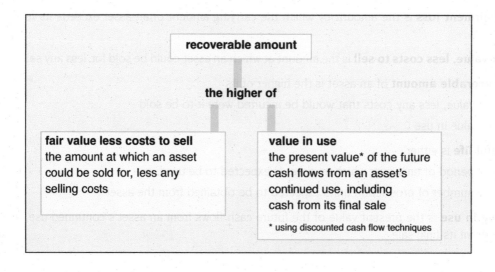

STEP 3   If an asset's carrying amount is greater than recoverable amount, then the asset is impaired and should be written down to its recoverable amount in the balance sheet. The amount of the impairment loss is shown as an expense in the income statement.

recognition of impairment losses

An impairment loss is to be recognised when the recoverable amount is less than the carrying amount. The asset is reduced to its recoverable amount and the impairment loss is shown as an expense in the income statement. After recognition of an impairment loss, depreciation/amortisation will need to be adjusted for future financial periods.

WORKED EXAMPLE: THE IMPAIRMENT REVIEW

situation

Initial Training plc is a large training organisation providing government-sponsored 'return-to-work' courses.

You are helping to prepare the company's year end financial statements and have been asked by your boss, the company accountant, to carry out an impairment review of non-current assets held at the training centre at Rowcester. Today you have obtained details of the two photocopiers in the print room at Rowcester:

- **Machine 1** is six years old and is a relatively slow photocopier based on old technology. The cost of this machine was £8,000 and depreciation to date (the year end) is £4,800, giving it a net book value of £3,200. Since the arrival of the other photocopier, this machine has been relegated to 'standby' use.

- **Machine 2** is only a few months old. It is a digital copier incorporating the latest technology. It is very fast and versatile, and has the capacity to meet the needs of the entire training centre. It cost £15,000 and depreciation to the end of the financial year will be £1,500, giving it a net book value of £13,500. This machine is much preferred by the staff who use it as a first choice.

solution

The impairment review you carry out is as follows:

Machine 1

- Carrying value (ie net book value): £3,200

- The company accountant has given you the following information to enable you to calculate the recoverable amount, the higher of:

  - fair value: £1,000 resale value of machine on the secondhand market (there would be no selling costs on disposal)

  - value in use: £2,000 being the present value of the future benefits from continued use as a standby machine

  Therefore the recoverable amount is £2,000.

- As the carrying value of £3,200 is greater than the machine's recoverable amount of £2,000, the asset is impaired. Accordingly, the amount of the impairment loss of £1,200 is to be shown as an expense in the income statement, and the value of the machine will be shown in the company's balance sheet at the recoverable amount of £2,000.

Machine 2

- Carrying value (ie net book value): £13,500

- You are given the following information to enable you to calculate the recoverable amount:

  the higher of

  - fair value: £10,000 resale value of machine on the secondhand market (there would be no selling costs on disposal)

  - value in use: £55,000 being the present value of the future benefits from continued use as the main machine

  Therefore recoverable amount is £55,000.

- As the carrying value of £13,500 is less than the machine's recoverable amount of £55,000, the asset is not impaired. Accordingly, the machine will be shown in the company's balance sheet at cost price less depreciation to date, ie a net book value of £13,500.

IAS 2 – INVENTORIES

The purpose of this standard is to set out the accounting techniques to be used when valuing inventories.

Companies often have inventories in various forms:

- raw materials, for use in a manufacturing business

- work-in-progress (partly manufactured goods) and finished goods (ready for sale) of a manufacturing business

- products bought for resale by a retailer

- service items, such as stationery, bought for use within a business

IAS 2 applies to all types of inventories.

The overriding principle of inventory valuation, as set out in IAS 2, is that inventories are to be valued at 'the lower of cost and net realisable value'.

Thus two different inventory values are compared:

- cost, which means the purchase price, plus any other costs incurred to bring the product to its present location and condition

- net realisable value, which is the estimated selling price less the estimated costs to get the product into a condition necessary to complete the sale

The lower of these two values is taken, and different items or groups of inventory are compared separately.

Inventory valuation is covered more fully in the next chapter – see Chapter 8.

Accounting for Liabilities

In this section we examine the accounting treatment of liabilities – non-current and current – as specified by the international accounting standards. A liability is defined by international accounting standards as: '*a present obligation of the entity arising from past events, the settlement of which is expected to result in an outflow from the entity of resources embodying economic benefits.*'

Note the three key parts of the definition:

- a present obligation of the entity (company)
- arising from past events
- the settlement of which is expected to result in an outflow from the entity

Thus a company which has bought goods or services on credit has a present obligation in the form of an amount owed to trade payables, which arises from past events such as a purchase order made last month, and which will result in settlement in the form of resources embodying economic benefits, ie payment will be made from the company's bank account.

In order to be recognised on the balance sheet, liabilities must be capable of being reliably measured. If the liability cannot be reliably measured then it will often be disclosed in the notes to the accounts.

The international accounting standards which follow set out the recognition and measurement criteria of different liabilities: *Provisions, Contingent Liabilities and Contingent Assets* (IAS 37) and *Events after the Reporting Period* (IAS 10).

IAS 37 – Provisions, Contingent Liabilities and Contingent Assets

The purpose of this standard is to achieve a consistent accounting treatment for provisions, contingent liabilities and contingent assets.

The key features covered by the standard are to ensure that companies disclose in the notes to the financial statements the bases of treatment used; in this way, users can understand the nature, timing and amount of provisions, contingent liabilities and contingent assets.

provisions

A provision is a liability of uncertain timing or amount, where:

- the company has an obligation as a result of a past event
- it is probable that the company will have to settle the obligation (eg payment will be made)
- a reliable financial estimate can be made of the obligation

If all of the above conditions are met, then the provision must be shown as a liability in the financial statements.

For provisions, IAS 37 uses the word 'probable' as being more likely to occur than not, ie a more than 50% likelihood of its occurrence.

Provisions differ from other liabilities such as trade payables and accruals. This is because, with provisions, there is uncertainty as to the timing or amount of the future expenditure required to settle. Contrast this with trade payables where the goods or services have been received or supplied and the amount due has either been invoiced or agreed with the supplier. Similarly, with accruals there is a liability to pay and, even if the amount may have to be estimated, the uncertainty is usually much less than for provisions.

The amount of the provision is shown as an expense in the income statement and as a liability in the balance sheet (either as a current or non-current liability). At each balance sheet date, the amount of provision is to be reviewed and adjusted to reflect the current best estimate. If a provision is no longer required, it is to be reversed and shown as income in the income statement.

Disclosure in the notes to the financial statements requires:

- – movements in the amount of provisions during the financial year
- – a description of the provisions and expected timings of any resulting expenditure
- – an indication of the uncertainties regarding the amount or timing of any resulting expenditure

contingent liabilities

A contingent liability is *either*:

- a possible obligation arising from past events whose outcome is based on uncertain future events
  or
- an obligation that is not recognised because it is not probable or cannot be measured reliably

Note that a contingent liability is a *possible* obligation, ie less than 50% likelihood of its occurrence (contrast this with the *probable* obligation of a provision, ie more than 50% likelihood of its occurrence).

A contingent liability is not recognised in the financial statements; however, it should be disclosed as a note to the statements to include:

- a description of the contingent liability
- an estimate of its financial effect
- an indication of the uncertainties regarding the amount or timing of any resulting expenditure

Note that where a contingent liability is considered to be remote (contrast with possible), then no disclosure is required in the notes to the financial statements.

contingent assets

A contingent asset is a possible asset arising from past events whose existence will be confirmed only by uncertain future events not wholly within the control of the business.

A business should not recognise a contingent asset in its financial statements (because it would not be prudent to recognise income that may never be realised). However, when the realisation of the profit is virtually certain, then the asset is no longer contingent and its recognition in the financial statements is appropriate.

A contingent asset is disclosed only where an inflow of economic benefits is probable; disclosure in the notes to the financial statements should include:

- a description of the contingent asset
- an estimate of its financial effect

Note that, where the asset is considered to be either possible or remote, then no disclosure is required in the notes to the financial statements.

summary

The following diagram summarises the ways in which provisions, contingent liabilities and contingent assets are to be handled in the financial statements.

PROVISIONS (more than 50% likelihood of occurrence)	CONTINGENT LIABILITIES (less than 50% likelihood of occurrence)	
Probable • provision recognised in financial statements as a liability • disclosure of provision in notes, giving details of the figure shown in the statements	**Possible** • no liability recognised in financial statements • disclosure of contingent liability in notes	**Remote** • no liability recognised in financial statements • no disclosure of contingent liability in notes
CONTINGENT ASSETS		
Probable • no asset recognised in financial statements • disclosure of contingent asset in notes	**Possible** • no asset recognised in financial statements • no disclosure of contingent asset in notes	**Remote** • no asset recognised in financial statements • no disclosure of contingent asset in notes

WORKED EXAMPLE: WHAT SHOULD BE SHOWN IN THE FINANCIAL
STATEMENTS?

situation

Wyvern Water Limited is a producer of spa water which is bottled at source high in the Wyvern Hills. The company also produces a very successful high energy drink – with a secret mix of Wyvern Water, glucose, and vitamins – marketed under the 'Dr Wyvern' label to sports enthusiasts.

You are helping to prepare the year end financial statements and have been asked to decide how the following should be reported in the year to 31 December 20-6.

1   Earlier in the year, a small batch of bottles of spa water was contaminated with oil from the bottling machinery. Although the problem was spotted by quality control checks, and most bottles were withdrawn from sale, some were sold to the public. In a few instances consumers of the water suffered severe stomach upsets and had to spend a night in hospital. These consumers are currently suing Wyvern Water for damages. The company's legal representatives consider that it is probable that the company will lose the case and that damages of £50,000 will be awarded against the company.

2   Wyvern Water holds worldwide patents and trademarks for the 'Dr Wyvern' energy drink. However, it has recently had letters from somebody claiming to be a Dr Wyvern who says that he devised the secret formula for the drink over fifty years ago. The mysterious Dr Wyvern is claiming royalties on sales of the drink for the past fifty years and says he will sue the company for £10 million if he is not paid. Wyvern Water has checked carefully and found that the formula for the high energy drink was devised ten years ago by its own development team and that all applicable patents and trademarks are held. The company has sought legal advice and been advised that it is extremely unlikely that the claimant's case, if it gets to court, will be successful.

3   During the year Wyvern Water Limited has formed a separate company, Wyvern Foods Limited, to manufacture 'homestyle' pies and cakes. Wyvern Water has given a guarantee to Mercia Bank plc in respect of bank overdraft facilities provided to Wyvern Foods. At 31 December 20-6 it is considered possible (but not probable) that Wyvern Water will have to make payment under the guarantee.

solution

1 Court case for damages

- The obligation is the potential liability to pay damages from a past event, ie the sale of contaminated bottled water.
- It is probable that the company will lose the case and have to pay damages.
- The amount of damages is reliably estimated at £50,000.
- The company will record a provision as an expense in its income statement and as a liability in its balance sheet.
- Details of the provision will be disclosed in the notes to the financial statements.

2 Claim for past royalties

- This is a possible obligation arising from past events, ie the sale of 'Dr Wyvern' energy drink.

- However, the possible obligation will be confirmed only by an uncertain future event – a court case.
- Legal advice considers the claimant's chances of success in a court case to be remote.
- This is a contingent liability, which will not be recognised in the accounts.
- Because the likelihood of losing the case is remote, there will be no disclosure of the contingent liability in the notes to the financial statements.

3 Bank guarantee
- The guarantee is a possible obligation arising from a past event, ie the giving of the bank guarantee.
- However, at 31 December 20-6, the obligation is not probable.
- This is a contingent liability, which will not be recognised in the accounts.
- Because the likelihood of having to meet the terms of the bank guarantee is possible (but not probable), details of the contingent liability will be disclosed in the notes to the financial statements.

IAS 10 – Events after the Reporting Period

Events after the reporting period are favourable or unfavourable events that take place after the financial statements have been prepared at the year end and before the time when the statements are authorised for issue to interested parties.

The purpose of this standard is to recognise that there may be events which occur, or information that becomes available after the end of the financial year that need to be reflected in the financial statements. For example, if a customer becomes insolvent after the year end and the amount owed is material, it may be necessary to make changes in the financial statements for the year to reflect this.

The key feature of the standard is that any such changes to the financial statements can only be made in the period

- after the end of the financial year, and
- before the financial statements are authorised for issue (usually by the board of directors)

Once the financial statements are authorised for issue, no alterations can be made.

IAS 10 distinguishes between

- adjusting events, and
- non-adjusting events

adjusting events

Adjusting events provide evidence of conditions that existed at the end of the reporting period. If the amount(s) involved are material, then the amounts shown in the financial statements should be changed. Examples of adjusting events include:

- the settlement after the end of the reporting period of a court case which confirms that a liability existed at the year end
- where a customer has become insolvent after the end of the reporting period and the debt has been included in the balance sheet figure of year end trade receivables

non-adjusting events

Non-adjusting events are conditions that arose after the reporting period. No adjustment is made to the financial statements. If such events are material, then they are disclosed by way of notes to the accounts. The notes would explain the nature of the event and, if possible, give the likely financial consequences of the event. Examples of non-adjusting events include:

- major purchase of assets
- losses of business capacity, eg caused by fire, flood or strikes
- a major restructuring of the business
- significant business commitments entered into after the end of the reporting period

Note that dividends proposed on ordinary shares after the end of the reporting period are not to be recognised as a liability in the balance sheet. Instead, they are non-adjusting events which are disclosed by way of a note – see also page 123 for more on the treatment of dividends in financial statements.

INCOME STATEMENT: IAS 18 – REVENUE

The purpose of this standard is to set out the accounting treatment to ensure that revenue is correctly shown in the income statement.

revenue

Revenue is the inflow of economic benefits arising from the ordinary activities of a business. Examples of revenue include sales of goods and services, and the receipt of interest, royalties and dividends.

In the financial statements, the recognition of revenue is based on the realisation concept. This means that financial transactions are recorded in the financial statements when legal title passes between buyer and seller – which may well not be at the same time as payment is made. For example, the income from credit sales is recorded at the time the sale is made – which is when legal title passes to the buyer – but payment will be made at a later date.

IAS 18 states that revenue is to be recorded at the fair value of the monies received or receivable.

The key feature of the standard is that it sets out the rules for the recognition of types of revenue:

- sale of goods and services
- interest, royalties and dividends

sale of goods and services

Revenue from the sale of goods and services is to be recognised when all of the following criteria have been met:

- the seller of the goods and services has transferred to the buyer the significant risks and rewards of ownership
- the seller retains no effective control over the goods and services
- the amount of revenue from the goods and services can be measured reliably
- it is probable that the economic benefits will flow to the seller of the goods and services
- the costs incurred, or to be incurred, in respect of the sale can be measured reliably

interest, royalties and dividends

Revenue for these items is to be recognised in the following way:

- for interest – using a time basis to calculate the interest
- for royalties – on an accrual basis in accordance with the royalty agreement
- for dividends – when the shareholder's right to receive payment is established

CHAPTER SUMMARY

- The regulatory framework of accounting forms the 'rules' of accounting and comprises accounting standards and company law.

- International accounting standards include IASs and IFRSs.

- The reasons for using international accounting standards are:
    - to provide a framework – the 'rules' – for preparing financial statements
    - to ensure that accountants follow the same set of rules
    - to reduce the number of different accounting treatments
    - to meet with the directors' duty to ensure that financial statements comply with accounting standards
    - to meet with the auditors' report requirements

- The benefits of international accounting standards are:
    - to standardise financial statements internationally
    - to reduce the variations of accounting treatments
    - to allow users of financial statements to make inter-firm comparisons

- IAS 8, *Accounting Policies, Changes in Accounting Estimates and Errors*, gives definitions of
  - accounting policies
  - accounting principles
  - accounting bases
  - errors

- IAS 16, *Property, Plant and Equipment*, sets out the accounting treatment for non-current assets such as land and buildings, machinery, office equipment, shop fittings and vehicles. It covers
  - recognition
  - initial measurement
  - cost and revaluation models
  - depreciation

- IAS 38, *Intangible Assets*, sets out the accounting treatment of expenditure on intangible assets. It covers
  - recognition
  - initial measurement
  - cost and revaluation models

- IAS 36, *Impairment of Assets*, sets out the accounting procedures to ensure that assets are shown in the balance sheet at no more than their value, or recoverable amount. The standard requires an impairment review to be carried out when there is evidence that impairment has taken place. The standard gives a number of indicators of impairment.

- IAS 2, *Inventories*, requires that inventories are valued at the lower of cost and net realisable value.

- IAS 37, *Provisions, Contingent Liabilities and Contingent Assets*, ensures a consistent accounting treatment for provisions, contingent liabilities and contingent assets. It requires that sufficient information is disclosed in the notes to the financial statements to enable users to understand their nature, timing and amount.

- IAS 10, *Events after the Reporting Period*, allows for events which may occur, or information that becomes available, in the period between the end of the financial year and the date the financial statements are authorised for issue to be reflected in the financial statements. The standard distinguishes between adjusting events and non-adjusting events.

- IAS 18, *Revenue*, sets out the accounting treatment to ensure that revenue is correctly shown in the income statement. It covers the rules for the recognition of revenue:
  - sale of goods and services
  - interest, royalties and dividends

In this chapter we have already seen how IAS 2, *Inventories*, requires that inventories are valued at the lower of cost and net realisable value. In the next chapter we look further at the techniques of inventory valuation and, in particular, at two methods of valuing the inventory of a business and the situations in which each might be used.

QUESTIONS

visit
www.osbornebooks.co.uk
to take an online test

An asterisk (*) after the question number means that the answer is given at the end of this book.

7.1*　Outline the reasons for, and benefits of, using international accounting standards when preparing and presenting financial statements.

7.2　Explain the terms

–　accounting principles

–　accounting bases

–　accounting policies

Give one example of each.

7.3　Beacon PLC is an international company which owns a large number of non-current assets throughout the world. It wishes to standardise its procedures for depreciation in accordance with IAS 16, *Property, Plant and Equipment*.

(a)　Define depreciation.

(b)　Outline the policy decisions Beacon PLC has to consider when accounting for IAS 16.

7.4*　The Betterland Company Limited purchased for its own use a freehold warehouse on 1 January 20-0 for £250,000. The directors decided to depreciate the warehouse over its estimated useful life of 50 years. At 1 January 20-5, the building is valued at £345,000, and the directors decide to incorporate this valuation into the financial statements from this date.

(a)　What is the amount to be transferred to revaluation surplus?

(b)　Assuming that the asset's life still has 46 years to run from 1 January 20-5, what will be the depreciation charge from 31 December 20-5 onwards?

7.5*　(a)　How does IAS 38, *Intangible Assets*, define an intangible asset?

(b)　What are the three key elements of an intangible asset set out in IAS 38, *Intangible Assets*?

(c)　How does IAS 38 require intangible assets to be recorded in the balance sheet at acquisition?

After acquisition, what methods are permitted by IAS 38 for the measurement of intangible assets?

7.6   (a)   Explain how an impairment review is carried out, and define the terms used.

        (b)   How is an impairment loss recorded in the financial statements?

        (c)   Machin Limited has three assets in use

	carrying amount	fair value less costs to sell	value in use
	£	£	£
Compressor	8,000	12,000	10,000
Fork lift truck	20,000	18,000	19,000
Dumper truck	10,000	7,000	13,000

        State which of the above assets is impaired and the amount by which it needs to be written down?

7.7   IAS 2, *Inventories*, states that inventories should be valued at the lower of cost and net realisable value.

        Outline what is meant by the terms 'cost' and 'net realisable value'.

7.8   Joe Yates runs a garage buying and selling second-hand cars. At the end of the financial year his inventories include the following cars. What is the correct valuation to be recorded according to IAS 2, *Inventories*?

	Cost £	Net realisable value £
Vauxhall Corsa	2,800	3,500
Landrover Discovery	10,000	15,000
Nissan Primera	3,400	2,600
Ford Focus	6,000	7,500
Volkswagon Polo	1,200	500

7.9*   IAS 37 deals with provisions, contingent liabilities and contingent assets. What is the difference between a provision and a contingent liability?

7.10*   State how a material provision and a material contingent liability should be treated and accounted for in financial statements.

7.11*   Define adjusting and non-adjusting events, giving an example of each.

7.12 Answer the following questions which the directors of Gernroder Limited have asked concerning the financial statements for the year ended 30 September 20-6. Where appropriate, make reference to international accounting standards to justify your answers.

(a) The auditors have asked us to reduce the value of some of our inventory from the cost of £156,590 to £101,640, which is the amount at which we sold the inventory after the year end. Why should something which happened after the year end be at all relevant to the balances at the year end?

(b) Our accountant knows that, in early October, we announced our proposal to pay a final dividend of £75,000 for the year but she hasn't shown a liability for it in the financial statements.

(c) We had to dismiss an employee in early October. The former employee has now started legal proceedings for unfair dismissal. Our lawyers tell us that the company will probably lose the case and think that a reliable estimate of damages awarded against us is £20,000. As we employed this person at the financial year end we feel that we ought to show the estimated amount of damages as an expense in the income statement and as a liability on the balance sheet.

7.13* IAS 18 deals with revenue.

(a) Explain the term 'revenue'.

(b) Give two examples of revenue.

7.14 The directors of Halls-Krosby plc have prepared the internal draft income statement for the year ended 31 March 2007. The company auditors have brought the following matters to the directors' attention. The auditors believe that the way the matters have been treated may not conform to existing accounting standards.

1. The company continues to grow by over 20% per year and the directors believe that goodwill should be included as an intangible fixed asset at a value of £7.5 million.

2. Some damaged inventory has been included in the final accounts at a value of £160,000 because a regular customer has indicated that he will purchase the inventory at selling price less 20%. When perfect, this type of inventory could be sold for £200,000. The inventory originally cost £100,000.

3. A piece of machinery that had cost £240,000 several years ago has recently had a major overhaul costing £85,000. The machinery has a written down value of £120,000. The engineering company that undertook the overhaul guarantees that the machine is now 'as good as new'. The directors have included the asset on the company balance sheet at £205,000.

REQUIRED

Identify the relevant international accounting standard to be applied to **each** of items 1, 2 and 3 and explain their treatment in the company's final accounts.

Assessment and Qualifications Alliance (AQA), Specimen Paper for 2010 – part question

7.15 You are employed by a firm of accountants and have been asked to prepare the financial statements of Corline PLC for the year to 31 March 20-5.

(a) Inventories are valued at the lower of cost and net realisable value in the accounts, in accordance with the IAS 2. The directors of Corline PLC would like you to explain how cost and net realisable value are derived.

(b) The directors of Corline PLC have drawn your attention to two matters and requested your advice on how these should be treated.

1. A customer owing £30,000 to Corline PLC on 31 March 20-5 went into liquidation on 3 April 20-5. The £30,000 is still unpaid and it is unclear whether any monies will be received.

2. The company is awaiting the outcome of a legal case; an independent lawyer has assessed that it is probable that the company will gain £25,000 from it.

Write notes for the directors of Corline PLC outlining the required treatment for these two events.

7.16 The following draft balance sheet of Groglin plc, an electrical goods retailer, has been prepared by the directors of the company:

GROGLIN plc	
BALANCE SHEET AT 31 DECEMBER 2008	
Assets	£
Non-current assets	
Property, plant and equipment	2,000,000
	2,000,000
Current assets	
Inventories	120,000
Trade receivables	16,000
Cash and cash equivalents	28,000
Suspense	200,000
	364,000
	2,364,000
Liabilities	
Current liabilities	
Trade payables	(84,000)
Net assets	2,280,000
Shareholders' equity	
Called up share capital	1,500,000
Retained earnings and other reserves	780,000
	2,280,000

Additional information:

After the preparation of the draft financial statements for the year ended 31 December 2008, the following items were discovered. They all need consideration when redrafting the balance sheet at 31 December 2008.

(1)   On 1 January 2008 Groglin plc purchased the rights to market computers in the UK from the MiniComp Corporation. Groglin plc paid £200,000 for the marketing rights.

The amount has been entered in a suspense account. The directors of Groglin plc estimate that the economic life of the marketing rights will be 5 years.

(2)   Groglin's sales have doubled over the past few years and the directors believe that they are now market leaders in their business sector. As a result, they propose to introduce a further £560,000 as additional goodwill. It is estimated that the economic life of the goodwill will be 8 years.

(3)   On 1 January 2008, property, plant and equipment were revalued from a new book value of £2,000,000 to £2,500,000. The revaluation had not been included in the company's books of account. Non-current assets are generally depreciated at 2% per annum, but no depreciation had been charged for the year ended 31 December 2008.

(4)   No provision has been made for doubtful debts. The directors feel that 3% of trade receivables would be appropriate.

(5)   The directors of Groglin plc have valued all closing inventories at cost. Included in the value of closing inventories were 10 microwave cookers that had been damaged. The microwave cookers cost £20 each and would normally sell for £50 each. The damaged microwave cookers could be sold for £30 each after the necessary repairs are carried out. The total cost of repairing the damaged microwave cookers will be £125.

REQUIRED

(a)   Identify the appropriate International Accounting Standard (IAS) for **each** of the (additional information) items 1 - 5.

(b)   Calculate the corrected retained earnings and other reserves balance at 31 December 2008, showing clearly the effect of each of the items 1 - 5.

(c)   Prepare a balance sheet at 31 December 2008 taking into accounts items 1 - 5.

(d)   Discuss the reasons why limited companies are required to comply with international accounting standards (IAS).

Assessment and Qualifications Alliance (AQA), Additional Specimen Questions

8 INVENTORY VALUATION

Companies may have inventories held in the form of raw materials, work-in-progress, finished goods, products bought for resale, and service items. Often the value of such inventories is high, representing a considerable sum of money and so it is important that it is valued consistently, and proper controls are kept over the physical inventory.

In this chapter we look at:

- valuation of inventories, including the application of IAS 2, *Inventories*
- FIFO (first in, first out) and AVCO (average cost) methods of inventory valuation
- use of a stores ledger record – or inventory card – to calculate the value of closing inventory
- effect on profits, in the short-term, of different methods of inventory valuation
- advantages and disadvantages of FIFO and AVCO
- importance of the inventory count and inventory reconciliation

INVENTORIES

Companies often have inventories in various forms:

- raw materials, for use in a manufacturing business
- work-in-progress (partly manufactured goods) and finished goods (ready for sale) of a manufacturing business
- products bought for resale by a retailer
- service items, such as stationery, bought for use within a business

Inventory is often kept in the stores or storeroom of a company and the person who looks after it is the storekeeper.

VALUATION OF INVENTORY

The inventories held by a business invariably have considerable value and tie up a lot of money. At the end of the financial year, it is essential for a company to make a physical inventory count and to value its inventory for use in the financial statements – in the calculation of profit, and for the balance sheet. This physical inventory count involves the company staff counting each item held. The inventory held is then valued as follows:

number of items held   x   cost per item   =   inventory value

The auditors of a company may make random checks to ensure that the inventory value is correct.

The value of inventory at the beginning and end of the financial year is used to calculate the figure for cost of sales. Therefore, the inventory value has an effect on profit for the year.

Inventory can be valued at *either*:

- cost, which means the purchase price plus any other costs incurred to bring the product (or service) to its present location and condition, *or*

- net realisable value, which is the estimated selling price less the estimated costs to get the product into a condition necessary to complete the sale

Inventory valuation is normally made at the lower of these two values, ie at the *lower of cost and net realisable value*. This valuation is taken from International Accounting Standard (IAS) No 2, *Inventories*. This valuation applies the prudence concept and is illustrated by the following diagram:

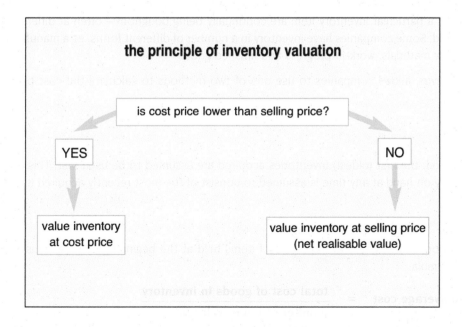

the principle of inventory valuation

is cost price lower than selling price?

YES

NO

value inventory
at cost price

value inventory at selling price
(net realisable value)

WORKED EXAMPLE: INVENTORY VALUATION

situation

The Clothing Store Limited bought a range of beachwear in the Spring, with each item costing £15 and retailing for £30. Most of the goods sell well but, by Autumn, ten items remain unsold. These are put on the bargain rail at £18 each. On 31 December, at the end of the store's financial year, five items remain unsold. At what price will they be included in the year end inventory valuation?

Twelve months later, three items still remain unsold and have been reduced further to £10 each. At what price will they now be valued in the year end inventory valuation?

solution

*   At 31 December, the five items will be valued at a cost of £15 each,
    ie 5 x £15 = £75.
*   Twelve months later, the three items remaining unsold will be valued at a net realisable value of £10 each, ie 3 x £10 = £30.

Important note: Inventories are never valued at selling prices when selling prices are above cost prices. The reason for this is that selling prices include profit, and to value inventory in this way would recognise the profit in the financial statements before it has been realised.

METHODS OF INVENTORY VALUATION

The difficulty in inventory valuation is in finding out the cost price of inventory – this is not easy when quantities of a particular inventory item are continually being bought in – often at different prices – and then sold. Some companies have inventory in a number of different forms, eg a manufacturer may well have raw materials, work-in-progress and finished goods.

IAS 2, *Inventories*, allows companies to use one of two methods to calculate the cost price of their inventory:

FIFO (first in, first out)

In this method, the first (oldest) inventories acquired are assumed to be used first. This means that the inventory on hand at any time is assumed to consist of the most recently acquired items.

AVCO (average cost)

In this method, the weighted average cost of items held at the beginning of the year is calculated, using the formula:

$$\text{weighted average cost} = \frac{\textbf{total cost of goods in inventory}}{\textbf{number of items in inventory}}$$

The weighted average cost is then used to value goods sold. A new weighted average cost must be calculated each time that further inventories are bought during the year.

Note that the use of a particular valuation method does not necessarily correspond with the method of physical distribution adopted in the stores of the business. For example, in a car factory one car battery of type X is the same as another, and no-one will be concerned if the storekeeper issues one from the last batch received, even if the FIFO system has been adopted. However, perishable goods are always physically handled on the basis of first in, first out, even if the inventory records use the AVCO method.

Having chosen a suitable inventory valuation method, a business would continue to use that method unless there were good reasons for making the change. This is in line with the consistency concept of accounting.

recording inventory values – stores ledger record

In order to be able to calculate accurately the price at which materials are issued and to ascertain a valuation of inventory, a stores ledger record – or inventory card – is used, as shown below. This method of recording inventory data is also used in the Worked Example which follows.

STORES LEDGER RECORD

Date	Receipts			Issues			Balance		
	Quantity	Cost	Total Cost	Quantity	Cost	Total Cost	Quantity	Cost	Total Cost
		£	£		£	£		£	£

Note that this price is the cost price to the business. It is not the selling price – inventory records are usually kept at cost price.

Note the following points:

- the layout of the stores ledger record – or inventory card – may vary slightly from one business to another
- many businesses use a computer system for their inventory records
- a blank stores ledger record, which may be photocopied, is available for free download from the Resources section of www.osbornebooks.co.uk
- whilst it is good learning practice to use a stores ledger record, many examination questions require a calculation of inventory value – this can be completed without a stores ledger record

WORKED EXAMPLE: STORES LEDGER RECORDS

situation

Ashok Patel runs a computer supplies company. One of the items stocked is the 'Zap' data disk.

To show how the stores ledger records would appear under FIFO and AVCO, the following data is used:

20-7

January	Opening inventory of 40 units at a cost of £3.00 each
February	Bought 20 units at a cost of £3.60 each
March	Sold 36 units for £6 each
April	Bought 20 units at a cost of £3.75 each
May	Sold 25 units for £6 each

What will be the profit for the period using the two inventory valuation methods?

solution

Note: In the FIFO method, units issued at the same time may be valued at different costs. This is because the quantities received, with their costs, are listed separately and used in a specific order. There may be insufficient units at one cost, eg see the May issue, below.

FIFO

STORES LEDGER RECORD

Date	Receipts			Issues			Balance		
20-7	Quantity	Cost	Total Cost	Quantity	Cost	Total Cost	Quantity	Cost	Total Cost
		£	£		£	£		£	£
Jan	Balance						40	3.00	120.00
Feb	20	3.60	72.00				40	3.00	120.00
							20	3.60	72.00
							60		192.00
March				36	3.00	108.00	4	3.00	12.00
							20	3.60	72.00
							24		84.00
April	20	3.75	75.00				4	3.00	12.00
							20	3.60	72.00
							20	3.75	75.00
							44		159.00
May				4	3.00	12.00			
				20	3.60	72.00			
				1	3.75	3.75	19	3.75	71.25

Note: In the 'Balance' columns, a new list of inventory quantities and costs is started after each receipt or issue. When inventory is issued, costs are used from the **top** of the list downwards.

AVCO

In this method, each quantity issued is valued at the weighted average cost per unit, and so is the balance in inventory. The complete list of different costs does not have to be re-written each time.

STORES LEDGER RECORD

Date	Receipts			Issues			Balance		
20-7	Quantity	Cost	Total Cost	Quantity	Cost	Total Cost	Quantity	Cost	Total Cost
		£	£		£	£		£	£
Jan	Balance						40	3.00	120.00
Feb	20	3.60	72.00				40	3.00	120.00
							20	3.60	72.00
							60	3.20	192.00
March				36	3.20	115.20	24	3.20	76.80
April	20	3.75	75.00				24	3.20	76.80
							20	3.75	75.00
							44	3.45	151.80
May				25	3.45	86.25	19	3.45	65.55

Note: Weighted average cost is calculated by dividing the quantity held into the value of the inventory. For example, at the end of February, the weighted average cost is £192 ÷ 60 units = £3.20, and at the end of April it is £151.80 ÷ 44 = £3.45.

The closing inventory valuations at the end of May 20-7 under the two methods show total cost prices of:

FIFO   £71.25
AVCO   £65.55

The difference comes about because different inventory valuation methods have been used.

effect on profit

In the example above, the selling price was £6 per unit. The effect on gross profit of using different inventory valuations is shown below.

		FIFO	AVCO
		£	£
Sales:	61 units at £6	366.00	366.00
Opening inventory:	40 units at £3	120.00	120.00
Purchases:	20 units at £3.60	147.00	147.00
	20 units at £3.75		
		267.00	267.00
Less Closing inventory:	19 units	71.25	65.55
Cost of sales		195.75	201.45
Gross profit = Sales − Cost of sales		170.25	164.55

Notice that the cost of sales figure is also obtainable by adding up the values in the 'Issues' column. You can also check this, both in Units and in Values:

opening inventory + receipts – issues = closing inventory

The Worked Example shows that in times of rising prices, as here, FIFO produces the higher reported profit and AVCO the lower. The reason for this is that, here, FIFO gives a higher closing inventory, which means that cost of sales is lower and profit is higher; by contrast, AVCO gives a lower closing inventory, which means that cost of sales is higher and profit is lower. Although the profit difference in this Worked Example is not significant, to a large company the difference could be a considerable money amount. However it is important to note that, over the life of a business, total profit is the same, whichever method is chosen: the closing inventory of one period becomes the opening inventory of the next and, in this way, profit is allocated to different years depending on which method is used.

ADVANTAGES AND DISADVANTAGES OF FIFO AND AVCO

FIFO (first in, first out)

advantages

- it is realistic, ie it assumes that goods are issued in order of receipt
- it is easy to calculate
- inventory valuation comprises the actual costs at which items have been bought
- the closing inventory valuation is close to the most recent costs
- it is one of the two methods which IAS 2, *Inventories*, allows companies to use
- acceptable for tax purposes

disadvantages

- costs at which goods are issued are not necessarily the latest prices, so cost of sales may not represent current prices
- in times of rising prices, profits are higher than with other methods (resulting in more tax to pay)
- the method is cumbersome as the list of different costs must be maintained

AVCO (average cost)

advantages

- over a number of accounting periods reported profits are smoothed, ie both high and low profits are avoided
- fluctuations in purchase costs are evened out so that issues per unit do not vary greatly
- logical, ie it assumes that identical units, when purchased at different times, have the same value
- closing inventory valuation is close to current market values (in times of rising prices, it will be below current market values)
- the calculations can be computerised more easily than the other methods
- it is one of the two methods which IAS 2, *Inventories*, allows companies to use
- acceptable for tax purposes

disadvantages

- a new weighted average has to be calculated after each receipt, and calculations may be to several decimal places
- because they are averaged, issues and inventory valuation are usually at costs which never existed
- issues may not be at current costs and, in times of rising prices, will be below current costs

The important point to remember is that a business must adopt a consistent inventory valuation policy, ie it should choose a method of finding the cost price, and not change it without good reason. FIFO and AVCO are the two methods allowed under IAS 2, *Inventories*, and a company might decide to use FIFO for one type of inventory and AVCO for another. The table on the next page provides a comparison of the FIFO and AVCO methods of inventory valuation. Note that the two methods are simply valuation techniques and do not affect the cash generated by the business, or the way in which the goods are physically moved.

CATEGORIES OF INVENTORY

IAS 2, *Inventories*, requires that, in calculating the lower of cost and net realisable value, note should be taken of:

- separate items of inventory, or
- groups of similar items

This means that the inventory valuation 'rule' must be applied to each separate item of inventory, or each group or category of similar inventories. The total cost cannot be compared with the total net realisable value, as is shown by the Worked Example which follows.

WORKED EXAMPLE: VALUING YEAR END INVENTORIES

situation

The year end inventories for the two main groups of inventory held by the Paint and Wallpaper Company Limited are found to be:

	Cost £	Net realisable value £
Paints	2,500	2,300
Wallpapers	5,000	7,500
	7,500	9,800

Which one of the following inventory valuations do you think is correct?

- (a) £7,500
- (b) £9,800
- (c) £7,300
- (d) £10,000

a comparison of the two main methods of inventory valuation

	FIFO	AVCO
method	The costs used for goods sold or issued follow the order in which the goods were received.	Does not relate issues to any particular batch of goods received, but uses a weighted average cost.
calculation	It is easy to calculate costs because they relate to specific receipts of goods.	More complex because of the need to calculate weighted average costs.
inventory valuation	Inventory valuations are based on the most recent costs of goods received.	Weighted average costs are used to value closing inventory.
acceptability under accounting standards	FIFO is acceptable under IAS 2, *Inventories*.	AVCO is acceptable under IAS 2, *Inventories*.
profits and taxation	In times of rising prices FIFO results in higher reported profits than AVCO, resulting in more tax being payable. This method is acceptable for tax purposes.	AVCO, by using a weighted average cost, smooths out some of the peaks and troughs of profit and loss. This method is acceptable for tax purposes.
administration	Use of FIFO will mean keeping track of each receipt of inventory until the goods are issued. This can be a time-consuming process.	There is no need to track each receipt as a weighted average cost is used. This also means it is easier to computerise the inventory records.
cost of sales	In a time of rising prices FIFO uses older, out of date prices for goods issued and cost of sales.	AVCO gives an average price for goods issued and cost of sales.

solution

Inventory valuation (c) is correct because it has taken the 'lower of cost and net realisable value' for each group of inventory, ie

	£
Paints (at net realisable value)	2,300
Wallpapers (at cost)	5,000
	7,300

You will also note that this valuation is the lowest possible choice, indicating that inventory valuation follows the prudence concept of accounting.

THE INVENTORY COUNT AND INVENTORY RECONCILIATION

the inventory count

A company needs to check regularly that the quantity of inventory held is the same as that recorded in the inventory records. This is done by means of an inventory count – counting the physical inventory on hand to check against the balance shown by the records, and to identify any theft or deterioration.

Inventory counting is carried out on either a periodic basis or continuously. A *periodic basis* involves carrying out an inventory count of all items held at regular intervals (often twice a year). *Continuous inventory counting* is a constant process where selected items are counted on a rotating basis, with all items being checked at least once a year (expensive, desirable or high-turnover items will need to be checked more frequently).

inventory reconciliation

The object of the inventory count is to see if the inventory records represent accurately the level of inventory held. The comparison between the inventory count and the inventory record is known as inventory reconciliation. This is an important process because

- an accurate inventory figure can then be used to value the inventory
- it will highlight any discrepancies which can then be investigated

Discrepancies and queries in inventory reconciliation need to be referred to the company's managers and any other people who may need to know, eg the firm's auditors who are organising the inventory count. If the discrepancy is a small shortfall in the physical inventory compared with the inventory record, it will be authorised for write-off. Larger discrepancies will need to be investigated, as they could have been caused by:

- an error on the inventory record, such as
  - a failure to record a receipt or an issue of goods
  - an administrative error, eg 100 items received recorded as 10 items
  - different items issued to those recorded, eg a size 8 issued instead of a size 10
  - an error in calculating the balance of inventory

- theft of inventory
- damaged inventory being disposed of without any record having been made

Once an accurate figure for closing inventory has been agreed it can then be used in the financial statements – to calculate profit, and for the balance sheet.

CHAPTER SUMMARY

- Companies may have inventories held in the form of raw materials, work-in-progress, finished goods, products bought for resale, and service items.

- At the end of the financial year, the company must make a physical inventory count and value its inventory for use in the financial statements – in the calculation of profit, and for the balance sheet.

- In order to be able to calculate accurately the price at which inventories of materials are issued and to ascertain a valuation of inventory, a stores ledger record – or inventory card – is used.

- The overriding principle of inventory valuation – set out in IAS 2, *Inventories* – is that inventories are to be valued at the lower of cost and net realisable value.

- IAS 2, *Inventories*, allows two methods to be used to value inventory:
  - FIFO (first in, first out)
  - AVCO (average cost)

- Having chosen an inventory valuation method, a company should apply it consistently.

- The use of either FIFO or AVCO may result in a different value for closing inventory and, hence, a different reported profit for a particular time period. However, over the life of a business, total profit is the same, whichever method is chosen.

- IAS 2, *Inventories*, requires that, in calculating the lower of cost and net realisable value, note should be taken of
  - separate items of inventory, or
  - groups of similar items

- An inventory count is carried out regularly to check that the quantity of inventory held is the same as that recorded in the inventory records. An inventory count is carried out on either a periodic basis or continuously.

- Inventory reconciliation is the process of comparing the inventory count and the inventory record. Small shortfalls in physical inventory may be authorised for write-off by the company's managers or auditors; larger discrepancies will need to be investigated to establish their cause.

This chapter completes your studies for AS Unit 3. However, this chapter prepares you for AS Unit 4 where you will be looking at aspects of management accounting.

QUESTIONS

visit
www.osbornebooks.co.uk
to take an online test

An asterisk (*) after the question number means that the answer is given at the end of this book.

8.1* Complete the following sentences:

(a) Inventory levels and movements are recorded on a ....

(b) The process of comparing the physical inventory with the inventory records is known as ....

(c) The international accounting standard that sets out the accounting treatment for the valuation of inventory is IAS ..., ...

(d) The usual basis for inventory valuation is at the lower of .... and ....

8.2* Breeden Bakery Limited makes 'homestyle' cakes which are sold to supermarket chains. The company uses the first in, first out (FIFO) method for valuing its inventories. Complete the following stores ledger record for wholewheat flour for May 20-7:

STORES LEDGER RECORD: wholewheat flour

Date	Receipts			Issues			Balance	
	Quantity kgs	Cost per kg	Total Cost	Quantity kgs	Cost per kg	Total Cost	Quantity kgs	Total Cost
20-7		£	£		£	£		£
Balance at 1 May							10,000	2,500
6 May	20,000	0.30	6,000				30,000	8,500
10 May				20,000				
17 May	10,000	0.35	3,500					
20 May				15,000				

8.3 The supplies department of Peoples Bank has the following movements of an item of inventory for June 20-4:

		units	cost per unit £	total cost £
1 June	Balance	2,000	2.00	4,000
15 June	Receipts	1,000	2.30	2,300
21 June	Issues	2,500		

You are to complete the following table for FIFO and AVCO:

Date 20-4	Description	FIFO £	AVCO £
21 June	Total issue value		
30 June	Total closing inventory value		

8.4 Wyezed Limited has two types of inventories, Wye and Zed. The company values Wye using a FIFO basis, and Zed on an AVCO basis.

The following are the inventory movements during the month of August 20-4:

Wye – FIFO basis

20-4		units	cost per unit £
1 Aug	Balance	5,000	5.00
10 Aug	Receipts	2,000	5.25
18 Aug	Receipts	3,000	5.50
23 Aug	Issues	8,000	

Zed – AVCO basis

20-4		units	cost per unit £
1 Aug	Balance	10,000	4.00
6 Aug	Receipts	5,000	4.30
19 Aug	Receipts	7,500	4.40
24 Aug	Issues	12,000	

(a)   **You are to** complete the stores ledger records, below, for Wye and Zed.

STORES LEDGER RECORD: Wye

FIFO

Date	Receipts			Issues			Balance		
20-4	Quantity	Cost	Total Cost	Quantity	Cost	Total Cost	Quantity	Cost	Total Cost
		£	£		£	£		£	£
1 Aug	Balance						5,000	5.00	25,000
10 Aug	2,000	5.25	10,500						
18 Aug	3,000	5.50	16,500						
23 Aug									

STORES LEDGER RECORD: Zed

AVCO

Date	Receipts			Issues			Balance		
20-4	Quantity	Cost	Total Cost	Quantity	Cost	Total Cost	Quantity	Cost	Total Cost
		£	£		£	£		£	£
1 Aug	Balance						10,000	4.00	40,000
6 Aug	5,000	4.30	21,500						
19 Aug	7,500	4.40	33,000						
24 Aug									

(b) At 31 August 20-4, the net realisable value of each type of inventory is:

* Wye £10,000
* Zed £46,000

Show the amount at which inventories should be valued on 31 August 20-4 in order to comply with IAS 2, *Inventories*.

8.5 From the following information prepare stores ledger records for product Alpha using:

(a) FIFO

(b) AVCO

* 20 units of the product are bought in January 20-7 at a cost of £3 each
* 10 units are bought in February at a cost of £3.60 each
* 8 units are sold in March
* 10 units are bought in April at a cost of £4.00 each
* 16 units are sold in May

Note: a blank stores ledger record, which may be photocopied, is available from the Resources section of www.osbornebooks.co.uk

8.6 JayKay Limited is formed on 1 January 20-7 and, at the end of its first half-year of trading, the stores ledger records show the following:

20-7	**PRODUCT JAY**		**PRODUCT KAY**	
	Receipts (units)	**Issues (units)**	**Receipts (units)**	**Issues (units)**
Jan	100 at £4.00		200 at £10.00	
Feb		80	100 at £9.55	
Mar	120 at £4.21			240
Apr	70 at £3.94		90 at £10.50	
May		140	150 at £10.00	
Jun	105 at £4.30			100

At 30 June 20-7, the net realisable value of each type of inventory is:

product Jay	£1,050.00
product Kay	£1,950.00
	£3,000.00

You are to:

- Complete stores ledger records for products Jay and Kay using (a) FIFO, (b) AVCO.

- The business has decided to use the FIFO method. Show the amount at which its inventories should be valued on 30 June 20-7 in order to comply with IAS 2, *Inventories*.

Note: a blank stores ledger record, which may be photocopied, is available from the Resources section of www.osbornebooks.co.uk

8.7* Go Games Limited sells computer games. At the end of the financial year, the company's inventories include:

300 copies of 'X1X' game that cost £40 each and will sell at only £30, because it is an out-of-date version.

260 copies of a newly-released game, 'X-TRA-G' that cost £56 each and will be sold for £90 each.

100 copies of a current version of 'X-TREME 2' game, which is expected to be up-dated to 'X TREME 3' in the near future. These cost £35 each and normally sell for £55, but because they may soon be out-of-date, Go Games Limited has reduced the price to £42 each.

You are to:

Calculate the total value of the inventory items described above, in order to comply with IAS 2, *Inventories*. Include an explanation of your calculations.

8.8* A football club shop sells replica club strip as well as other goods and clothing. The club strip has recently been changed and the old version will have to be sold at greatly reduced prices. At the end of the financial year, the inventories in the shop include:

	Cost	Net realisable value
	£	£
Replica strip (old version)	3,800	2,500
Replica strip (new version)	8,400	11,000
	12,200	13,500

You are to:

Determine the total value of the inventory items above, in order to comply with IAS 2, *Inventories*.

8.9* Denise Watson sells one type of agricultural machine, a mini-baler. She provides the following information for April 2008.

Denise held 2 mini-balers in inventory at 1 April 2008. They cost £1,200 each.

Date	Purchases	Sales
1 April	3 @ £1,200	
2 April		4 @ £2,900
7 April	4 @ £1,350	
17 April		4 @ £3,000
21 April	8 @ £1,400	
24 April		7 @ £3,000

Total purchases for the month: £20,200. Total sales for the month: £44,600

Denise has calculated her gross profit to be £24,782, using the weighted average cost method (AVCO) of valuing her inventory.

She sells her mini-balers in the order in which she purchases them. For this reason, she believes she should change her method of valuing inventory to the first in first out method (FIFO).

REQUIRED

(a) Calculate gross profit for the month of April 2008 using the FIFO method of valuing inventory.

(b) Discuss one advantage and one disadvantage of using the weighted average cost method (AVCO) of valuing inventory. Advise whether she should change her method of valuing inventory.

Assessment and Qualifications Alliance (AQA), Second Specimen Paper for 2010

8.10 Tom Greenacre buys and sells one model of caravan. He provides the following information for April 2007.

On 1 April, there was one caravan in inventory, which had cost £17,700.

Date	Purchases	Sales
10 April	2 @ £18,000 each	
18 April		2 @ £23,000 each
26 April	3 @ £18,400 each	
30 April		2 @ £23,000 each

REQUIRED

(a) Calculate the value of closing inventory at 30 April 2007, using the weighted average cost (AVCO) method of inventory valuation

(b) Discuss whether or not a change from the weighted average cost (AVCO) method to the first in first out (FIFO) method would be beneficial to Tom's business.

Assessment and Qualifications Alliance (AQA), 2007

8.11*   Your friend, Gerry Gallagher, has recently set up in business selling plastic toys.

The transactions for his first month of trading are:

1 April	Bought 500 toys at £1.50 each
3 April	Sold 250 toys at £2.50 each
7 April	Bought 1,000 toys at £1.40 each
14 April	Sold 600 toys at £2.60 each
20 April	Sold 300 toys at £2.70 each
27 April	Bought 1,050 toys at £1.62 each

At the end of April he asks you to help him to value his closing inventory.

He has heard that other firms in the toy trade value their inventory using either FIFO or AVCO.

He asks you to do the calculations for him, and also to work out his gross profit using each of the two inventory valuation methods. He comments that he 'will use the inventory valuation that gives the higher profit' because he wants to impress his bank manager.

You are to:

(a)   Calculate his closing inventory valuation using each of the two methods. (Note: do not use a stores ledger record.)

(b)   Calculate the gross profit for the month, using each of the two methods.

(c)   Respond to his comment.

8.12   You work as an accounts assistant at Kurt Plastics PLC and, for the last few days, you have been carrying out an inventory count and an inventory reconciliation. There are discrepancies with two inventory lines:

INVENTORY NUMBER	UNIT PRICE	INVENTORY RECORD	PHYSICAL INVENTORY
146	£2 each	10	8
523	£200 each	100	90

You take this information to the company accountant who asks what actions you would take to deal with these discrepancies.

REQUIRED

(a)   What is the purpose of an inventory count?

(b)   What is meant by inventory reconciliation?

(c)   How will you respond to the company accountant? Give your reasons.

A2 Accounting Unit 4

Further Aspects of Management Accounting

Unit 4 for AQA A2 Accounting develops further the knowledge and understanding of management accounting techniques you acquired in AS Unit 2 'Financial and Management Accounting'. The areas covered by Unit 4 include:

- manufacturing accounts – preparing and commenting on the final accounts of manufacturing businesses

- marginal, absorption and activity based costing – selecting and applying the cost concepts to be used in decision-making, including the use of break-even analysis

- standard costing and variance analysis – the purpose of standard costing, including the calculation and interpretation of variances

- capital investment appraisal techniques – payback and net present value

- budgeting – preparing and commenting on budgets and forecast operating statements and balance sheets

- other factors affecting decision-making, such as social accounting

9 MANUFACTURING ACCOUNTS

Until now your studies in accounting have been concerned with businesses that trade in goods, ie buy and sell goods without carrying out a manufacturing process. However, many firms buy raw materials and manufacture products which are then sold as finished goods. The final accounts for a manufacturer include a manufacturing account which brings together all the elements of cost making up the production cost. In this chapter we will:

● consider the manufacturing process
● study the elements of cost
● prepare a manufacturing account
● calculate transfer prices and factory profit

THE MANUFACTURING PROCESS AND ELEMENTS OF COST

The diagram below shows, in outline, the manufacturing process and the costs incurred at each stage.

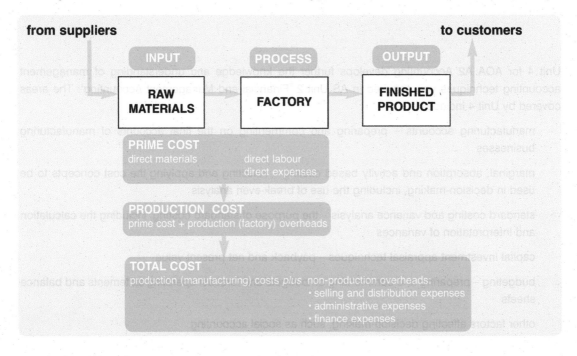

from suppliers   **to customers**

INPUT   PROCESS   OUTPUT

RAW MATERIALS   FACTORY   FINISHED PRODUCT

PRIME COST
direct materials   direct labour
                   direct expenses

PRODUCTION COST
prime cost + production (factory) overheads

TOTAL COST
production (manufacturing) costs *plus* non-production overheads:
     • selling and distribution expenses
     • administrative expenses
     • finance expenses

Note that there are four main elements of cost which make up the manufacturing (or production) cost:

1   **direct materials** – the raw materials that are required in manufacturing the finished product

2   **direct labour** – this is the cost of the workforce engaged in production, eg machine operators (note that the wages of factory supervisors are a production overhead and are usually described as 'indirect labour')

3   **direct expenses** – these include any special costs that can be identified with each unit produced, eg a royalty payable for the use of patents or copyrights for each unit made, or the hire of specialist machinery to carry out a particular manufacturing task

4   **production (factory) overheads** – all the other costs of manufacture, eg wages of supervisors, rent of factory, depreciation of factory machinery, heating and lighting of factory

Prime cost is the basic cost of manufacturing a product before the addition of production overheads. It consists of the first three costs, ie:

direct materials + direct labour + direct expenses = prime cost

Production cost is the factory cost of making the product after the addition of production overheads, and is:

prime cost + production (factory) overheads = production (or manufacturing) cost

FINAL ACCOUNTS OF A MANUFACTURER

The final accounts of a manufacturer are structured as follows:

		Direct materials
MANUFACTURING	*add*	Direct labour
ACCOUNT	*add*	Direct expenses
	equals	PRIME COST
	add	Production (factory) overheads
	equals	PRODUCTION (OR MANUFACTURING) COST
		Revenue (Sales)
INCOME	*less*	Production cost
STATEMENT	*equals*	GROSS PROFIT
	less	Non-production overheads, eg
		• selling and distribution expenses
		• administrative expenses
		• finance expenses
	equals	PROFIT FOR THE YEAR

Note that a manufacturing business also prepares a balance sheet.

We will now study the manufacturing account, and the income statement in more detail.

MANUFACTURING ACCOUNT

A manufacturing account must be prepared at the end of the financial year for a manufacturing business.

The bottom line of this financial statement provides **the production cost of goods completed for the period**. Total production cost is defined as:

direct costs (prime cost) + production overheads = production cost

The manufacturing account includes all the **direct costs** (prime cost) of making the products, together with the **production overheads**. Finished goods are sent from the factory to the warehouse, from which they are sold to customers. The accounts reflect this movement: the cost of producing the finished goods – adjusted for the value of any work-in-progress (partly finished goods) not yet completed – is carried forward from the manufacturing account to the trading account. The calculations are explained step by step below.

manufacturing account calculation

	cost of raw materials used (or consumed)
add	direct labour costs
add	direct expenses
equals	prime cost
add	production (factory) overheads
adjust for	value of any work-in-progress
equals	production cost of goods completed

calculating the production cost of goods completed

step 1   raw materials used in the factory

The first step in the manufacturing account is to calculate the direct cost of the **raw materials** actually used. The closing inventory (the inventory not used) is deducted from the opening inventory plus the purchases, and so it follows that the remainder must have been used (see diagram on the next page):

opening inventory of raw materials + purchases – closing inventory of raw materials

= cost of raw materials used (or consumed)

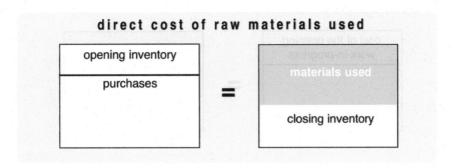

direct cost of raw materials used

step 2   calculating prime cost

In addition to the direct cost of materials used, the cost of direct labour and any direct expenses, eg royalties for the use of a patented or copyrighted process, must be added. The total of all the direct costs is the prime cost.

step 3   adding production (factory) overheads

Production overheads are added to the prime cost to give the **production cost**. Production overheads are the overheads relating to the factory.

Note that some overheads – eg rent and rates – may be split between the factory and the office. The factory part of the total figure is included in the manufacturing account at this stage and the office part will be included in the income statement.

step 4   adjusting for work-in-progress

Work-in-progress – or partly finished goods in course of manufacture – remains in the factory: it cannot be sold because it is not complete. Therefore there is an adjustment at the end of the manufacturing account to ensure that the cost of closing work-in-progress is removed from the total of all production costs, leaving just the cost of producing the finished (completed) goods.

Note also that if there is any work-in-progress brought forward at the start of the period, its value must be included in the manufacturing account. The calculation for the production cost of goods completed is:

	production cost
add	opening inventory of work-in-progress
less	closing inventory of work-in-progress
equals	production cost of goods completed

This figure (production cost of goods completed) is the bottom line of the manufacturing account and is passed to the income statement. However, manufacturing businesses may add a factory profit before making the transfer to the income statement – this aspect of manufacturing accounts is covered on page 231.

The work-in-progress adjustment is illustrated as follows:

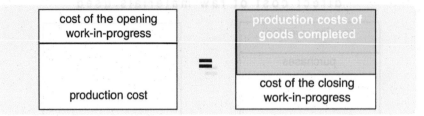

INCOME STATEMENT AND BALANCE SHEET

The income statement and balance sheet follow on from the manufacturing account.

income statement

In the first part of the income statement the manufacturer sells its manufactured goods to its customers. It is also in effect 'buying' the finished goods from its own factory. Instead of 'purchases' of goods from outside suppliers, we now have the 'production cost' of goods completed coming from the factory. This figure is brought forward from the manufacturing account as explained above.

The cost of sales is therefore calculated as:

	opening inventory of finished goods
add	production cost of goods completed
less	closing inventory of finished goods
equals	cost of sales

The expenses section of the income statement of a manufacturing business is prepared in exactly the same way as for any other business. Notice that the **factory** costs have already been dealt with in the manufacturing account, so the income statement deals only with **non-production** (usually warehouse and office) expenses.

balance sheet

The balance sheet of a manufacturing business is prepared in exactly the same way as for any other business. The only difference is that, in the current assets section, there will be the three different forms of inventory – raw materials, work-in-progress and finished goods. These are set out as shown in the balance sheet extract in the diagram opposite.

summary so far . . .

The diagram opposite illustrates how the manufacturing account and income statement are constructed. This shows where the three inventory adjustments – for raw materials, work-in-progress and finished goods – are made in the accounts, and how the closing inventories are shown in the balance sheet.

The two Worked Examples that follow on pages 226-230 put these principles into practice.

inventory adjustments in the final accounts

Note: the inventory adjustment in the manufacturing account and income statement is to *add* opening inventory and to *deduct* closing inventory

MANUFACTURING ACCOUNT

direct materials

prime cost — direct labour

direct expenses

add

production overheads

equals

production cost

> adjustment made for the change in inventory of raw materials used

> adjustment made for the change in inventory of work-in-progress

INCOME STATEMENT

sales

less

cost of sales

equals

gross profit

less

office & warehouse (non-production) expenses

equals

profit for the year

> adjustment made for the change in inventory of finished goods

BALANCE SHEET (extract)

Current Assets

Inventories – raw materials

– work-in-progress

– finished goods

> closing inventory of raw materials from manufacturing account

> closing inventory of work-in-progress from manufacturing account

> closing inventory of finished goods from income statement

WORKED EXAMPLE 1: MANUFACTURING ACCOUNTS

> This Worked Example shows the layout of the final accounts for a manufacturing business, together with notes highlighting important points.

Alpha Manufacturing Company Limited makes paving slabs. The layout of its manufacturing account and income statement for the year 20-2 is as follows:

ALPHA MANUFACTURING COMPANY LIMITED
MANUFACTURING ACCOUNT AND INCOME STATEMENT
FOR THE YEAR ENDED 31 DECEMBER 20-2

	£	£
Opening inventory of raw materials		5,000
Add Purchases of raw materials		50,000
		55,000
Less Closing inventory of raw materials		6,000
COST OF RAW MATERIALS USED (OR CONSUMED)		49,000
Direct labour		26,000
Direct expenses		2,500
PRIME COST		77,500
Add Production (factory) overheads:		
Indirect materials	2,000	
Indirect labour	16,000	
Rent of factory	5,000	
Depreciation of factory machinery	10,000	
Factory light and heat	4,000	
		37,000
		114,500
Add Opening inventory of work-in-progress		4,000
		118,500
Less Closing inventory of work-in-progress		3,000
PRODUCTION (OR MANUFACTURING) COST OF GOODS COMPLETED		115,500
Revenue		195,500
Opening inventory of finished goods	6,500	
Production (or manufacturing) cost of goods completed	115,500	
	122,000	
Less Closing inventory of finished goods	7,500	
COST OF SALES		114,500
Gross profit		81,000
Less Non-production overheads:		
Selling and distribution expenses	38,500	
Administrative expenses	32,000	
Finance expenses	3,500	
		74,000
Profit for the year		7,000

BALANCE SHEET EXTRACT AS AT 31 DECEMBER 20-2

		£	£	£
Current Assets				
Inventories	– raw materials	6,000		
	– work-in-progress	3,000		
	– finished goods	7,500		
			16,500	

points to note

1 The first step in the manufacturing account is to calculate the cost of **raw materials used**.

2 The next step is to calculate the **prime cost** of production.

3 The manufacturing account collects together all 'factory' costs, ie prime cost plus production overheads.

4 If there is any work-in-progress, an adjustment is made at the end of the manufacturing account. This ensures that the figure carried forward is the **production cost of the goods completed** in the period.

5 The figure for revenue (sales) goes into the top line of the income statement as usual.

6 **Cost of sales** is calculated in the normal way, except that the production or 'factory' cost replaces the 'purchases' of goods for sale. The production cost of goods completed is transferred from the manufacturing account.

7 **Gross profit = sales – cost of sales,** as usual.

8 The income statement then continues with all **non-production** (non-factory) ie **warehouse and office expenses**.

9 In the balance sheet, all three forms of inventory – raw materials, work-in-progress, finished goods – held at the end of the year are listed in the **current assets** section.

unit cost of goods manufactured

When the production cost has been ascertained, the unit cost can be calculated as follows:

$$\text{Unit cost} = \frac{\text{Production cost of goods completed}}{\text{Number of units completed}}$$

For example, if the manufacturing account of Alpha Manufacturing Company, on the previous page, represented production of 200,000 units of output, the unit cost for the year was:

$$\text{Unit cost} = \frac{£115,500}{200,000} = £0.58 \text{ per unit}$$

WORKED EXAMPLE 2: MANUFACTURING ACCOUNTS

> This Worked Example shows the calculations that are required in order to prepare the final accounts of a manufacturing business.

situation

Trevellas Manufacturing Limited is a small business which makes surf boards. The following figures relate to the year ended 31 December 20-5.

	Opening Inventory 1 January 20-5	Closing Inventory 31 December 20-5
	£	£
Inventory of raw material	15,275	14,385
Inventory of work-in-progress	3,800	3,250
Inventory of finished goods	27,350	26,000

	£
Purchases of raw materials	43,850
Factory wages (direct)	22,725
Factory indirect expenses	12,500
Depreciation of factory machinery	1,500
Rent and rates*	4,000
General administrative expenses	13,250
Sales (revenue) of finished goods	168,000
Depreciation of vehicles	1,400
Vehicle running expenses	2,550
Selling expenses	13,090

Note: at 31 December 20-5, rent of £2,000 is owing.

*Rent and rates are three-quarters for the factory and one-quarter for the office.

You are to prepare the manufacturing account and income statement for Trevellas Manufacturing Limited, for the year ended 31 December 20-5, together with the balance sheet extract showing inventories.

solution

When preparing these accounts from given data, it is useful to mark against each item where it will go. Remember that the inventories of raw materials and work-in-progress are dealt with in the manufacturing account. The finished goods inventories appear in the income statement.

Purchases of raw materials and all 'factory' expenditure go into the manufacturing account. In the case of rent and rates, the factory part must be calculated:

Factory rent and rates = (£4,000 + £2,000) x three-quarters = £4,500 ⟶ manufacturing account

Non-production rent and rates = £6,000 x one-quarter = £1,500 ⟶ income statement

Note: always adjust for accruals and prepayments before calculating the appropriate costs for manufacturing account and income statement.

All other costs relating to the office (administration) and selling and distribution (including vehicles) are entered in the income statement.

Revenue (sales) is shown in the income statement.

TREVELLAS MANUFACTURING LIMITED

MANUFACTURING ACCOUNT FOR THE YEAR ENDED 31 DECEMBER 20-5

	£	£
Opening inventory of raw materials	15,275	
Add Purchases of raw materials	43,850	
	59,125	
Less Closing inventory of raw materials	14,385	
COST OF RAW MATERIALS USED (OR CONSUMED)		44,740
Direct labour (factory wages)		22,725
PRIME COST		67,465
Add Production (factory) overheads		
Factory indirect expenses	12,500	
Factory machinery depreciation	1,500	
Factory rent and rates	4,500	18,500
		85,965
Add Opening inventory of work-in-progress		3,800
		89,765
Less Closing inventory of work-in-progress		3,250
PRODUCTION COST OF GOODS COMPLETED		86,515

TREVELLAS MANUFACTURING LIMITED
INCOME STATEMENT FOR THE YEAR ENDED 31 DECEMBER 20-5

	£	£
Revenue		168,000
Opening inventory of finished goods	27,350	
Production cost of goods completed	86,515	
	113,865	
Less: Closing inventory of finished goods	26,000	
COST OF SALES		87,865
Gross profit		80,135
Less Non-production overheads:		
Selling and distribution expenses (see note 1, below)	17,040	
Administrative expenses (see note 2, below)	14,750	
		31,790
Profit for the year		48,345

Note 1: Selling and distribution expenses include:

	£
Depreciation of vehicles	1,400
Vehicle running expenses	2,550
Selling expenses	13,090
	17,040

Note 2: Administrative expenses include

	£
Rent and rates (one-quarter)	1,500
General administrative expenses	13,250
	14,750

BALANCE SHEET EXTRACT AS AT 31 DECEMBER 20-5

	£	£	£
Current Assets			
Inventories – raw materials	14,385		
– work-in-progress	3,250		
– finished goods	26,000		
		43,635	

TRANSFER PRICES AND FACTORY PROFIT

Often manufacturing businesses transfer completed goods from the factory to the warehouse at, for example, 'factory cost plus ten per cent' (the transfer price). The objective in doing this is for the factory to make a notional profit which is added into profit for the year at a later stage. This gives the unit cost of goods manufactured a more realistic value which can be compared with the cost of buying in completed goods from an outside source. Also, by showing a factory profit, the profit (or loss) from trading activities (as distinct from manufacturing) can be identified separately.

Referring back to the manufacturing account of Alpha Manufacturing Company Limited on page 226 and amending the figures to allow for a factory 'profit' of ten per cent, the final part of the manufacturing account, and the income statement appear as follows:

	£	£
PRODUCTION COST		115,500
Factory profit of 10 per cent		11,550
PRODUCTION COST OF GOODS COMPLETED (transfer price)		127,050
Revenue		195,500
Opening inventory of finished goods 6,500 + 10% profit	*7,150	
Production (or manufacturing) cost of goods completed	127,050	
	134,200	
Less Closing inventory of finished goods 7,500 + 10% profit	*8,250	
COST OF SALES		125,950
Gross profit		69,550
Less Non-production overheads:		
Selling and distribution expenses	38,500	
Administrative expenses	32,000	
Finance expenses	3,500	
		74,000
Loss from trading		(4,450)
Factory profit	11,550	
Less increase in provision for unrealised profit	100	
		11,450
Profit for the year		7,000

* adjustments to finished goods inventories are explained on the next page

Note that the final profit for the year is unchanged, but the manufacturing cost is higher, and gross profit is lower. The factory profit is added back in the income statement, after showing separately the profit or loss from trading. The reason for doing this is to make the factory and the warehouse into separate profit centres which show the contribution of each to the overall profitability of the business.

provision for unrealised profit on finished goods inventories

A business using the 'factory profit' method values inventories of finished goods at manufacturing cost plus manufacturing profit. For example, Alpha Manufacturing Company Limited whose manufacturing account is shown above, values its finished goods inventories as:

Opening inventory at 1 January 20-2

manufacturing cost £6,500 + manufacturing profit of 10 per cent £650 = £7,150

Closing inventory at 31 December 20-2

manufacturing cost £7,500 + manufacturing profit of 10 per cent £750 = £8,250

The logic behind valuing finished goods inventories in this way is to show more clearly the profit from the separate sections of the business, ie manufacturing and trading. It will apply particularly where goods are both manufactured and bought in as finished goods from outside manufacturers. The income statement now compares 'like with like', ie own-manufactured goods are priced to include a profit, while the bought-in goods include the supplier's profit. At the end of the financial year the closing inventory of own-manufactured goods includes an element of unrealised profit.

Under International Accounting Standard No 2, *Inventories* (see Chapter 8), inventories are to be shown in the balance sheet at cost price if purchased, or cost of production if manufactured. (Note that if net realisable value is lower than cost, then this will be used instead.) In order to comply with IAS 2, it is necessary to account for the element of unrealised profit included in the finished goods inventory valuation. This is done by calculating the provision for unrealised profit, which is used to adjust downwards the closing inventory figure in the balance sheet to cost price.

For example, using the adjusted finished goods opening and closing inventory figures of £7,150 (above) and £8,250 (which include manufacturing profits of £650 and £750 respectively), the calculation of the change in unrealised profit is as follows:

	£
Unrealised profit at start of year	650
Unrealised profit at end of year	750
Increase in provision for unrealised profit	100

Here the unrealised profit has increased by £100. This increase is deducted from factory profit shown in the income statement as follows:

	£	£
Factory profit	11,550	
Less increase in provision for unrealised profit	100	
		11,450

If there is a fall in the value of finished goods inventory during the year, then there will be a decrease in the provision for unrealised profit, and this will be added to the factory profit shown in the income statement.

In the balance sheet, the figure for finished goods inventories at 31 December 20-2 is adjusted as follows:

Current Assets	£	£
Inventory of finished goods	8,250	
Less Provision for unrealised profit	750	
Adjusted inventory of finished goods		7,500

As can be seen this reduces the closing inventory value of finished goods to cost price, and enables the balance sheet valuation to comply with IAS 2 and the concept of prudence.

calculating the figures for unrealised profit

When we are told a figure for inventory which includes unrealised profit, how do we work out the amount of unrealised profit?

The calculation is as follows:

$$\text{inventory figure (including unrealised profit)} \quad \times \quad \frac{\text{profit percentage}}{100 + \text{profit percentage}}$$

For example, inventory of £7,150 includes a manufacturing profit of 10 per cent:

$$£7,150 \quad \times \quad \frac{10}{100 + 10} \quad = \quad £650 \text{ unrealised profit}$$

Thus the inventory without the manufacturing profit is

$$£7,150 \quad - \quad £650 \quad = \quad £6,500$$

This can, of course, be calculated as follows:

$$£7,150 \quad \times \quad \frac{100}{100 + 10} \quad = \quad £6,500$$

CHAPTER SUMMARY

- A manufacturing account brings together all the elements of cost which make up production (or manufacturing) cost.

- A manufacturing account shows prime cost and the production (or manufacturing) cost:
  - the prime cost is the total of all direct costs.
  - the production (or manufacturing) cost is the total of direct costs and production overheads, ie prime cost plus production overheads.

- Manufacturing businesses usually have three types of inventory:
  - raw materials
  - work-in-progress
  - finished goods

- The total value of all three kinds of inventory is shown on the balance sheet of a manufacturing business.

- Raw materials and work-in-progress remain in the factory and are therefore dealt with in the manufacturing account:

  opening inventory of raw materials + purchases – closing inventory of raw materials
  = cost of raw materials used

  total production cost + cost of the opening work-in-progress – cost of the closing work-in-progress
  = production cost of finished goods

- Finished goods are transferred from the factory to the warehouse: their cost of production is similarly transferred from the manufacturing account to the income statement. A transfer price can be used to enable a factory to earn a notional profit.

- In the income statement, cost of sales is calculated as follows:

	opening inventory of finished goods
add	production cost of finished goods
less	closing inventory of finished goods

- The income statement continues with non-production costs, such as warehouse and office expenses.

In this chapter manufacturing accounts have provided us with an introduction to identifying costs with various sections of the business – the factory, the warehouse, the office. In the next chapter we develop our study of management accounting by focusing on the nature of fixed, semi-variable, and variable costs, and the calculation of contribution.

QUESTIONS

An asterisk (*) after the question number means that the answer is given at the end of this book.

9.1* Allocate the following costs to

- manufacturing account
- income statement

(a) factory rent

(b) production supervisors' wages

(c) insurance of factory buildings

(d) depreciation of office photocopier

(e) sales commission

(f) raw materials purchased

(g) advertising

9.2* The following figures relate to the accounts of Barbara Francis, who operates a furniture manufacturing business, for the year ended 31 December 20-8:

	£
Inventories of raw materials, 1 January 20-8	31,860
Inventories of raw materials, 31 December 20-8	44,790
Inventories of finished goods, 1 January 20-8	42,640
Inventories of finished goods, 31 December 20-8	96,510
Purchases of raw materials	237,660
Sale of finished goods	796,950
Rent and rates	32,920
Manufacturing wages	234,630
Manufacturing power	7,650
Manufacturing heat and light	2,370
Manufacturing sundry expenses and maintenance	7,355
Administrative salaries	138,700
Advertising	22,170
Office expenses	7,860
Depreciation of manufacturing plant and machinery	7,450

Rent and rates are to be 75% to manufacturing and 25% to administration.

(a) You are to prepare manufacturing account and income statement for the year ended 31 December 20-8, to show clearly:

- cost of raw materials used
- prime cost
- cost of production (factory) overheads
- production cost of goods completed
- cost of sales
- gross profit for the year
- profit for the year

(b) During 20-8 the business manufactured 575 units of output. Calculate the unit cost for the year.

(c) Explain to Barbara Francis why you have presented the accounts in such a form, and what they show.

9.3* Noriv plc is a manufacturing business. The following figures have been extracted from the company's ledgers as at 31 May 2003.

		£
Inventories as at 1 June 2002:	raw materials	21,450
	work-in-progress	14,780
	finished goods	58,620
Sales		657,000
Purchases of raw materials		234,090
Direct labour costs		260,000
Indirect labour costs		82,800
Factory overheads (excluding labour costs)		138,000
Manufacturing royalties		6,560
Returns inwards		1,000
Returns outwards		980
Carriage inwards		750
Carriage outwards		1,340

Additional information:

- At 31 May 2003 inventories were valued as follows:

	£
Raw materials	22,170
Work-in-progress	13,750
Finished goods	60,650

- At 31 May 2003 factory wages accrued and unpaid amounted to £8,000. One-quarter of this was for indirect labour and the remainder was for direct labour.

- Depreciation of factory machinery for the year was £25,000.

REQUIRED

(a)   Selecting from the information given, prepare an extract from the manufacturing account for the year ended 31 May 2003 to show prime cost.

(b)   Explain what is meant by 'work-in-progress'.

Assessment and Qualifications Alliance (AQA), 2003

9.4   Jacqui King plc is a manufacturing business. The following figures have been extracted from the company's books of account as at 30 November 2001.

		£
Inventories as at 1 December 2000:	raw materials	47,600
	work-in-progress	23,000
	finished goods	76,400
Sales		3,780,000
Purchases of raw materials		498,000
Factory overheads (excluding labour costs)		548,000
Factory labour costs		959,400
Office salaries		365,000
Royalties		17,000
Provisions for depreciation:	factory machinery	48,000
	delivery vehicles	56,000
	office equipment	11,000

Additional information:

- At 30 November 2001 inventories were valued as follows: £
  Raw materials at cost   50,900
  Work-in-progress at cost   24,100
  Finished goods at cost   79,200

- Factory labour costs are apportioned:
  2/3 to direct labour, and
  1/3 to indirect labour

REQUIRED

(a)   Prepare the manufacturing account for the year ended 30 November 2001 for Jacqui King plc, selecting from the information given.

The account should show clearly the totals for raw materials consumed, prime cost and total production cost.

(b)   Explain the term 'royalties'.

Assessment and Qualifications Alliance (AQA), 2002

9.5*   Cheung Lee runs a business which manufactures garden chairs. He transfers the production
        cost of completed chairs from the manufacturing account to the trading account at cost plus
        25%.

        Cheung provides you with the following information for the year ended 31 December 20-8:

	1 January 20-8	31 December 20-8
Inventory of finished goods at cost plus 25%	£56,000	£60,500

        Provision for unrealised profit at 1 January 20-8 was £11,200.

        REQUIRED

        (a)   Calculate the adjustment to the provision for unrealised profit to be shown in the
               income statement for the year ended 31 December 20-8.

        (b)   Draw up a balance sheet extract at 31 December 20-8 which shows the treatment of
               the provision for unrealised profit calculated in (a).

        (c)   Explain why Cheung Lee makes a provision for unrealised profit in the final accounts.

9.6   Malcolm plc is a manufacturing company producing bathroom and kitchen tiles.
        The tiles are transferred from the manufacturing account to the income statement at cost
        plus 25%.
        The cost of finished goods at 31 December 2007 was £680,000.
        Transfer price was £850,000.
        Factory gross profit for the year was £170,000.

        All inventories of finished goods are valued at the transfer price shown below.

	31 December 2007	31 December 2008
Inventories of finished goods	£20,000	£24,000

        REQUIRED

        (a)   Calculate the provision for unrealised profit at

               (i)   31 December 2007

               (ii)   31 December 2008

(b) From your calculations, complete the entries for the year ended 31 December 2008.

Malcolm plc

Income statement for the year ended 31 December 2008

	£
Factory gross profit	170,000
Provision for unrealised profit	_____
Adjusted factory gross profit	_____

Malcolm plc

Balance sheet as at 31 December 2008

	£
Current asset	
Inventory of finished goods	
Provision for unrealised profit	
Adjusted inventory of finished goods	_____
	_____

Assessment and Qualifications Alliance (AQA), 2001 (with dates amended)

9.7 Dewray plc manufactures bedroom furniture.

All completed furniture is transferred to the income statement at cost plus 20%.

The following figures have been extracted from the trial balance of the company as at 31 December 2002 after calculating prime cost.

	Dr	Cr
	£000	£000
Prime cost	1,207	
Factory overheads	915	
Factory machinery at cost	150	
Office equipment at cost	60	
Provision for depreciation – factory machinery		90
– office equipment		18
Provision for unrealised profit		26
Inventories as at 1 January 2002		
work-in-progress at cost	34	
finished goods at cost plus 20%	156	
Revenue (Sales)		3,460

Additional information:

- All non-current assets are depreciated at 10% per annum on cost.

	£000
• Inventories as at 31 December 2002 – raw materials at cost	75
work-in-progress at cost	36
finished goods at cost plus 20%	192

REQUIRED

(a) Starting with the prime cost of £1,207,000, prepare a summarised manufacturing account for the year ended 31 December 2002.

(b) Prepare an income statement to show gross profit for the year ended 31 December 2002.

(c) Calculate the amount of the adjustment to the provision for unrealised profit to be shown in the income statement for the year ended 31 December 2002.

The amount of the adjustment to the provision for unrealised profit to be shown in the income statement is: £...........................

(d) Explain how the amount calculated in (c) should be shown in the income statement.

(e) Complete the following extract from the balance sheet.

Dewray plc

Balance sheet extract as at 31 December 2002

Current assets

Inventory – raw materials ....

– work-in-progress ....

– finished goods ....

Assessment and Qualifications Alliance (AQA), 2003

9.8 Cathy Yow manufactures garden furniture. The following balances have been extracted from her books of account as at 31 December 2001.

	£
Inventories as at 1 January 2001: raw materials at cost	9,000
work-in-progress at cost	3,000
finished goods at cost plus 25%	8,750
Purchases of raw materials	63,600
Direct labour costs	146,800
Factory overhead costs	106,790
Administrative expenses	140,500
Manufacturing royalties	8,140
Sales	568,720
Plant and machinery at cost	400,000
Provision for depreciation of plant and machinery 1 January 2001	160,000
Office equipment at cost	115,000
Provision for depreciation of office equipment 1 January 2001	75,000
Provision for unrealised profit 1 January 2001	1,750

Additional information:

- Factory output is transferred to the income statement at factory cost plus 25%.

- Inventories as at 31 December 2001 were valued as follows:

	£
raw materials at cost	9,400
work-in-progress at cost	3,100
finished goods at cost plus 25%	9,250

- Direct labour costs accrued at 31 December 2001 amounted to £3,450.

REQUIRED

(a) Prepare the prime cost section **only** of the manufacturing account for the year ended 31 December 2001 for Cathy Yow, selecting from the information given.

(b) Calculate the amount to be charged to the income statement for the adjustment to the provision for unrealised gross profit.

The adjustment is £.............................

(c) Explain why Cathy needs to make provision for unrealised profit in her final accounts.

Assessment and Qualifications Alliance (AQA), 2002

9.9*

Tutorial note:

This is a part question – the other parts of the question can be seen in Chapter 13 as question 13.14.

On 31 December 2006 the following balances were extracted from the books of account of Osborne Melbourne Ltd, a manufacturer of electrical hedge cutters.

	£
Direct factory wages	390,500
Factory canteen expenses	37,150
Factory machinery at cost	720,000
Machine maintenance	12,000
Machine set-up costs	40,000
Purchases of raw materials	188,360
Royalties	10,080
Inventories at 1 January 2006 – raw materials at cost	48,560
– work-in-progress at cost	28,420

Additional information:

1. Inventories at 31 December 2006 – raw materials at cost 50,120
 – work-in-progress at cost 31,400

2. The factory machinery is depreciated at 2% per annum, using the straight-line method.

3. At 31 December 2006 the company owed wages to its factory workers of £9,500.

4. The factory canteen costs had been prepaid by £1,150.

5. During the year 30,000 hedge cutters had been produced.

REQUIRED

(a) Prepare a manufacturing account for Osborne Melbourne Ltd for the year ended 31 December 2006.

(b) Calculate the manufacturing cost per hedge cutter.

Assessment and Qualifications Alliance (AQA), Specimen Paper for 2010 (part of question)

9.10 Catherine Donovan manufactures furniture. Completed furniture is transferred from her manufacturing account to her income statement at cost plus 25%. She provides the following information for the year ended 31 December 2006:

	Dr	Cr
	£	£
Inventory at 1 January 2006 – raw materials	9,840	
– finished goods	23,500	
Purchases of raw materials	126,430	
Direct wages	274,700	
Factory supervisors' wages	63,150	
Administrative staff wages	124,490	
Rates	6,400	
Indirect expenses – office	198,160	
– factory	337,171	
Manufacturing royalties	55,000	
Machinery at cost	400,000	
Office equipment at cost	80,000	
Provision for depreciation – machinery		160,000
– office equipment		30,000
Provision for unrealised profit		4,700

Additional information at 31 December 2006:

1. Rates paid in advance amounted to £400.

2. Rates are apportioned three-quarters to the factory and one-quarter to the office.

3. Depreciation is provided on all non-current assets at 10% using the straight-line method.

4. Inventory of raw materials were £10,211.

5. Inventory of finished goods were £25,600.

6. Inventory of work-in-progress increased by £580 during the year.

REQUIRED

(a) Prepare a manufacturing account for the year ended 31 December 2006.

(b) Calculate the change in the provision for unrealised profit for the year ended 31 December 2006.

> Catherine has calculated her gross profit on trading for the year ended 31 December 2006 to be £312,400.

REQUIRED

(c)   Calculate the **total** gross profit from manufacturing and trading for the year ended 31 December 2006, showing how the provision for unrealised profit is treated.

(d)   Explain to Catherine the reason for making a provision for unrealised profit in her books of account.

Assessment and Qualifications Alliance (AQA), 2007

9.11* Tecyl Products is a manufacturing business. It transfers all goods manufactured to the income statement at production cost plus 20%.
The following figures relate to inventories held by the business.

	as at 1 December 2002	as at 30 November 2003
	£	£
Inventory of raw materials	27,000	28,000
work-in-progress	9,000	8,500
finished goods	22,200	23,400
Provision for unrealised profit	3,700	3,900

REQUIRED

(a)   Calculate the amount of provision for unrealised profit to be entered in the income statement for the year ended 30 November 2003.

What effect will the change have on the gross profit?

(b)   Show in detail how the information relating to **all** inventories should be shown on the balance sheet as at 30 November 2003.

(c)   Explain why it is necessary for Tecyl Products to provide for unrealised profit.

Assessment and Qualifications Alliance (AQA), 2004

9.12 Amandeep Pawar owns a manufacturing business. She transfers all goods from the factory to the income statement at cost plus 20%. She has prepared her manufacturing account, and the total cost of production (**before** the addition of factory profit) was £720,000.

Amandeep provides the following information.

(1)   Sales for the year ended 31 December 2005 were £1,430,972.

(2) Inventories | as at 1 January 2005 | as at 31 December 2005

	as at 1 January 2005 £	as at 31 December 2005 £
Raw materials at cost	6,780	7,140
Work-in-progress at cost	9,630	9,880
Finished goods at cost plus 20%	27,804	31,776

(3) Administrative expenses for the year were £478,221.

REQUIRED

(a) Calculate the change in the provision for unrealised profit for the year ended 31 December 2005.

(b) Prepare an income statement for the year ended 31 December 2005.

Assessment and Qualifications Alliance (AQA), 2006

9.13 S H Matt runs a manufacturing business. Finished goods are transferred from the manufacturing account to the trading account at cost plus 40%.

The following extracts are taken from the two most recent balance sheets.

Balance sheet	At 31 March 2007 £	£	At 31 March 2008 £	£
Inventories				
Raw materials		12,468		10,980
Work-in-progress		8,647		9,946
Finished goods	29,876		31,906	
Less provision for unrealised profit	8,536		?	
		21,340		?

REQUIRED

(a) Prepare a balance sheet extract for inventories, having calculated the following:

(i) the provision for unrealised profit to be included in the balance sheet extract at 31 March 2008

(ii) the cost of the closing inventory of finished goods at 31 March 2008

(b) Calculate the provision for unrealised profit to be shown in the income statement for the year ended 31 March 2008.

(c) Outline **two** reasons why S H Matt transfers goods to the income statement at cost plus a profit.

Assessment and Qualifications Alliance (AQA), Second Specimen Paper for 2010

10 COSTS AND CONTRIBUTION

The last chapter covered manufacturing accounts and provided an introduction to the identification of costs with the various sections of the business. In this chapter we continue this theme and begin to study cost and management accounting, which produces reports for managers and directors to help with making decisions, and planning and control of the business.

In the chapter we cover:

- the purpose of cost and management accounting
- the terms 'direct costs' and 'indirect costs'
- the nature of costs – fixed, semi-variable and variable
- marginal costing
- the calculation of contribution and how it can be used in management decision-making

COST AND MANAGEMENT ACCOUNTING

the purpose of cost and management accounting

Cost and management accounting enables the managers of a business to know the cost of the firm's output – whether a product or a service – and the revenue from sales. Managers need answers to detailed questions about costs in order to assist them with:

- decision-making
- planning for the future
- control of expenditure

Cost and management accounting is widely used by all types of businesses – the cost of a hospital operation, the cost of building a new hospital ward, the cost of tuition to a student, the cost of a swim at a sports centre, the cost of a passenger's bus journey, the cost of a new road – are all just as important as the cost of making a product. A business, whether it provides a service or makes a product, needs to keep its costs under review; in order to do this it needs accurate cost information. Thus cost accounting will provide answers to questions such as:

What does it cost us to provide a student with a day's accountancy course?

What does it cost us to carry out a hip replacement operation?

What does it cost us to make a pair of trainers?

What does it cost us to serve a burger and fries?

What does it cost us to provide a week's holiday in Spain?

Cost and management accounting helps managers with production planning and decision-making, such as:

- short-term decisions, eg "how many do we need to make and sell in order to break-even?"
- long-term decisions, eg "we need to buy a new machine for the factory – shall we buy Machine Exe or Machine Wye?"

The dividing line between cost accounting and management accounting is not always clear. Usually the cost accountant is the person who obtains and analyses information about costs. The management accountant then interprets the information and prepares reports for management purposes.

financial accounting and cost and management accounting

Financial accounting and cost and management accounting are types of accounting which, although they produce different reports and statements, obtain their information from the same set of transactions carried out by the business over a given period. The following diagram illustrates these types of accounting.

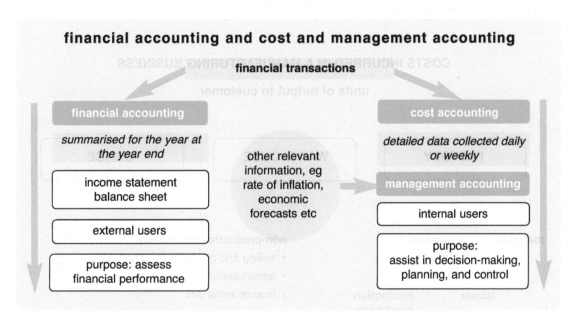

Financial accounting uses the financial information relating to transactions carried out over a period of time. The information is processed through the accounting records and extracted in the form of final accounts – income statement, and balance sheet. The statements are often required to be produced by law, eg the Companies Act, and are available to external user groups such as shareholders, suppliers, banks, HM Revenue & Customs, Companies House.

Cost and management accounting uses the same data to produce reports containing financial information on the recent past and projections for the future. The reports are available to internal users only, such as managers, directors, and owners (but not to shareholders generally). There is no legal requirement to produce this information and the content of the report and the principles used can be suited to the activities of the business and the requirements of its managers. The information is prepared as frequently as it is required, and speed is often vital as the information may go out-of-date very quickly.

CLASSIFICATION OF COSTS

Within any business, whether it manufactures a product or provides a service, there are certain costs involved at various stages to produce the units of output. The diagram below shows the costs which are incurred by the three main sections or 'areas' of a manufacturing business (see also Chapter 9).

These three separate sections are:

- **factory** – where production takes place and the product is 'finished' and made ready for selling
- **warehouse** – where finished goods are stored and from where they are despatched when they are sold
- **office** – where the support functions take place – marketing, sales, administration, finance and so on

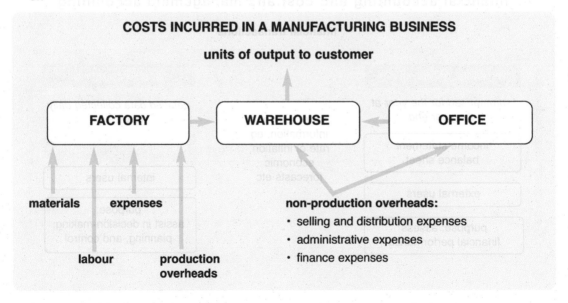

Note that while the diagram above shows the costs of a manufacturing business, it can be adapted easily to fit non-manufacturing businesses and organisations, such as a shop, a hospital, a school or college, a church or a club. While the output of these organisations differs from that of a manufacturer, nevertheless they still incur costs at various stages of the 'production' process.

In order to prepare information for the managers of a business, costs must be **classified**, ie organised into sets in a way which the managers will find useful. We will look at how costs can be classified in two ways:

* by element, which focuses on direct costs and indirect costs
* by behaviour, which focuses on fixed costs, semi-variable costs and variable costs

CLASSIFICATION OF COSTS BY ELEMENT

Businesses and organisations incur many different kinds of cost in the production of goods or 'output', including costs of the warehouse and the office. The most basic way of splitting up costs is according to the type of expenditure under the headings:

* **materials**, eg the components to make a car
* **labour**, eg wages of an employee
* **expenses**, eg rent and rates, telephone charges, insurance

Note: materials, labour, and expenses are often referred to as the three *elements of cost*.

Splitting costs into these three elements applies to both manufacturing and service businesses. The classification provides important information to managers as they can see the breakdown of the total into different kinds of cost.

Within each of the three elements of materials, labour and expenses, some costs can be identified directly with each unit of output. For example:

* the cost of components used in making cars
* the wages of workers on a production line in a factory

These are termed **direct costs**. In manufacturing, the total of all the direct costs is called the **prime cost** of the output. Costs which cannot be identified directly with each unit of output are **indirect costs** or overheads. We can therefore define these two types of cost as follows:

a direct cost is a cost that can be identified directly with each unit of output

indirect costs (overheads) are all costs other than those identified as 'direct costs'; they cannot be identified directly with specific units of output

Note: the way in which costs can be classified as direct or indirect is often referred to as the *nature of costs*.

There are many examples of overheads, including:

* telephone charges
* insurance premiums
* cost of wages of non-production staff, such as managers, secretaries, cost accountants and so on
* running costs of delivery vehicles
* depreciation charge for non-current assets

Note particularly the last two examples. In cost accounting, as in financial accounting, we distinguish between capital and revenue expenditure. In our analysis of costs we are referring to revenue expenditure, and therefore include the running costs and depreciation of non-current assets, rather than the capital cost of their purchase.

The direct and indirect costs for a manufacturing business are illustrated in the table below.

	DIRECT COSTS	INDIRECT COSTS
MATERIALS	The cost of raw materials from which the finished product is made.	The cost of all other materials, eg grease for machines, cleaning materials.
LABOUR	Wages paid to those who work the machinery on the production line or who are involved in assembly or finishing of the product.	Wages and salaries paid to all other employees, eg managers and supervisors, maintenance staff, administration staff.
EXPENSES	Any expenses which can be attributed to particular units of output, eg royalties payable to the designer of a product, fees linked directly to specific output and paid to people who are not employees.	All other expenses, eg rent, rates, telephone, lighting and heating costs, depreciation of non-current assets, insurance, advertising, etc. These are costs which cannot be linked directly with units of output.
TOTAL	**TOTAL DIRECT COST = PRIME COST**	**TOTAL INDIRECT COST = TOTAL OVERHEADS**

CLASSIFICATION OF COSTS BY BEHAVIOUR

In cost accounting, it is important to appreciate the *behaviour* of costs – in particular to understand that not all costs increase or decrease directly in line with increases or decreases in output or activity. By nature, costs are:

- fixed, or
- semi-variable, or
- variable

The diagram on the next page shows the differences between these.

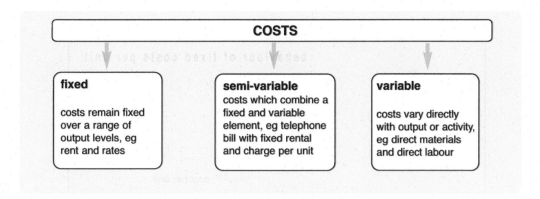

It is important to know the behaviour of costs and how they are affected by changes in the level of output. For example, a business decides to increase its output by 25% – will all costs increase by 25%? Fixed costs, such as rent and rates, are likely to remain unchanged, provided that there is capacity for the increased output within the existing building. Variable costs, such as direct materials and direct labour, are likely to increase by 25% as they generally vary directly with output (unless any economies of scale can be achieved). Semi-variable costs, such as the telephone bill, will increase as the extra business generates more phone calls; however, the increase should certainly be much less than 25%.

We shall be studying the relationship between fixed and variable costs in detail in the next chapter. In particular, we will be looking at the technique of break-even analysis – the point at which costs are exactly equal to income. For the moment we will see how the differing behaviour of costs is shown in the form of a graph.

fixed costs

These are costs that do not normally change when the level of output or activity changes.   For example, the cost of insuring a car factory against business risks will not vary in line with the number of cars produced – it is a fixed cost and varies with time rather than activity.

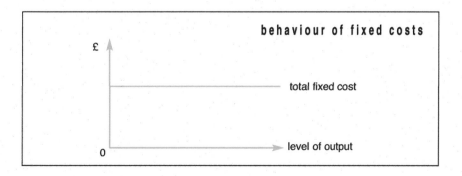

Note that money amounts are shown on the vertical axis and the level of output or activity on the horizontal axis.

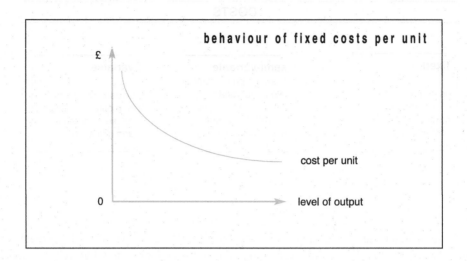

For fixed costs, the *cost per unit* falls as output increases, as follows:

For example, with rent of £40,000 per year:

*   at output of 4,000 units, equals £10 per unit
*   at output of 10,000 units, equals £4 per unit

Whilst it is sensible to seek to achieve maximum output in order to reduce the cost per unit, fixed costs do not remain fixed at all levels of production. For example, a decision to double production is likely to increase the fixed costs – an increase in factory rent, for example, because an additional factory may need to be rented. Fixed costs are often described as *stepped fixed costs*, because they increase by a large amount all at once; graphically, the cost behaviour is shown as a step:

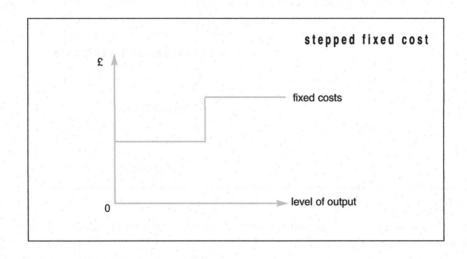

semi-variable costs

These are costs where a part of the cost acts as a variable cost, and a part acts as a fixed cost. For example, some fuel bills are semi-variable: there is a fixed 'standing charge' and a variable 'unit charge'.

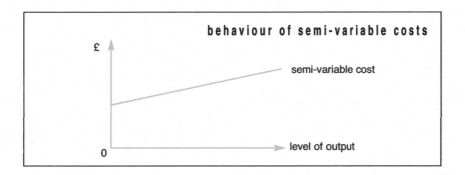

variable costs

These are the costs where the cost varies in proportion to the level of output or activity. For example, if a car manufacturer makes more cars it will use more metal – a variable cost. Note however that the cost per unit remains constant at all levels of output.

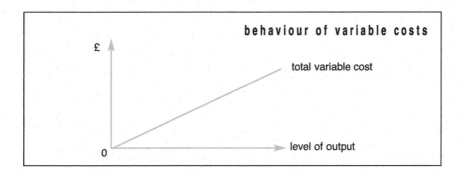

fixed and variable costs in decision-making

Identifying costs as being fixed, semi-variable or variable helps with decision-making – the business might be able to alter the balance between fixed and variable costs in order to increase profits. A product could be made:

- either by using a labour-intensive process, with a large number of employees supported by basic machinery, or

- by using expensive machinery in an automated process with very few employees

In the first case, the cost structure will be high variable costs (direct labour) and low fixed costs (depreciation of machinery). In the second case, there will be low variable costs, and high fixed costs.

Management will need to examine the relationship between the costs – together with the likely sales figures, and the availability of finance with which to buy the machinery – before making a decision.

More specifically, a knowledge of the behaviour of costs can be used to help management to identify the point at which costs are exactly equal to income – known as the break-even point (covered in the next chapter).

Marginal Costing

To help with decision-making, costs are classified as either variable costs or fixed costs (semi-variable costs are divided into their fixed and variable components). For example, a car manufacturer will need to identify:

- the variable costs of each car
- the total fixed costs of running the business over a period of time

The classification of costs as fixed or variable is used in **marginal costing** to work out how much it costs to produce each extra unit of output.

marginal cost is the cost of producing one extra unit of output

The marginal cost for a car manufacturer is therefore the cost of producing one extra car.

Marginal cost is often – but not always – the total of the variable costs of producing a unit of output. For most purposes, marginal costing is not concerned with fixed costs (such as the rent of a factory); instead it is concerned with variable costs – direct materials, direct labour, direct expenses, and variable production overheads – which increase as output increases. For most decision-making, the marginal cost of a unit of output is, therefore, the variable cost of producing one more unit.

Knowing the marginal cost of a unit of output enables the managers of a business to focus on the **contribution** provided by each unit. The contribution is the amount of money coming in from sales after marginal/variable costs have been paid. The formula for calculating contribution is:

selling price per unit less variable cost per unit = contribution per unit

Contribution can be calculated on a per unit basis (as here), or for a batch of output (eg 1,000 units), or for a whole business.

It follows that the difference between the sales income and the variable costs of the units sold in a period is the **total contribution** that the sales of all the units in the period make towards the fixed costs of the business. Once these are covered, the remainder of the contribution is profit.

Thus a business can work out its profit, using a marginal costing statement, for any given period from the total contribution and fixed costs figures:

total contribution less total fixed costs = profit

A marginal costing statement can be prepared in the following format:

	sales revenue
less	variable costs
equals	contribution
less	fixed costs
equals	profit

Note from the marginal costing statement how the contribution goes firstly towards the fixed costs and, when they have been covered, secondly contributes to profit.

The relationship between marginal costing, contribution and profit is shown in the Worked Example which follows.

WORKED EXAMPLE: MARGINAL COSTING

situation

The Wyvern Bike Company makes 100 bikes each week and its costs are as follows:

Direct materials	£3,000
Direct labour	£2,500
Indirect costs	£3,500

Investigations into the behaviour of costs has revealed the following information:
- direct materials are variable costs
- direct labour is a variable cost
- of the indirect costs, £1,500 is a fixed cost, and the remainder is a variable cost

The selling price of each bike is £120.

You are to:
- calculate the marginal cost of producing each bike
- show the expected contribution per bike
- prepare a marginal costing statement to show clearly the total contribution and the total profit each week

solution

Marginal cost per bike

	£
Variable costs per unit:	
direct materials (£3,000 ÷ 100)	30
direct labour (£2,500 ÷ 100)	25
indirect costs (£2,000* ÷ 100)	20
marginal cost per bike	75

* £3,500 – £1,500 fixed costs

Contribution per bike

		£
	selling price per bike	120
less	variable cost per bike	75
equals	contribution per bike	45

Marginal costing statement

		£	£
	sales £120 x 100 bikes		12,000
less	variable costs:		
	direct materials	3,000	
	direct labour	2,500	
	indirect costs	2,000	
			7,500
equals	total contribution		4,500
less	fixed costs (indirect costs)		1,500
equals	profit for the week		3,000

ADVANTAGES OF A MARGINAL COSTING STATEMENT

A marginal costing statement is of benefit to the managers of a business because:

- contribution, ie selling price less variable cost, is clearly identified
- with the marginal cost of output identified, the managers can focus on the contribution provided by the output
- the effect on costs of changes in sales revenue can be calculated

- it helps with decision-making in the forms of
  - costing a project
  - make or buy
  - acceptance of additional work
  - price setting
  - optimum use of scarce resources

(We will look at the role of marginal costing in decision-making in Chapter 14.)

CHAPTER SUMMARY

- Cost and management accounting provides information to help the managers of a business with decision-making, planning and control.

- The main elements of cost are
  - materials
  - labour
  - expenses

  Each of these can be direct or indirect.

- Direct costs can be identified directly with each unit of output.

- Indirect costs (overheads) cannot be identified directly with specific units of output.

- By behaviour, costs are fixed, or semi-variable, or variable.

- A fixed cost remains fixed over a range of output levels and varies with time rather than activity.

- A variable cost varies directly with output.

- A semi-variable cost combines a fixed and variable element.

- The marginal cost is the cost of producing one extra unit of output.

- Knowing the marginal cost of a unit of output enables the managers of a business to focus on the contribution of each unit.

- Contribution per unit = selling price per unit less variable cost per unit.

- A business can work out its profit, using a marginal costing statement, for any given period from the total contribution and fixed cost figures:

  total contribution less total fixed costs = profit

In the next chapter we develop the relationship between fixed and variable costs in the form of break-even analysis.

QUESTIONS

An asterisk (*) after the question number means that the answer is given at the end of this book.

10.1* (a) Explain how costs are classified (i) by element, and (ii) by behaviour.

(b) Analyse each of the following costs by behaviour (ie fixed, or semi-variable, or variable):

- raw materials
- factory rent
- telephone bill with fixed rental and charge per call unit
- direct labour, eg production workers paid on the basis of work done
- indirect labour, eg supervisors' salaries
- commission paid to sales staff

Taking the costs in turn, explain to a friend, who is about to set up a furniture manufacturing business, why you have analysed each as fixed, or semi-variable, or variable. Answer the comment, "What difference does it make anyway, they are all costs that have to be paid."

10.2* Explain the behaviour of the costs shown by the following graphs. (Study the graphs and read the notes that follow on the next page).

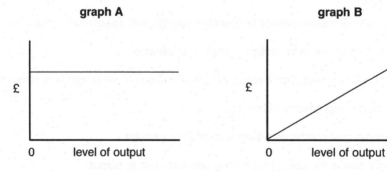

graph A   graph B

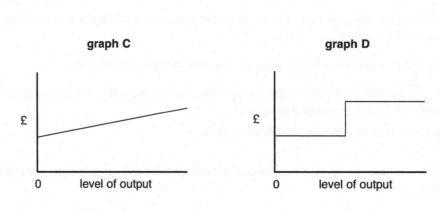

graph C   graph D

notes to the graphs

Graph A shows the cost of factory rent.

Graph B shows the wages of production-line employees who are paid on a piecework basis (ie on the basis of goods produced).

Graph C shows the cost of a photocopier with a fixed rental and a cost per unit copied.

Graph D shows the cost of factory rent in an expanding business.

10.3* Classify the following costs (tick the appropriate column):

	fixed	semi-variable	variable
(a) rates of business premises			
(b) royalty paid to designer for each unit of output			
(c) car hire with fixed rental and charge per mile			
(d) employees paid on piecework basis (ie on the basis of goods produced)			
(e) straight-line depreciation			
(f) direct materials			
(g) telephone bill with fixed rental and charge per call unit			
(h) office salaries			

10.4 Each of the following types of costs is incurred by Seedy Limited, a company that makes music CDs:

(a) factory rates

(b) CD cases

(c) production workers paid a basic wage plus a bonus per CD made

(d) production supervisors paid a fixed salary

(e) blank CDs

(f) factory rent

(g) cellophane for packaging individual CDs

(h) royalties paid to recording artists for each CD made

You are to state whether each of the above costs behaves as a fixed, semi-variable, or variable cost.

10.5 You have been asked to organise a day of lectures on costing techniques for students. You will need to advertise the event, and hire a suitable room in a local hotel, and speakers. You will also need to provide lunch and course materials for each person who books a place, and decide how much to charge them each for the day.

Using your own estimates for the relevant costs and price, you are to:

(a) calculate the total fixed costs for the event

(b) calculate the total variable costs per delegate

(c) decide the price to be charged per delegate and then calculate the contribution per delegate

(d) assuming that thirty delegates attend, prepare a marginal costing statement to show clearly the total contribution and the profit or loss for the event

10.6* Newman Electronics Ltd manufactures one product which sells for £32 per unit.

The company plans to manufacture 40,000 units.

Annual costs are expected to be:

	£
variable costs	360,000
semi-variable costs of which £80,000 are fixed	280,000
other fixed costs	340,000

In the year ended 31 March 2003 46,000 units were produced and sold.

REQUIRED

(a) Define the following:

    (i) fixed costs

    (ii) variable costs

    (iii) semi-variable costs

(b) Calculate the expected contribution per unit. State the formula used.

(c) Prepare a statement for Newman Electronics Ltd for the year ended 31 March 2003 to show clearly the total contribution and the total profit for the year.

Assessment and Qualifications Alliance (AQA), 2003

10.7 John Walker Limited manufactures high quality trainers. The management of the company is considering next year's production and has asked you to help with certain financial decisions.

The following information is available:

wholesale selling price (per pair)	£40
direct materials (per pair)	£15
direct labour (per pair)	£12
overheads (fixed)	£245,000 per year

The company is planning to manufacture 25,000 pairs of trainers next year.

You are to:

(a) calculate the marginal cost per pair of trainers

(b) calculate the contribution per pair of trainers

(c) prepare a marginal costing statement to show the profit or loss if 25,000 pairs of trainers are sold

10.8 Pinder Ltd manufactures parachutes.

The cost of producing one parachute is:

	£
materials (£4 per metre)	10
labour (£8 per hour)	16
other variable costs	8

Total fixed costs for the year are expected to be £134,000.

Each parachute sells for £44. The company expects to sell 22,000 parachutes each year.

The production manager intends to purchase new advanced machinery, which will reduce the time taken to produce one parachute by 25%.

In order to operate the machinery the workforce must be retrained for two months at a cost of £32,000. If the retraining is completed satisfactorily the workforce will receive a 12.5% pay rise.

It is expected that not all the workforce will wish to be retrained.

REQUIRED

(a)   Define the term "contribution".

(b)   Calculate the contribution per unit:

    (i)   before the proposed purchase of the machinery

    (ii)   after the proposed purchase of the machinery

(c)   Assess the effect the proposed purchase of the machinery will have on the profitability of Pinder Ltd.

Assessment and Qualifications Alliance (AQA), 2002

10.9*   Perpend plc manufactures and sells electrical heat pumps.

It is expected that 600 pumps will be produced in August 2001. At this level of production the following costs would arise:

	£
Materials: Unassembled pump kit	20
Labour: 3 employees working in the Assembly Dept at £5 per hour	15
Other variable costs (one-fifth of labour cost per pump)	3
Total fixed costs are expected to be £2,400	
Each pump is sold at a 20% mark-up on cost	

In order to increase production the Production Manager has introduced a bonus scheme within the Assembly Department. It will be paid in September for each pump manufactured in excess of the expected production level of 600 pumps.

The bonus is valued at £3 per pump, but this figure is not to be included in the calculation for the variable overhead cost.

The Purchasing Manager has also negotiated a 10% discount on pump materials. The discount will take effect from 1 September and will only apply to each pump kit purchased in excess of 400 kits.

REQUIRED

(a) Distinguish between fixed costs and variable costs. State one example of each.

(b) Calculate the total cost if 650 pumps are manufactured in September.

Total cost of 650 pumps:	£
Materials:	
Labour:	
Other variable costs:	
Fixed costs:	
Total costs:	

Assessment and Qualifications Alliance (AQA), 2001

10.10 Which Direction Ltd produces compasses that sell for £20 each.

The following costs relate to the six months ended 31 December 2003, when 5,000 compasses were produced and sold.

	£
Direct labour	23,000
Direct materials	35,000
Other direct costs	21,000

Of the other direct costs, £12,000 are fixed costs.

REQUIRED

(a) Distinguish between direct and indirect costs.

(b) Calculate the marginal cost of one compass.

(c) Prepare a marginal costing statement for the six months ended 31 December 2003. Show the total contribution and the profit for the period.

(d) Explain *one* advantage of producing a marginal costing statement.

Assessment and Qualifications Alliance (AQA), 2004

11 BREAK-EVEN ANALYSIS

This chapter looks at the relationship between fixed costs and variable costs: the behaviour of these costs has been examined already in Chapter 10. We shall now study the relationship between them in break-even analysis, which is the point at which a business makes neither a profit nor a loss.

In this chapter we look at:

● the behaviour of fixed and variable costs

● break-even point

● break-even analysis, by calculation, by table, by graph

● interpretation of break-even

● limitations of break-even analysis

● margin of safety, ie the amount by which sales exceed the break-even point

● target profit, and the contribution sales ratio

● use of break-even analysis

FIXED AND VARIABLE COSTS

In Chapter 10 we have seen that the main elements of cost for most businesses comprise:

* materials
* labour
* expenses (overheads)

We know that, by behaviour, costs are:

* fixed, or
* semi-variable, or
* variable

In brief, fixed costs remain fixed over a range of output levels, despite other changes. Variable costs vary directly with changes in output levels. Semi-variable costs combine both a fixed and variable element, eg the telephone bill comprises the fixed rental for the line, together with the variable element of call charges.

Do remember that the behaviour of costs can change as the business changes. For example, a fixed cost, such as factory rent, is only likely to be fixed at or near current production levels: if output is doubled or trebled, then it is likely that an additional factory will need to be rented. In this way, the fixed cost becomes a stepped fixed cost.

For the purposes of break-even analysis we need to distinguish between fixed and variable costs, and to be able to pick out from semi-variable costs the amounts of the fixed and variable elements.

BREAK-EVEN POINT

Break-even is the point at which neither a profit nor a loss is made.

The break-even point (bep) is the output level (units manufactured or services provided) at which the income from sales is just enough to cover all the costs. Break-even is the point at which the profit (or loss) is zero. The output level can be measured in a way that is appropriate for the particular business; it is commonly measured in units of output.

The formula for break-even in units of output is:

$$\frac{fixed\ costs\ (£)}{*contribution\ per\ unit\ (£)} = break\text{-}even\ point\ (in\ units\ of\ output)$$

* selling price – variable costs

In order to use break-even analysis, we need to know:

- selling price (per unit)
- costs of the product
  - variable costs (such as materials, labour) per unit
  - overhead costs, and whether these are fixed or variable
- limitations, such as maximum production capacity, maximum sales

The Worked Example of Fluffy Toys Limited which follows shows how the break-even point can be determined.

WORKED EXAMPLE: BREAK-EVEN

situation
Fluffy Toys Limited manufactures soft toys, and is able to sell all that can be produced. The variable costs (materials and direct labour) for producing each toy are £10 and the selling price is £20 each. The fixed costs of running the business are £5,000 per month. How many toys need to be produced and sold each month for the business to cover its costs, ie to break-even?

solution
This problem can be solved by calculation, by constructing a table, or by means of a graph. Which method is used depends on the purpose for which the information is required:

- the **calculation method** is quick to use and is convenient for seeing the effect of different cost structures on break-even point

- the **table method** shows the amounts of fixed and variable costs, sales revenue, and profit at different levels of production

- the **graph method** is used for making presentations – for example, to the directors of a company – because it shows in a visual form the relationship between costs and sales revenue, and the amount of profit or loss at different levels of production

Often the calculation or table methods are used before drawing a graph. By doing this, the break-even point is known and suitable scales can be selected for the axes of the graph in order to give a good visual presentation.

calculation method

The contribution per unit is:

	selling price per unit	£20
less	variable costs per unit	£10
equals	contribution per unit	£10

Each toy sold gives a contribution (selling price, less variable costs) of £10. This contributes towards the fixed costs and, in order to break-even, the business must have sufficient £10 'lots' to meet the fixed costs. Thus, with fixed costs of £5,000 per month, the break-even calculation is:

$$\frac{fixed\ costs\ (£)}{contribution\ per\ unit\ (£)} = \frac{£5,000}{£10} = 500\ toys\ each\ month$$

The break-even point (in units of output) is 500 toys each month.

table method

units of output	fixed costs A	variable costs B	total cost C A + B	sales revenue D	profit/(loss) D – C
	£	£	£	£	£
100	5,000	1,000	6,000	2,000	(4,000)
200	5,000	2,000	7,000	4,000	(3,000)
300	5,000	3,000	8,000	6,000	(2 000)
400	5,000	4,000	9,000	8,000	(1,000)
500	5,000	5,000	10,000	10,000	nil
600	5,000	6,000	11,000	12,000	1,000
700	5,000	7,000	12,000	14,000	2,000

graph method

A graphical presentation uses money amounts as the common denominator between fixed costs, variable costs, and sales revenue.

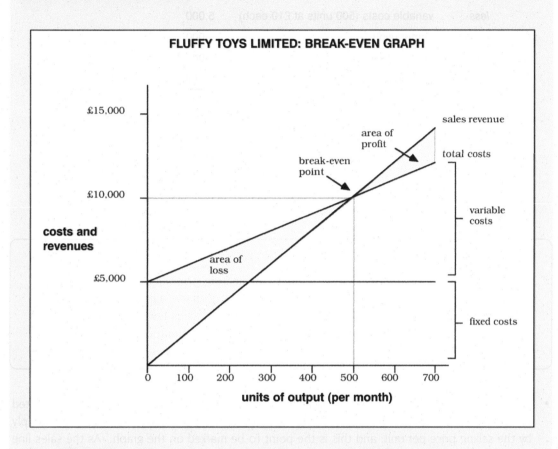

notes to the graph

- It is usual for the vertical axis to show money amounts, while the horizontal axis shows units of output/sales – the reason for this is that the amount of money depends on the volume of activity, ie output/sales.

- The fixed costs are unchanged at all levels of output, in this case they are £5,000.

- The variable costs commence, on the vertical axis, *from the fixed costs amount, not from 'zero'.* This is because the cost of producing zero units is the fixed costs.

- The fixed costs *and* the variable costs added together form the *total costs line.*

- The point at which the total costs and sales revenue lines cross is the break-even point.

- From the graph we can read off the break-even point both in terms of units of output, 500 units on the horizontal axis, and in sales revenue and total costs, £10,000 on the vertical axis.

- The 'proof' of the break-even chart is:

		£
	sales revenue (500 units at £20 each)	10,000
less	variable costs (500 units at £10 each)	5,000
equals	contribution	5,000
less	fixed costs	5,000
equals	profit/loss	nil

HINTS FOR DRAWING A BREAK-EVEN GRAPH

> Tutorial note:
>
> It is unlikely that, in the AQA A2 Accounting examination, you will be asked to draw a break-even graph. However, practice at drawing graphs does give a good understanding of the relationship between fixed and variable costs and sales revenue. It also helps with those examination questions that present you with a graph and require you to interpret aspects of it.

- In most break-even charts all lines are straight. This means that only two points need be plotted for each line; for example, with sales, choose a number that is the maximum expected, multiply by the selling price per unit, and this is the point to be marked on the graph. As the sales line always passes through zero, there are now two points along which to draw a straight line.

- When drawing a break-even graph it is often difficult to know what total value to show on each axis, ie how many units, and/or how much in costs and revenues. As a guide, look for a maximum output or sales level that will not be exceeded: this will give the horizontal axis. Multiply the maximum sales, if known, by the unit selling price to give the maximum sales revenue for the vertical axis. If the figure for maximum sales is not known, it is recommended that the break-even point is calculated before drawing the graph so that the extent of the graph can be established.

- A common error is to start the total costs from the zero point instead of the fixed costs line.

- Although fixed costs are likely to be unchanged within a fairly narrow range of outputs, watch out for stepped fixed costs (see page 252). For example, a major expansion of output may require that additional premises are rented: thus the fixed cost of rent will increase at a particular point (and is shown graphically as a step). Such a stepped fixed cost has a direct effect on total costs.

INTERPRETATION OF BREAK-EVEN

When interpreting break-even, it is all too easy to concentrate solely on the break-even point. The graph, for example, tells us much more than this: it also shows the profit or loss at any level of output/sales contained within the graph. To find this, simply measure the gap between sales revenue and total costs at a chosen number of units, and read the money amounts off on the vertical axis (above break-even point it is a profit; below, it is a loss). For example, the graph in the Worked Example shows a profit or loss at:

- 650 units = £1,500 profit
- 600 units = £1,000 profit
- 400 units = £1,000 loss

Break-even analysis, whether by calculation, by table, or by graph, can be used by all types of businesses, as well as other organisations. For example, a shop will wish to know the sales it has to make each week to meet costs; a sports centre will wish to know the ticket sales that have to be made to meet costs; a club or society might wish to know how many raffle tickets it needs to sell to meet the costs of prizes and of printing tickets.

Once the break-even point has been reached, the additional contribution forms the profit. For example, if the business considered in the Worked Example was selling 650 toys each month, it would have a total contribution of 650 x £10 = £6,500; of this the first £5,000 will be used to meet fixed costs, and the remaining £1,500 represents the profit (which can be read off the break-even graph). This can be shown by means of a marginal costing statement as follows:

		£
	sales revenue (650 units at £20 each)	13,000
less	variable costs (650 units at £10 each)	6,500
equals	contribution (to fixed costs and profit)	6,500
less	monthly fixed costs	5,000
equals	profit for month	1,500

A quick way of calculating the profit is to use the following formula:

(selling price – variable costs) per unit x volume* – fixed costs = profit

* the level of output or activity

ie (£20 – £10) x 650 – £5,000 = £6,500 – £5,000 = £1,500 profit

LIMITATIONS OF BREAK-EVEN ANALYSIS

The problem of break-even analysis is the assumption that the relationship between sales revenue, variable costs and fixed costs remains the same at all levels of production. This is a rather simplistic view because, for example, in order to increase sales, a business will often need to offer bulk discounts, so reducing the sales revenue per unit at higher levels. The limitations of break-even analysis can be summarised as follows:

- The assumption is made that all output is sold. There is no point in preparing the cost data, calculating the break-even point, and estimating the profits to be made if the product will not sell in sufficient quantities. However, break-even analysis is useful for a new business in order to establish the level of sales that must be achieved to reach break-even point. The feasibility of reaching that level of sales must then be considered by the owner.

- The presumption is made that there is only one product. While separate break-even analysis can be made for different products, it is difficult to make the calculations for a mix of products.

- All costs and revenues are expressed in terms of straight lines. However, this relationship is not always so. As indicated above, selling prices may vary at different quantities sold; in a similar way, variable costs alter at different levels as advantage is taken of the lower prices to be gained from bulk buying, and/or more efficient production methods.

- Fixed costs do not remain fixed at all levels of output; instead, there may be stepped fixed costs (see page 252).

- It is not possible to extrapolate the graph or calculation; 'extrapolation' means extending the lines on the graph beyond the limits of the activity on which the graph is based. For example, in the Worked Example, the graph cannot be extended to, say, 1,000 units of output and the profit read off at this point. The relationship between sales revenues and costs will be different at much higher levels of output – different methods of production might be used, for example.

- The profit or loss shown by the graph or calculations is probably only true for figures close to current output levels – the more that output changes from current figures, the less accurate will be the expected profit or loss.

- External factors – such as the state of the economy, interest rates, the rate of inflation, etc – are not considered by break-even analysis.

- A further disadvantage of break-even analysis is that it concentrates too much attention on the break-even point. While this aspect is important, other considerations such as ensuring that the output is produced as efficiently as possible, and that costs are kept under review, are just as important.

BREAK-EVEN: MARGIN OF SAFETY

The **margin of safety** is the amount by which sales exceed the break-even point. Margin of safety can be expressed as:

- a number of units, ie sales volume – break-even point (units)
- a sales revenue amount, ie sales volume – break-even point (units) x selling price
- a percentage, using the following formula

$$\frac{current\ output - break-even\ output}{current\ output} \times \frac{100}{1}$$

WORKED EXAMPLE: MARGIN OF SAFETY

Referring back to the Fluffy Toys Limited Worked Example (pages 265-268), if current output is 700 units, while the break-even point is 500 units, the margin of safety is:

- 200 units (ie 700 – 500)
- £4,000 of sales revenue (ie 200 units at £20 each)
- 29 per cent, ie $\frac{700 - 500}{700} \times \frac{100}{1}$

In interpreting this margin of safety we can say that production/sales can fall by these values before the business reaches break-even point and ceases to make a profit.

Margin of safety is especially important in times of recession as it expresses to management the amount of the 'cushion' which current production/sales gives beyond the break-even point. Where there is a comparison to be made between two or more products, each with different margins of safety, the product with the highest margin of safety is looked on favourably; however, margin of safety is only one factor in decision-making.

BREAK-EVEN: TARGET PROFIT

A further development of break-even is to calculate the output that needs to be sold in order to give a certain amount of profit – the **target profit**. This is calculated as follows:

$$\frac{fixed\ costs\ (£) + target\ profit\ (£)}{contribution\ per\ unit\ (£)} = number\ of\ units\ of\ output$$

WORKED EXAMPLE: TARGET PROFIT

If Fluffy Toys Limited (pages 265-268) required a profit of £2,000 per month, the calculation is:

$$\frac{£5,000 + £2,000}{£10} = 700 \text{ units, with a sales value of £14,000*}$$

* 700 units at £20 each = £14,000

This target profit can then be shown by means of a profit statement as follows:

		£
	sales revenue (700 units at £20 each)	14,000
less	variable costs (700 units at £10 each)	7,000
equals	contribution (to fixed costs and profit)	7,000
less	monthly fixed costs	5,000
equals	target profit for month	2,000

Alternatively, it can be calculated as follows:

(selling price – variable costs) per unit x volume – fixed costs = profit

ie (£20 – £10) x 700 – £5,000 = £7,000 – £5,000 = £2,000

Note that target profit can also be calculated by making use of the contribution sales ratio (see below).

CONTRIBUTION SALES RATIO

The contribution sales (CS) ratio – also known as the profit volume (PV) ratio – expresses the amount of contribution in relation to the amount of the selling price:

$$\frac{contribution \ (£)}{selling \ price \ (£)} = contribution \ to \ sales \ ratio$$

The ratio, or percentage, can be calculated on the basis of a single unit of production or for the whole business.

In break-even analysis, if fixed costs are known, we can use the CS ratio to find the sales value at which the business breaks-even, or the sales value to give a target amount of profit.

WORKED EXAMPLE: CONTRIBUTION SALES RATIO

Referring back to Fluffy Toys Limited, the CS ratio (per unit) is:

$$\frac{\text{contribution (£)}}{\text{selling price (£)}} = \frac{£10^*}{£20} = 0.5 \text{ or } 50\%$$

* selling price £20 – variable costs £10 = contribution £10

Fixed costs are £5,000 per month, so the sales revenue needed to break-even is:

$$\frac{\text{fixed costs (£)}}{\text{CS ratio}} = \frac{£5,000}{0.5 \text{ (see above)}} = \underline{£10,000}$$

As the selling price is £20 per toy, we can get back to the break-even in units of output as follows:
£10,000 ÷ £20 = 500 units

If the directors of Fluffy Toys Limited wish to know the sales revenue that must be made to achieve a target profit of £2,000 per month, the CS ratio is used as follows:

$$\frac{\text{fixed costs + target profit}}{\text{CS ratio}} = \text{required level of sales}$$

$$\frac{£5,000 + £2,000}{0.5} = \underline{£14,000}$$

As the selling price is £20 per toy, we can get to the units of output as follows:

£14,000 ÷ £20 = 700 units to achieve a target profit of £2,000.

WHEN TO USE BREAK-EVEN ANALYSIS

Break-even analysis is used by businesses in a variety of situations:

before starting a new business

The calculation of break-even point is important in order to see the level of sales needed by the new business in order to cover costs, or to make a particular level of profit. The feasibility of achieving the level can then be considered by the owner of the business, and other parties such as the bank manager.

when making changes within a business

The costs of a major change will need to be considered by the owners and/or managers. For example, a large increase in production will, most likely, affect the balance between fixed and variable costs. Break-even analysis will be used as part of the planning process to ensure that the business remains profitable.

to measure profits and losses

Within the limitations of break-even analysis, profits and losses can be estimated at different levels of output from current production. (Remember that this can be done only where the new output is close to current levels and where there is no major change to the structure of costs – ie it is not possible to extrapolate.)

to answer 'what if?' questions

Questions such as 'what if sales fall by 10 per cent?' and 'what if fixed costs increase by £1,000?' can be answered – in part at least – by break-even analysis. The effect on the profitability of the business can be seen, subject to the limitations noted earlier. A question such as 'what if sales increase by 300 per cent?' is such a fundamental change that it can only be answered by examining the effect on the nature of the fixed and variable costs and then re-calculating the break-even point.

to evaluate alternative viewpoints

There are often different ways of production; this is particularly true of a manufacturing business. For example, a product could be made:

- either by using a labour-intensive process, with a large number of employees supported by basic machinery, or
- by using expensive machinery in an automated process with very few employees.

In the first case, the cost structure will be high variable costs (labour) and low fixed costs (depreciation of machinery). In the second case, there will be low variable costs and high fixed costs. Break-even analysis can be used to examine the relationship between the costs which are likely to show a low break-even point in the first case, and a high break-even point in the second. In this way, the management of the business is guided by break-even analysis; management will also need to know the likely sales figures, and the availability of money with which to buy the machinery.

CHAPTER SUMMARY

● Break-even analysis distinguishes between fixed costs and variable costs.

● Break-even is the point at which neither a profit nor a loss is made.

● The relationship between sales revenue, and fixed costs and variable costs is used to ascertain the break-even point, by means of a calculation, a table, or a graph.

● The break-even calculation is:

$$\frac{fixed\ costs\ (£)}{contribution\ per\ unit\ (£)} = break\text{-}even\ point\ (number\ of\ units)$$

● Break-even analysis can show:
  - break-even point in units of output
  - break-even point in value of sales
  - profit or loss at a given level of output/sales

● The limitations of break-even analysis are that:
  - the assumption is made that all output is sold
  - the presumption is that there is only one product
  - costs and revenues are expressed in straight lines
  - fixed costs do not remain fixed at all levels of output
  - it is not possible to extrapolate the break-even graph or calculation
  - the profit or loss is probably only true for figures close to current output levels
  - external factors are not considered
  - it concentrates too much on break-even point

● Margin of safety is the amount by which sales exceed the break-even point.

● Target profit uses break-even analysis to calculate the output that needs to be sold in order to give a certain amount of profit.

● The contribution sales ratio – also known as the profit volume ratio – expresses the amount of contribution in relation to the amount of the selling price.

● Break-even analysis is often used:
  - before starting a new business
  - when making changes to a business
  - to measure profits or losses
  - to answer 'what if?' questions
  - to evaluate alternative viewpoints

In the next chapter we look at absorption costing and activity based costing, and compare them with marginal costing.

QUESTIONS

An asterisk (*) after the question number means that the answer is given at the end of this book.

11.1 Bright Limited estimates that costs and revenue for next month will be:

selling price	£10 per unit
variable cost	£5 per unit
fixed costs for the month	£7,500

Maximum output is 3,000 units per month

You are to complete the following table:

units of output	fixed costs	variable costs	total cost	sales revenue	profit/(loss)
	£	£	£	£	£
0					
500					
1,000					
1,500					
2,000					
2,500					
3,000					

11.2* Cuddly Toys Limited manufactures a popular children's teddy bear. At present production is limited by the capacity of the factory to 50 bears each week. The following information is available:

Selling price per teddy bear	£20
Materials per teddy bear	£4
Direct labour per teddy bear	£5
Weekly fixed expenses	
• factory rent and rates	£100
• fuel and power	£20
• other costs	£34

You are to find the weekly break-even point by the graphical method, and to check your answer by calculation.

11.3* Mike Etherton, a manufacturer of cricket bats, has the following monthly costs:

Material cost	£8 per bat
Labour cost	£12 per bat
Selling price	£35 per bat
Overheads (fixed)	£12,000

You are to:

(a) Prepare a table showing costs, sales revenue, and profit or loss for production of bats in multiples of 100 up to 1,200.

(b) Draw a graph showing the break-even point.

(c) Prove your answer by calculation.

(d) Read off the graph the profit or loss if 200 bats, and 1,200 bats are sold each month: prove the answer by calculation.

(e) If production is currently 1,000 bats per month, what is the margin of safety, expressed as a percentage and in units?

11.4 Riley Limited has made the following estimates for next month:

Selling price	£25 per unit
Variable cost	£10 per unit
Fixed costs for the month	£300,000
Forecast output	30,000 units
Maximum output	40,000 units

You are to carry out the following tasks:

(a) Calculate:
 • the contribution sales ratio
 • the break-even point in units
 • the break-even point in sales revenue
 • the margin of safety at the forecast output
 • the number of units to generate a profit of £100,000

(b) Calculate the profit at:
 • the forecast output • the maximum output

(c) One of the managers has suggested that, if the selling price were reduced to £20 per unit, then sales would be increased to the maximum output. For this new strategy, you are to calculate:
 – the contribution sales ratio
 – the break-even point in units
 – the break-even point in sales revenue
 – the margin of safety at maximum output
 – the forecast profit at maximum output

Write an email to the general manager advising whether you believe that the new strategy should be implemented.

11.5   Melvin Books Ltd manufactures bookmarks, which sell for £1.00 each.

The bookmarks are made by people working at home, who are paid 20p for every bookmark they produce. The raw materials bought to make one bookmark cost 30p. Salespeople sell the bookmarks and are paid 10p for each bookmark which they sell. The administration costs £42,000 per year. Business rates of £20,400 are also paid annually.

REQUIRED

(a)   Classify each cost by completing the following table and total each column:

	Total fixed costs £	Variable costs per unit in pence
Wages		
Raw materials		
Salespeople's wages		
Administration costs		
Business rates		
Total		

(b)   (i)   State the formula used to calculate the contribution per unit.

(ii)   Calculate the contribution per unit.

(iii)   Why is the amount of contribution per unit important?

(c)   Calculate:

(i)   The number of bookmarks which must be manufactured and sold per year for the business to break-even. State the formula used.

(ii)   The total revenue at this level of sales.

(iii)   The profit or loss achieved by Melvin Books Ltd if 150,000 bookmarks are sold.

Assessment and Qualifications Alliance (AQA), 2002

11.6* Suddley Ltd manufactures a single product.

For the year ending 31 March 2002 each unit is expected to sell for £50.

The expected costs per unit for the year ended 31 March 2002 are:

	£
Materials	12
Labour	16
Variable overheads	7

The annual fixed overheads are expected to be £450,000.

Suddley Ltd has a maximum annual production capacity of 37,500 units.

REQUIRED

(a)   Define and calculate:

    (i)   the contribution per unit

    (ii)   the break-even point in £s and units.

State the formula used in each case.

    (i)   Formula: ....

           Definition: ....

           ....

           Calculation: ....

           ....

    (ii)   Formula: ....

           Definition: ....

           ....

           Calculation: ....

           ....

(b)   In the graph on the next page, the letters **A, B, C** and **D** have been used to identify particular lines or terms used in accounting.

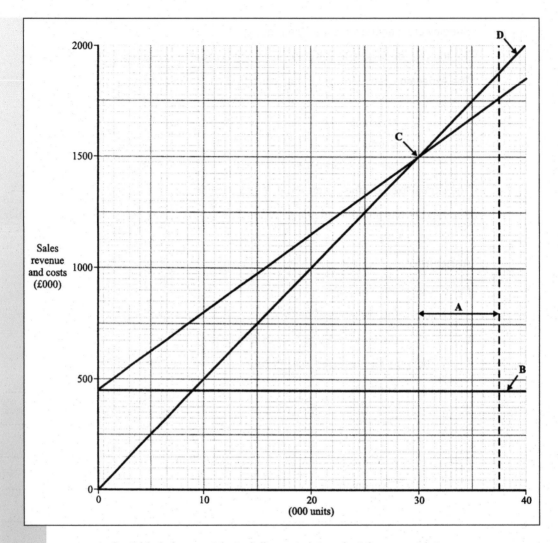

In the table below, match each line or term against the correct letter.

Line or term	A, B, C or D
Fixed costs	
Total sales revenue	
Break-even point	
Margin of safety	

(c)   From the graph, calculate the profit made from the sale of 35,000 units.

(d)   Explain two possible consequences for Suddley Ltd if the selling price is reduced to £47 per unit.

Assessment and Qualifications Alliance (AQA), 2001

11.7* "Break-even analysis has its limitations in decision-making."

Discuss four limitations of break-even analysis.

11.8

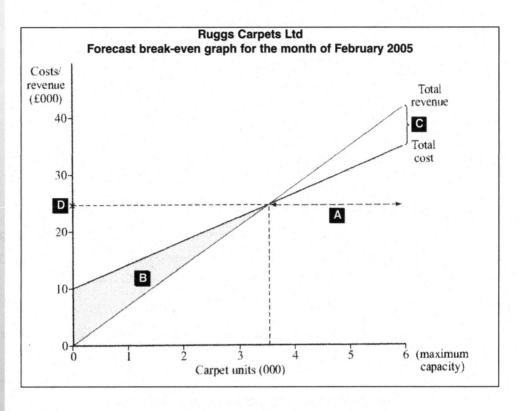

REQUIRED

(a) From the above graph, identify what each letter shows:

A ....

B ....

C ....

D ....

(b) Explain one disadvantage of using a break-even graph to identify the break-even point.

Assessment and Qualifications Alliance (AQA), 2005

11.9   Jackson Ltd manufactures a single product.

The costs per unit are expected to be:

        materials: 3 metres at £5 per metre

        labour: 15 minutes at £12 per hour

        variable manufacturing overheads at £3 per unit

The total fixed overheads are expected to be £52,500 per year.

Each unit is sold at marginal cost plus 20%.

REQUIRED

(a)   Define the term 'marginal cost'.

(b)   Calculate the marginal cost per unit.

(c)   Calculate the selling price per unit.

(d)   Calculate total revenue at the break-even point.

(e)   Evaluate the usefulness of break-even analysis as an aid to decision-making.

Assessment and Qualifications Alliance (AQA), 2007

11.10*   The following break-even graph relates to Bungay Books Ltd, for the year ending 31 December 2004.

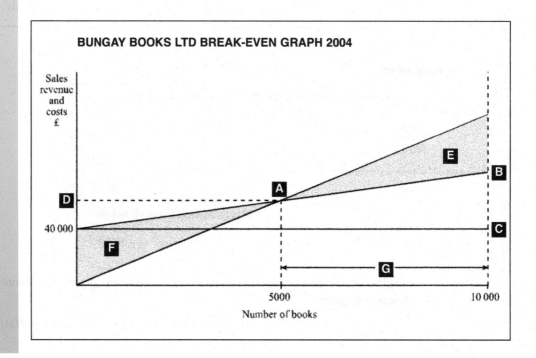

Additional information: the selling price is £15 per book.

REQUIRED

(a) Identify each of the following shown in the graph:

A ....

B ....

C ....

D ....

Area E ....

Area F ....

G ....

(b) (i) Calculate the value indicated at point D on the graph.

(ii) Calculate the marginal cost per unit.

(iii) Calculate the contribution per unit.

Assessment and Qualifications Alliance (AQA), 2005

11.11   Tracey Kent owns a photographer's studio. Each portrait sells for £38 and costs £12 to produce. Unfortunately, for the year ending 30 November 2004 her fixed overheads are expected to rise from the previous year's figure of £42,250 to £52,000.

REQUIRED

(a) State the formula used to calculate the number of portraits required to break even.

(b) Calculate the number of portraits required to break even for:

(i) the year ended 30 November 2003

(ii) the year ending 30 November 2004

(c) Calculate the required change in selling price for the year ending 30 November 2004, if Tracey wishes to maintain the same level of break-even as that for the year ended 30 November 2003.

(d) Evaluate this change in selling price. Is there any alternative action that Tracey could take?

Assessment and Qualifications Alliance (AQA), 2004

12 ABSORPTION AND ACTIVITY BASED COSTING

In the previous two chapters we have seen how marginal costing distinguishes between fixed and variable costs in order to calculate contribution and the break-even point.

In this chapter we look in detail at other costing methods and cover:

- an explanation of cost units and cost centres
- an overview of the main costing systems and their purposes
- the use of absorption costing, comparing it with marginal costing
- the use of activity based costing, including an explanation of cost drivers and cost pools
- a comparison of the cost methods of marginal, absorption, and activity based costing

COST UNITS AND COST CENTRES

The costing methods of absorption costing, activity based costing and standard costing make use of cost centres and cost units. Before we look in detail at these costing systems we need to explain cost units and cost centres.

Cost units are units of output to which costs can be charged.

A cost unit can be:

- a unit of production from a factory such as a car, a television, an item of furniture
- a unit of service, such as a passenger-mile on a bus, a transaction on a bank statement, an attendance at a swimming pool, a call unit on a telephone

Within an individual business – particularly in the service industry – there may well be several cost units that can be used. For example, in a hotel the cost units in the restaurant will be meals, and for the rooms, the cost units will be guest nights.

Costs also need to be charged to a specific part of a business – a **cost centre.**

Cost centres are sections of a business to which costs can be charged.

A cost centre in a manufacturing business, for example, is a department of a factory, a particular stage in the production process, or even a whole factory. In a college, examples of cost centres are the teaching departments, or particular sections of departments such as the college's administrative office. In a hospital, examples of cost centres are the hospital wards, operating theatres, specialist sections such as the X-ray department and the pathology department.

Collecting costs together in cost centres assists with control of the business. The manager of a cost centre can be held responsible for its costs.

COSTING METHODS

The main costing methods used in cost and management accounting are:

- absorption costing – the total costs of the whole business are absorbed amongst all of the cost units
- marginal costing – the cost of producing one extra unit of output
- activity based costing – the overheads of the business are charged to output on the basis of activities
- standard costing – a pre-determined cost for materials, labour and overheads is set in advance of production

The diagram on the next page shows the purpose of each of these costing methods. The use of each costing method is dependent on the information needs of the business:

- do we require a figure for profit? (use absorption costing)
- why are the overheads so high for the production line making 'Product Exe'? (use activity based costing)
- can we afford to sell 1,000 units each month to Megastores Limited at a discount of 20 per cent? (use marginal costing)
- how much will it cost us to make 'Product Wye' next month? (use standard costing)

Note that absorption costing, marginal costing, and activity based costing are all methods that can be used in conjunction with standard costing, if required.

In this chapter we study absorption costing – making comparisons with marginal costing – and activity based costing. Standard costing, together with the use of variance analysis, is covered in detail in Chapter 15.

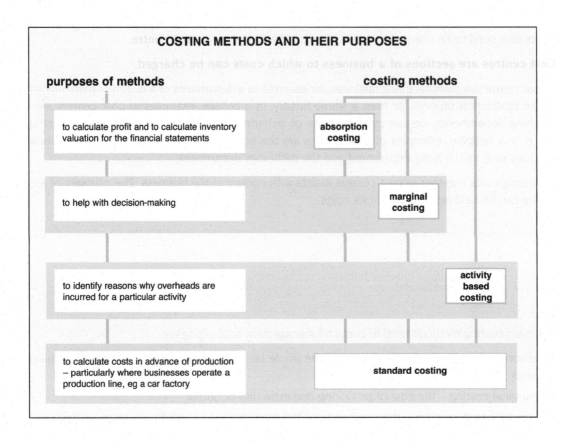

ABSORPTION COSTING

Absorption costing absorbs the total costs of the whole business amongst all of the cost units.

Absorption costing answers the question, "What does it cost to make one unit of output?"

The absorption cost of a unit of output is made up of the following costs:

		£
	direct materials	x
add	direct labour	x
add	direct expenses	x
add	overheads (fixed and variable)	x
equals	ABSORPTION COST	x

Note that:

- the overheads of a business comprise both the factory and the office costs of indirect materials, indirect labour, and indirect expenses
- under some circumstances, absorption costing includes only production costs, ie it excludes all costs beyond production, such as selling and distribution expenses, administrative expenses, and finance expenses.

WORKED EXAMPLE: ABSORPTION COSTING

situation

The Wyvern Bike Company makes 100 bikes each week and its costs are as follows:

Weekly costs for producing 100 bikes	
	£
direct materials (£30 per bike)	3,000
direct labour (£25 per bike)	2,500
PRIME COST	5,500
overheads (fixed)	3,500
TOTAL COST	9,000

- there are no direct expenses incurred by the company
- the selling price of each bike is £100

What is the absorption cost of producing one bike, and how much profit does the company make each week?

solution

The absorption cost of producing one bike is:

$$\frac{\text{total cost (direct and indirect costs)}}{\text{units of output}} = \frac{£9,000}{100 \text{ bikes}} = £90 \text{ per bike}$$

With a selling price of £100 per bike, the profit statement is:

			£
	selling price	(100 bikes x £100)	10,000
less	total cost		9,000
equals	PROFIT		1,000

As the Worked Example shows, each cost unit bears an equal proportion of the costs of the overheads of the business. Because of its simplicity, absorption costing is a widely used system which tells us how much it costs to make one unit of output. It works well where the cost units are identical, eg 100 identical bikes, but is less appropriate where some of the cost units differ in quality, eg 100 bikes, of which 75 are standard models and 25 are handbuilt to the customers' specifications. It also ignores the effect of changes in the level of output on the cost structure. For example, if the bike manufacturer reduces output to 50 bikes a week:

- will direct materials remain at £30 per bike? (buying materials in smaller quantities might mean higher prices)

- will direct labour still be £25 per bike? (with lower production, the workforce may not be able to specialise in certain jobs, and may be less efficient)

- will the overheads remain fixed at £3,500? (perhaps smaller premises can be used and the factory rent reduced)

In the next chapter we will see how, under absorption costing, overheads are charged to output using direct labour and machine hour methods. Such overhead absorption rates allow different products to be charged with the amount of overheads that reflect the direct labour or machine hours used in their production.

MARGINAL COSTING AND ABSORPTION COSTING COMPARED

Marginal costing tells the management of a business the cost of producing one extra unit of output, while the distinction between fixed and variable costs forms the basis of break-even analysis. Nevertheless, costing methods should ensure that all the costs of a business are recovered by being charged to production. This is achieved by means of absorption costing. A comparison between these two methods of costing is as follows:

- *marginal costing*

  As we have seen in Chapter 10, marginal costing recognises that fixed costs vary with time rather than activity, and identifies the cost of producing one extra unit. For example, the rent of a factory relates to a certain time period, eg one month, and remains unchanged whether 100 units of output are made or whether 500 units are made; by contrast, the production of one extra unit will incur an increase in variable costs, ie direct materials, direct labour and direct expenses – this increase is the marginal cost.

- *absorption costing*

  As we have seen in this chapter, absorption costing absorbs all production costs into each unit of output. Thus each unit of output in a factory making 100 units will bear a greater proportion of the factory rent than will each unit when 500 units are made in the same time period.

The diagram on the next page demonstrates how the terms in marginal costing relate to the same production costs as those categorised under absorption costing terms. When using marginal costing it is the behaviour of the cost – fixed or variable – that is important, not the origin of the cost.

ABSORPTION COSTING	MARGINAL COSTING
direct costs direct materials direct labour direct expenses	**variable costs** variable direct materials variable direct labour variable direct expenses variable overheads
indirect costs variable overheads fixed overheads	**fixed costs** fixed direct costs fixed overheads

marginal costing and absorption costing: profit comparisons

Because of the different ways in which marginal costing and absorption costing treat fixed costs, the two methods produce different levels of profit when there is a closing inventory figure. This is because, under marginal costing, the closing inventory is valued at variable production cost; by contrast, absorption cost includes a share of fixed production costs in the closing inventory valuation. This is illustrated in the Worked Example which follows, looking at the effect of using marginal costing and absorption costing on the profit statement of a manufacturing business.

Note that the marginal cost approach helps with management decision-making – eg break-even, and other short-term decisions (covered in Chapter 13). However, for financial accounting, absorption costing must be used for inventory valuation purposes in order to comply with IAS 2, *Inventories* (see page 201). Under IAS 2, the closing inventory valuation is based on the costs of direct materials, direct labour, direct expenses (if any), and production overheads. Note that non-production overheads are not included, as they are charged in full to the profit statement in the year to which they relate.

WORKED EXAMPLE: MARGINAL AND ABSORPTION COSTING

situation

Chairs Limited commenced business on 1 January 20-7. It manufactures a special type of chair designed to alleviate back pain. Information on the first year's trading is as follows:

number of chairs manufactured	5,000
number of chairs sold	4,500
selling price	£110 per chair
direct materials	£30 per chair
direct labour	£40 per chair
fixed production overheads	£100,000

The directors ask for your help in producing profit statements using the marginal costing and absorption costing methods. They say that they will use 'the one that gives the higher profit' to show to the company's bank manager.

solution

CHAIRS LIMITED

PROFIT STATEMENT FOR THE YEAR ENDED 31 DECEMBER 20-7

	MARGINAL COSTING		ABSORPTION COSTING	
	£	£	£	£
Sales revenue 4,500 chairs at £110 each		495,000		495,000
Variable costs				
Direct materials at £30 each	150,000		150,000	
Direct labour at £40 each	200,000		200,000	
	350,000			
Less Closing inventory (marginal cost)				
500 chairs at £70 each	35,000			
		315,000		
CONTRIBUTION		180,000		
Fixed production overheads		100,000	100,000	
			450,000	
Less Closing inventory (absorption cost)				
500 chairs at £90 each			45,000	
Less Cost of sales				405,000
PROFIT		80,000		90,000

Notes:

- Closing inventory is always calculated on the basis of this year's costs:

  marginal costing, variable costs only, ie £30 + £40 = £70 per chair

  absorption costing, variable and fixed costs, ie £450,000 ÷ 5,000 chairs = £90 per chair

- The difference in the profit figures is caused by the closing inventory figures: £35,000 under marginal costing and £45,000 under absorption costing – the same costs have been used, but fixed production overheads have been treated differently.

- Only fixed production overheads are dealt with differently using the techniques of marginal and absorption costing – both methods charge non-production overheads *in full* to the profit statement in the year to which they relate.

With marginal costing, the full amount of the fixed production overheads has been charged in this year's profit statement; by contrast, with absorption costing, part of the fixed production overheads (here, £10,000) has been carried forward to next year in the inventory valuation. Because of this, profit will always be higher under absorption costing in accounting periods of increasing inventory levels.

With regard to the directors' statement that they will use 'the one that gives the higher profit', two points should be borne in mind:

- A higher profit does *not* mean more money in the bank.
- The two costing methods simply treat fixed production overheads differently and, in a year when there is no closing inventory, total profits *to date* are exactly the same – but they occur differently over the years.

Note that, for financial accounting purposes, Chairs Limited will have to use the absorption cost closing inventory valuation of £45,000 in order to comply with IAS 2, *Inventories*.

ACTIVITY BASED COSTING

Activity based costing (ABC) charges overheads to output on the basis of activities.

Activity based costing is a relatively new costing method which has developed from absorption costing, but adopts a different approach to charging overheads to output. ABC identifies what causes overheads to be incurred, rather than simply charging total overheads for a particular period.

Traditional costing systems usually charge overheads to output on the basis of direct labour hours (or labour cost), or machine hours. For example, for each labour hour – or machine hour – required by the output, £x of overheads is charged through an *overhead absorption rate* (see Chapter 13). While this method may be suitable for industries which are labour intensive, or where production requires the use of heavy machinery, it is not always appropriate for today's capital intensive, low-labour industries, as the example which follows shows.

example

ExeWye Limited manufactures two products, Exe and Wye. Product Exe is produced on a labour-intensive production line, using basic machinery; product Wye is produced using the latest 'state of the art' computer-controlled machinery, which requires few employees.

ExeWye Limited's elements of cost are:

direct materials, total	£500,000	
– product Exe	£250,000	
– product Wye	£250,000	
direct labour, total	£250,000	(25,000 hours)
– product Exe	£200,000	(20,000 hours)
– product Wye	£50,000	(5,000 hours)

overheads (fixed), total   £250,000

– a major proportion of these relate to maintenance and depreciation of the computer controlled machinery used to make product Wye

ExeWye Limited uses labour hours as the basis by which to charge overheads to production. Therefore, the overhead will be split between the two products as:

overhead for product Exe = four-fifths (ie 20,000 out of 25,000 hours) of total overheads of £250,000 = £200,000

overhead for product Wye = one-fifth (ie 5,000 out of 25,000 hours) of total overheads of £250,000 = £50,000

Thus, the majority of the overhead is charged to the labour-intensive production line (product Exe), and relatively little to the capital intensive line (product Wye). As a major proportion of the costs relates to product Wye, this has the effect of undercosting this product (and overcosting product Exe). Instead, a more appropriate costing system is needed, and activity based costing can be used to charge overheads to output on the basis of activities.

the use of cost drivers

Cost drivers are activities which cause costs to be incurred.

In the example looked at above, the cost driver used to charge overheads to output was – inappropriately – labour costs. Instead of using a cost driver linked to the volume of business (as above), activity based costing uses cost drivers linked to the *way in which business is conducted*: this concept is illustrated in the example which follows:

example

AyeBee Limited manufactures two products, Aye and Bee. Product Aye is produced in batches of 500 units of output; product Bee is produced in batches of 100 units of output. Each unit of production – whether Aye or Bee – requires one direct labour hour.

Production of each batch of Aye and Bee requires the following overheads:

• the machinery to be set up at a cost of £400 per batch (to cover the engineer's time, test running of the machinery, etc)

• quality inspection at a cost of £200 per batch (to cover the inspector's time, cost of rejects, etc)

In a typical week the company produces 500 units of product Aye, ie one batch of 500 units, and 500 units of product Bee, ie five batches of 100 units. Thus the set-up and quality inspection costs for the week will be:

6 set-ups at £400 each	=	£2,400
6 quality inspections at £200 each	=	£1,200
TOTAL		£3,600

Note: each 'box' represents one set-up and one quality inspection

As each unit of output requires one direct labour hour, ie product Aye 500 hours, product Bee 500 hours, the overhead costs of set-ups and quality inspection, using traditional costing systems, will be charged to output as follows:

product Aye	=	£1,800
product Bee	=	£1,800
TOTAL		£3,600

We can see that this is an incorrect basis on which to charge overheads to output, because product Aye required just one set-up and one quality inspection, while product Bee took five set-ups and five quality inspections. By using the system of activity based costing, with set-up and inspection as cost drivers, we can charge overheads as follows:

product Aye

1 set-up at £400	=	£400
1 quality inspection at £200	=	£200
TOTAL		£600

product Bee

5 set-ups at £400	=	£2,000
5 quality inspections at £200	=	£1,000
TOTAL		£3,000

By using the activity based costing system, there is a more accurate reflection of the cost of demand on the support functions of set-up and quality inspection: it reduces the cost of 500 units of product Aye by £1,200 (ie £1,800 – £600) and increases the cost of 500 units of product Bee by £1,200 (ie from £1,800 to £3,000). This may have implications for the viability of product Bee, and for the selling price of both products.

other cost drivers

Cost drivers must have a close relationship with an activity, which can then be related to output. In the example, we have seen the cost of set-ups and quality inspections used as cost drivers. Examples of other activities and their cost drivers include:

activity	**cost driver**
• processing orders to suppliers	• number of orders
• processing invoices received from suppliers	• number of invoices
• processing orders to customers	• number of orders
• processing invoices issued to customers	• number of invoices

As has been seen in the example above, by using activity based costing, the emphasis is placed on which activities cause costs. It answers the question why costs are incurred, instead of simply stating the amount of the cost for a given period. By using ABC, the responsibility for the cost is established and so steps can be taken to minimise it for the future.

the use of cost pools

Cost pools are groups of overhead costs that are incurred by the same activity.

When using activity based costing it is advisable to group together those overhead costs which are incurred by the same activity in a cost pool. For example, the purchasing costs for goods to be used in production will include the wages of the firm's purchasing staff, the cost – or proportionate cost – of the purchasing office, the cost of telephone/post/email relating to purchasing.

The use of a cost pool makes the application of costs through cost drivers that much easier – there is no need to seek a separate cost driver for each overhead cost, when similar activities can be grouped together.

using activity based costing

The steps to applying activity based costing are illustrated in the following diagram:

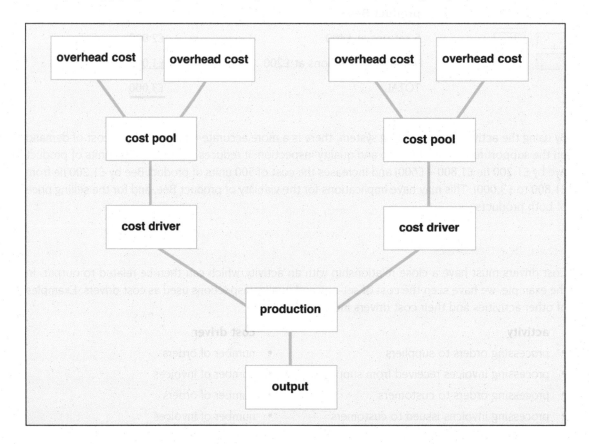

- The first step is to group together in a cost pool the overhead costs which are incurred by the same activity, for example, the purchasing costs for goods to be used in production.
- The second step is to identify the factor which influences the costs – the cost driver. Once identified, the rate for each cost can be calculated. For example, the cost driver could be the cost of placing an order for the purchase of goods to be used in production.
- The third step is to charge the rate for each cost to production based on the use of the activity. For example, if a product requires two purchase orders to be placed, it will be charged with the cost of two activities.

advantages of using activity based costing

The main advantages of using ABC:

- cost information is more accurate because cost drivers are used to identify the activity which causes costs to be incurred
- it is more objective because it is able to identify the overhead costs relating to different products, rather than the overheads of the whole business
- with its focus on overhead costs ABC gives the management of a business a good understanding of why costs are incurred and how they will be altered by changes in production
- it leads to the more accurate calculation of selling prices because overhead costs are analysed to the products which use the activities
- it may identify areas of waste and inefficiency
- management decision-making is improved, eg in pricing policy
- ABC is appropriate for capital-intensive industries where overheads are high and complex in nature

COMPARISON OF COSTING METHODS

The table, on the next page, gives a comparison between marginal costing, absorption costing, and activity based costing, including a note on the usefulness and the limitations of each. The Worked Example on page 297 compares these three costing methods in a practical situation.

A further costing method, standard costing, is discussed in Chapter 15.

COMPARISON OF COSTING METHODS

	marginal costing	absorption costing	activity based costing
main use	• to help with decision-making (see Chapter 14) in the forms of – costing a project – make or buy – acceptance of additional work – price setting – optimum use of scarce resources	• to calculate profit • to calculate inventory valuation for the financial statements	• to identify what causes overheads to be incurred for a particular activity
how does it work?	• costs are classified as either fixed or variable • contribution to fixed costs is calculated as selling price less variable costs	• overheads are charged to output, often on the basis of direct labour hours or machine hours	• cost drivers are identified • overheads are charged to output on the basis of activities
main focus	• marginal cost • contribution	• all overheads charged to output • calculating profit • calculating inventory values	• identifying cost drivers as a way of charging overheads to output
usefulness	• concept of contribution is easy to understand • useful for decision-making – such as the optimum use of scarce resources (see Chapter 14) – but no consideration of overheads	• acceptable under IAS 2, *Inventories* • appropriate for traditional industries where overheads are charged to output on the basis of direct labour hours or machine hours	• acceptable under IAS 2, *Inventories* • more accurate calculation of selling prices because overheads are considered • appropriate for capital-intensive industries where overheads are high and complex in nature
limitations	• costs have to be identified as either fixed or variable • all overheads have to be recovered, otherwise a loss will be made • not acceptable under IAS 2, *Inventories* • calculation of selling prices may be less accurate than other costing methods	• not as useful in decision-making as marginal costing • may provide less accurate basis for calculation of selling prices where overheads are high and complex in nature	• time-consuming to set up and record costs (because of the detail required) • the selection of cost drivers can be difficult • the cost drivers and cost pools need to be kept up-to-date • common costs – such as rent and rates – still need to be recovered

WORKED EXAMPLE: WHICH COSTING METHOD TO USE?

situation

EssTee Limited manufactures two products, Ess and Tee.

Weekly production is 500 units of each product. Each unit of production – whether Ess or Tee – requires one direct labour hour.

Products are made in batches – before a batch can be made the production machinery must be set up, checked for accuracy and test run. Each batch produced has to be inspected to ensure that it is of the required standard, with any rejects being identified.

Currently the company uses absorption costing.

Details of each product are:

Product Ess

– made in batches of 500 units

– selling price per unit, £100

– direct materials per unit, £30

– direct labour per unit, £10

Product Tee

– made in batches of 100 units

– selling price per unit, £80

– direct materials per unit, £20

– direct labour per unit, £10

Fixed production costs each week are:

– set-up costs of machinery, £12,000

– inspection costs of production, £6,000

These costs are currently absorbed on the basis of direct labour hours.

The management accountant of EssTee Limited asks for your help to show how marginal costing, absorption costing and activity based costing will deal differently with the costs.

solution

Marginal costing

		Product Ess		Product Tee		Total
		£	£	£	£	£
	sales revenue		50,000		40,000	
less	variable costs:					
	direct materials	15,000		10,000		
	direct labour	5,000		5,000		
			20,000		15,000	
equals	contribution		30,000		25,000	55,000
less	fixed production costs					18,000
equals	profit for the week					37,000

- With marginal costing, the focus is on the contribution – both by product and in total.
- Fixed production costs are treated as a period cost – ie cost of time (such as a week, as here) rather than being product related.

Absorption costing

		Product Ess		Product Tee		Total
		£	£	£	£	£
	sales revenue		50,000		40,000	
less	direct materials	15,000		10,000		
	direct labour	5,000		5,000		
	PRIME COST	20,000		15,000		
	fixed production costs	*9,000		*9,000		
	TOTAL COST		29,000		24,000	
equals	profit for the week		21,000		16,000	37,000

* 500 direct labour hours for each product per week, so fixed production costs are
£18,000 ÷ 2 = £9,000 per product.

- With absorption costing, the focus is on profit – both by product and in total.
- Overhead costs are absorbed by production before profit is calculated.

Activity based costing

Fixed production costs:	set-ups		inspections	
	number	£	number	£
product Ess	1	2,000	1	1,000
product Tee	5	10,000	5	5,000
		12,000		6,000

- set-ups: £12,000 ÷ 6 = £2,000 per set-up
- inspections: £6,000 ÷ 6 = £1,000 per inspection

		Product Ess		Product Tee		Total
		£	£	£	£	£
	sales revenue		50,000		40,000	
less	direct materials	15,000		10,000		
	direct labour	5,000		5,000		
	PRIME COST	20,000		15,000		
	fixed production costs					
	set-ups	2,000		10,000		
	inspections	1,000		5,000		
	TOTAL COST		23,000		30,000	
equals	profit for the week		27,000		10,000	37,000

- With activity based costing, which is a development of absorption costing, the focus is on identifying the overhead costs for a particular activity.
- It gives more accurate costing information and shows that smaller batches (as here with product Tee) cost more to produce.

CHAPTER SUMMARY

- The costing methods of absorption costing, activity based costing and standard costing make use of cost centres and cost units.

- Cost units are units of output to which costs can be charged.

- Cost centres are sections of a business to which costs can be charged.

- The main costing methods are
  - absorption costing
  - marginal costing (covered in chapter 10)
  - activity based costing
  - standard costing (covered in Chapter 15)

- Absorption costing absorbs the total costs of the whole business amongst all of the cost units.

- Activity based costing (ABC) charges overheads to output on the basis of activities.

- ABC makes use of cost drivers and cost pools.

- Cost drivers are activities which cause costs to be incurred.

- Cost pools are groups of overhead costs that are incurred by the same activity.

In the next chapter we look at the allocation and apportionment of overhead costs, together with the use of overhead absorption rates to charge overhead costs to production.

QUESTIONS

An asterisk (*) after the question number means that the answer is given at the end of this book.

12.1

(a) Distinguish between cost units and cost centres.

(b) Suggest one cost unit and two cost centres for:

- a firm of accountants

- a parcel delivery company

- a college of further education

- a mixed farm, growing crops and raising cattle

12.2 Suggest likely cost centres for each of the following:

- A theatre in a provincial town, where touring productions are staged. The theatre has a bar and a confectionery counter. Ticket sales are dealt with by the theatre's own box office, and the plays are advertised locally.

- A garage, which sells new and used cars of two different makes. Cars are also repaired, serviced and valeted.

12.3* Coffeeworks Limited manufactures coffee machines for domestic use. The management of the company is considering next year's production and has asked you to help with certain financial decisions.

The following information is available:

selling price (per machine)	£80
direct materials (per machine)	£25
direct labour (per machine)	£20
overheads (fixed)	£270,000 per year

The company is planning to manufacture 15,000 coffee machines next year.

(a) calculate the marginal cost per coffee machine

(b) calculate the absorption cost per coffee machine

(c) prepare a profit statement to show the profit or loss if 15,000 coffee machines are sold

12.4 Cook-It Limited makes garden barbecues. The management of the company is considering the production for next year and has asked for help with certain financial decisions.

The following information is available:

wholesale selling price (per barbecue)	£90
direct materials (per barbecue)	£30
direct labour (per barbecue)	£25
fixed overheads	£150,000 per year

The company is planning to manufacture 10,000 barbecues next year.

REQUIRED

You are to calculate:

- the marginal cost per barbecue

- the absorption cost per barbecue

- the profit or loss if 10,000 barbecues are sold

12.5* Maxxa Limited manufactures one product, the Maxx. For the month of January 20-7 the following information is available:

number of units manufactured	4,000
number of units sold	3,000
selling price	£8 per unit
direct materials for month	£5,000
direct labour for month	£9,000
fixed production overheads for month	£6,000

There was no inventory of finished goods at the start of the month. Both direct materials and direct labour are variable costs.

REQUIRED

You are to produce profit statements using marginal costing and absorption costing methods.

12.6 Activtoys Limited commenced business on 1 January 20-1. It manufactures the 'Activ', an outdoor climbing frame. Information on the first year's trading is as follows:

number of climbing frames manufactured	1,500
number of climbing frames sold	1,300
selling price	£125 per frame
direct materials	£25 per frame
direct labour	£30 per frame
fixed production overheads	£82,500

REQUIRED

(a)   The directors ask for your help in producing profit statements using the marginal costing and absorption costing methods. They say that they will use "the one that gives the higher profit" to show to the company's bank manager.

(b)   Write a note to the directors explaining the reason for the different profit figures and commenting on their statement.

12.7 Durning Limited manufactures one product, the Durn. For the month of April 20-4 the following information is available:

number of units manufactured	10,000
number of units sold	8,000
selling price	£4 per unit
direct materials for month	£8,000
direct labour for month	£16,000
fixed production overheads for month	£10,000

There was no finished goods inventory at the start of the month. Both direct materials and direct labour are variable costs.

REQUIRED

(a)   produce profit statements for April 20-4, using:

- marginal costing

- absorption costing

(b)   explain briefly the reason for the difference between recorded profits under the alternative costing methods

12.8* Stan Bede Ltd manufactures one product with a selling price of £60 per unit.

Sales and production are expected to be 9,000 units per quarter.

Inventory of finished goods at the beginning of the year will be 1,000 units and will be maintained at this level.

The cost per unit is expected to be:

	£
Direct labour	12.25
Direct material	16.25
Production overhead (variable and fixed)	18.00
Selling and administrative overhead	6.50
Total	53.00

Fixed production overhead is expected to be £49,500 per quarter. Selling and administrative overhead is to be treated as a fixed cost.

REQUIRED

(a)   State the absorption cost per unit.

(b)   Calculate the marginal cost per unit for the first quarter.

(c)   Prepare a statement comparing the forecast profit for the first quarter, using

   (i)   marginal costing

   (ii)   absorption costing

Assessment and Qualifications Alliance (AQA), 2005

12.9 The budgeted profit for Jayne Bonde plc is expected to be £60,000 per month, using the marginal costing method of cost accounting.

Em, the financial accountant, would like to change to the absorption method of cost accounting in June. She believes that this method will enable the company to record a higher level of profit.

The fixed production costs are £90,000 per month, which will be absorbed on the basis of the normal production of 12,000 units.

The fixed non-production costs are £50,000 per month.

The budgeted variable production costs remain unchanged at £70 per unit.

The selling price is expected to be £90 per unit.

REQUIRED

(a) (i)   Calculate the absorption rate per unit.

(ii) Calculate the budgeted total production cost per unit, using the absorption rate calculated in (a) (i).

> For the month of June, opening inventory is 500 units, production is expected to be 12,000 units, but only 10,000 units are expected to be sold.

REQUIRED

(b) Calculate the budgeted profit for the month of June. Use the absorption costing method.

(c) Assess how the change in profit, resulting from the adoption of the absorption method, could affect the shareholders.

Assessment and Qualifications Alliance (AQA), 2006

12.10* (a) Explain the term 'activity based costing'.

(b) Explain the term 'cost driver'.

Assessment and Qualifications Alliance (AQA), Additional Specimen Questions

12.11

> Activity based costing was developed as an alternative to absorption costing.

REQUIRED

(a) Explain how activity based costing is used to calculate the cost of a product.

(b) Explain two benefits of using activity based costing as opposed to using absorption costing.

Assessment and Qualifications Alliance (AQA), Additional Specimen Questions

12.12*

> The financial director of Hansons Ltd is considering changing the method of calculating the selling price from marginal cost plus a mark-up, to activity based costing (ABC) plus a mark-up.

Discuss the benefits of using ABC instead of marginal costing.

Assessment and Qualifications Alliance (AQA), Second Specimen Paper for 2010

12.13

Mereford Manufacturing Limited makes two products, Aye and Bee. Product Aye is made in batches of 10,000 units, and Product Bee is made in batches of 1,000 units. Each batch has the following set-up and quality inspection costs:

- set-up £250
- quality inspection £150

Each week, the company produces 50,000 units of Aye and 50,000 units of Bee. At present the company charges overheads to output on the basis of labour hours, which are 500 hours per week for Aye and 500 hours for Bee.

(a) calculate the overheads charged to Aye and Bee each week, on the basis of labour hours

(b) calculate the overheads charged to Aye and Bee each week, using activity based costing with the cost drivers of set-up and quality inspection

(c) advise the management of Mereford Manufacturing Limited which is the more appropriate method of charging overheads to output

12.14

ExeWye Limited manufactures two products, Exe and Wye.

Weekly production is 1,000 units of each product. Each unit of production – whether Exe or Wye – requires two direct labour hours.

Products are made in batches – before a batch can be made the production machinery must be set up, checked for accuracy and test run. Each batch produced has to be inspected to ensure that it is of the required standard, with any rejects being identified.

Currently the company uses absorption costing.

Details of each product are (see next page):

Product Exe
- made in batches of 500 units
- selling price per unit, £200
- direct materials per unit, £60
- direct labour per unit, £20

Product Wye
- made in batches of 100 units
- selling price per unit, £160
- direct materials per unit, £40
- direct labour per unit, £20

Fixed production costs each week:
- set-up costs of machinery, £24,000
- inspection costs of production, £12,000

These costs are currently absorbed on the basis of direct labour hours.

REQUIRED

Show how marginal costing, absorption costing, and activity based costing will deal differently with the costs.

13 OVERHEADS AND OVERHEAD ABSORPTION

In this chapter, we examine how overheads – the cost of indirect materials, indirect labour and indirect expenses – are calculated for a product or service and are added to the direct costs. We will be studying:

- the need to recover the cost of overheads through units of output
- the collection of overhead costs together in cost centres
- the process of allocating and apportioning the cost of overheads into the units of output
- the different bases of apportionment of overheads
- apportionment of service department costs
- two commonly-used overhead absorption rates and their relative merits
- the application of overhead absorption rates to actual work done
- the use of cost-plus pricing

OVERHEADS

In Chapter 10, Costs and Contribution, we saw (page 250) that costs could be classified as follows:

DIRECT MATERIALS	INDIRECT MATERIALS
+ DIRECT LABOUR	+ INDIRECT LABOUR
+ DIRECT EXPENSES	+ INDIRECT EXPENSES
= TOTAL DIRECT COSTS OR PRIME COST	= TOTAL OVERHEADS

Direct costs can be identified directly with each unit of output, but indirect costs or overheads cannot be identified directly with each unit of output.

Overheads do not relate to particular units of output but must, instead, be shared amongst all of the cost units (*units of output to which costs can be charged*) to which they relate. For example, the cost of the factory rent must be included in the cost of the firm's output.

The important point to remember is that all the overheads of a business, together with the direct costs (materials, labour and expenses), must be covered by money flowing in from the firm's output – the sales of products or services. This point is demonstrated in the Worked Example which follows.

WORKED EXAMPLE: OVERHEAD ABSORPTION

situation

CoolHeads is a new hairdressing business, being set up by Nathan and Morgan in a rented shop.

Nathan and Morgan are preparing their price list. They must set the prices sufficiently high to cover all their costs and to give them a profit.

They have details of the costs of all the materials they need (shampoos, colourings and so on) from a specialist supplier. Nathan and Morgan have decided the rate to charge to the business for their own work and they do not intend to employ anyone else for the time being.

But there are other costs which they will also incur – their overheads – and they are not so sure how they will work these into their pricing structure. Nathan asks:

'What about the shop rent and the business rates we have to pay? What about the electricity, the insurance, the telephone bill and all the advertising we have to do? How are we going to cover these costs?'

'How much will it cost us in total to deal with each customer?'

'How do we make sure that we are going to make a profit?'

solution

For pricing purposes, Nathan and Morgan need to include overheads in the cost of each item on their price list.

In a small business like this, the whole business could be a single cost centre. All the overheads could be allowed for in a single rate to charge for a haircut.

Suppose Nathan and Morgan estimate that their total overheads for the first year of trading will be £27,000. They expect to be working on hairstyling for 1,500 hours each during the year, ie a total of 3,000 hours between them.

Therefore, they could decide in advance that each hour of their work should be charged £27,000 ÷ 3,000 = £9 for overheads. A job that takes two hours to complete would then be charged 2 x £9 = £18 for overheads.

Notice that in a service business such as hairdressing, direct materials costs are likely to be relatively small in comparison with the cost of direct labour and overheads. It is essential for Nathan and Morgan to consider the cost of overheads when they are setting their prices and the labour hourly rate is one way of doing this. This is called an 'overhead absorption rate' and we will look in more detail at this idea later in this chapter.

In larger businesses, overheads are usually classified by function under headings such as:

- factory or production expenses, eg factory rent and rates, indirect factory labour, indirect factory materials, heating and lighting of factory
- selling and distribution expenses, eg salaries of sales staff, vehicle costs, delivery costs
- administrative expenses, eg office rent and rates, office salaries, heating and lighting of office, indirect office materials
- finance expenses, eg bank interest, bank charges

Each of these functions or sections of the business is likely to be a separate cost centre (*a section of a business to which costs can be charged*).

In order to deal with the overheads we need to know how the whole business is split into cost centres. This will depend on the size of the business and the way in which the work is organised.

Collecting Overheads in Cost Centres

allocation of overheads

Some overheads belong entirely to one particular cost centre, for example:

- the salary of a supervisor who works in only one cost centre
- the rent of a separate building in which there is only one cost centre
- the cost of indirect materials that have been issued to one particular cost centre

Overheads like these can therefore be allocated to the cost centre to which they belong.

Allocation of overheads is the charging to a particular cost centre of overheads that are incurred entirely by that cost centre.

apportionment of overheads

Overheads that cannot be allocated to a particular cost centre have to be shared or **apportioned** between two or more cost centres.

Apportionment of overheads is the sharing of overheads over a number of cost centres to which they relate. Each cost centre is charged with a proportion of the overhead cost.

For example, a department which is a cost centre within a factory will be charged a proportion of the factory rent and rates. Another example is where a supervisor works within two departments, both of which are separate cost centres: the indirect labour cost of employing the supervisor is shared between the two cost centres.

With apportionment, a suitable **basis** – or method – must be found to apportion overheads between cost centres; the basis selected should be related to the type of cost. Different methods might be used for each overhead – the example on the next page indicates some methods that can be used.

OVERHEAD	BASIS OF APPORTIONMENT
rent, rates	floor area (or volume of space) of cost centres
heating, lighting	floor area (or volume of space) of cost centres
buildings insurance	floor area (or volume of space) of cost centres
buildings depreciation	floor area (or volume of space) of cost centres
machinery insurance	cost or net book value of machinery and equipment
machinery depreciation	value of machinery; or machine usage (hours)
canteen	number of employees in each cost centre
supervisory costs	number of employees in each cost centre, or labour hours worked by supervisors in each cost centre

It must be stressed that apportionment is used for those overheads that cannot be allocated to a particular cost centre. For example, if a college's Business Studies Department occupies a building in another part of town from the main college building, the rates for the building can clearly be allocated to the Business Studies cost centre. By contrast, the rates for the main college building must be apportioned amongst the cost centres on the main campus.

review of allocation and apportionment

It is important that the allocation and apportionment of overheads are reviewed at regular intervals to ensure that the methods being used are still valid. For example:

- *allocation*

  The role of a supervisor may have changed – whereas previously the supervisor worked in one department only, he or she might now be working in two departments.

- *apportionment*

  Building work may have expanded the floor area of a department, so that the apportionment basis needs to be reworked for costs such as rent and rates.

Any proposed changes to allocation and apportionment must be discussed with senior staff and their agreement obtained before any changes to methods are implemented. Accounting staff will often have to consult with staff (such as managers and supervisors) working in operational departments, to discuss how overheads are charged to their departments, and to resolve any queries.

apportionment and ratios

It is important to understand the method of apportionment of overheads using ratios. For example, overheads relating to buildings are often shared in the ratio of the floor area used by the cost centres.

Now read through the example below which shows the use of ratios in apportionment, and then the Worked Example on the next page.

example of apportionment using ratios

AyeBee Limited has four cost centres: two production departments, Aye and Bee, and two non-production cost centres, stores and maintenance. The total rent per year for the business premises is £12,000. This is to be apportioned on the basis of floor area, given as:

	production dept Aye	production dept Bee	stores	maintenance
Floor area (square metres)	400	550	350	200

Step 1

Calculate the total floor area: 400 + 550 + 350 + 200 = 1,500 square metres

Step 2

Divide the total rent by the total floor area: £12,000 ÷ 1,500 = £8

This gives a rate of £8 per square metre.

Step 3

Multiply the floor area in each cost centre by the rate per square metre. This gives the share of rent for each cost centre. For example, in Production Department Aye, the share of rent is 400 x £8 = £3,200. The results are shown in the table:

	production dept Aye	production dept Bee	stores	maintenance
Floor area (square metres)	400	550	350	200
Rent apportioned	£3,200	£4,400	£2,800	£1,600

Step 4

Check that the apportioned amounts agree with the total rent:

£3,200 + £4,400 + £ 2,800 + £1,600 = £12,000.

WORKED EXAMPLE: OVERHEAD ALLOCATION AND APPORTIONMENT

situation

Pilot Engineering Limited, which makes car engine components, uses some of the latest laser equipment in one department, while another section of the business continues to use traditional machinery. Details of the factory are as follows:

Department Exe is a 'hi-tech' machine shop equipped with laser-controlled machinery which cost £80,000. This department has 400 square metres of floor area. There are three machine operators: the supervisor spends one-third of the time in this department.

Department Wye is a 'low-tech' part of the factory equipped with machinery which cost £20,000. The floor area is 600 square metres. There are two workers who spend all their time in this department: the supervisor spends two-thirds of the time in this department.

The overheads to be allocated or apportioned are as follows:

1	Factory rates (ie business rates)	£12,000
2	Wages of the supervisor	£21,000
3	Factory heating and lighting	£2,500
4	Depreciation of machinery	£20,000
5	Buildings insurance	£2,000
6	Insurance of machinery	£1,500
7	Specialist materials for the laser equipment	£2,500

How should each of these be allocated or apportioned to each department?

solution

The recommendations are:

1 Factory rates – apportioned on the basis of floor area.

2 Supervisor's wages – apportioned on the basis of time spent, ie one-third to Department Exe, and two-thirds to Department Wye. If the time spent was not known, an alternative basis could be established, based on the number of employees.

3 Factory heating and lighting – apportioned on the basis of floor area.

4 Depreciation of machinery – apportioned on the basis of machine value.

5 Buildings insurance – apportioned on the basis of floor area.

6 Insurance of machinery – apportioned on the basis of machine value.

7 Specialist materials for the laser equipment – allocated to Department Exe because this cost belongs entirely to Department Exe.

It is important to note that there are no fixed rules for the apportionment of overheads – the only proviso is that a fair proportion of the overhead is charged to each department which has some responsibility for the cost being incurred. Methods of apportionment will need to be reviewed at regular intervals to ensure that they are still valid; changes can only be implemented with the agreement of senior staff.

The apportionment of overheads for Pilot Engineering Limited is as follows (sample workings are shown below the table):

overhead	basis of apportionment	total	dept Exe	dept Wye
		£	£	£
Factory rates	Floor area	12,000	4,800	7,200
Wages of supervisor	Time spent	21,000	7,000	14,000
Heating and lighting	Floor area	2,500	1,000	1,500
Dep'n of machinery	Machine value	20,000	16,000	4,000
Buildings insurance	Floor area	2,000	800	1,200
Machinery insurance	Machine value	1,500	1,200	300
Specialist materials	Allocation	2,500	2,500	–
		61,500	33,300	28,200

For example, the floor areas of the two departments are:

Dept Exe	400	square metres
Dept Wye	600	square metres
Total	1,000	square metres

Factory rates are apportioned as follows:

$$\frac{£12,000}{1,000} = £12 \text{ per square metre}$$

Dept Exe rates	£12 x 400	=	£4,800
Dept Wye rates	£12 x 600	=	£7,200
Total			£12,000

Note that overhead apportionment is often, in practice, calculated using a computer spreadsheet.

SERVICE DEPARTMENTS

Many businesses have departments which provide services within the business; for example, maintenance, transport, stores or stationery. Each service department is likely to be a cost centre, to which a proportion of overheads is charged. As service departments do not themselves have any cost units to which their overheads may be charged, the costs of each service department must be re-apportioned to the production departments (which do have cost units to which overheads can be charged). A suitable basis of re-apportionment must be used, for example:

- the overheads of a maintenance department might be re-apportioned to production departments on the basis of value of machinery or equipment, or on the basis of time spent in each production department
- the overheads of a stores or stationery department could be re-apportioned on the basis of value of goods issued to production departments
- the overheads of a subsidised canteen could be re-apportioned on the basis of the number of employees

Re-apportionment of service department overheads is considered in the next section.

RE-APPORTIONMENT OF SERVICE DEPARTMENT OVERHEADS

The overheads of service departments are charged to production cost centres using the **elimination method** with either:

- direct apportionment, where service departments provide services to production departments only, or
- step-down, where service departments provide services to production departments and to some other service departments

To illustrate re-apportionment, we will apply the elimination method to a business with two production departments, Cee and Dee, and two service departments, stores and maintenance. After allocation and apportionment of production overheads, the totals are:

	total	production dept Cee	production dept Dee	stores	maintenance
	£	£	£	£	£
Overheads	20,400	10,000	5,000	2,400	3,000

elimination method, with direct apportionment

Here the service departments do not provide services to one another. Their costs are directly apportioned to production departments using a suitable basis. In the example on the previous page:

- stores overheads are re-apportioned on the basis of the number of stores requisitions – department Cee has made 150 requisitions; department Dee has made 50
- maintenance overheads are re-apportioned on the value of machinery – department Cee has machinery with a net book value of £20,000, department Dee's machinery has a value of £10,000

Using direct apportionment, the overheads of the service departments are re-apportioned as shown in the table below. The method of calculation using ratios is the same as we used for apportionment.

Notice that the total is taken out of the service cost centre column when it is shared between the production cost centres.

	total	production dept Cee	production dept Dee	stores	maintenance
	£	£	£	£	£
Overheads	20,400	10,000	5,000	2,400	3,000
Stores	–	1,800	600	(2,400)	–
Maintenance	–	2,000	1,000	–	(3,000)
	20,400	13,800	6,600	–	–

Thus all the overheads have now been charged to the production departments where they can be 'absorbed' into the cost units which form the output of each department. We will see how the absorption is carried out later in this chapter.

elimination method, with step-down

This is used where, as well as to production departments, one service department provides services to another.

Using the example above, the stores department deals with requisitions from the maintenance department, but no maintenance work is carried out in the stores department. Under the elimination method with step-down, we re-apportion firstly the overheads of the stores department (because it does not receive any services from the maintenance department), and secondly the overheads of the maintenance department (see next page).

- number of stores requisitions
  - department Cee   150
  - department Dee   50
  - maintenance   50

- value of machinery
  - department Cee   £20,000
  - department Dee   £10,000

The re-apportionment of the production overheads of the service departments, using step-down, is as follows:

	total	production dept Cee	production dept Dee	stores	maintenance
	£	£	£	£	£
Overheads	20,400	10,000	5,000	2,400	3,000
Stores	–	1,440	480	(2,400)	480
			–		*3,480
Maintenance	–	2,320	1,160	–	(3,480)
	20,400	13,760	6,640	–	–

* Note that a new total is calculated for the maintenance department before it is re-apportioned. £480 from stores is added to the original £3,000 overheads in the maintenance department.

All the overheads have now been charged to the production departments.

ALLOCATION AND APPORTIONMENT – A SUMMARY

The diagram on the next page summarises the allocation and apportionment of overheads that we have seen in this chapter. It shows:

- allocation of overheads directly to cost centres
- apportionment of overheads on an equitable basis to cost centres
- re-apportionment of service department costs to production cost centres

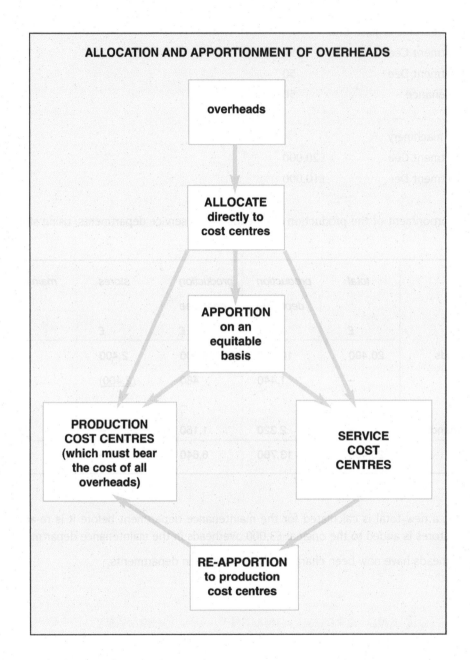

ALLOCATION AND APPORTIONMENT OF OVERHEADS

overheads

ALLOCATE
directly to
cost centres

APPORTION
on an
equitable
basis

PRODUCTION
COST CENTRES
(which must bear
the cost of all
overheads)

SERVICE
COST
CENTRES

RE-APPORTION
to production
cost centres

OVERHEAD ABSORPTION

Once overheads have been allocated or apportioned to production cost centres, the final step is to ensure that the overheads are charged to cost units. In the language of cost accounting this is known as 'absorption' or 'recovery', ie the cost of overheads is charged to the cost units which pass through that particular production department.

We saw in the Worked Example on page 309 (CoolHeads hairdressing) how overheads could be allowed for when deciding on selling prices.

Similarly, if you take a car to be repaired at a garage, the bill may be presented as follows:

	£
Parts	70.00
Labour: 3 hours at £40 per hour	120.00
Total	190.00

Within this bill are the three main elements of cost: materials (parts), labour and overheads. The last two are combined as labour – the garage mechanic is not paid £40 per hour; instead the labour rate might be £15 per hour, with the rest, ie £25 per hour, being absorption of the overhead and the profit of the garage. Other examples are accountants and solicitors, who charge a 'rate per hour', part of which is used to contribute to the cost of overheads and profit.

To be profitable, a business must ensure that its selling prices more than cover all its costs:

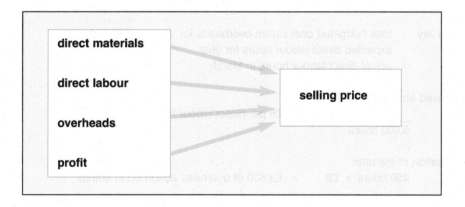

calculating overhead absorption rates

In order to absorb the overheads of a department, there are two steps to be followed:

1   calculation of the overhead absorption rate (OAR)

2   application of this rate to actual work done

The overhead absorption rate is calculated using estimated or budgeted figures as follows, for a given time period:

$$OAR = \frac{\textit{total budgeted cost centre overheads}}{\textit{total planned work in the cost centre}}$$

The amount of work must be measured in a suitable way, usually:

- labour hours, or
- machine hours

These methods are illustrated below.

labour hour method

With this method, production overhead is absorbed on the basis of the number of direct labour hours worked.

1 Calculation of the overhead absorption rate, using budgeted (expected) figures:

$$\frac{\textit{total cost centre overheads}}{\textit{total direct labour hours (in cost centre)}} = \textit{cost per labour hour}$$

2 Application of the rate:

direct labour hours worked x overhead absorption rate
= overhead absorbed and charged to production

---

example

Department Jay	total budgeted cost centre overheads for year	£40,000
	expected direct labour hours for year	5,000
	actual direct labour hours in March	450

1 Overhead absorption rate:

$$\frac{£40,000}{5,000 \text{ hours}} = £8 \text{ per direct labour hour}$$

2 Application of the rate:

450 hours x £8 = £3,600 of overhead absorbed in March

---

machine hour method

Here the production overhead is absorbed on the basis of machine hours.

1 Calculation of the overhead absorption rate, using budgeted (expected) figures:

$$\frac{\textit{total cost centre overheads}}{\textit{total machine hours (in cost centre)}} = \textit{cost per machine hour}$$

2 Application of the rate:

machine hours worked x overhead absorption rate
= overhead absorbed and charged to production

example

Department Kay   total budgeted cost centre overheads for year   £216,000
expected machine hours for year   36,000
actual machine hours in March   3,500

1   Overhead absorption rate:

$$\frac{£216,000}{36,000 \text{ hours}} = £6 \text{ per machine hour}$$

2   Application of the rate:

3,500 hours x £6 = £21,000 of overhead absorbed in March

which method to use?

Only one overhead absorption rate will be used in a particular department (cost centre), and the method selected must relate to the reason why the costs are incurred. For example, a cost centre which is machine based, where most of the overheads incurred relate to machinery, will use a machine hour basis.

The labour hour method is popular where the cost centre is labour intensive (eg the garage mentioned earlier). Overheads are absorbed on a time basis – a cost unit that requires twice the labour of another cost unit will be charged twice the overhead. However this method will be inappropriate where some units are worked on by hand while others quickly pass through a machinery process and require little labour time.

A machine hour rate is particularly appropriate where expensive machinery is used in the department. However, it would be unsuitable where not all products pass through the machine but some are worked on by hand: in the latter case, no overheads would be charged to the cost units.

It is important to select the best method of overhead absorption for the particular business, otherwise wrong decisions will be made on the basis of the costing information. The particular absorption method selected for a department will need to be reviewed at regular intervals to ensure that it is still valid. For example, the labour hour method is unlikely to continue to be appropriate where a machine has been brought in to automate processes that were previously carried out by hand. As noted earlier, any proposed changes must be discussed with senior staff and their agreement obtained before any changes to methods are implemented. The changes will need to be discussed with staff (such as managers and supervisors) working in operational departments to explain how overheads will be charged to their departments in the future, and any queries will need to be resolved.

using a pre-determined rate

Most businesses calculate a pre-determined overhead absorption rate (OAR) for each department. This is then applied to all production passing through that department.

The OAR is calculated in advance using estimates – this avoids having to calculate the rate regularly, which may result in changes over quite short time periods. Instead the rate is smoothed out over fluctuations in cost and activity over a longer accounting period.

COST-PLUS PRICING

Cost-plus pricing can be used in conjunction with absorption costing to determine the selling price of products. Cost-plus pricing uses the cost price of making a product or providing a service and adds on a percentage of the cost to give the selling price, ie

cost price + profit = selling price

Cost is usually calculated on the basis of the full cost of absorption costing (or activity based costing) which adds together all the costs of each unit. Profit is calculated as a percentage mark-up on cost price (ie the profit, being a percentage of cost price, is added to cost price to give selling price).

Cost-plus pricing can also be used in connection with marginal costing although the percentage mark-up on cost price will need to be higher in order to achieve the same selling price as under absorption costing. This is illustrated in the Worked Example below.

The disadvantage of using cost-plus pricing is that the selling price may be uncompetitive with other, similar products or services. This could lead to an insufficient number of units of output being sold to recover costs.

WORKED EXAMPLE: USING COST-PLUS PRICING

situation

Leathercraft Limited makes high quality seats for aircraft. Its costs per seat are:

	£
Direct materials	70
Direct labour	30
PRIME COST	100
Fixed overheads	25
TOTAL COST	125

The company is currently reviewing its selling prices and is considering cost-plus pricing based on a 20 per cent mark-up on absorption cost (ie profit is 20 per cent of cost price, which is added to cost price to give selling price).

The company is also considering using cost-plus pricing as a mark-up on the marginal cost of each seat. What is the mark-up on marginal cost that will give the same selling price as under absorption cost?

solution

percentage mark-up on absorption cost
selling price is calculated as:

	£
total cost per seat	125
20 per cent mark-up (20% x £125)	25
selling price per seat	150

percentage mark-up on marginal cost

The variable costs are £100 per seat (materials £70, labour £30).

To achieve a selling price of £150 per seat, the marginal cost must be marked up by 50 per cent, ie

$$\frac{\text{profit}}{\text{marginal cost}} = \frac{£50}{£100} = 50\%$$

Note here how the percentage mark-up is much greater for marginal cost than for absorption cost in order to achieve the same selling price. Clearly this is because the mark-up for marginal cost is based on a lower starting cost than for absorption cost.

important note

Using cost-plus pricing does not mean that Leathercraft Limited will be able to sell its seats at the price of £150 each. It might be that customers will find a supplier who is able to produce seats of the same quality but at a cheaper price. This could lead Leathercraft Limited into selling an insufficient number of seats to recover its costs. In these circumstances decisions about price setting will have to be taken and these are covered in the next chapter.

CHAPTER SUMMARY

- Direct costs can be identified directly with each unit of output.

- Indirect costs (overheads) do not relate to particular units of output, but must be shared amongst all the cost units to which they relate.

- Overheads are:
    - allocated to a specific cost centre, if they belong entirely to that cost centre
    - apportioned between cost centres, if they are shared

- Apportionment is done on a suitable basis, using ratios of floor area, numbers of employees, etc.

- Methods of allocation and apportionment should be reviewed regularly.

- The total overheads allocated and apportioned to the service cost centres are then re-apportioned to the production cost centres using the elimination method.

- After re-apportionment of the service cost centre overheads, the total overheads in each production cost centre can be calculated.

- All the above steps can be carried out using expected or budgeted overhead amounts.

- Overhead absorption rates (OAR) are calculated using the total expected or budgeted overheads in each cost centre.

- An OAR is calculated as follows:

    $$\text{overhead absorption rate} = \frac{\text{total budgeted cost centre overheads}}{\text{total planned work in cost centre}}$$

    where the planned amount of work may be measured, often in terms of direct labour hours or machine hours.

- Two commonly-used OARs are labour hour and machine hour.

- Overhead absorption rates are applied to the actual work carried out. A direct labour hour absorption rate is applied as follows, for example:

    $$\text{labour hours worked} \times \text{overhead absorption rate} = \text{overhead absorbed}$$

- Cost-plus pricing is where a mark-up is added to the cost price in order to determine the selling price.

In the next chapter we look at how costs can be used to help with decision-making in business.

QUESTIONS

An asterisk (*) after the question number means that the answer is given at the end of this book.

13.1* Distinguish between:

- allocation of overheads

- apportionment of overheads

13.2* Wyvern Fabrication Company has two production departments – moulding and finishing.

The company absorbs overheads on the basis of machine hours and the following overhead analysis information is available to you (note that service department overheads have already been apportioned to production departments):

OVERHEAD ANALYSIS SHEET		
	MOULDING	FINISHING
Budgeted total overheads (£)	9,338	3,298
Budgeted machine hours	1,450	680
Budgeted overhead absorption rate (£)		

Details of a particular job of work are as follows:

JOB NUMBER 1234: OVERHEAD ANALYSIS SHEET		
	MOULDING	FINISHING
Machine hours	412	154
Budgeted overhead absorption rate (£)		
Overhead absorbed (£)		

You are to:

(a) Calculate the overhead absorption rate for each of the two departments and complete the overhead analysis sheet.

(b) Calculate the production overhead absorbed by job number 1234 and complete the job overhead analysis sheet.

(c) Suggest an alternative overhead absorption rate that the company might use and comment on the circumstances that would make it appropriate.

13.3 Mereford Management College is a private college that has two teaching departments – accountancy and management.

The College charges overheads on the basis of lecturer hours. The following overhead analysis information is available to you (note that support services overheads – such as the administration office, reprographics department and learning resources – have already been apportioned to the teaching departments):

OVERHEAD ANALYSIS SHEET for January 20-8		
	Accountancy Department	Management Department
Budgeted total overheads (£)	22,143	17,251
Budgeted lecturer hours	1,525	1,300
Budgeted overhead absorption rate (£)		

Details of a particular course – 'Finance for Managers' – that is taught in both the accountancy and management departments are as follows:

OVERHEAD ANALYSIS SHEET Course: Finance for Managers		
	Accountancy Department	Management Department
Lecturer hours	45	20
Budgeted overhead absorption rate (£)		
Overhead absorbed by course (£)		

You are to:

(a) calculate the overhead absorption rate for each of the two departments and complete the overhead analysis sheet

(b) calculate the overhead absorbed by the 'Finance for Managers' course and complete the course overhead analysis sheet

13.4* ABC Limited is a manufacturing business with three cost centres: Departments A, B and C. The following are the expected factory overheads for the forthcoming year:

Rent and rates	£7,210
Depreciation of machinery	£10,800
Supervisor's salary	£12,750
Insurance of machinery	£750

Departmental information is:

	Dept A	Dept B	Dept C
Floor area (sq m)	300	150	250
Value of machinery	£25,000	£15,000	£10,000
Number of production-line employees	8	4	3

You are to:

(a) Apportion the overheads to the cost centres, stating the basis of apportionment.

(b) Calculate the overhead absorption rate (to two decimal places) of each department, based on labour hours. Note that the factory works a 37 hour week for 48 weeks in a year.

13.5 Wye Engineering Limited offers specialist engineering services to the car industry. It has two production departments – machining and finishing – and a service department which maintains the machinery of both departments. Expected production overheads for the forthcoming year are:

	£
Rent and rates	5,520
Buildings insurance	1,320
Insurance of machinery	1,650
Lighting and heating	3,720
Depreciation of machinery	11,000
Supervisory salaries	30,000
Maintenance department salary	16,000
Factory cleaning	4,800

The following information is available:

	Machining	Finishing	Maintenance
Floor area (square metres)	300	200	100
Number of employees	6	3	1
Value of machinery	£40,000	£15,000	–

The factory works a 35 hour week for 47 weeks each year.

You are to:

(a)   Prepare an analysis of production overheads showing the basis of allocation and apportionment to the three departments of the business.

(b)   Re-apportion the service department overheads to production departments on the basis of value of machinery.

(c)   Calculate an overhead absorption rate based on labour hours for each of the two production departments.

(d)   Discuss an alternative overhead absorption rate that the company could use.

13.6*   Mercia Tutorial College has two teaching departments – business studies and general studies – and two service departments – administration and technical support. The overheads of each department are as follows:

		£
•	business studies	40,000
•	general studies	20,000
•	administration	9,600
•	technical support	12,000

The basis for re-apportioning the overheads of the service departments is:

•   technical support, on the value of equipment in each department – business studies, £50,000; general studies, £25,000; administration, £25,000

•   administration, on the number of students in the teaching departments – business studies 500; general studies, 250

You are to use the elimination method with step-down to re-apportion the two service department overheads to the two teaching departments.

13.7*   Rossiter and Rossiter is a firm of chartered accountants, with two partners. Overhead costs for next year are estimated to be:

	£
Office rent	10,000
Office salaries	30,000
Rates	4,800
Heating and lighting	2,400
Stationery	2,000
Postage and telephone	5,100
Car expenses	5,600

The two partners plan to work for 47 weeks next year. They will each be in the office for 40 hours per week, but will be working on behalf of their clients for 35 hours per week.

(a)   What is the overhead absorption rate per partner hour?

(b)   If each partner wishes to earn a salary of £50,000 per year, what is the combined hourly rate per partner, which includes overheads and their salaries?

(c)   If both partners actually work on their clients' behalf for 37 hours per week, what will be the total over-absorption of overheads for the year?

13.8

A friend of yours is about to start in business making garden seats. She plans to make two different qualities – 'Standard' and 'De Luxe'. Costs per unit for direct materials and labour are expected to be:

	Standard	De Luxe
	£	£
Direct materials	12.50	20.00
Direct labour:		
3 hours at £8.00 per hour	24.00	–
3.5 hours at £10.00 per hour	–	35.00
	36.50	55.00
Machine hours	1	2.5

Production overheads are expected to be £1,000 per month.

Production is expected to be 80 'Standard' seats and 40 'De Luxe' seats per month.

(a)   Suggest two different methods by which overheads can be absorbed.

(b)   Calculate the production cost of each of the two qualities of garden seats using the two different methods of overhead absorption.

(c)   Compare the results of your calculations and suggest to your friend the most appropriate method of overhead absorption for this business.

13.9*

Durning Limited manufactures and sells household furniture. The company's operations are organised by departments, as follows:

*   Warehouse

*   Manufacturing

*   Sales

*   Administration

The fixed overheads of the company for November 20-7 were as follows:

	£
Depreciation of non-current assets	9,150
Rent	11,000
Other property overheads	6,200
Administration overheads	13,450
Staff costs:	
– warehouse	3,600
– indirect manufacturing	9,180
– sales	8,650
– administration	5,940
Total fixed overheads	67,170

The following information is also relevant:

Department	% of floor space occupied	Net book value of non-current assets £000
Warehouse	15%	120
Manufacturing	60%	400
Sales	10%	20
Administration	15%	60
	100%	600

Overheads are allocated and apportioned between departments using the most appropriate basis.

REQUIRED

(a)   Please refer to the text and table on the opposite page.

Manufacturing fixed overheads are absorbed on the basis of budgeted machine hours. The budgeted number of machine hours for November 20-7 was 10,000 hours.

REQUIRED

(b)   Calculate the budgeted fixed overhead absorption rate for the manufacturing department for November 20-7.

For use with Question 13.9 (a) on previous page

Complete the following table showing the allocation and apportionment of fixed overheads between the four departments.

Fixed overheads for November 2004	Basis	Total £	Warehouse £	Manufacturing £	Sales £	Administration £
Depreciation of non-current assets		9,150				
Rent		11,000				
Other property overheads		6,200				
Administration overheads		13,450				
Staff costs		27,370				
		67,170				

13.10 Wyvern Private Hospital plc has two patient wards – a day care ward for minor operations where the patients go home at the end of the day, and a surgical ward for patients who remain in the hospital for several days. There are two service departments – the operating theatre and administration.

The overheads of each department for last month were as follows:

		£
•	day care ward	28,750
•	surgical ward	42,110
•	operating theatre	32,260
•	administration	9,075

The basis for re-apportioning the overheads of the service departments is:

*   operating theatre, on the number of operations carried out – day care ward, 160; surgical ward, 120

*   administration, on the number of staff in each department – day care ward, 10; surgical ward, 25; operating theatre, 20

You are to use the elimination method with step-down to re-apportion the two service department overheads to the two patient wards.

13.11 Fox Furniture Limited makes tables and chairs for school and college use. There are two production lines – tables and chairs – and two service departments – stores and maintenance.

The overheads of each department for last month were as follows:

		£
•	tables	12,000
•	chairs	8,000
•	stores	3,000
•	maintenance	2,000

The basis for re-apportioning the overheads of the service departments is:

*   stores, on the number of requisitions – tables, 100; chairs, 80; maintenance, 20

*   maintenance, on the value of equipment in each department – tables, £30,000; chairs, £20,000

You are to use the elimination method with step-down to re-apportion the two service department overheads to the two production departments.

13.12 Milestone Motors Limited sells and services cars. The company's operations are organised into four departments, as follows:

- New car sales
- Used car sales
- Servicing
- Administration

The fixed overheads of the company for the four weeks ended 28 April 20-4 were as follows:

	£
Depreciation of non-current assets	8,400
Rent	10,000
Other property overheads	4,500
Staff costs:	
– new car sales	11,080
– used car sales	7,390
– servicing	9,975
– administration	6,850
Administration overheads	3,860
Total fixed overheads	62,055

The following information is also relevant:

Department	% of floor space occupied	Net book value of non-current assets £000
New car sales	40%	50
Used car sales	30%	30
Servicing	20%	100
Administration	10%	20
	100%	200

Overheads are allocated and apportioned using the most appropriate basis. The total administrative overheads are then re-apportioned to the three departments using the following percentages.

- New car sales   20%
- Used car sales   30%
- Servicing   50%

REQUIRED

(a)   Please refer to the text and table on the next page.

> Servicing department fixed overheads are absorbed on the basis of budgeted direct labour hours. The budgeted number of direct labour hours for the servicing department during the four weeks ended 28 April 20-4 was 1,025 hours.

REQUIRED

(b)   Calculate the budgeted fixed overhead absorption rate per direct labour hour for the servicing department during the period.

For use with Question 13.12 (a) on previous page

Complete the following table showing:

- the basis for allocation or apportionment of each overhead;
- the allocation and apportionment of fixed overheads between the four departments;
- the re-apportionment of the total administration overheads.

Fixed overheads for four weeks ended 28 April 20-4	Basis	Total £	New Car Sales £	Used Car Sales £	Servicing £	Administration £
Depreciation of non-current assets		8,400				
Rent		10,000				
Other property overheads		4,500				
Staff costs		35,295				
Administration overheads		3,860				
		62,055				( )
Administration		62,055				–

13.13   Dario Uno produces a single product.

The following information is available for the year ending 31 October 2007.

(1)   The expected costs per unit are:

materials 40 metres at £2.50 per metre;

labour 3 hours at £16 per hour.

(2)   The expected production is 26,000 units per year.

(3)   The fixed overheads of £39,000 are absorbed using labour hours.

(4)   The selling price is based on full cost plus 20%.

REQUIRED

(a)   Calculate the overhead absorption rate per hour.

(b)   Calculate the selling price per unit.

(c)   Compare the advantages of using absorption costing with the advantages of using marginal costing to set a selling price.

Assessment and Qualifications Alliance (AQA), 2007

13.14

Tutorial note:

Parts (a) and (b) of this question have been seen already in Chapter 9 as question 9.9.

The costs that you will need from parts (a) and (b) of this question are:

	£
Factory canteen expenses	36,000
Factory machinery depreciation	14,400
Machine maintenance	12,000
Machine set-up costs	40,000

Osborne Melbourne Ltd has two production departments: Machining and Assembly. It also has two service departments: Maintenance and the Canteen.

The following information is available for the year ended 31 December 2006:

	Machining	Assembly	Maintenance	Canteen
Area (square metres)	6,000	20,000	2,000	1,000
Machine net book value	£200,000	£400,000	–	–
Machine hours	30,000	60,000	–	–
Labour hours	40,000	12,000	–	–
Number of employees	150	300	100	50
Number of machine set-ups	12	8	–	–
Number of machines	6	8	–	–

The overheads of the service departments are allocated to the production departments on the following bases.

	Maintenance	Canteen
Machining	20%	60%
Assembly	80%	30%
Maintenance	–	10%

REQUIRED

(c)   Prepare a statement to show the total overheads allocated and apportioned to **each** of the two production departments. Identify the bases used.

(d)   Calculate the overhead absorption rates for **each** of the two production departments. Identify the bases used. Give a reason for each choice.

The financial director of Osborne Melbourne Ltd is considering changing the method of overhead allocation to activity based costing (ABC) instead of absorption costing.

REQUIRED

(e)   Explain the term "cost drivers".

(f)   Identify the cost drivers for each of the following overheads:

   factory canteen expenses

   factory machine maintenance

   factory machine set-up costs

Assessment and Qualifications Alliance (AQA), Specimen Paper for 2010 (part of question)

13.15* Duchy Private Hospital Limited carries out a large number of minor operations for day patients. For next year it plans 2,500 operations based on the following costs:

annual costs for 2,500 minor operations

	£
Direct materials (£100 per operation)	250,000
Direct labour (£200 per operation)	500,000
PRIME COST	750,000
Fixed overheads	250,000
TOTAL COST	1,000,000

The hospital is reviewing its pricing policy for minor operations and is considering cost-plus pricing based on a 20 per cent mark-up on absorption cost.

(a) Calculate the price per minor operation using cost-plus pricing.

(b) The hospital is also considering using cost-plus pricing as a mark-up on marginal cost. What is the mark-up on marginal cost that will give the same price per minor operation as under absorption cost?

14 COSTING IN DECISION-MAKING

In this chapter we study how costing methods can help with decision-making in business. In particular we see that, whilst absorption costing is important because costs must be covered, marginal costing can help with a number of different circumstances, including:

- make or buy decisions
- acceptance of additional work
- price setting
- optimum use of scarce resources

INTRODUCTION

In the long term every business that seeks to make profits must cover its costs and make a profit from the sale of its output. As we have seen in the previous chapter, this often involves the use of cost-plus pricing techniques which add a percentage to absorption cost. However, it is common to use marginal cost to help with analysing the outcome of output, pricing, and cost situations – in other words the analysis of 'what if' scenarios. Nevertheless, an important point to bear in mind is that, overall, if the business is to be profitable, the selling prices used must give sufficient contribution to meet its fixed costs and provide an acceptable level of profit.

We have already seen in Chapter 10 that the marginal cost is the cost of producing one extra unit of output. Marginal costing techniques recognise that fixed costs vary with time rather than activity. For example, the rent of premises relates to a certain time period – such as a week, month or year – and remains unchanged whether there are 100 units of output or 300 (always assuming that the capacity of the premises is at least 300 units). By contrast, one extra unit of output will incur an increase in the variable costs, such as direct materials and direct labour; this increase is the marginal cost.

A knowledge of marginal costing techniques helps with decision-making in the forms of:

- make or buy decisions
- acceptance of additional work
- price setting
- optimum use of scarce resources

The key to each of these, as we shall see shortly, is the contribution from the sale of units of output. Contribution is calculated as:

	unit selling price
minus	unit marginal cost
equals	contribution to fixed costs and profit

We have already seen, in Chapter 11, how contribution is used as part of the calculation for break-even.

MAKE OR BUY DECISIONS

A make or buy decision is a management decision whether to make a product, or supply a service, 'in-house', or to buy in the product/service from an outside supplier.

Examples of make or buy decisions include:

- a car manufacturer needing many different components to make the car – some components will be manufactured in-house while others will be bought from outside suppliers
- a hospital facing the decision whether to provide a payroll accounting service itself, or to buy in the service from an outside contractor

There are a number of considerations before taking a make or buy decision, including:

- for how long will we need this product or service?
- can we find a supplier to make the product or provide the service for us?
- is the supplier's product or service to the specification that we require?
- how much do we want to be reliant on another business?
- what are the costs involved in the decision and the effect on our profits?
- what happens if there are problems with the supplier, eg poor quality, late delivery?
- what happens at the end of the make or buy contract?

the effect on fixed and variable costs

Make or buy decisions affect the cost structure of the business, particularly the relationship between fixed and variable costs. For example, a business seeking to increase output can:

- either expand its own production facilities – which will mainly affect its fixed costs (ie rent of premises, depreciation of new machinery and equipment), with a smaller effect on variable costs

- or buy in from outside suppliers – which will mainly affect its variable costs (ie bought in units are classed as direct materials), with a smaller effect on fixed costs

The first course of action takes a long-term view and assumes that the increase in production can be sustained for a number of years. The second course of action is rather more flexible (ie the number of units bought in can be varied to meet demand) and could be either a long-term arrangement, or for the short-term with, perhaps, the possibility of expanding in-house production facilities in the future.

the use of marginal costing

When considering make or buy decisions, comparisons need to be made between:

- the marginal cost of the product from in-house supply

  and

- the price quoted by the outside supplier

The lower price is, in financial terms, the better choice; however there may well be non-financial aspects to consider, such as quality, reliability, etc.

opportunity cost

Opportunity cost is the benefit that is foregone when a particular course of action is taken.

In make or buy decisions we must consider the resources used (eg factory or office space, machines and equipment) when goods or services are provided in-house. The use of these resources may cause other work to be lost or curtailed. The loss of contribution from this other work needs to be added to the marginal cost in order to make the decision. The make or buy decision is expressed now as a comparison between:

- the marginal cost of making the product in-house, plus the contribution from lost or curtailed work

  and

- the price quoted by the outside supplier

The lower price is the better choice in financial terms.

WORKED EXAMPLE: A MAKE OR BUY DECISION

situation

Wyvern Alarms Limited manufactures high quality security alarms called 'Wyvern Super'. These are sold to alarm companies who install and maintain them.

Until now, Wyvern Alarms has been proud of its in-house production line – materials are bought in, and all manufacturing and assembly is carried out at its factory in Wyvern. The company is finding that demand for its products is increasing. The point has been reached when decisions must be taken about buying in components from outside suppliers.

The management accountant of Wyvern Alarms has obtained a price from a potential supplier for control boxes. These comprise a metal box with a hinged, lockable cover. The box is spray painted in white, with the company logo applied by means of a transfer. It is not considered that quality will be compromised if this item is bought in from an outside supplier.

These are the two alternatives:

1   The cost of making each control box in-house at the current level of 5,000 units each year is:

	£
direct materials	2.50
direct labour	5.50
variable overheads	1.50
fixed overheads	5.50
total cost	15.00

There is no other use for the specialist production machinery required to make this product.

2   An outside supplier has quoted a price of £10 per unit (based on Wyvern's requirements of 5,000 units each year).

Should the management of Wyvern Alarms 'make' or 'buy' ?

solution

The marginal cost of producing each control box is:

	£
direct materials	2.50
direct labour	5.50
variable overheads	1.50
marginal cost	9.50

The comparison is then:

*   marginal cost of in-house manufacturer, £9.50 x 5,000 units = £47,500

*   price quoted by outside supplier, £10 x 5,000 units   = £50,000

As there is no other use for the production machinery currently being used, the decision should be to continue making this component in-house.

Note that if there was an alternative use for the production machinery, the comparison then becomes:

*   marginal cost of in-house manufacture, plus contribution from alternative work

*   price quoted by outside supplier

In this Worked Example, a contribution of more than £2,500 per year from the production machinery, would make the buy-in a better financial proposition. However, before making the final decision, the management of Wyvern Alarms need to consider social accounting issues, such as making employees redundant, the effect on their local community – see Chapter 18 for a fuller discussion of these issues.

ACCEPTANCE OF ADDITIONAL WORK

Once a business is profitable at its current level of output, it can make additional sales at a selling price above marginal cost, but below absorption cost, and so increase its profits. However, in order to increase profits, the additional sales must be sourced from spare production capacity within the business. For example, if in order to sell 1,000 extra units, a new factory has to be bought with a production capacity of one million units, then it seems unlikely that the additional sales will prove to be profitable!

The key to increasing profit from the acceptance of additional work is to ensure that a contribution to profit is made from the additional work. The Worked Example below illustrates this principle.

WORKED EXAMPLE: ACCEPTING ADDITIONAL WORK

situation

The Wyvern Bike Company produces 100 bikes a week, and sells them for £200 each. Its costs are as follows:

weekly costs for producing 100 bikes

	£
Direct materials (£40 per bike)	4,000
Direct labour (£50 per bike)	5,000
PRIME COST	9,000
Overheads (fixed)	5,000
TOTAL COST	14,000

The management of the company has been approached by a mail order warehouse which wishes to buy:

* *either* 50 bikes each week at a price of £120

* *or* 100 bikes each week at a price of £80

The bikes can be produced in addition to existing production, with no increase in overheads. The additional work is not expected to affect the company's existing sales. How would you advise the management?

solution

The *absorption cost* of producing one bike is £140 (£14,000 ÷ 100 bikes). The mail order warehouse is offering either £120 or £80 per bike. On the face of it, with an absorption cost of £140, both orders should be rejected. However, as there will be no increase in fixed overheads, we can use *marginal costing* to help with decision-making.

The *marginal cost* per bike is £90 (direct materials £40, plus direct labour £50 per bike), and so any contribution, ie selling price less marginal cost, will be profit:

- **50 bikes at £120 each**

  Although below absorption cost, the offer price of £120 is above the marginal cost of £90 and increases profit by the amount of the £30 extra contribution, ie (£120 – £90) x 50 bikes = £1,500 extra profit.

- **100 bikes at £80 each**

  This offer price is below absorption cost of £140 and marginal cost of £90; therefore there will be a fall in profit if this order is undertaken of (£80 – £90) x 100 bikes = £1,000 reduced profit.

weekly profit statements	Existing production of 100 units	Existing production + 50 units @ £120 each	Existing production + 100 units @ £80 each
	£	£	£
Sales revenue (per week):			
100 bikes at £200 each	20,000	20,000	20,000
50 bikes at £120 each	–	6,000	–
100 bikes at £80 each	–	–	8,000
	20,000	26,000	28,000
Less production costs:			
Direct materials (£40 per unit)	4,000	6,000	8,000
Direct labour (£50 per unit)	5,000	7,500	10,000
Overheads (fixed)	5,000	5,000	5,000
PROFIT	6,000	7,500	5,000

The conclusion is that the first order from the mail order warehouse should be undertaken, and the second declined.

summary

The general rule about accepting additional work is that there needs to be a contribution to profit. Other factors to consider are:

- the additional work should not take the place of products or services that can be sold at above absorption cost
- there must be spare capacity to produce the additional products or services

- customers who pay normal prices must not be aware of the special prices being offered for additional work

- if marginal costing is used for special prices, it may be difficult to maintain normal prices for other customers

- a customer buying at special prices may undercut the prices charged by other customers who have bought at normal prices

In the short-term a business may choose to sell some of its output at below marginal cost, ie at a negative contribution. This will have the effect of reducing profit but might be done in order to:

- use as a 'loss leader' (a product sold cheaply, often below cost) to attract customers who, it is expected, will then buy other, profitable, items

- develop relations with new customers and/or markets, with the intention of increasing prices in the future

- sell a range of products, eg a garage might service cars cheaply with the expectation that any faults found will be repaired at their normal charges

- keep together a skilled workforce in times of economic slowdown

- ensure continual availability of the product or service

Note that a negative contribution is only sustainable in the short-term and, in the longer-term, additional work must make a contribution to profit.

PRICE SETTING

A price is the amount of money that is agreed between a buyer and a seller which enables the exchange of a product – goods or a service – to take place.

There are three main factors that a business must consider when deciding the price at which to sell its products or services:

- *the need to make a profit* – in the long-term, selling price must be higher than total cost

- *prices of competing products or services* – the selling price is determined largely by what other suppliers of the product or service are charging

- *under-used capacity* – selling some of the output at a cut price, eg selling unsold tickets cheaply at a theatre just before the performance, or off-peak travel on trains and buses

For each of these factors which determine price, there is a related pricing strategy:

- *the need to make a profit* – the pricing strategy is *cost-plus pricing*

- *prices of competing products* – the pricing strategy is *market led pricing/competitive pricing*

- *under-used capacity* – the pricing strategy is *marginal cost/contribution pricing*

cost-plus pricing

The calculation for cost-plus pricing, which has been seen already in Chapter 13, is:

cost price   +   profit   =   selling price

Cost is usually calculated on the basis of absorption cost, but can also be on the basis of marginal cost.

market-led pricing

When a business has a product or service for which there is considerable demand and over which it has sole rights, it may be able to set and maintain its own price level (subject to government intervention on the grounds of monopoly pricing). Most businesses, however, must set their prices in comparison with other suppliers of the same or similar products and services – in other words, they must use competitive pricing. In the economy of the free market, buyers will tend to buy from the supplier than can produce the product, or supply the service, at least cost. Thus, in an ideal world (but not always in reality), inefficient suppliers will be forced out of the market and, in order to re-establish themselves, will have to look carefully at their costings and/or production techniques.

There are many examples of market-led or competitive pricing, some of which benefit the buyer:

* ***the price of similar products***

  Supermarket shelves, as an example, often contain 'rival' brands of the same product, eg tins of baked beans, cans of cola drink. Whilst each manufacturer will always tell you that their product is infinitely superior to that of their rivals, market-led pricing means that there is little, if any, difference in price. Whilst supermarket 'own brand' products are usually cheaper, the pricing is still market-led, ie a smaller margin below the price of branded goods.

* ***the price of seasonal products, such as fresh fruit***

  Usually the market leads the price, eg a supplier of strawberries cannot charge significantly more than the competitors.

* ***price cutting***

  In recent years there have been many examples of price cutting started by one retailer and then spreading across the whole industry, ie the price cutting has been market led. Examples include air fares, clothes and holidays.

marginal cost/contribution pricing

Marginal cost is useful in price setting because it determines the minimum price to be charged for products or services. This is appropriate for pricing additional sales at a special reduced rate after sales have already been made at the normal selling price. The rule is simple: once fixed costs have been covered by the contribution from normal sales, then additional sales must cover, as a minimum, their variable costs – at above variable cost, the contribution will be profit.

Optimum Use of Scarce Resources

Scarce resources, or limiting factors, are those aspects of a business which limit output.

Examples of scarce resources include:

- availability of materials
- availability of skilled labour
- availability of productive capacity, eg machine hours
- availability of storage facilities
- finance
- the quantity of the output which can be sold – whether a manufactured product or a service

At any one time there is usually one main scarce resource. It is essential to minimise its effect by optimising resources and maximising profit. After one scarce resource has been dealt with, another one then affects the business – for example, once a shortage of materials has been resolved, the scarce resource might well become a lack of skilled labour.

Where a business sells more than one product, under normal circumstances it will be best to switch output to the product that gives the highest contribution in relation to sales. For example, a company makes two products, Exe and Wye, with the following costs and revenues:

	Product	Exe £	Wye £
	Selling price per unit	100	200
less	Unit variable costs	60	140
equals	Contribution per unit	40	60

With no limiting factors, the company should concentrate on making and selling product Exe. The reason for this is that the contribution/sales percentage is 40 per cent (£40 ÷ £100) when compared with product Wye, where it is 30 per cent (£60 ÷ £200).

Where there is a scarce resource, for example the availability of skilled labour, a business will switch production to the product which gives the highest contribution from each unit of the limiting factor (eg contribution per direct labour hour). Thus the key to optimising the use of scarce resources is to:

maximise the contribution per unit of scarce resources

Following this rule will always maximise profits. Where there is a maximum level of output for the selected product, this product should be produced to the full if possible, and any units of scarce resources which remain unused should be 'spilled over' to the next best product. This is illustrated in the Worked Example which follows.

WORKED EXAMPLE: OPTIMUM USE OF SCARCE RESOURCES

situation

Sound Systems Limited is a small company which makes reproduction radios to 1930s' designs (but with 21st century sound quality!). Two models are made – the 'Windsor' and the 'Buckingham'. Both products require skilled direct labour which cannot be increased in the short term. Demand for the company's products is increasing rapidly and, while the company is taking steps to train new employees, the managing director is unsure of the 'mix' of products that should be produced each week.

Costs and revenues are as follows:

		Windsor	Buckingham
		£	£
	Selling price per unit	50	100
less	Unit variable costs	30	70
equals	Contribution per unit	20	30

- each radio takes two direct labour hours to make
- the number of direct labour hours each week is 260
- the weekly fixed overheads of the business are £2,000
- demand for the Windsor model is currently 100 radios per week, and for the Buckingham it is 80 radios per week

Give the production manager your recommendations for next week's production, supporting your views with a forecast profit statement.

solution

Ignoring, for the moment, the scarce resource of direct labour, the better model for the company to produce is the Windsor, because this gives a higher contribution/sales percentage:

- Windsor: £20 contribution on £50 of sales = 40 per cent
- Buckingham: £30 contribution on £100 of sales = 30 per cent

However, as direct labour is the scarce resource, the company should maximise the contribution from each hour of direct labour, as follows:

		Windsor	Buckingham
	Contribution per unit	£20	£30
	Direct labour hours per unit	2	2
equals	Contribution per direct labour hour	£10	£15
	Ranking	2	1

To optimise use of the scarce resource of direct labour, the company should produce all of the Buckingham model that can be sold, ie 80 per week, as follows:

	Total hours available per week	260
less	80 units of Buckingham at 2 hours each	160
equals	hours remaining to produce units of Windsor	100

Therefore production of Windsor will be 100 hours ÷ 2 hours = 50 units per week

The weekly production plan of Sound Systems will be 50 units of Windsor and 80 units of Buckingham. However, by taking this action, insufficient Windsor models will be produced to meet demand. This may make it difficult to re-establish the Windsor in the market when full production of this model can be resumed following the completion of training of new employees.

The forecast profit statement for next week will be as follows:

		Windsor £	Buckingham £	Total £
	Sales revenue:			
	50 Windsor at £50 per unit	2,500		2,500
	80 Buckingham at £100 per unit		8,000	8,000
		2,500	8,000	10,500
less	Variable costs:			
	50 Windsor at £30 per unit	1,500		1,500
	80 Buckingham at £70 per unit		5,600	5,600
equals	Contribution	1,000	2,400	3,400
less	Fixed overheads			2,000
equals	Profit			1,400

summarising the use of scarce resources

The procedures for decision-making with scarce resources are:

- calculate the *contribution per unit of scarce resource* to make the decision as to which product to manufacture – the one with the highest contribution per unit of scarce resource will maximise profits

- calculate the profit statement using the *number of units of output* (and not the number of units of scarce resource)

- where there is a maximum level of output for the selected product, use as much of the scarce resource as possible, and then 'spill over' any unused scarce resource to the next best product (as in the Worked Example)

Note that, where there are scarce resources, fewer of one or more products will be produced causing a shortfall in the market. It may be difficult to re-establish these products when full production can be resumed after the availability of the scarce resource has been resolved. The problem is that often customers want availability of all products and, if one isn't fully available, they won't buy the others (think of a store closing its carpet department and the effect on sales in the furniture department).

MARGINAL COSTING: OTHER POINTS

In this chapter we have seen how marginal costing techniques can be useful in decision-making. Nevertheless, there are a number of points that must be borne in mind:

* **fixed costs must be covered**

    A balance needs to be struck between the output that is sold at above marginal cost and the output that is sold at absorption cost. The total contribution from output needs to cover the fixed costs of the business and provide a profit.

* **separate markets for marginal cost**

    It is sensible business practice to separate out the markets where marginal cost is used. For example, a business would not quote a price based on absorption cost to retailer A and a price based on marginal cost to retailer B, when A and B are both in the same town! It would be better to seek new markets in which to sell with prices based on marginal cost.

* **effect on customers**

    One of the problems of using marginal cost pricing to attract new business is that it is difficult to persuade the customer to pay closer to, or above, absorption cost later on. Thus one of the dangers of using marginal cost is that profit margins can be squeezed quite dramatically if the technique is used too widely.

* **problems of product launch on marginal cost basis**

    There is great temptation in business to launch a new product at the keenest possible price – below absorption cost (but above marginal cost). If the product is highly successful, it could well alter the cost structure of the business. However, it could also lead to the collapse of sales of older products so that most of the company's sales are derived from output priced on the marginal cost basis – it may then be difficult to increase prices to above absorption cost levels.

* **special edition products**

    Many businesses use marginal costing techniques to sell off older products at a keen price. For example, car manufacturers with a new model due in a few months' time will package the old model with 'special edition' badging and sell it at a low price (but above marginal cost)

CHAPTER SUMMARY

- A business, seeking to make a profit, must cover its costs and make a profit from the selling prices of its output.

- Cost-plus pricing adds a percentage to absorption cost.

- Marginal cost is the cost of producing one extra unit of output.

- Marginal costing techniques can help with decision-making.

- A make or buy decision is a management decision whether to make a product/supply a service 'in-house', or to buy in the product/service from an outside supplier.

- Make or buy decisions compare the marginal cost of the product from in-house supply with the price quoted by the outside supplier.

- Acceptance of additional work is where a business is able to sell output as 'special orders' at a price above marginal cost, but below absorption cost – always provided that the fixed costs are covered by the contribution from normal sales.

- The factors to consider when setting a selling price for products or services are:
  - the need to make a profit
  - prices of competing products or services
  - the availability of any under-used capacity

- The main pricing strategies are:
  - cost-plus pricing
  - market-led pricing/competitive pricing
  - marginal cost/contribution pricing

- Scarce resources, or limiting factors, are those aspects of a business which limit output. Scarce resources should be allocated to the output which maximises the contribution per unit of scarce resources.

- Using marginal costing techniques, decision makers must bear in mind:
  - fixed costs must be covered
  - separate markets for marginal cost
  - effect on customers
  - problems of product launch on a marginal cost basis
  - special edition products

In the next chapter we focus on standard costing, one of the four main methods of costing, and look at its purpose, advantages, and its role in variance analysis.

QUESTIONS

visit
www.osbornebooks.co.uk
to take an online test

An asterisk (*) after the question number means that the answer is given at the end of this book.

14.1 Investigate applications of marginal costing in a service business, for example:

- – hotel
- – transport
- – cinema or theatre
- – holiday companies

- Identify the benefits and possible restrictions to customers
- Identify the benefits and potential problems for the supplier

14.2 Pentland Pumps Limited manufactures electric pumping equipment used in industry and agriculture. At present all parts are made in-house from raw materials. The company is considering buying in pump motors from an outside supplier in order to release facilities for a new product, an 'olde worlde' handpump for decorative (and practical) use.

The following information is available:

- the cost of making each pump motor in-house at the current level of production of 3,500 pumps per year is:

	£
direct materials	40.00
direct labour	25.00
variable overheads	20.00
fixed overheads	15.00
total cost	100.00

- an outside supplier has quoted a price of £95 per motor
- if pump motors are bought in from an outside supplier, the company will be able to make 750 'olde worlde' handpumps each year, with a selling price of £250 per unit and variable costs of £150 per unit

You are to advise the management of Pentland Pumps Limited whether or not, in financial terms, the motors should be bought in from the outside supplier

14.3* Westfield Limited makes 2,000 units of product Exe each month. The company's costs are:

monthly costs for making 2,000 units of Exe (£)	
direct materials	6,000
direct labour	4,000
production overheads (fixed)	8,000
total cost	18,000

Each unit of Exe is sold for £12.

The management of the company has been approached by a buyer who wishes to purchase:

- *either* 200 units of Exe each month at a price of £6 per unit

- *or* 500 units of Exe each month at a price of £4 per unit

The extra units can be produced in addition to existing production, with no increase in overheads. The special order is not expected to affect the company's existing sales. How would you advise the management?

You are to prepare monthly profit statements showing current profits and the expected profits from the two proposed options. Using this data, advise the management of Westfield Limited as to the best course of action.

14.4* Popcan Limited manufactures and sells a soft drink which the company sells at 25p per can. Currently output is 150,000 cans per month, which represents 75 per cent of production capacity. The company has an opportunity to use the spare capacity by producing the product for a supermarket chain which will sell it under their own label. The supermarket chain is willing to pay 18p per can.

You are to prepare, from the data set out below, monthly profit statements showing current profits and the expected profits from the new proposal. Using this data, advise the management of Popcan Limited as to whether the supermarket's offer should be accepted.

POPCAN LIMITED	
Costs per can	
	pence
Direct materials	5
Direct labour	5
Production overheads (variable)	4
Production overheads (*fixed)	6
* fixed production overheads are apportioned on the basis of current output	

14.5   Mercia Airways is a local airline which flies to short-haul destinations within the UK and Europe. The costs of weekly flight MA 005 to Rome, which uses a 100 seater aircraft are as follows:

direct materials	£12.50 per passenger
direct labour	£10.00 per passenger
direct expenses	£2.50 per passenger
fixed overheads	£3,500 per flight

For next week's flight, sixty seats have been sold at a standard-class fare of £100 each.

REQUIRED

(a)   Calculate the absorption cost per seat on this flight with sixty seats sold.

(b)   Calculate the marginal cost per seat.

(c)   Calculate the profit or loss if no further tickets are sold for this flight.

(d)   Refer to the text below and advise the marketing manager whether either of the two suggested possibilities should be considered; explain your reasoning, and illustrate your answer with profit statements.

The marketing manager thinks it unlikely that any further standard-class fares will be sold. There are two possibilities that she must consider:

*   to release the surplus seats to a firm that sells cheap flights: the airline will receive £45 for each seat sold and, from past experience, the marketing manager expects thirty seats to be sold

*   to sell all forty spare seats to a local newspaper, which will offer them as prizes for a 'spot-the-ball' competition: the newspaper will pay £35 per seat

---

14.6   The Last Company Ltd is famous for its 'Snowdon' range of hill-walking boots. The management of the company is considering the production for next year and has asked for help with certain financial decisions.

The following information is available:

wholesale selling price (per pair)	£60
direct materials (per pair)	£20
direct labour (per pair)	£18
fixed overheads	£200,000 per year

The company is planning to manufacture 12,500 pairs of boots next year.

REQUIRED

(a)   You are to calculate:

- the absorption cost per pair

- the marginal cost per pair

- the profit or loss if 12,500 pairs of boots are sold

(b)   An internet sales company, Zambesi Ltd, has approached The Last Company Ltd with a view to selling the 'Snowdon' boot through its website. Zambesi Ltd offers two contracts:

- either 2,500 pairs of boots at £45 per pair

- or 5,000 pairs of boots at £37 per pair

As The Last Company Ltd usually sells through specialist shops, it is not expected that 'normal' sales will be affected. These 'special orders' are within the capacity of the factory, and fixed overheads will remain unchanged.

You are to advise the management whether these offers should be accepted. Illustrate your answer with profit statements.

14.7* Select a business with which you are familiar.

(a)   Investigate the scarce resources currently affecting the business. Suggest possible solutions.

(b)   Identify the opportunities for using marginal costing to increase sales.

14.8* Dean Limited makes two products – Aye and Bee. Both products are made from the same type of direct materials. These materials are currently in short supply. At present the company can obtain only 500 kilos of the direct materials each week. The production manager wishes to know the 'mix' of products that should be produced each week. The information available is:

	Product	Aye	Bee
	Selling price per unit	£150	£200
less	Unit variable costs	£120	£150
equals	Contribution per unit	£30	£50
	Kilos of direct materials per unit	2	4
	Demand per week (in units)	200	150

The weekly fixed overheads of the business are £4,000.

REQUIRED

Advise the production manager of your recommendations for next week's production. Support your views with a forecast profit statement.

14.9* Sesame Shoes Limited manufactures shoes at its factory in Wyvern. It has three shoe ranges – the 'Madrid', the 'Paris', and the 'Rome'. The expected monthly costs and sales information for each range is as follows:

Product	'Madrid'	'Paris'	'Rome'
Sales and production units*	5,000	3,000	500
Machine hours per month	2,500	1,200	375
Total sales revenue	£150,000	£120,000	£30,000
Total direct materials	£50,000	£45,000	£10,000
Total direct labour	£25,000	£24,000	£6,000
Total variable overheads	£10,000	£9,000	£1,250

* note: a unit is a pair of shoes

The total expected monthly fixed costs relating to the production of all shoes are £72,800.

REQUIRED

(a) Complete the table below to show for each product range the expected contribution per unit.

Product	'Madrid' £	'Paris' £	'Rome' £
Selling price per unit			
Less: Unit variable costs			
Direct materials			
Direct labour			
Variable overheads			
Contribution per unit			

(b)   If the company only manufactures the 'Madrid' range, calculate the number of units it would need to make and sell each month to cover the fixed costs of £72,800.

(c)   The breakdown of a machine used in the manufacture of shoes has reduced available machine time from 4,075 to 3,000 hours. The finance director asks you to calculate the contribution of each unit (pair of shoes) per machine hour.

Using the data from (a), complete the table below.

Product	'Madrid'	'Paris'	'Rome'
Contribution per unit			
Machine hours per unit			
Contribution per machine hour			

(d)   Using the data from (c), calculate how many units of each of product ranges 'Madrid', 'Paris', and 'Rome' the company should make and sell in order to maximise its profits using 3,000 machine hours.

14.10   Wyvern Porcelain Limited produces decorated porcelain figures which are sold in quality shops both in the UK and abroad. The figures are especially popular with holidaymakers from other countries who visit the factory and see the figures being made.

There are three ranges of porcelain figures – 'people', 'animals' and 'birds'. The expected monthly costs and sales information for each range is as follows:

Product	'People'	'Animals'	'Birds'
Sales and production units*	1,000	2,000	2,700
Labour hours per month	1,500	1,000	900
Total sales revenue	£60,000	£55,000	£47,250
Total direct materials	£5,000	£6,000	£5,400
Total direct labour	£15,000	£10,000	£9,000
Total variable overheads	£10,000	£9,000	£8,000

* note: a unit is a porcelain figure

The total expected monthly fixed costs relating to the production of all porcelain figures are £45,400.

REQUIRED

(a)   Complete the table below to show for each product range the expected contribution per unit.

Product	'People' £	'Animals' £	'Birds' £
Selling price per unit			
Less: Unit variable costs			
Direct materials			
Direct labour			
Variable overheads			
Contribution per unit			

(b)   If the company only produces the 'People' range, calculate the number of units it would need to make and sell each month to cover the fixed costs of £45,400.

(c)   Making and painting the porcelain figures are highly skilled tasks, and unskilled labour cannot be brought in to cover for absent staff.

Unfortunately, because of staff illness, the available labour hours are reduced from 3,400 to 2,800. The finance director asks you to calculate the contribution of each unit (porcelain figure) per labour hour.

Using the data from (a), complete the table below.

Product	'People'	'Animals'	'Birds'
Contribution per unit			
Labour hours per unit			
Contribution per labour hour			

(d)   Using the data from (c), calculate how many units of each of product ranges 'People', 'Animals' and 'Birds' the company should make and sell in order to maximise its profits using 2,800 labour hours.

14.11*   Mark Maxmus Ltd is the sole manufacturer of the MxMs.

The company currently produces 400 units a month.

The direct costs per unit are:

		£
Materials	(2 metres @ £3 per metre)	6
Labour	(2 hours @ £8 per hour)	16

The total indirect fixed costs for each month are £2,840.

The selling price is always set at 120% of the total cost per unit.

If production exceeds 500 units in any one month, overtime will be paid at a rate of £10 per hour for each extra hour.

The company has received an order from a new customer. This order will increase total production for each of the following months to 560 units.

REQUIRED

(a)   Distinguish between direct costs and indirect costs.

(b)   Calculate the total cost per unit if the order is accepted and 560 units are produced.

(c)   Calculate the change between the new selling price and the original selling price.

(d)   Explain one effect of this change in selling price on the company's present customers.

Assessment and Qualifications Alliance (AQA), 2006

14.12   Drew Armstrong manufactures and sells two products, an ink pen and a novelty ruler.

	Selling price per unit	Direct costs per unit	Expected demand for the next 3 months
Ink pen	£8.00	£6.20	4,200
Novelty ruler	£2.50	£0.60	8,400

Drew is working at full capacity but, due to staff long-term sickness, he can only produce 3,000 ink pens and 6,000 novelty rulers over this period.

He is worried that he will lose customers during these three months. Drew can buy the deficit of goods from a rival supplier who will supply the ink pen for £3.10 and the novelty ruler for £0.40. However, these goods will only be partly completed. The ink pen will require extra costs of £4.00 per pen and the novelty ruler will require extra costs of £1.10 per ruler.

REQUIRED

(a) (i) Define the term 'contribution'.

(ii) State the formula used to calculate contribution per unit.

(b) Calculate the **total** contribution to satisfy expected demand:

(i) if Drew manufactures both products himself and there is no staff sickness;

(ii) if there is staff sickness and he buys in the deficit of goods.

(c) Explain whether Drew Armstrong should buy in the deficit of goods for the next three months.

> At the end of the three months, Drew finds out that the staff on long-term sickness leave cannot return in the immediate future. It will be expensive to appoint and train replacement staff. Alternatively, he can purchase a new machine that will significantly increase production. The purchase of the new machine will be financed by a long-term loan. Drew believes that, after installation, he can make 5% of the workforce redundant and retrain some of the remaining staff.

REQUIRED

(d) Explain the possible effects of the purchase of the new machine on the current staff.

Assessment and Qualifications Alliance (AQA), 2006

14.13   Halls Hampers Ltd manufactures a single product. The company is located in a deprived area of a city. The year ended 31 May 2007, was a difficult year with the factory only operating at 60% capacity. The company needs to raise £80,000 to cover debts.

Additional information for the year ended 31 May 2007

Selling price per unit	£40
Annual sales in units	12,000
Variable cost per unit	£12
Overheads (of which £18,000 is variable)	£256,500

Orders have been received from two new overseas customers. However, only one new order can be accepted. Whichever order is undertaken, a new overseas agent will be required at an annual cost of £14,000.

Order JJH

For 6,000 units for a total invoice price of £180,000.

A delivery charge will be payable of 2% of the selling price. Modifications will have to be made to some of the factory machines at a cost of £19,000. Consequently, some of the staff will need to be retrained at a cost of £8,000. Future orders from this customer are almost guaranteed.

Order JHB

For 8,000 modified units for a total invoice price of £256,000.

A delivery charge will be payable of 2.5% of the selling price. Extra temporary staff will be required at a cost of £28,000. Once the order is finished, these staff will no longer be needed. No further orders are expected from this customer.

For the year ending 31 May 2008 there are not expected to be many changes to the sales price or the amount of overheads. However the variable cost is expected to rise to £14 per unit.

The new order chosen will be in addition to the current level of sales.

REQUIRED

(a)   Distinguish between fixed, semi-variable and variable costs. Give one example of each.

(b)   Define the term 'contribution'.

(c)   Calculate the total contribution for the year ended 31 May 2007.

(d)   Calculate the break-even point in units.

(e)   Prepare comparative profit statements for **each** new order for the year ending 31 May 2008.

(f)   Discuss which order Halls Hampers Ltd should accept. Give reasons for your choice.

Assessment and Qualifications Alliance (AQA), Second Specimen Paper for 2010

14.14   C J Lewison Ltd manufactures two products, Caz and Jaz.

The following information is available.

	Caz	Jaz
Direct materials	3 kg @ £6 per kg	2 kg @ £6 per kg
Direct labour	2 hrs @ £8 per hour	3 hrs @ £8 per hour

The factory operates at full capacity, using 42,000 labour hours.

Demand during the year is expected to be:

Caz	12,000 units @ £42 per unit
Jaz	8,000 units @ £45 per unit

REQUIRED

(a)   Calculate the contribution per unit per labour hour.

(b)   Calculate the optimum production plan that CJ Lewison Ltd should implement to maximise annual profit.

In order to meet total demand for its products, the company is considering buying-in from other suppliers. The costs of buying-in the units are:

Caz	£35 per unit + 10% delivery charge
Jaz	£38 per unit + 15% delivery charge

REQUIRED

(c)   Explain whether C J Lewison Ltd should buy-in the shortfall in expected demand.

Assessment and Qualifications Alliance (AQA), 2005

14.15* Stewart Ltd manufactures three products: the Meton, the Nevon and the Obon.

The following budgeted information is available for the coming year.

	Meton	Nevon	Obon
Maximum budgeted production	40,000 units	30,000 units	15,000 units
Direct materials cost per kg	£5	£6	£3
Material kilograms per unit	4 kg	3 kg	5.5 kg
Direct labour cost per hour	£8	£8	£8
Labour hours per unit	1 hour	0.50 hour	0.25 hour
Selling price per unit	£48	£49	£54

The budgeted total overheads for the year are £822,500.

REQUIRED

(a)   Calculate the total labour hours necessary to achieve budgeted production.

(b)   Calculate the overhead absorption rate for the total overheads of £822,500. Use the direct labour hour basis.

(c)   Calculate the direct cost per unit and the total cost per unit of **each** of the products, using absorption costing.

(d)   Calculate the optimum production plan, using the contribution per limiting factor per unit, if only 50,000 labour hours are available.

Assessment and Qualifications Alliance (AQA), 2004

14.16   Rist Ltd manufactures two products, JHB1 and JJH2.

The following information is available:

	JHB1	JJH2
Selling price per unit	£50	£50
Labour hours per unit at £8 per hour	4 hours	2 hours
Materials per unit at £4 per metre	2 metres	4 metres
Expected demand	15,000 units	20,000 units

Unfortunately, due to a machine breakdown, there are only 80,000 labour hours available.

Annual fixed costs are expected to be £420,000.

REQUIRED

(a)   Prepare the optimum production plan that would maximise profits.

Any shortfall in the production of either product could be purchased from another supplier at a cost of:

JHB1   £45 each

JJH2   £40 each

REQUIRED

(b)   Explain whether any shortfall should be purchased from this supplier.

(c)   Calculate the total profit if the optimum production plan is used and if any shortfall is purchased.

Assessment and Qualifications Alliance (AQA), Specimen Paper for 2010

15 STANDARD COSTING AND VARIANCE ANALYSIS

This chapter focuses on standard costing, which can be used in conjunction with marginal costing, absorption costing and activity based costing.

Standard costing is used to calculate costs – materials, labour and overheads – in advance of production. It is a way of controlling costs: standard costs are compared with actual costs by calculating variances, and action is taken where appropriate to improve performance.

In this chapter we look at the:

- purpose of standard costing
- advantages and disadvantages of standard costing
- role of standard costing in variance analysis
- main variances for materials, labour and sales
- interrelationships of variances
- reconciliation of budget and actual figures

PURPOSE OF STANDARD COSTING

Standard costing sets pre-determined/budgeted cost for materials, labour and overheads in advance of production.

All businesses need methods of controlling the costs of materials, labour and overheads that go to make up the finished product (we shall see, in Chapter 17, how budgets can be set and controlled). Imagine a factory where the cost and amount of materials to make the product is not known, where the hours of work and rates of pay have not been recorded and where there is no indication of the cost of overheads. Under such circumstances, the costs could not be controlled, and it would be impossible to quote a price for the product to a customer. Therefore many businesses establish a standard or budgeted cost for their output. Thus a standard cost can be calculated for things as diverse as a product manufactured in a factory, a hospital operation, servicing a car and a meal in a restaurant.

Standard costing is ideal for situations where components are identical and manufacturing operations are repetitive.

The standard cost for units of output is calculated or budgeted in advance of production and working on the assumption of either an *ideal standard* (ie no poor quality material, no idle time, no machine breakdowns), or an *attainable standard*, which allows for a pre-determined amount of loss or wastage and a given level of efficiency.

Standard costs are set for:

- **materials**

    The quantity and quality of each type of direct material to be used in production, and the price of such materials is pre-determined. Standard materials cost is the expected quantity and quality of materials multiplied by expected material price.

- **labour**

    The direct labour hours required to manufacture a quantity of goods, and the cost of the labour is pre-determined. Standard labour cost is the expected labour hours multiplied by expected wage rates.

- **overheads**

    The expected quantity of output within a time period divided into the expected overheads will determine the standard overhead cost.

Note that standard costing is used in conjunction with the other costing methods, ie the standard cost is set in advance of production using absorption costing or marginal costing , or activity based costing methods.

advantages and disadvantages of standard costing

The main *advantages of standard costing* are that it can be used:

- to help with *decision-making* – for example, with price setting
- to assist in *planning* – for example, to plan the quantity and cost of resources needed for production
- as a means of *controlling* costs – standard costs are compared with actual costs and variances calculated so that action can be taken by the responsible manager or department when appropriate

In addition to these, there may be other benefits:

- the detailed study of current production techniques that is needed to set up a standard costing system may reveal hidden inefficiencies and unnecessary expenditure
- the close monitoring of costs should increase the awareness of cost consciousness of both employees and management, and encourage them to achieve the standard costs which have been set
- standard costing lends itself to exception reporting – results are reported only when they are outside a pre-set range and so, in this way, major variations from standard are spotted and dealt with quickly, eg with a standard cost of £10,000 a difference of £10 would not be investigated, whereas a £1,000 difference would be investigated, this being the exception

The main *disadvantages of standard costing* are:

- the standard cost of making a product or providing a service may be set incorrectly, leading either to reduced sales because the product is priced too high, or to increased sales which are being sold at too low a price to make a profit

- prices of materials, labour and overheads may fluctuate frequently (eg the price of raw materials) so that the standard cost quickly goes out-of-date

- while a standard cost represents one way of making the product or providing a service there may be others – eg switching production from a labour-intensive process to a machine-intensive production line

- the use of variance analysis may be more complex than a variance from the standard cost, eg the use of better quality materials might lead to increased output and lower labour costs

setting standards

In standard costing, it is important that care should be taken over the setting of standards. Poorly set standards will be of no help to the management of a business when the figures are used in further analysis.

The main departments within an organisation which can provide information to enable standards to be set are:

- **Purchasing**

   The buying department of a business will be able to determine prices, and their expected trends, of materials used.

- **HR (Human Resources)**

   This department will have current wage and salary rates, together with bonus and overtime details, of the various grades of employees; forecasts of changes can also be ascertained.

- **Management services**

   Often called work study, this department will determine the standard amount of time that each work-task in the production process should take.

- **Production**

   This department has overall responsibility for production and will know the quantities of materials required for each unit of production, and the value of production will be linked to the overhead costs.

WORKED EXAMPLE: SETTING A STANDARD COST

situation

AMC Engineering Limited manufactures car bumper mouldings. It has been asked by its major customer, Okassa Limited to prepare a quotation for mouldings for a new car, which is code-named OK10. The elements of cost for 100 mouldings have been calculated by AMC Engineering as:

		£	£

materials: polycarbonate (of specified quality), 200 kilos at £1.10 per kilo

finishing material, 10 litres at £5.40 per litre

labour: 10 hours at £5.75 per hour

3 hours at £8.50 per hour

overheads: 13 hours at £20 per hour

What is the standard cost of producing 100 bumper mouldings?

solution

	£	£
materials		
polycarbonate: 200 kilos at £1.10 per kilo	220.00	
finishing material: 10 litres at £5.40 per litre	54.00	
		274.00
labour		
10 hours at £5.75 per hour	57.50	
3 hours at £8.50 per hour	25.50	
		83.00
		357.00
overheads		
13 hours at £20 per hour		260.00
STANDARD COST		617.00

This standard cost will then be used by AMC Engineering to help establish the selling price to the customer, ie: standard cost + profit = selling price.

THE ROLE OF STANDARD COSTING IN VARIANCE ANALYSIS

A variance is the calculated difference between the standard cost/expected revenue and the actual cost/revenue.

A business using the standard costing system monitors the outcomes by comparing the standard costs set with the results that actually occurred and by calculating variances. An outline of the monitoring process is shown in the diagram which follows on the next page.

THE MONITORING PROCESS FOR STANDARD COSTS

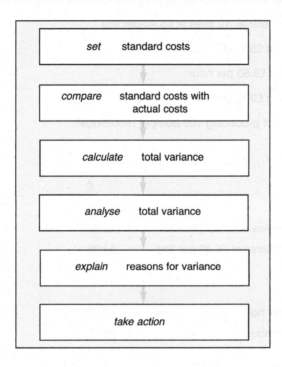

set	standard costs
compare	standard costs with actual costs
calculate	total variance
analyse	total variance
explain	reasons for variance
	take action

The full amount by which the actual cost of a product differs from the standard cost is known as the cost variance. It is calculated by deducting actual cost from standard cost, for example:

cost of making 1,200 garden walling blocks

	£	
standard cost	1,000	
actual cost	980	
COST VARIANCE	20	*FAV

* Variances are either favourable (FAV) or adverse (ADV):
 – favourable is where actual cost is less than standard cost
 – adverse is where actual cost is more than standard cost

The cost variance is made up of the variances for each of the main elements of cost – materials, labour and overheads. Note that we do not study overhead variances in AQA A2 Accounting. The variance for each element can be further analysed into a number of sub-variances which are used to identify the *reasons* for the variance.

A summary of the cost variances and sub-variances for materials and labour is shown in the diagram below.

SUMMARY OF COST VARIANCES AND SUB-VARIANCES FOR MATERIALS AND LABOUR

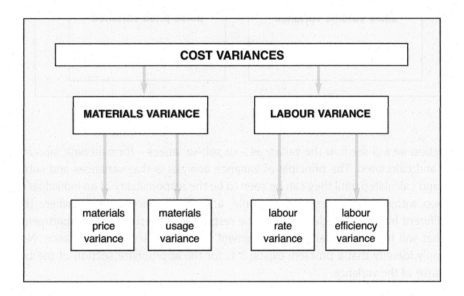

As the diagram shows, the cost variance can result from a combination of different factors:

- **materials variance**
- price variance, caused by a price rise (or price fall) in the cost of materials
- usage variance, caused by a change in the amount of materials used

The materials price variance and usage variance make up the materials variance.

- **labour variance**
- rate variance, caused by a rise in pay rates, or the need to use a different grade of employee (at a higher or lower wage rate)
- efficiency variance resulting in more or less hours worked

The labour rate variance and efficiency variance make up the labour variance.

Tutorial note: overheads variances are not studied in AQA A2 Accounting.

As well as cost variances, there are also variances for sales, as follows:

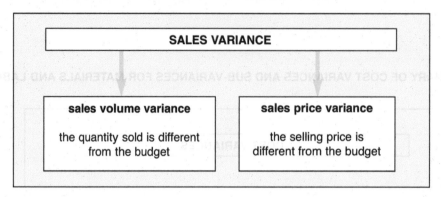

In the next section we will see how the variances – or sub-variances – for materials, labour and sales are identified and calculated. The principle of variance analysis is that variances and sub-variances are identified and calculated until they can be seen to be the responsibility of an individual employee, or small section within the business. For example, a materials price variance, where the cost of materials is different from the standard cost, is the responsibility of the buying department; it is this department that will have to explain to management the reason(s) for any variance. Note that a variance can only identify that a problem exists; it is for the appropriate section of the business to identify the cause of the variance.

MATERIALS VARIANCES

Materials variance is the difference between the standard cost of material and the actual cost of material for the actual production.

The materials variance =

the standard cost of material for the actual output	minus	the actual cost of material

This can be expressed as:

(standard quantity x standard price) – (actual quantity x actual price)

The materials variance is analysed into the **materials price variance** and the **materials usage variance.** As their names suggest, the first sub-variance measures the amount of the cost difference due to the price of material, and the second, the cost difference due to the amount of material used.

material price variance

The material price variance =

| the standard cost of the actual quantity of material used | minus | the actual cost of the actual quantity of material used |

This can be expressed as:

actual quantity x (standard price – actual price)

material usage variance

The material usage variance =

| the standard quantity of material for the actual production at standard price | minus | the actual quantity of material used at standard price |

This can be expressed as:

standard price x (standard quantity – actual quantity)

Tutorial note:

The above formulas have been presented so that positive answers will give rise to favourable variances, and a negative answer will mean the variance will be adverse. However it is best to determine favourable or adverse from logic since formulas can be remembered incorrectly. Simply, if it costs more than standard, or the usage is more than standard, the variance must be adverse.

linking of materials variances

Materials variances are often linked in the following way:

- the use of cheaper material of lower quality may result in a favourable price variance, but may lead to an adverse usage variance as the material may be more difficult to work with and have higher wastage (eg the use of cheap paper in a computer printer may jam the printer)
- the use of more expensive material of higher quality may result in an adverse price variance, but may lead to a favourable usage variance because the material is easier to work with and there is less wastage

WORKED EXAMPLE: CALCULATING MATERIALS VARIANCES

situation

Wyvern Walling is a manufacturer of garden wall blocks. The management accountant has prepared the following costs for a batch of 1,200 wall blocks:

- the standard price of concrete is 25p per kilo
- the standard usage is 1,200 kilos

The results achieved for the latest batch are:

- the actual price of concrete used was 30p per kilo
- the actual usage was 900 kilos

In short, the concrete has cost more, but less has been used for each wall block.

What are the variances for materials costs?

solution

Here both the price and usage have differed from the standard to give the following *materials variance*:

(standard quantity x standard price) – (actual quantity x actual price)

(1,200 kgs x 25p per kg) – (900 kgs x 30p per kg) =

£300 – £270 = £30 FAVOURABLE

While the total materials variance is favourable by £30, as both price *and* usage differ from standard, the sub-variances must be calculated:

material price sub-variance

actual quantity x (standard price – actual price)

900 kgs x (25p – 30p) = £45 ADVERSE

material usage sub-variance

standard price x (standard quantity – actual quantity)

25p x (1,200 kgs – 900 kgs) = £75 FAVOURABLE

MATERIALS VARIANCE £30 FAVOURABLE

For a batch of 1,200 wall blocks, the materials variance is £30 FAV. Although materials have cost more, this extra cost has been more than offset by the reduced usage. It might be that the higher price paid has meant that better quality materials have been purchased resulting in less wastage.

Labour Variances

Labour variance is the difference between the standard cost of labour and the actual cost of labour for the actual production.

The labour variance =

the standard cost of labour for the actual output	minus	the actual cost of labour

This can be expressed as:

(standard hours x standard rate) – (actual hours x actual rate)

Labour variance is analysed into two sub-variances in a similar way to materials variances. The **labour rate variance** measures the labour cost difference due to the rate paid, and the **labour efficiency variance** measures the cost difference due to the amount of labour time used. The concept of labour 'rate' is similar to materials 'price', and labour 'efficiency' is similar to materials 'usage'. This makes remembering the calculation method and interpreting the variances much easier.

labour rate variance

The labour rate variance =

the standard cost of the actual labour hours worked	minus	the actual cost of the actual labour hours worked

This can be expressed as:

actual labour hours x (standard rate – actual rate)

Note how similar this is to the materials price variance.

labour efficiency variance

The labour efficiency variance =

standard labour hours for actual production at standard rate	minus	actual labour hours worked at standard rate

This can be expressed as:

standard rate x (standard hours – actual hours)

This also has a strong resemblance to the materials usage variance; we are simply considering the efficiency of the workforce instead of the quantity of material.

linking of labour variances

Labour variances are often linked in the following way:

- the use of a lower grade of staff may result in a favourable labour rate variance, but may lead to an adverse labour efficiency variance as they will be less skilled at carrying out the work

- the use of a higher grade of staff may result in an adverse labour rate variance, but may lead to a favourable labour efficiency variance as they will be more skilled and so will get the work done more quickly and to a higher standard

WORKED EXAMPLE: CALCULATING LABOUR VARIANCES

situation

The management accountant of Wyvern Walling has prepared the following labour costs for a batch of 1,200 wall blocks.

- the standard cost of direct labour is £6.00 per hour
- the standard time is 50 hours per batch

The results achieved for the latest batch are:

- the actual cost of direct labour was £5.00 per hour
- the actual production took 65 hours

In short, the wage rates are lower, but the employees have not worked as efficiently as expected.

What are the variances for labour costs?

solution

Here both the rate and efficiency have differed from the standard to give the following *labour variance*:

(standard hours x standard rate) – (actual hours x actual rate)

(50 hours x £6.00 per hour) – (65 hours x £5.00 per hour) =

£300 – £325 = £25 ADVERSE

Note: The calculation gives a negative figure of £25; this means that the actual cost is more than the standard cost, ie it is adverse, and profits will reduce. By contrast, a favourable cost variance is a positive figure, ie the actual cost is less than the standard cost, and profits will increase.

While the labour variance is adverse by £25, as both rate and efficiency differ from standard, the sub-variances must be calculated:

labour rate sub-variance

actual hours	x	(standard rate – actual rate)		
65 hours	x	(£6.00 – £5.00)	= £65	FAVOURABLE

labour efficiency sub-variance

standard rate	x	(standard hours – actual hours)		
£6.00	x	(50 hours – 65 hours)	= £90	ADVERSE
LABOUR VARIANCE			= £25	ADVERSE

For a production run of 1,200 wall blocks, the labour variance is £25 ADV. Although the workforce has been paid less (or lower grade employees have been used), this cost saving has been more than offset by lower efficiency.

Sales Variances

Sales variance is the difference between the standard sales revenue and the actual sales revenue for the product or service.

The sales variance =

the standard sales revenue for the product or service	minus	the actual sales revenue for the product or service

This can be expressed as:

(standard quantity x standard price) – (actual quantity x actual price)

The sales variance is analysed into two sub-variances. The **sales volume variance** measures the sales income difference due to the quantity sold, and the **sales price variance** measures the sales income difference due to the price received.

sales volume variance

The sales volume variance =

the standard quantity of sales at the standard selling price	minus	the actual quantity of sales at the standard selling price

This can be expressed as:

standard price x (standard quantity – actual quantity)

sales price variance

The sales price variance =

the actual quantity of sales at the standard selling price	minus	the actual quantity of sales at the actual selling price

This can be expressed as:

actual quantity x (standard price – actual price)

Tutorial note:

Take care when determining whether sales variances are favourable or adverse – it is better to use logic. Simply, if more have been sold than standard, or the selling price is higher than standard, the variance must be favourable.

linking of sales variances

Sales variances are often linked in the following way:

* a lower selling price may result in an adverse sales price variance, but may lead to a favourable sales volume variance as more of the product is sold
* a higher selling price may result in a favourable sales price variance, but may lead to an adverse sales volume variance as customers switch to cheaper products

WORKED EXAMPLE: CALCULATING SALES VARIANCE

situation

The management accountant of Wyvern Walling has prepared the following estimates for sales:

* expected sales next week are 5,000 wall blocks
* expected selling price is £1.00 per wall block

At the end of the week the results are:

* actual sales for the week were 4,500 wall blocks
* actual selling price was £1.10 per wall block

In short, the sales volume is lower than estimated, but the selling price is higher.

What are the variances for sales?

solution

Here both sales volume and price have differed from what was estimated to give the following *sales variance*:

(standard quantity x standard selling price) – (actual quantity sold x actual selling price)

(5,000 wall blocks x £1.00 each)	–	(4,500 wall blocks x £1.10 each)	=
£5,000	–	£4,950	= £50 ADVERSE

This adverse variance will reduce profits by £50. As both sales volume *and* price differ from what was estimated, the sub-variances must be calculated:

sales volume sub-variance

standard price   x   (standard quantity – actual quantity)

£1.00   x   (5,000 – 4,500)   = £500   ADVERSE

sales price sub-variance

actual quantity   x   (standard price – actual price)

4,500   x   (£1.00 – £1.10)   = £450   FAVOURABLE

SALES VARIANCE   = £50   ADVERSE

The sales variance for the week is £50 ADV – the selling price is higher, but fewer wall blocks have been sold. The reduction in the volume of sales has not been offset by the higher selling price.

THE INTERRELATIONSHIPS OF VARIANCES

Once you are familiar with the figures used for calculating variances, and with what each variance means, it is necessary then to consider the possible causes of variances. It should be possible to think your way logically through each situation in order to assess its impact on variances. In the A2 examination you may calculate, or be given, a number of variances and asked to suggest the possible causes. When doing this, think about the *interrelationships of variances* where a situation causes more than one variance. Examples include:

- buying cheaper material of lower quality may result in a favourable price variance but, if there is higher wastage, may lead to an adverse usage variance
- using a higher grade of labour may result in an adverse labour rate variance but, because of the greater skill of the workforce, may lead to a favourable labour efficiency variance
- using better quality material, which is more expensive, may affect not just material variances but labour variances too – a lower grade of labour might be used and, because of the good quality material, labour efficiency might be improved, resulting in both labour sub-variances being favourable

- reducing the selling price of a product is likely to give an adverse sales price variance but, if more is sold, a favourable sales volume variance
- the quality of materials and/or the grade of labour used is likely to affect the sales variances – customers are less likely to buy products made cheaply, but may be prepared to pay a price premium for a well-made quality product

The following table gives examples of possible causes of variances. Please read it carefully, and ensure that you can appreciate the logic of including each item, and its effect. There may be situations where you can envisage the cause creating further variances, since the table is not intended to be exhaustive.

'A' or 'F' refers to whether adverse or favourable variances may result.

	Material price	Material usage	Labour rate	Labour efficiency	Sales volume	Sales price
Possible Cause:						
Poorly set standard	A or F	A or F	A or F	A or F		
Different material supplier	A or F					
Different material quality	A or F	A or F		A or F		
Unexpected discounts	F					
Higher grade staff		F	A	F		
Lower grade staff		A	F	A		
Unexpected pay rise			A			
High inflation	A		A			
Low inflation	F		F			
Improved production machinery		F		F		
Exchange rate fluctuations	A or F					A or F
Reduction in selling price					F	A
Increase in selling price					A	F

RECONCILIATION STATEMENTS

Variances can be brought together in a reconciliation statement which may take the form of:

- a profit reconciliation statement, or
- a cost reconciliation statement, or
- a sales reconciliation statement

Reconciliation statements set out the variances and demonstrate to the management of a business how the forecast profit or cost or revenue has been affected by variances to give the actual profit or cost or revenue for the period. It is then for management to decide which variances require further investigation and, where appropriate, they can be passed to the responsible department with a request for an explanation.

profit reconciliation statement

This statement reconciles the forecast (or budgeted) profit with the actual profit in the following way:

WYVERN WALLING

PROFIT RECONCILIATION STATEMENT FOR THE WEEK ENDED ....

	£	£	£
	ADV	FAV	
Forecast profit			1,000
Material price variance	45		
Material usage variance		75	
Labour rate variance		65	
Labour efficiency variance	90		
	135	140	5
Actual profit			1,005

Note that, for a profit reconciliation statement, favourable cost variances are added to increase profit, while adverse cost variances are deducted to reduce profit.

---

cost reconciliation statement

This statement reconciles the forecast (or budgeted) total cost with the actual total cost in the following way:

WYVERN WALLING

COST RECONCILIATION STATEMENT FOR THE WEEK ENDED ....

	£	£	£
	ADV	FAV	
Forecast total cost			500
Material price variance	45		
Material usage variance		75	
Material rate variance		65	
Labour efficiency variance	90		
	135	140	(5)
Actual total cost			495

Note that, for a cost reconciliation statement, favourable cost variances are deducted because they reduce costs, while adverse cost variances are added because they increase costs.

A further version of the cost reconciliation statement, which is often asked in the AQA examination, is to prepare a statement reconciling the forecast (or budgeted) variable production costs with the actual variable production costs. Here it is necessary to calculate all costs on the basis of actual output rather than budgeted output. This technique is known as *flexing the budget*.

Flexing the budget to actual output is illustrated in the following Worked Example which also requires the calculation of cost sub-variances.

WORKED EXAMPLE: RECONCILING THE VARIANCES

situation

Sally Johnson plc manufactures one product, the SJ 003.

The forecast variable production costs per unit are:

	£
Direct materials (5 metres at £4.00 per metre)	20.00
Direct labour (2 hours 20 minutes at £9.00 per hour)	21.00
	41.00

Forecast production for May 2009 is 5,000 units.

The actual variable production costs for May 2009 were:

	£
Direct materials (32,000 metres)	112,000
Direct labour (13,500 hours)	125,550
	237,550

The actual variable production costs for May were based on an actual production level of 6,000 units.

(a)   Calculate the

– material price and usage variances

– labour rate and efficiency variances

(b)   Prepare a statement which reconciles the forecast variable production costs with the actual variable production costs.

solution

(a)   Material price variance:

32,000 metres x (£4.00 – *£3.50)	= £16,000	FAVOURABLE

* £112,000 ÷ 32,000 metres

Material usage variance:

£4.00 x (*30,000 metres – 32,000 metres)	= £8,000	ADVERSE

* 6,000 units produced x 5 metres

Labour rate variance:

13,500 hours x (£9.00 – *£9.30)	= £4,050	ADVERSE

* £125,550 ÷ 13,500 hours

Labour efficiency variance:

£9.00 x (*14,000 – 13,500 hours)	= £4,500	FAVOURABLE

* 6,000 units produced x 2 hours 20 minutes (note 20 minutes = 1/3rd of an hour) = 12,000 + 2,000 hours = 14,000 hours

(b)

SALLY JOHNSON PLC

VARIABLE PRODUCTION COSTS RECONCILIATION STATEMENT FOR MAY 2009

	£ ADV	£ FAV	£
Materials:			
5 metres x £4.00 per metre x 6,000 units produced			120,000
Labour:			
2 hours 20 minutes x £9.00 per hour x 6,000 units produced			126,000
Forecast variable production costs			246,000
Material price variance		16,000	
Material usage variance	8,000		
Labour rate variance	4,050		
Labour efficiency variance		4,500	
	12,050	20,500	(8,450)
Actual variable production costs			237,550

Notes:

- The reconciliation statement is based on actual production of 6,000 units (and not on the forecast production of 5,000 units), ie the budget is flexed.
- Because we are dealing with costs, adverse variances are added and favourable variances are deducted.
- The management of Sally Johnson plc will wish to study the interrelationships between the labour and materials variances, for example:
  - favourable material price variance could indicate that the material is of poorer quality which has led to an adverse material usage variance because there is more wastage
  - adverse labour rate variance may have been caused because a higher grade of labour has had to be used with the skills to work with poorer quality material, while the more skilled workforce has been more efficient in production

sales reconciliation statement

This statement reconciles the forecast (or budgeted) sales revenue with the actual total revenue in the following way:

WYVERN WALLING

SALES RECONCILIATION STATEMENT FOR THE WEEK ENDED ....

	£
Forecast sales (5,000 wall blocks at £1.00 each)	5,000
Sales volume variance (ADV)	(500)
Sales price variance (FAV)	450
Actual sales (4,500 wall blocks at £1.10 each)	4,950

Note that, for a sales reconciliation statement, favourable sales variances are added to increase revenue, while adverse sales variances are deducted to reduce revenue.

CHAPTER SUMMARY

- Standard costing sets a pre-determined/budgeted cost for materials, labour and overheads in advance of production.

- Standard costing can be used:
  - to help with *decision-making*
  - to assist in *planning*
  - as a means of *controlling* costs

- A variance is the calculated difference between the standard cost/expected revenue and the actual cost/revenue.

- With standard costing, variances and sub-variances can be calculated for materials, labour and overheads. Note that overheads variances are not studied in AQA A2 Accounting.

- Materials variance = (standard quantity x standard price) – (actual quantity x actual price).

- Materials price variance = actual quantity x (standard price – actual price).

- Materials usage variance = standard price x (standard quantity – actual quantity).

- Labour variance = (standard hours x standard rate) – (actual hours x actual rate).

- Labour rate variance = actual labour hours x (standard rate – actual rate).

- Labour efficiency variance = standard rate x (standard hours – actual hours).

- As well as materials and labour variances, there are also variances for sales.

- Sales variance = (standard quantity x standard price) – (actual quantity x actual price).

- Sales volume variance = standard price x (standard quantity – actual quantity).

- Sales price variance = actual quantity x (standard price – actual price).

- The *interrelationships of variances* is where one variance has an effect on another variance.

- Variances can be brought together in a *reconciliation statement* which may take the form of:
  - a profit reconciliation statement, or
  - a cost reconciliation statement, or
  - a sales reconciliation statement

  Such statements demonstrate to the management of a business how the forecast profit/cost/revenue has been affected by variances to give the actual profit/cost/revenue.

- A reconciliation of forecast costs with actual costs requires all costs to be based on actual output (rather than budgeted output) – this is known as flexing the budget.

In the next chapter we look at how business decision-making can be helped by the use of capital investment appraisal techniques.

QUESTIONS

visit
www.osbornebooks.co.uk
to take an online test

An asterisk (*) after the question number means that the answer is given at the end of this book.

15.1   (a)   What is meant by standard costing?

        (b)   What are the main advantages to a business in using such a costing method?

15.2*   Calculate the materials variance for each of the following, and analyse the variance between a price variance and a usage variance. (Indicate whether each variance is *adverse* or *favourable*.)

Material: sheet steel

Standard quantity	0.5 sq metres
Standard price	£5 per sq metre
Actual quantity	0.5 sq metres
Actual price	£6 per sq metre

Material: alloy

Standard quantity	2 kgs
Standard price	£1.50 per kg
Actual quantity	2.5 kgs
Actual price	£1.50 per kg

Material: flour

Standard quantity	0.5 kgs
Standard price	50p per kg
Actual quantity	0.6 kgs
Actual price	40p per kg

Material: gelling fluid

Standard quantity	3 litres
Standard price	£1.50 per litre
Actual quantity	2.5 litres
Actual price	£2 per litre

15.3* Calculate the labour variance for each of the following, and analyse the variance between a rate variance and an efficiency variance. (Indicate whether each variance is *adverse* or *favourable*.)

> *Casting*
>
> | | |
> |---|---|
> | Standard hours | 5 hours |
> | Standard rate | £10 per hour |
> | Actual hours | 6 hours |
> | Actual rate | £10 per hour |
>
> *Machining*
>
> | | |
> |---|---|
> | Standard hours | 2 hours |
> | Standard rate | £13 per hour |
> | Actual hours | 2 hours |
> | Actual rate | £15 per hour |
>
> *Finishing*
>
> | | |
> |---|---|
> | Standard hours | 1 hour |
> | Standard rate | £12 per hour |
> | Actual hours | 1.25 hours |
> | Actual rate | £12.80 per hour |
>
> *Packing*
>
> | | |
> |---|---|
> | Standard hours | 1 hour |
> | Standard rate | £8 per hour |
> | Actual hours | 0.75 hours |
> | Actual rate | £7.20 per hour |

15.4 From the following data you are to calculate:

(a) material price variance

(b) material usage variance

(c) materials variance

(Indicate whether each variance is *adverse* or *favourable*.)

	standard price	standard quantity	actual price	actual quantity
Material A	£5 per kg	100 kgs	£4 per kg	120 kgs
Material B	£20 per unit	120 units	£22 per unit	100 units
Material C	£10 per litre	600 litres	£9 per litre	500 litres
Material D	£2 per metre	300 metres	£3 per metre	250 metres

15.5   From the following data you are to calculate:

(a)   labour rate variance

(b)   labour efficiency variance

(c)   labour variance

(Indicate whether each variance is *adverse* or *favourable*.)

	standard hours	standard rate	actual hours	actual rate
Product 1	8	£10.00	7	£11.00
Product 2	3	£9.00	4	£10.00
Product 3	24	£12.00	30	£11.50
Product 4	12	£16.00	15	£17.00

15.6   The following information is available for the manufacture of 600 ornamental clay garden pots, showing variances for materials and labour:

	standard cost		*actual cost*		*variances*		
		£		£		£	
materials	900 kilos		800 kilos		price	40	ADV
	at 75p per kilo	675	at 80p per kilo	640	usage	75	FAV
					materials	35	FAV
labour	150 hours		140 hours		rate	140	ADV
	at £10.00 per hour	1,500	at £11.00 per hour	1,540	efficiency	100	FAV
					labour	40	ADV

REQUIRED

(a)   Show how the variances for materials and labour have been calculated.

(b)   Explain why the variances may have occurred and how they will be used to monitor costs.

15.7* The directors of Mikhail Manufacturing Ltd forecast a profit of £72,100 for the year ended 31 March 2007. The company operates a system of standard costing.

At the year end, it was discovered that the number of units sold and total sales revenue were as expected. Production levels were also as expected. However, the following information is available for materials and labour.

	Standard	Actual
Material price per metre	£4	£3.50
Metres of material	1,200 metres	1,250 metres
Labour rate per hour	£12	£13
Hours of labour	600 hours	520 hours

REQUIRED

(a) Define the term 'variance', used in standard costing.

(b) Calculate **both** the material price variance **and** the material usage variance for the year ended 31 March 2007.

(c) Calculate **both** the labour rate variance **and** the labour efficiency variance for the year ended 31 March 2007.

(d) Prepare a profit reconciliation statement to calculate the actual profit for the year ended 31 March 2007.

Assessment and Qualifications Alliance (AQA), 2007

15.8 Jayne Bonde plc manufactures one product, the GB007.

The budgeted variable production costs per unit were:

	£
Direct materials (5.5 metres at £8 per metre)	44
Direct labour (4 hours and 20 minutes at £6 per hour)	26
	70

Budgeted production for the month of May was 10,000 units.

The actual costs for May were:

	£
Materials (60,000 metres)	585,000
Labour (60,000 hours)	360,000

The actual costs for May were based on an actual production level of 12,000 units.

REQUIRED

(a)   Calculate:

    (i)   the material price and usage variances

    (ii)   the labour rate and efficiency variances

(b)   Prepare a statement reconciling the budgeted variable production costs with the actual variable production costs.

(c)   Explain the interrelationships between the labour and material variances.

Assessment and Qualifications Alliance (AQA), 2006

15.9*   Dounes Ltd manufactures one product.

The following variances have been calculated for the year ended 31 December 2004.

	£	
Material price	1,400	Adverse
Material usage	600	Favourable
Labour rate	2,400	Favourable
Labour efficiency	900	Adverse
Sales price	1,800	Adverse
Sales volume	200	Favourable

Budgeted total cost was £124,600.

REQUIRED

(a)   Explain the term 'variance'.

(b)   Explain one possible cause of each variance.

(c)   Calculate the actual total cost for the year ended 31 December 2004.

Assessment and Qualifications Alliance (AQA), 2005

15.10 AJ Dan plc manufactures a single product.

The standard costs per unit are:

          direct materials   – 5 kg at £18 per kg

          direct labour   – 40 minutes at £12 per hour

The company expects to manufacture and sell 15,000 units each month.

In April 2008 the actual results were:

- direct materials cost was £1,200,000 for 80,000 kg
- direct labour cost was £150,000 for 15,000 hours

The company actually manufactured and sold 15,240 units.

REQUIRED

(a)   Calculate the direct material price and usage variances for April 2008.

(b)   Calculate the direct labour rate and efficiency variances for April 2008.

(c)   Prepare a statement reconciling the standard total direct cost of the actual output with the actual total direct cost. Show the variances.

(d)   Discuss **two** uses of this reconciliation statement.

Assessment and Qualifications Alliance (AQA), Second Specimen Paper for 2010

15.11* Handley Ltd manufacture gold club bags. The accountant has calculated the following sub-variances for the year ended 31 March 2007.

	£	
Material price variance	1,400	adverse
Material usage variance	2,600	favourable
Labour rate variance	750	adverse
Labour efficiency variance	600	favourable

Budgeted profit for the year was £123,450.

REQUIRED

(a)   Calculate the actual profit for the year ended 31 March 2007.

(b)   Explain a possible reason for **each** of the four sub-variances.

(c)   Identify **one** sub-variance which the managers of Handley Ltd should investigate and explain any possible actions they could take.

Assessment and Qualifications Alliance (AQA), Specimen Paper for 2010

15.12*   Nathan's Nicknaks Ltd sells a single product at £6 per unit. The company's expected sales for the year ended 30 April 2005 were 12,000 units.

At the year end, the company had actually sold 14,000 units for £70,000.

REQUIRED

(a)   Calculate the sales price variance. State the formula used.

(b)   Calculate the sales volume variance. State the formula used.

(c)   Explain why each of these variances may have occurred.

Assessment and Qualifications Alliance (AQA), 2005

15.13   Zelah Ltd sells a single product, the Zel, at £5 per unit. The company's forecast sales for the year ended 31 December 20-9 were 20,000 units.

At the year end, the company had actually sold 18,000 units for £108,000.

REQUIRED

(a)   Calculate the sales price variance and state the formula used.

(b)   Calculate the sales volume variance and state the formula used.

(c)   Prepare a statement reconciling the forecast revenue with the actual revenue.

(d)   Explain why the sales variances may have occurred.

16 CAPITAL INVESTMENT APPRAISAL

In this chapter we see how accounting information is used to help a business to make decisions involving capital investment projects. For example, if we need a new photocopier for the office, shall we buy a Toshiba or a Canon model?

The main methods of capital investment appraisal are:

● payback period

● discounted cash flow, also known as net present value

In this chapter we will explain what capital investment appraisal involves, and then study these two methods by means of a Worked Example, and make comparisons between them.

WHAT IS CAPITAL INVESTMENT APPRAISAL?

Capital investment appraisal enables a business to make decisions as to whether or not to invest in a particular capital investment project and, where there are alternatives, to assist in deciding in which to invest.

You will readily appreciate that, whether at home or at work, resources are limited and, as a result, there is a need to use them in such a way as to obtain the maximum benefits from them. To do this it is necessary to choose between various financial alternatives available; for example, on a personal level, we have to make decisions such as:

Should I save my spare cash in a bank's instant access account, or should I deposit it for a fixed term?

Should I save up for a car, or should I buy on hire purchase?

Which make of car, within my price range, should I buy?

Should I rent a house or should I buy, taking out a mortgage?

While these decisions are personal choices, the management of businesses of all sizes are faced with making choices, as are other organisations such as local authorities and central government.

The management of any business is constantly having to make decisions on what goods or services to produce, where to produce, how to produce, and how much to produce. For each major choice to be made, some method of appraisal has to be applied to ensure that, whatever decisions are taken, they are consistent with the objectives of the business. This means that it is necessary to look at all the alternatives available and to choose the one that is going to give the most benefit. For example, a business may have to decide whether to replace its existing machinery with new, more up-to-date machinery. If it decides on new machinery, it then has to choose between different makes of machine and different models, each having a different cost and each capable of affecting output in a different way. The decision will affect the performance of the business – its profit or loss and its cash flow.

WHAT IS A CAPITAL INVESTMENT PROJECT?

A capital investment project is the spending of money now in order to receive benefits (or reduce costs) in future years; it is illustrated in the diagram below.

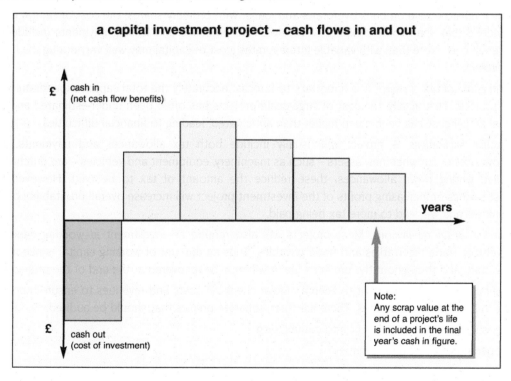

Here, the cost of the investment, or capital expenditure, is being spent at the start – either at the very beginning of the project (often stated as 'year 0'), or during the first year. The difference between these two is illustrated by the following:

- buying a new photocopier is a cash outflow at the beginning of the project
- the installation of a new production line may well incur cash outflows during the first year

The cost of the investment brings benefits (or reduced costs) in future years for as long as the project lasts. Any expected scrap value at the end of the project's life is included in the final year's net cash inflow.

INVESTMENT APPRAISAL IN CONTEXT

Businesses need to apply capital investment appraisal methods to ensure that the decisions they make are the correct choices. As well as the cash flows in and out for a capital investment project, a number of other factors need to be considered before a decision is made. These factors include:

- *Source of finance.* Where is the money coming from to finance the project? Is it from a cash surplus, an existing or new bank overdraft and loans? A large project may warrant a share or debenture (loan) issue to raise specific finance. Assets such as machinery, equipment and vehicles are often financed using hire purchase and leasing.

- *Cost of capital.* All finance has a cost – invariably expressed as a rate of return. The rate of return will be different for each source of finance – from the interest foregone on cash surpluses, to that which must be paid on bank overdrafts and loans. With ordinary shares, the cost of capital is the dividend that shareholders expect to receive. Hire purchase and leasing payments include the interest cost. Note that, with variable interest rates, cost of capital may well vary during the life of a project.

- *Total estimated cost of project.* It is important to forecast accurately the total capital expenditure cost of projects. Historically, the cost of large-scale projects has often been under-estimated and the final actual cost has been much higher than anticipated, leading to financial difficulties.

- *Taxation implications.* A project will usually include both tax allowances and payments. The allowances occur when new assets – such as machinery, equipment and vehicles – are purchased; called writing down allowances, these reduce the amount of tax to be paid. However, the cost savings or increasing profits of the investment project will increase overall profitability of the business and will lead to more tax being paid.

- *Working capital requirements.* Most projects will also require an investment in working capital – inventory, trade receivables and trade payables. Thus an amount of working capital is needed at the start, and throughout the project's life. It will only be recovered at the end of the project.

- *Audit of project.* It is important to keep a regular check on costs and revenues to ensure that they are in line with the estimates. There are three separate phases that should be audited:

  – costs of bringing the project into commission

  – operational costs and revenues

  – decommissioning costs

- *Other considerations*

  Economic climate – recession or period of growth.

  Political implications – a possible change of government may affect investment decisions.

  Commissioning – the length of time that it will take for the project to be up and running.

  Training – the costs and implications of staff training.

Location – where the project is to be located, and subsequent effects on the culture of the business.

Capacity – effect on overall output of the business.

Product life cycle – the implications on the project of the stage of the output within the product life cycle.

WORKED EXAMPLE: MAKING THE DECISION

situation

A business is investing in a new project and has to make the choice between Project Aye and Project Bee. The initial cost and the net cash flow (income, less expenses but not depreciation) to the business have been calculated over five years for each project as follows:

	PROJECT AYE	PROJECT BEE
Initial cost at the beginning of the project	£20,000	£28,000
Net cash inflow:		
Year 1	£8,000	£10,000
Year 2	£12,000	£10,000
Year 3	£5,000	£8,000
Year 4	£4,000	£9,000
Year 5	£2,000	£9,000

- At the end of year 5, both projects will have a scrap value of £1,000; this amount is already included in the year 5 cash inflows.

- Only one project can be undertaken.

- The business requires an annual rate of return of 10 per cent on new projects.

Which project should be chosen?

solution

The two methods commonly used to appraise a capital investment project such as this are:

- payback period

- discounted cash flow, also known as net present value

These methods will be considered in this chapter in order to help the business to make its decision.

PAYBACK PERIOD

Payback is the period of time it takes for the initial cost of capital investment to be repaid from net cash flow inflows.

From the Worked Example of Projects Aye and Bee, seen earlier, the cash flows and the cumulative cash flows (ie net cash flows to date) are shown in the table below. From this information it can be seen that project Aye costs £20,000 (paid out at the beginning of the project) and it is expected that the net cash flow over the first two years will equal the cost. The payback period for Project Aye is, therefore, two years, while that for Project Bee is three years. So, using payback, Project Aye is preferable because it has the shorter payback period.

WORKED EXAMPLE: PAYBACK CALCULATIONS

	PROJECT AYE			PROJECT BEE	
Year	Cash Flow	Cumulative Cash Flow		Cash Flow	Cumulative Cash Flow
	£	£		£	£
0	(20,000)	(20,000)		(28,000)	(28,000)
1	8,000	(12,000)		10,000	(18,000)
2	12,000	–		10,000	(8,000)
3	5,000	5,000		8,000	–
4	4,000	9,000		9,000	9,000
5	2,000	11,000		9,000	18,000

The payback period is indicated by the shading

Although these payback periods work out to exact years, they rarely do so in practice. Be prepared to calculate part years in the examination. For example, if Project Aye had an initial cost of £22,000, the payback would require £2,000 of the £5,000 cash flow in year 3. The payback period would then be:

- 2 years + (£2,000/£5,000 x 12 months)
  = 2 years and 4.8 months, or

- 2 years + (£2,000/£5,000 x 52 weeks)
  = 2 years and 20.8 weeks, or

- 2 years + (£2,000/£5,000 x 365 days)
  = 2 years and 146 days

Note that, in calculating part years, we are making the assumption that cash flows occur at an even rate throughout the year – this may not be the case for all projects – sales (and costs) may be higher at certain times: for example, retailers are likely to have high sales in the pre-Christmas shopping period.

The shorter the payback period the better, particularly where high technology or fashion projects are concerned – they may be out-of-date before they reach the end of their useful lives.

Earlier cash flows are likely to prove more accurate estimates than later cash flows. Thus, if two projects have the same payback, the one with the greater cash flow in the early years is preferred.

For example, consider two projects with a payback period of two years from the following cash flows:

	Wye	Zed
Year 1	£8,000	£12,000
Year 2	£12,000	£8,000

While both projects have the same payback period of two years, Zed is the preferred project under the payback method because of earlier cash flows.

advantages of payback

- it is easy to calculate
- it is easy to understand
- it places emphasis on the earlier cash flows, which are more likely to be accurate than later cash flows
- an ideal capital investment appraisal method for high technology projects

disadvantages of payback

- all cash flows after the payback period are ignored
- within the payback period it fails to consider the timing of net cash flows, eg Project Aye would still have had a payback of two years even if the cash flows for years one and two had been reversed (as noted above, greater cash flows in earlier years are to be preferred)
- the effects of inflation are ignored
- the time value of money is ignored, unlike the discounted cash flow method
- the life of the asset is not considered
- the estimates of cash flows may be inaccurate

DISCOUNTED CASH FLOW

Discounted cash flow is a method of capital investment appraisal which recognises that money has a time value – it compares net cash flows, at their present values, with the initial cost of the capital investment to give a net present value of the capital project.

A quick example of a discounted cash flow decision is where a friend asks you to lend her £1 and offers to repay you either tomorrow, or in one year's time. Which will you choose? The answer is clear: you would want the money back sooner rather than later because, if you don't intend to spend it, you can always save it in a bank, where it will earn interest. Thus the rate of interest represents the time value of money.

Using £1 as an example, if it is saved with a bank at an interest rate of 10 per cent* per year, it will increase as follows:

* an interest rate of 10 per cent per year on a savings rate is too good to be true but is used here for illustrative purposes!

original investment	£1.00
interest at 10% on £1	£0.10
value at end of first year	£1.10
interest at 10% on £1.10	£0.11
value at end of second year	£1.21

This uses the technique of compound interest. So, with interest rates of 10 per cent per year, we can say that the future value of £1 will be £1.10 at the end of year one, £1.21 at the end of year two, and so on; thus £1 set aside now will gain in value so that, at some time in the future, we will have access to a larger sum of money. However, supposing that we were to receive £1 at the end of year one, what is it worth to us now? To find the answer to this, we need to carry out the following calculation:

$$£1 \quad \times \quad \frac{100}{110^*} \quad = \quad £0.91$$

* 100 per cent, plus the rate of interest (in this example, 10 per cent).

Therefore, if we had £0.91 now and invested it at 10 per cent per year, we would have £1 at the end of year one. We can say that the *present value* of £1 receivable in one year's time is £0.91. In the same way, £1 receivable in two years' time is £0.83, calculated as follows:

$$£1 \quad \times \quad \frac{100}{110} \quad \times \quad \frac{100}{110} \quad = \quad £0.83$$

We can build up a *table of factors* (for 10 per cent interest rate) as shown below:

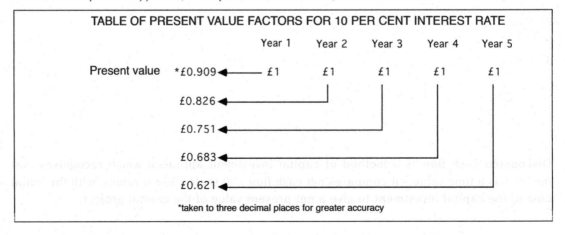

TABLE OF PRESENT VALUE FACTORS FOR 10 PER CENT INTEREST RATE

	Year 1	Year 2	Year 3	Year 4	Year 5
Present value *£0.909	£1	£1	£1	£1	£1
£0.826					
£0.751					
£0.683					
£0.621					

*taken to three decimal places for greater accuracy

Note that there is no need to learn how to calculate present value factors – the correct factors will always be given to you in the examination.

The table of factors reminds us of the basic principle that *money has a time value* and, from this, the further into the future that we expect to receive money, then the lower is its *present value*. Thus the present value (or discount) factors relate to interest rates which represent the cost of capital (ie either the rate of return that the business expects on its money, or the rate of interest it has to pay when borrowing).

Let us now return to the Worked Example where a business has to choose between Projects Aye and Bee. We will look at this assuming a cost of capital – or rate of return – of 10 per cent. For each project, the expected net cash flows are multiplied by the relevant factor to give the *discounted cash flow*; the difference between total discounted cash flow and the initial cost is the *net present value* of the project.

WORKED EXAMPLE: DISCOUNTED CASH FLOW CALCULATIONS

Project Aye

	Cash Flow £		Discount Factor		Discounted Cash Flow £
Year 0*	(20,000)	x	1.000	=	(20,000)
Year 1	8,000	x	0.909	=	7,272
Year 2	12,000	x	0.826	=	9,912
Year 3	5,000	x	0.751	=	3,755
Year 4	4,000	x	0.683	=	2,732
Year 5	2,000	x	0.621	=	1,242
			Net Present Value	=	4,913

* Year 0 is the beginning of the project when the initial cost is paid. Some projects such as the installation of a new production line – may well incur cash outflows during the first year.

Notes:

- The initial cost is shown in brackets because it is a cost, whereas the net cash inflows are positive amounts. Net Present Value is the net sum of all the discounted cash inflows and outflows.

- When using discount factors, the assumption is made that cash flows occur at the end of each year – apart, that is, from the Year 0 initial cash flow.

Project Bee

	Cash Flow £		Discount Factor		Discounted Cash Flow £
Year 0	(28,000)	x	1.000	=	(28,000)
Year 1	10,000	x	0.909	=	9,090
Year 2	10,000	x	0.826	=	8,260
Year 3	8,000	x	0.751	=	6,008
Year 4	9,000	x	0.683	=	6,147
Year 5	9,000	x	0.621	=	5,589
			Net Present Value	=	7,094

Here, with a cost of capital – or rate of return – of 10 per cent, Project Bee is better, producing a considerably higher net present value than Aye. Note that both projects give a positive net present value at 10 per cent: this means that either project will be of benefit to the business but Bee is preferable; a negative net present value would indicate that a project should not go ahead.

Thus, using a discounted cash flow method, future cash flows are brought to their present value; this means that, the further on in time that cash flows are receivable, the lower is the net present value.

advantages of discounted cash flow

- all cash flows are considered
- the time value of money is used
- the timing of cash flows is taken into account
- although more complex to calculate than payback, when using a table of factors the calculations are easy to make

disadvantages of discounted cash flow

- the cost of capital rate – or rate of return – is, in practice, difficult to ascertain and may also vary over the life of the project
- the meaning of net present value is not always clear to users of the information
- when comparing two projects, the one with the higher net present value does not always represent the better project for the business – other factors need to be considered, eg quality of output, compatibility with existing equipment and systems
- the estimates of cash flows may be inaccurate

Tutorial note: in the AQA Examination, do not abbreviate the terms 'net present value' and 'discounted cash flow'.

CAPITAL INVESTMENT APPRAISAL: COMPARISON

It is unlikely that a business will rely on one investment appraisal method only; instead both methods might need to be satisfied before a capital project is given the go-ahead. Supposing, for example, that the business in the Worked Example which has to choose between Projects Aye and Bee, applied the following criteria: "projects must have a payback period not exceeding two-and-a-half years, and must have a positive net present value at a 10 per cent rate of return." How do the two projects compare?

	Project Aye	Project Bee
Payback period	2 years	3 years
Net present value at 10 per cent	£4,913	£7,094

Under the criteria that the business has laid down, Aye would be chosen. However, Bee seems a better project on the net present value basis and is only rejected because it does not meet the payback period requirement. However, the capital expenditure required for Bee is £8,000 greater than Aye, being £28,000 compared with £20,000; so it seems that Project Aye is, on balance, the better of the two.

OTHER CONSIDERATIONS

As well as the numerical techniques that can be used for capital investment appraisal, a business must consider a number of other factors before making the final decision. These include:

- **Total implications.** The effect of the project on the business as a whole will include implications for
  - sales, with possible increases in output
  - output, with changes in techniques, eg a switch from labour-intensive to machine-intensive output
  - staff, with possible redundancies, training needs, pay structure
  - working capital required for the project
  - needs, such as premises, transport, materials
- **Cost of finance.** Possible changes in the cost of capital will have a direct effect on the viability of the project. For example, an increase in the general level of interest rates will reduce the project's overall profitability. Projects are often financed through fixed interest rate loans, or through hire purchase and leasing, thus establishing some part of the finance at fixed rates; however, invariably working capital is financed by a bank overdraft at variable interest rates.
- **Taxation considerations.** The project will include the implications of both tax allowances and charges. However, a change in the level of taxation will affect the viability of the project.
- **Forecasting techniques.** These can be used to answer 'what if?' questions: for example, "what if sales increase by 25 per cent?" or "what if materials costs fall by 5 per cent?" In this way, a business can see how the project is affected by changes to any of the data used in the appraisal.

- **Size of the investment.** A major project can be destabilising for a small business if cash inflows prove to be lower than expected.

REPORTING DECISIONS

Capital investment appraisal decisions often have to be reported to managers, or other appropriate people, in a clear and concise way. The information should include recommendations which are supported by well-presented reasoning.

To conclude, we include a written report addressed to the General Manager of the business on Projects Aye and Bee, which we have looked at in this chapter. The company has the following criteria: "projects must have a payback period not exceeding two-and-a-half years, and must have a positive net present value at a 10 per cent cost of capital."

REPORT

To:	General Manager
From:	A2 Accounting Student
Date:	Today

Projects Aye and Bee

Introduction
- This report applies capital investment appraisal methods to these two projects.
- In this appraisal, the cash inflows and outflows used are those that have been given.

Report
- Please refer to the calculation sheet (tutorial note: on page 396 and 399-400).
- Both projects are acceptable from a financial viewpoint because they each return a positive net present value at a discount rate of 10%, as follows: Project Aye £4,913; Project Bee £7,094. These calculations assume that net cash inflows occur at the end of each year.
- The payback periods are: Project Aye, 2 years; Project Bee, 3 years.

Conclusion
- Project Aye meets both the company requirements of payback within two-and-a-half years, and a positive net present value at a 10 per cent rate of return.
- Project Bee does not meet the payback requirement, but does have a positive net present value at a 10 per cent rate of return.
- Project Aye has a lower net present value than Project Bee.
- On balance, Project Aye is recommended:
  - lower initial cost
  - high cash inflows in the first two years
  - quick payback
  - positive net present value

THE USE OF DISCOUNTED CASH FLOW TO MINIMISE COSTS

In this chapter we have used discounted cash flow to appraise capital investment projects, ie capital expenditure at the start of the project with cash inflows over the life of the project. A further use of discounted cash flow is to minimise costs – eg making a choice between alternative electricity or telephone suppliers. The same principles are applied as with capital investment projects but, because we are looking at costs, the preferred choice will be the one with the lower net present cost. This is shown by the following:

- Estimated annual electricity costs from two suppliers, based on a three-year contract:

	POWER UK	MERCIAN ENERGY
Year 1	£2,000	£1,500
Year 2	£2,000	£2,000
Year 3	£2,000	£2,500

- At a cost of capital of 10 per cent, with factors of 0.909, 0.826 and 0.751 for years 1, 2 and 3 respectively, the net present costs of the two suppliers are:

	POWER UK			MERCIAN ENERGY		
			£			£
Year 1	(2,000) x 0.909	=	(1,818)	(1,500) x 0.909	=	(1,364)
Year 2	(2,000) x 0.826	=	(1,652)	(2,000) x 0.826	=	(1,652)
Year 3	(2,000) x 0.751	=	(1,502)	(2,500) x 0.751	=	(1,878)
Net Present Cost			(4,972)			(4,894)

The preferred supplier – based solely on the calculations – is Mercian Energy, because it has the lower net present cost.

Net present cost can be used in a number of circumstances – both in business and personally – such as:

- choosing a utility supplier
- making finance cost comparisons when buying a car, etc
- comparing loan/mortgage deals from banks

CHAPTER SUMMARY

- Capital investment appraisal uses two main methods to help in decision-making:

  – payback period

  – discounted cash flow, also known as net present value

- Capital investment appraisal enables a business to make decisions as to whether or not to invest in a particular capital investment project and, where there are alternatives, to assist in deciding in which to invest

- Businesses often use a combination of appraisal methods before making decisions about capital projects.

- Payback is the length of time it takes for the initial cost of a capital investment to be repaid from net cash inflows.

- Discounted cash flow is a method of capital investment appraisal which recognises that money has a time value – it compares net cash flows, at their present values, with the initial cost of the capital investment to give a net present value of the capital project.

- Cost of capital is the percentage cost of financing an investment – either the rate of return that the business expects on its money, or the rate of interest it has to pay when borrowing.

- Before deciding on a capital project, other factors include:

  – total implications for the business

  – cost of finance, and effect of changes

  – taxation

  – forecasting techniques to answer 'what if?' questions

  – size of the investment relative to the size of the business

In the next chapter we look at how costs and revenues can be incorporated into the budgets of a business, the preparation of budgets, and their uses in the control of a business.

QUESTIONS

An asterisk (*) after the question number means that the answer is given at the end of this book.

16.1* Sesame Shoes Limited is appraising the financial effects of a project to develop a new range of shoes. The company requires an annual rate of return of 10% on any new project.

The following information relates to this project.

	Year 0	Year 1	Year 2	Year 3	Year 4	Year 5
	£	£	£	£	£	£
Design costs	95,000	–	–	–	–	–
Sales revenue	–	60,000	80,000	100,000	100,000	50,000
Variable costs	–	30,000	40,000	50,000	50,000	25,000
10% discount factor	1.000	0.909	0.826	0.751	0.683	0.621

REQUIRED

Calculate for the new project:

(a) the payback period

(b) the net present value

16.2* Robert Smith is considering two major capital investment projects for his business. Only one project can be chosen and the following information is available:

	Project Exe	Project Wye
	£	£
Initial cost at the beginning of the project	80,000	100,000
Net cash inflows, year: 1	40,000	20,000
2	40,000	30,000
3	20,000	50,000
4	10,000	50,000
5	10,000	40,000

The initial cost occurs at the beginning of the project and you may assume that the net cash inflows will arise at the end of each year. Robert Smith requires an annual rate of return of 12 per cent. Neither project will have any residual value at the end of five years.

The discount factors at 12 per cent are:

Year 1	0.893
Year 2	0.797
Year 3	0.712
Year 4	0.636
Year 5	0.567

REQUIRED

(a) Produce numerical assessments of the two projects based on the following capital investment appraisal methods:

- the payback period

- the net present value

(b) Write a report to Robert Smith on the relative merits of the capital investment appraisal methods, advising which capital investment, if either, should be undertaken.

16.3* The Wyvern Bike Company is planning to introduce a new range of bikes in addition to its existing range. The company requires an annual rate of return of 12 per cent on any new project. The Managing Director has asked you to appraise the financial effects of introducing the new range. The following information relates to this project.

	Year 0 £	Year 1 £	Year 2 £	Year 3 £	Year 4 £	Year 5 £
Development costs	40,000	60,000	–	–	–	–
Sales revenue	–	–	75,000	90,000	150,000	100,000
Variable costs	–	–	30,000	36,000	60,000	40,000
10% discount factor	1.000	0.893	0.797	0.712	0.636	0.567

REQUIRED

(a)   Calculate for the new project:
- the payback period
- the net present value

(b)   Use the data from part (a) to prepare a report to the Managing Director on the new bike project. Your report should:
- identify **two** additional items of information relevant to appraising this project
- make a recommendation to accept or reject the project based on its net present value

16.4   The following information relates to two major capital investment projects being considered by Newell Limited. For financial reasons, only one project can be accepted.

	Project Ess	Project Tee
	£	£
Initial cost at the beginning of the project	100,000	115,000
Net cash inflows, year: 1	40,000	50,000
2	60,000	35,000
3	20,000	30,000
4	20,000	30,000
5	10,000	30,000
Expected scrap value* at end of year 5	5,000	7,500

Note: remember to add the expected scrap value to the year 5 net cash inflow.

The initial cost occurs at the beginning of the project and you may assume that the net cash inflows will arise at the end of each year. Newell Limited requires an annual rate of return of 10 per cent.

The discount factors at 10 per cent are:

Year 1	0.909
Year 2	0.826
Year 3	0.751
Year 4	0.683
Year 5	0.621

REQUIRED

(a) Produce numerical assessments of the two projects based on the following capital investment appraisal methods:

• the payback period

• the net present value

(b) Write a report to the Managing Director on the relative merits of the project appraisal methods, and advising which capital investment, if either, should be undertaken.

16.5 The Chester Carpet Company is considering a capital investment project to purchase a new machine for the production department.

The machine will cost £65,000 and will have a useful life of four years. The cash inflows are expected to be:

	£
Year 1	17,000
Year 2	25,000
Year 3	31,000
Year 4	24,000

At the end of the project, the machine will be sold as scrap for an expected amount of £4,000. The expected scrap value should be added to the year 4 cash inflow.

The Chester Carpet Company requires an annual rate of return of 10 per cent for net present value, and a maximum payback period of three years.

REQUIRED

(a) Use the working paper on the next page to calculate the net present value and the payback period of the proposed project. Calculate all money amounts to the nearest £.

(b) Write a report to the General Manager evaluating the proposal from a financial viewpoint. State any assumptions you have made in your analysis.

THE CHESTER CARPET COMPANY

Working paper for the financial appraisal of a new machine

for the production department

DISCOUNTED CASH FLOW

Year	Cash Flow	Discount Factor at 10%	Discounted Cash Flow
	£		£
0	_____	1.000	_____
1	_____	0.909	_____
2	_____	0.826	_____
3	_____	0.751	_____
4	_____	0.683	_____

Net Present Value

PAYBACK PERIOD

Year	Cash Flow	Cumulative Cash Flow
	£	£
0	_____	_____
1	_____	_____
2	_____	_____
3	_____	_____
4	_____	_____

Payback period =   _____

16.6 The research department of Zelah Chemical Company has discovered a wonder drug which cures the symptoms of the common cold within a matter of hours. The company has decided to develop the new drug – to be called 'Zelahcold' – and the Managing Director has asked you to appraise the financial effects of this project.

For all new projects the company requires an annual rate of return of 10 per cent for net present value, and a maximum payback period of three years.

The following information relates to this project.

	Year 0 £	Year 1 £	Year 2 £	Year 3 £	Year 4 £	Year 5 £
Development costs	110,000	–	–	–	–	–
Sales revenue	–	55,000	90,000	120,000	120,000	120,000
Variable costs	–	35,000	30,000	40,000	40,000	35,000
10% discount factor	1.000	0.909	0.826	0.751	0.683	0.621

REQUIRED

(a) Calculate for the new project:
- the payback period
- the net present value

(b) Use the data from part (a) to prepare a report to the Managing Director on the new product. Your report should:
- identify **two** additional items of information relevant to appraising this project
- make a recommendation to accept or reject the project

16.7 Em is the financial accountant of Jayne Bonde plc. She is proposing to replace all of the existing machinery at a cost of £2,400,000. The new machinery will produce 14,000 units per month, and total costs are expected to be £1,130,000 per month.

The selling price of each unit is £90.

All cash flows are expected to occur evenly throughout the month. It is presumed that all production will be sold each month.

Ignore depreciation.

REQUIRED

(a) Calculate the payback period of the new machinery.

(b) Explain **two** limitations of using payback as a method of capital investment appraisal.

Assessment and Qualifications Alliance (AQA), 2006

16.8* Tom Drake wishes to purchase a new machine. He has calculated the payback period of two machines:

	Cost £	Payback period Years
Machine 1	60,000	4
Machine 2	90,000	5

Both machines are expected to last 10 years with regular yearly cash flows.

REQUIRED

(a) Define the term "payback".

(b) Calculate the estimated total cash flows that each machine would generate over its lifetime.

(c) Explain how these calculations will aid Tom Drake in deciding which machine to purchase.

Assessment and Qualifications Alliance (AQA), 2004

16.9 Roberta uses one machine to manufacture her products. This machine was purchased six years ago for £160,000. It has an expected useful economic life of ten years, and currently produces 6,000 units per annum.

Although this machine is still in good working order, Roberta is considering replacing it with a more up-to-date machine at a cost of £350,000. This new machine is expected to increase the annual production by 20% and will last ten years. Roberta will have to borrow to finance the purchase of this machine.

Each unit is sold for £80, and will cost £60 to manufacture.

The discount factors at 14% are:

Year 1	0.877
Year 2	0.769
Year 3	0.675
Year 4	0.592

REQUIRED

(a) Calculate the net present value of the new machine.

(b) Advise Roberta whether she should purchase the new machine. Justify your recommendation.

Assessment and Qualifications Alliance (AQA), 2005

16.10* Robert intends to purchase a new machine costing £60,000.

The cost of capital is 8%.

The discount factors are:

Year 1	0.926
Year 2	0.857
Year 3	0.794
Year 4	0.735

The annual net cash flow is expected to be £26,000 per annum for the next three years.

REQUIRED

(a)   Calculate the payback period for the new machine.

(b)   Calculate the net present value for the machine.

(c)   Assess the usefulness of the net present value method of capital investment appraisal.

Assessment and Qualifications Alliance (AQA), 2007

16.11* Wesley Rise wishes to purchase a machine with an initial cost of £180,000 plus a delivery charge of £20,000. The machine is expected to last 5 years.

The cost of capital is 12%.

The discount factors are:

Year 1	0.893
Year 2	0.797
Year 3	0.712
Year 4	0.636
Year 5	0.567

The cash inflows generated by the machine are expected to be:

	£
Year 1	60,000
Year 2	80,000
Year 3	120,000
Year 4	120,000
Year 5	80,000

The cash outflows are expected to be £40,000 each year. A major overhaul of the machine is expected to be carried out at a cost of £20,000 in year 4.

REQUIRED

(a)   Calculate the payback period for the machine.

(b)   Calculate the net present value for the machine.

(c)   Advise whether the machine should be purchased. Give reasons for your decision.

Assessment and Qualifications Alliance (AQA), 2005

16.12 The directors of Beard Bakeries Ltd have decided to replace one of the blending machines. The following information relates to two possible replacement machines.

	Machine A	Machine B
Cost	£30,000	£80,000
Annual production	12,000 cakes	15,000 cakes
Cost per cake	£1.50	£1.00
Expected life of machine	2 years	3 years

Additional information

- The cost of capital is 10%.

- It is assumed that revenues and costs are paid at the end of each year.

- Each cake is expected to sell for £3.00.

- It is assumed that everything produced is sold.

- The following is an extract from the net present values table for £1:

	10%
Year 1	0.909
Year 2	0.826
Year 3	0.751

REQUIRED

(a) Calculate the expected total net cash flow for the life of **each** of the machines.

(b) Calculate the net present value for **each** machine using the expected annual net cash flows.

(c) Identify which machine Beard Bakeries Ltd should purchase. Give a reason for your choice.

Assessment and Qualifications Alliance (AQA), Specimen Paper for 2010

17 FURTHER ASPECTS OF BUDGETING

In AS Accounting we have already seen how budgeting is used by businesses as a method of financial planning for the future and, in particular, saw how a cash budget is prepared. Budgets are prepared for important aspects of the business – sales, production, purchases, labour, trade receivables, trade payables, cash – which give detailed plans of the business for the next three, six or twelve months. The budgets are brought together in a master budget which comprises a forecast operating statement – a forecast income statement – and a forecast balance sheet.

In this further chapter on budgeting we will be looking at:

● how budgets can be used to control the business by means of budgetary control

● budgets for sales, production, purchases, labour, trade receivables, trade payables and cash

● how the budgets link into the master budget, which is made up of a forecast operating statement and balance sheet

BUDGETARY CONTROL

Budgetary control is the process of using budgets to monitor actual results against budgeted figures.

The principle of budgetary control

BUDGET FIGURES

ACTUAL FIGURES

MONITOR AND COMPARE

CONTROL AND TAKE ACTION

The principle illustrated in the diagram on the previous page is that, once a budget has been agreed by managers, budgetary control is used as a mechanism to compare actual results with what was planned to happen in the budget. As the period covered by the budget progresses, budget reports are prepared – often monthly – and the 'actual' and 'variance' columns are completed and the cumulative figures for the year-to-date are recorded. An example of a budget report is shown below. You will see that the owner of the business should be pleased with the results shown.

Fitta Homegym – sales budget report

	Income: December			Income: Year-to-date		
	budget	actual	variance	budget	actual	variance
	£	£	£	£	£	£
Retail sales	200,000	250,000	50,000 FAV	2,750,000	3,125,000	375,000 FAV
Mail order	225,000	200,000	25,000 ADV	1,275,000	1,350,000	75,000 FAV
Total sales	425,000	450,000	25,000 FAV	4,025,000	4,475,000	450,000 FAV

The management of a business will be monitoring the budget during the year and will be watching closely for variances between the budgeted and actual figures. As we have already seen in chapter 15, there are two types of variance:

- a **favourable variance** (FAV), where the results are better than expected
- an **adverse variance** (ADV), where the results are worse than expected

Details of variances are used to:

- **feed back** information to the budget holders responsible for the budget so that, where necessary, corrective action can be taken
- **feed forward** into the planning process for the next period's budgets

benefits of budgetary control

- planning – the formal framework of budgets is used to predict future activities of the business, and potential problems will be highlighted
- co-ordination – individual budgets, eg sales, production, purchases, trade receivables, trade payables, are integrated into the master budget
- control – comparison is made of actual results against the budget
- communication – between managers and other staff in order to achieve the objectives of the business
- motivation – of staff to ensure that budgets are met
- evaluation of performance – to compare the budget against the actual results, and to see where improvements can be made
- decision-making – about production, sales and costs

limitations of budgetary control

- costs and benefits – the benefit must exceed the cost of budgetary control
- accuracy – some information used in the budget may be inaccurate and may distort the budget
- demotivation – of staff who have not been involved in planning the budget, or who are set too high a level to achieve
- disfunctional management – where different sections of the business are not co-ordinated there may be departmental rivalry
- set too easy – where budgets are set at too low a level they will not enable the business to use its resources to best advantage
- may restrict activities – budgets may be inflexible so that staff are unable to take advantage of opportunities, eg to buy materials in bulk at an advantageous price earlier than budgeted but which would result in an overspend

WHAT BUDGETS ARE PREPARED?

A budget is a financial plan for a business, prepared in advance and generally covering a period of up to 12 months.

Budgets are planned for specific sections of the business: these budgets can then be controlled by a budget holder, who may be the manager or supervisor of the specific section. Such budgets include:

- sales budget
- production budget
- purchases budget
- labour budget
- trade receivables budget
- trade payables budget
- cash budget

The end result of the budgeting process is often the production of a master budget, which takes the form of forecast operating statements – forecast income statement – and forecast balance sheet (a forecast cash flow statement is often also included in the master budget). The master budget is the 'master plan' which shows how all the other budgets 'work together'. The diagram on the next page shows how all the budgets are linked to each other.

The starting point for the budgeting process is generally the sales budget, because it is usually sales that determine the other activities of the business. Consequently the order in which the budgets will be prepared is usually:

- **sales budget** – what can the business expect to sell in the coming months?
- **production budget** – how can the business make/supply all the items which it plans to sell?

- **purchases budget** – what does the business need to buy to make/supply the goods it plans to sell?

- **labour budget** – what will be the cost of labour to make/supply the goods?

- **trade receivables budget** – how much will the business receive from sales?

- **trade payables budget** – how much will the business have to pay for purchases?

- **cash budget** – what money will be flowing in and out of the bank account? – will an overdraft be needed?

- **master budget** – a summary of all the budgets to provide a forecast operating statement – forecast income statement – and a forecast balance sheet

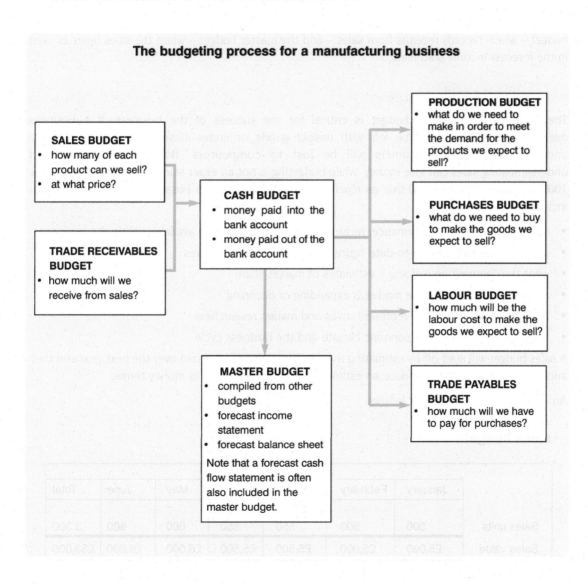

The budgeting process for a manufacturing business

SALES BUDGET
- how many of each product can we sell?
- at what price?

TRADE RECEIVABLES BUDGET
- how much will we receive from sales?

CASH BUDGET
- money paid into the bank account
- money paid out of the bank account

PRODUCTION BUDGET
- what do we need to make in order to meet the demand for the products we expect to sell?

PURCHASES BUDGET
- what do we need to buy to make the goods we expect to sell?

LABOUR BUDGET
- how much will be the labour cost to make the goods we expect to sell?

MASTER BUDGET
- compiled from other budgets
- forecast income statement
- forecast balance sheet

Note that a forecast cash flow statement is often also included in the master budget.

TRADE PAYABLES BUDGET
- how much will we have to pay for purchases?

Sales Budget

A sales budget is used to estimate sales in units and revenue. It is linked to the production budget, the trade receivables budget and the master budget.

The sales budget is often the starting point for the budgeting process in any type of business. It is the plan which will project the sales of:

- products made by a **manufacturing** business, eg cars, DVDs, breakfast cereals
- services provided by a **service** business, eg holidays, educational courses, bus and train journeys

It is from the sales budget that a business is able to estimate what it needs to produce, thus giving a link between the sales and production budgets. Sales budget also links to the trade receivables budget – which records receipts from sales – and the master budget – when the sales figure is used in the forecast income statement.

planning the sales budget

The accuracy of the sales budget is critical for the success of the business. If a business overestimates sales, it will be left with unsold goods or under-utilised services; if sales are underestimated, then customers will be lost to competitors. Both overestimating and underestimating sales can lose money. While budgeting is not an exact science, and is unlikely to be 100% accurate, it is essential that as much accurate information as possible is gathered; this can include:

- details of past sales performance, including seasonal variations – available within the business
- present sales figures – up-to-date figures from sales representatives
- what the competition is doing – estimates of market share
- assessment of whether the market is expanding or declining
- forecasts made – by sales representatives and market researchers
- trading conditions – the economic climate and the business cycle

A sales budget will start off by estimating the number of units to be sold over the next year and then applying a selling price to produce an estimate of the income figure in money terms.

An example of a sales budget follows:

sales budget

	January	February	March	April	May	June	Total
Sales units	500	500	550	550	600	600	3,300
Sales value	£5,000	£5,000	£5,500	£5,500	£6,000	£6,000	£33,000

Note how the budget uses:

budget periods – the subdivision of the budget into monthly, four-weekly (which divides a 52-week year into 13 four-weekly periods), or weekly

budget headings – the subdivision of the budget into sales units and sales value

The total column is not always shown, but it does provide a target for the six-month period.

Production Budget

A production budget shows the level of production in units needed to meet the demand for expected sales and identifies any production problems that may need to be resolved. It is linked to the purchases and labour budgets.

When a business has established its sales budget it is then in a position to work out its production budget (for a manufacturing business), or its operating budget (for a service). Note that production/operating budgets are normally prepared using units of output (rather than money amounts).

A production budget links to purchases budget – which records the materials that need to be bought – and the labour budget – which shows the labour hours and the cost needed to produce the goods.

planning the production budget

When planning a production/operating budget, management must gather together information about the business' resources and consider a range of external factors in order to assess what can and cannot be achieved. These include:

- **timing** When during the year are the products required? Are there any seasonal fluctuations (Christmas cards, fireworks) which will produce uneven demands on production facilities? Will the business need to hold inventories of products in advance?

- **capacity** Can the existing production facilities cope with the expected demand? Will new non-current assets be needed? Should some work be subcontracted to other businesses?

- **labour cost** Does the business have the right number of staff with the necessary skills? Will more staff be needed? Will there need to be training? Will overtime need to be worked, or is an additional shift required?

- **materials** Can the right quality and quantity of materials be obtained at the right price?

When all of this information has been gathered and analysed, the business should then be in a position to prepare the production budget, taking into account:

- the projected monthly sales (in units)
- the number of units of goods in inventory at the beginning and end of each month

The production budget is usually prepared in terms of units of production. Some of the factors listed above will need to be considered, for example:

- there may be a maximum level of inventory that can be held in the warehouse/stores
- management may require that each month's closing inventory is a set percentage of next month's sales

WORKED EXAMPLE: PRODUCTION BUDGET

This production budget (in units) has been prepared where there are the following constraints:
- each month's closing inventory is to be 20% of the following month's sales units
- the maximum capacity of the warehouse is 100 units

production budget

	January	February	March	April	May	June	Total
	units	units	units	units	units	units	units
Sales	250	300	280	600	325	300	2,055
Opening inventory	(50)	(60)	(56)	(100)	(65)	(60)	(50)
Closing inventory	60	56	*100	65	60	**65	65
Production	260	296	324	565	320	305	2,070

*   maximum capacity of the warehouse

**   sales in July are estimated to be 325 units, so closing inventory at the end of June is budgeted to be 65 units

Tutorial notes:
- To calculate the production units for each month, deduct the opening inventory from sales and add the closing inventory. For example, in January:

		Units
	sales	250
less	opening inventory	50
add	closing inventory	60
equals	production	260

Opening inventory is deducted because it is used for sales for the month – for example in January, if there were to be no closing inventory, production would need to be 250 units – 50 units opening inventory = 200 units; however, closing inventory is 60 units, so production needs to be 260 units.

- The total column, on the right-hand side of the budget, can be used as a cross-check of the monthly figures.

benefits of a production budget

The use of a production budget enables a business to:

- identify the production capacity available
- schedule resources – eg cash, materials, labour – effectively
- meet sales demand
- make best use of spare capacity

PURCHASES BUDGET

A purchases budget shows the number and value of the goods that need to be bought in order to meet the demands of the production department. It is linked to the trade payables budget and the master budget.

Purchases budget is a development of the sales and production budgets. It is used to work out the level of purchases that will have to be made:

- either, to meet the requirements for materials in the production process of a manufacturing business
- or, to provide the goods to be sold in a shop

Purchases budget is expressed in terms of units of goods to be bought, together with the purchases cost.

Purchases budget links to the trade payables budget – which records payments made for purchases – and the master budget – where the purchases figure is used in the forecast income statement.

planning the purchases budget

The layout for this budget is very similar to that for production, using sales, opening inventory and closing inventory to calculate purchases in units. A bottom row shows the money amounts of purchases.

As with the production budget, there may be factors to consider when preparing the purchases budget, for example:

- there may be a maximum level of inventory that can be held in the warehouse/stores
- management may require that each month's closing inventory is a set percentage of next month's sales
- there must be a link to the production budget so that sufficient goods are bought to meet the requirements of the production department

WORKED EXAMPLE: PURCHASES BUDGET

This purchases budget has been prepared where there are the following constraints:
- each month's closing inventory is to be 50% of the following month's sales units
- the maximum capacity of the warehouse is 350 units
- the purchase cost of each unit is £10

Sales units are shown in the budget; sales in July are estimated to be 640 units.

---

purchases budget

	January	February	March	April	May	June	Total
	units	units	units	units	units	units	units
Sales	500	550	600	780	570	620	3,620
Opening inventory	(250)	(275)	(300)	(350)	(285)	(310)	(250)
Closing inventory	275	300	*350	285	310	**320	320
Purchases	525	575	650	715	595	630	3,690
Purchases cost	£5,250	£5,750	£6,500	£7,150	£5,950	£6,300	£36,900

*　maximum capacity of the warehouse

**　sales in July are estimated to be 640 units, so closing inventory at the end of June is budgeted to be 320 units

---

Tutorial notes:
- To calculate the number of units to be purchased each month, deduct the opening inventory from sales and add the closing inventory.
- The total column, on the right-hand side of the budget, can be used as a cross-check of the monthly figures.
- The row for purchases cost is included in the purchases budget and is the number of units to be bought multiplied by the purchase cost of each unit.

LABOUR BUDGET

A labour budget is used to plan and control the labour hours and labour costs of production-line employees.

A labour budget links with the production budget to ensure that a business will have the right number of labour hours available for the planned level of production. It is not only the right number of hours available, but other factors to consider include:

- are staff of the correct grade available?
- do we need to train any staff to bring them to the grade needed?
- do we need to recruit more staff?
- do we have too many staff and, if so, do we need to consider redundancies?

The use of a labour budget allows any shortfalls in labour hours to be identified so that corrective action can be taken. Shortfalls in the right number and grade of staff available may mean that labour costs increase because, in order to keep production going, it is necessary to:

- hire in temporary staff
- pay overtime
- work extra shifts
- use more skilled and more expensive staff than is necessary

planning the labour budget

Working from the production budget the number of labour hours to make each unit of output needs to be determined. At the same time the grade of staff needed to carry out the work and their pay rate needs to be known. If there are any pay rises expected to be paid within the budget period, these should be allowed for when preparing the budget.

A labour budget consists of the number of labour hours expected for each budget period – eg weekly, four-weekly or monthly. The rate paid to staff is then used to calculate an estimate of the labour cost.

An example of a labour budget follows:

labour budget

	January	February	March	April	May	June	Total
Labour hours	400	450	450	500	500	450	2,750
Labour cost	£4,000	£4,500	£4,500	£5,000	£5,000	£4,500	£27,500

An adaptation of labour budget can be used to show the:

- labour hours required to meet planned production
- labour hours available
- any surplus or shortfall of labour hours

The surplus or shortfall indicates that action needs to be taken:

− a surplus of hours available in some months could be used to manufacture inventory in advance of months when the budget shows a shortfall, subject to the costs of manufacturing and storing the extra inventory

− a surplus of hours available could indicate that the business is employing too many staff for its production needs, and should consider reducing overtime, cutting back on the number of shifts, laying off temporary staff, or making some staff redundant

− a shortfall of hours available could indicate that the business needs to consider increasing overtime, working additional shifts, taking on temporary staff, recruiting permanent staff, or training other staff to work on this production

An example of a labour budget showing surpluses and shortfalls of labour hours follows:

labour budget

	January	February	March	April	May	June	Total
Production in units	200	225	225	250	250	225	1,375
Labour hours at 2 hours per unit	400	450	450	500	500	450	2,750
Labour hours available	450	450	450	450	500	500	2,800
Surplus/(shortfall) of labour hours	50	−	−	(50)	−	50	50

- the surplus hours in January could be used to make extra units to be held in inventory until April
- the surplus hours in June could be used to build up inventory before employees begin their summer holidays

benefits of a labour budget

The use of a labour budget enables a business to:

- plan and control the cost of labour
- identify any surplus or shortfall in the number of labour hours available for planned production, allowing corrective action to be taken and changes made to overtime and shift working
- plan labour requirements for future production, identifying when more or fewer labour hours will be needed, and linking to recruitment or redundancy issues for the Human Resources Department

TRADE RECEIVABLES BUDGET

A trade receivables budget is used to estimate the timing and amount of receipts from trade receivables and is linked to the sales budget, the cash budget and the master budget.

This is an important budget for those businesses that make a large proportion of their sales on credit. The period of credit allowed to customers – the time between making a sale and receiving payment – affects the cash flow of the business in that this period is being financed by the seller. It is important that, as well as having good products and being able to sell them, cash flows in from customers without delay and by the due date. It is a shortage of cash that causes most business failures.

A trade receivables budget links directly to the cash budget (see page 428) – which records receipts from trade receivables – and the master budget – where the amount of trade receivables is shown as an asset on the forecast balance sheet.

planning the trade receivables budget

The information needed to plan the trade receivables budget is:

–   the amount of credit sales (from the sales budget)

–   the expected receipts from trade receivables (from the cash budget)

–   the expected cash discount allowed to trade receivables (from the cash budget)

–   the normal trade terms under which credit sales are made (eg 30 days net, 2% cash discount for settlement within 7 days)

–   the trade receivables' collection period, ie $\dfrac{\text{Trade receivables}}{\text{Credit sales}}$ x 365 days (or 52 weeks or 12 months)

–   details of any bad debts written off

WORKED EXAMPLE: TRADE RECEIVABLES BUDGET

This trade receivables budget has been prepared from the following information:

–   credit sales are budgeted to be £30,000 per month for January to March, and £40,000 for April to June

–   receipts from trade receivables are budgeted to be £28,000 per month for January and February, £35,000 per month for March and April, and £39,000 per month for May and June

–   cash discount allowed is budgeted to be £500 per month

–   bad debts of £500 per month are to be written off in January and February

–   the figure for trade receivables at 1 January is £33,000

trade receivables budget

	January	February	March	April	May	June	Total
	£000	£000	£000	£000	£000	£000	£000
Opening trade receivables	33	34	35	29.5	34	34.5	33
Credit sales	30	30	30	40	40	40	210
Receipts	(28)	(28)	(35)	(35)	(39)	(39)	(204)
Discount allowed	(0.5)	(0.5)	(0.5)	(0.5)	(0.5)	(0.5)	(3)
Bad debts written off	(0.5)	(0.5)	–	–	–	–	(1)
Closing trade receivables	34	35	29.5	34	34.5	35	35

Tutorial notes:

*   The figure for closing trade receivables is calculated as follows:

    opening trade receivables + credit sales – receipts – discount allowed – bad debts

*   The total column may be used as a cross-check of the monthly figures

effect of bad debts

As seen in the Worked Example, bad debts written off affect the trade receivables budget in the following ways:

–   the bad debt is shown in the trade receivables budget as an expense
–   the business receives less cash than was expected

The effect of bad debts is to reduce the bank balance of the business or to increase its bank overdraft by the amount written off. The profitability of the business will also be affected as the amount will have to be written off as an expense in income statement.

improving trade receivables control

To reduce the incidence of bad debts, businesses should seek to improve their trade receivables control by taking the following measures:

*   take two credit references from new customers
*   use 'pro-forma' invoices – where the customer pays against the invoice and before goods are delivered – until credit references are received

- set credit limits for each customer – eg £500, £1,000 – to give a limit to possible bad debts
- offer cash discounts for prompt settlement, eg 2% cash discount for settlement within 7 days; however, ensure that cash discounts are not too generous as there is a cost in offering them
- issue statements of account to customers regularly, eg monthly
- chase up overdue accounts with letters, phone calls and emails
- threaten to charge interest on overdue accounts
- take legal action against overdue trade receivables but, in view of the high costs involved, ensure that such action will be cost effective

TRADE PAYABLES BUDGET

A trade payables budget is used to estimate the timing and amount of payments to trade payables and is linked to the purchases budget, the cash budget and the master budget.

An important aspect of running a business is to ensure that trade payables are paid on time. Delaying payment beyond the due date may well mean that suppliers refuse to deliver any further goods, which will lead to production problems and have an effect on the whole business. Suppliers usually offer a period of credit, and so the period between taking delivery of the goods and making payment for them gives the buyer a period when its purchases are being financed by the seller. Nevertheless, the buyer needs to ensure that cash is available in the bank account to meet trade payables payments as they fall due.

A trade payables budget links directly to the cash budget (see next page) – which records payments to trade payables – and the master budget – where the amount of trade payables is shown as a liability on the forecast balance sheet.

planning the trade payables budget

The information needed to plan the trade payables budget is:

- the amount of credit purchases (from the purchases budget)
- the expected payments to trade payables (from the cash budget)
- the expected cash discount received from trade payables (from the cash budget)
- the normal trade terms under which credit purchases are made
- the trade payables' collection period, ie $\dfrac{\text{Trade payables}}{\text{Credit purchases}}$ x 365 days (or 52 weeks or 12 months)

WORKED EXAMPLE: TRADE PAYABLES BUDGET

This trade payables budget has been prepared from the following information:

- credit purchases are budgeted to be £25,000 per month in July and August, £30,000 per month in September and October, and £35,000 per month in November and December
- payments to trade payables are budgeted to be £26,000 per month for July to September, and £33,000 per month for October to December
- cash discount received is budgeted to be £300 per month
- the figure for trade payables at 1 July is £29,000

trade payables budget

	July	Aug	Sep	Oct	Nov	Dec	Total
	£000	£000	£000	£000	£000	£000	£000
Opening trade payables	29	27.7	26.4	30.1	26.8	28.5	29
Credit purchases	25	25	30	30	35	35	180
Payments	(26)	(26)	(26)	(33)	(33)	(33)	(177)
Discount received	(0.3)	(0.3)	(0.3)	(0.3)	(0.3)	(0.3)	(1.8)
Closing trade payables	27.7	26.4	30.1	26.8	28.5	30.2	30.2

Tutorial notes:

- The figure for closing trade payables is calculated as follows:

    opening trade payables + credit purchases – payments – discount received

- The total column may be used as a cross-check of the monthly figures

CASH BUDGET

Tutorial note: the cash budget has been studied already as part of AS Accounting. For the purposes of revision, and to provide a link to forecast financial statements, some study material is repeated.

A cash budget details the forecast cash/bank receipts and payments, usually on a month-by-month basis, for the next three, six or twelve months, in order to show the forecast bank balance at the end of each month throughout the budget period.

From the cash budget, the managers of a business can decide what action to take when a surplus of cash is shown to be available or, as is more likely, when a bank overdraft needs to be arranged.

layout of a cash budget

A format for a cash budget, with example figures, follows.

Mike Anderson, trading as 'Art Supplies' **Cash budget for the six months ending 30 June 20-8**						
	Jan £	Feb £	Mar £	Apr £	May £	Jun £
Receipts						
Capital introduced	20,000					
Trade receivables	–	–	3,000	6,000	6,000	10,500
Total receipts for month	20,000	–	3,000	6,000	6,000	10,500
Payments						
Non-current assets	8,000					
Inventory	5,000					
Trade payables	–	2,000	4,000	4,000	7,000	7,000
Operating expenses	1,600	1,600	1,600	1,600	1,600	1,600
Drawings	1,000	1,000	1,000	1,000	1,000	1,000
Total payments for month	15,600	4,600	6,600	6,600	9,600	9,600
Net cash flow	4,400	(4,600)	(3,600)	(600)	(3,600)	900
Add bank balance (overdraft) at beginning of month	–	4,400	(200)	(3,800)	(4,400)	(8,000)
Bank balance (overdraft) at end of month	4,400	(200)	(3,800)	(4,400)	(8,000)	(7,100)

sections of a cash budget

A cash budget consists of three main sections:

* receipts for the month
* payments for the month
* summary of bank account

Receipts are analysed to show the amount of money that is expected to be received from cash sales, trade receivables, sale of non-current assets, capital introduced/issue of shares, loans received etc.

Payments show how much money is expected to be paid in respect of cash purchases, trade payables, expenses (often described in cash budgets as operating expenses), purchases of non-current assets, repayment of capital/shares and loans. Note that non-cash expenses (such as depreciation and doubtful debts) are not shown in the cash budget.

The **summary of the bank account** at the bottom of the cash budget shows **net cash flow** (total receipts less total payments) added to the bank balance at the beginning of the month, and resulting in the estimated closing bank balance at the end of the month. An overdrawn bank balance is shown in brackets.

benefits of a cash budget

The use of a cash budget enables a business to:

- plan future expenditure, eg the financing of new non-current assets
- control costs and revenues to ensure that either
  - a bank overdraft is avoided (so saving interest and charges payable), or
  - a bank overdraft or loan can be arranged in advance
- reschedule payments where necessary to avoid bank borrowing, eg delay the purchase of non-current assets
- co-ordinate the activities of the various sections of the business, eg the production department buys in materials not only to meet the expected sales of the sales department but also at a time when there is cash available
- communicate the overall aims of the business to the various sections and to check that the cash will be available to meet their needs
- identify any possible cash surpluses in advance and take steps to invest the surplus on a short-term basis (so earning interest)

THE MASTER BUDGET

A master budget takes the form of a forecast operating statement – forecast income statement – and a forecast balance sheet. (A forecast cash flow statement is also often included in the master budget.)

A cash budget does not indicate the profits (or losses) being made by a business. It does not follow that a cash budget which reveals an increasing bank balance necessarily indicates a profitable business. A **master budget** is the next logical step once all other budgets, including the cash budget, have been prepared.

WORKED EXAMPLE: MASTER BUDGET

situation

A friend of yours, Mike Anderson, has recently been made redundant from his job as a sales representative for an arts and crafts company. Mike has decided to set up in business on his own selling art supplies to shops and art societies. He plans to invest £20,000 of his savings into the new business. He has a number of good business contacts, and is confident that his firm will do well. He thinks that some additional finance will be required in the short term and plans to approach his bank for this.

Mike has prepared a cash budget for his new business (see previous page) and asks for your assistance in producing a forecast operating statement for the next six months, together with a forecast balance sheet at 30 June 20-8.

He provides the following information:

* The business, which is to be called 'Art Supplies' will commence in January 20-8.

* Non-current assets costing £8,000 will be bought in early January. These will be paid for immediately and are expected to have a five-year life, at the end of which they will be worthless.

* An initial supply of goods costing £5,000 will be bought and paid for at the beginning of January, and will be maintained at this level.

* Monthly purchases of inventories will then be made at a level sufficient to replace forecast sales for that month, ie the goods he expects to sell in January will be replaced by purchases made in January, and so on.

* Forecast monthly sales are:

January	February	March	April	May	June
£3,000	£6,000	£6,000	£10,500	£10,500	£10,500

* The selling price of goods is fixed at the cost price plus 50 per cent; for example, the goods he expects to sell in January for £3,000 will have cost him £2,000 (two-thirds of the selling price), ie his mark-up is 50%.

* To encourage sales, he will allow two months' credit to customers; however, only one month's credit will be received from suppliers of goods (but the initial goods will be paid for immediately).

* Operating expenses of the business, including rent of premises, but excluding depreciation of non-current assets, are estimated at £1,600 per month and are paid for in the month in which they are incurred.

* Mike intends to draw £1,000 each month in cash from the business.

solution

Mike Anderson, trading as 'Art Supplies'		
Forecast income statement for the six months ending 30 June 20-8		
	£	£
Revenue		46,500
Opening inventory	5,000	
Purchases £46,500 x 2/3	31,000	
	36,000	
Less Closing inventory	5,000	
Cost of sales		31,000
Gross profit		15,500
Less expenses:		
Running expenses	9,600	
Depreciation of non-current assets		
(68,000 ÷ 5 years) ÷ 2, ie six months	800	
		10,400
Profit for the six months		5,100

Mike Anderson, trading as 'Art Supplies'
Forecast balance sheet as at 30 June 20-8

	£	£
Non-current Assets		
At cost		8,000
Less provision for depreciation		800
Net book value		7,200
Current Assets		
Inventory	5,000	
Trade receivables £10,500 x 2 months	21,000	
	26,000	
Less Current Liabilities		
Trade payables	7,000	
Bank overdraft	7,100	
	14,100	
Net Current Assets		11,900
NET ASSETS		19,100
FINANCED BY		
Capital		
Opening capital		20,000
Add profit for the six months		5,100
		25,100
Less Drawings		6,000
		19,100

Notes:
- purchases are two-thirds of the sales values (because selling price is cost price plus 50 per cent)
- customers pay two months after sale, ie trade receivables from January settle in March
- suppliers are paid one month after purchase, ie trade payables from January are paid in February

---

Points to note when preparing forecast final accounts:

- The sales figure used is the total amount of goods sold, whether paid for or not (sales made, but not yet paid for, are recorded as trade receivables in the balance sheet).

- Likewise, the figure for purchases is the total of goods bought, with amounts not yet paid for recorded as trade payables in the balance sheet.

- Depreciation, which *never* appears in the cash budget, is shown amongst the expenses in the income statement, and deducted from the cost of the non-current asset in the balance sheet. (Note that, in the example above, depreciation is for a period of six months.)

benefits of the master budget

The master budget involves preparation of a forecast operating statement – forecast income statement – and a forecast balance sheet. These benefit a business in a number of ways:

- the forecast profit can be calculated and compared with the actual profit of the previous year
- the forecast profit shows the effect of changes in the selling price of products, the volume of units sold, the buying price, and in overhead expenses
- management of a business can take action by reviewing their selling prices, volume of sales, buying prices, and overhead expenses
- the actual profit for the year can be compared with the forecast profit, and any differences can be investigated

differences between cash and profit

While cash budget shows the forecast bank balance during the budget period, the master budget shows the forecast profit for the budget period. Sometimes people in business get confused between 'cash' and 'profit' and may say: "I am making a profit, but why is my bank overdraft increasing."

The difference between cash and profit is:

- cash is money in the bank or held as physical cash (eg in a cash till)
- profit is a calculated figure which shows the surplus of income over expenditure for the period; it takes note of adjustments for accruals and prepayments and non-cash items such as depreciation and provision for doubtful debts; it does not include capital expenditure (ie the purchase of non-current assets, or owner's drawings/dividends).

The reasons why a business can be making a profit but its bank balance is reducing (or its bank overdraft is increasing) include:

- capital expenditure – the purchase of non-current assets reduces cash but profit is affected only by the amount of depreciation on the asset
- increase in trade receivables – if more goods are being sold, this should lead to an increase in profit but, until trade receivables pay, there is no benefit to the bank balance
- decrease in trade payables – if trade payables are paid earlier than usual there will be no effect on profit but the bank balance will reduce (or a bank overdraft will increase)
- increase in inventory – if more inventory is purchased there will be an increase in profit as it is sold, but paying for the inventory will reduce the money at bank (or increase an overdraft)
- prepayment of expenses at the year end – as the prepayment is an expense for next year, early payment will have no effect on the current year's profit, but the bank balance will be affected by the payment
- repayment of a loan – this has no effect on profits (although loan interest may be reduced), but the bank balance will be affected by the repayment
- drawings/dividends paid to owners – will have no effect on profit, but the bank balance will be affected by the payment

Clearly the above will work in reverse for a business that is making reduced profits (or losses) but whose bank balance is increasing (or its bank overdraft is reducing).

Note that a cash flow statement (see Chapter 6) demonstrates the link between profit and changes in cash. The master budget often also includes a forecast cash flow statement.

CHAPTER SUMMARY

- Budgetary control is the process of using budgets to monitor actual results against budgeted figures.

- The benefits of budgetary control are
  - planning future activities
  - co-ordination into master budget
  - control of the business
  - communication within the business
  - motivation of staff
  - evaluation of performance
  - decision-making for production, sales and costs

- The limitations of budgetary control are
  - costs may exceed benefits
  - accuracy of information
  - demotivation of staff
  - disfunctional management
  - budgets may be set too easy
  - budgets may restrict activities

- A budget is a financial plan for a business, prepared in advance and generally covering a period of up to 12 months.

- Budgets are prepared for each section of the business, eg sales, production, purchases, labour, trade receivables, trade payables, cash.

- Responsibility for budgets is given to managers and supervisors – the budget holders.

- The master budget is compiled from the budgets of a business.

- The master budget comprises:
  - forecast income statement
  - forecast balance sheet
  A forecast cash flow statement is often also included in the master budget.

In the next chapter we turn our attention to the way in which businesses make decisions in the context of social accounting, eg the effects of decisions on the workforce, the local economy and the environment.

QUESTIONS

visit
www.osbornebooks.co.uk
to take an online test

An asterisk (*) after the question number means that the answer is given at the end of this book.

17.1 AggieSurf is a manufacturer of surfboards. It is owned by Sally Johnson as a sole trader business. There are five employees and annual turnover is approximately £400,000 per year.

REQUIRED

(a) Explain two benefits of budgetary control to Sally Johnson.

(b) Suggest three budgets which Sally could use in the business to provide an adequate system of budgetary control.

(c) Advise Sally of the relevant factors to consider when implementing budgetary control.

17.2* Davidson Reproductions Ltd produces tables. The production manager has collected the following information in order to produce a production budget for the next four months.

1. Demand is expected to be 1,200 tables in month 1. This should reduce by 10% in month 2, but thereafter increase by 5% each month, based on the demand for the previous month.

2. The inventory at the end of each month is to be maintained at a level of 20% of the following month's sales but due to a storage constraint should not exceed 240 tables.

3. The inventory at the start of month 1 is 100 tables.

REQUIRED

Produce a production budget for the next four months. Round up to the nearest whole table.

	Month 1 (tables)	Month 2 (tables)	Month 3 (tables)	Month 4 (tables)
Sales	....	....	....	....
Opening inventory	....	....	....	....
Closing inventory	....	....	....	....
Production	....	....	....	....

Assessment and Qualifications Alliance (AQA), 2003

17.3

Lee's Landscapes Ltd supplies plants for residential gardens.

The results for the year ended 31 March 2003 are:

	£
Sales	150,000
Purchases	110,000
Trade receivables	12,000
Trade payables	11,000

All sales and purchases are on credit terms.

Total sales for the year ending 31 March 2004 are expected to be:

April – June	£20,000 per month
July – October	£15,000 per month
November – March	£5,000 per month

As at 31 March 2004 trade receivables and trade payables are expected to be £14,000 and £10,000 respectively.

There is no closing inventory. The profit margin is 25%.

The business prepares budgets on a two-monthly basis.

REQUIRED

(a)   Prepare a purchases budget for the year ending 31 March 2004.

	April and May £000	June and July £000	August and September £000	October and November £000	December and January £000	February and March £000
Sales						
Margin						
Purchases						

(b)   (i)   Calculate the trade receivables' collection period for each of the last two years. State the formula used.

Formula ....

....

Year ending 31 March 2003	Year ending 31 March 2004
....	....
....	....
....	....

   (ii)   Calculate the trade payables' payment period for each of the last two years. State the formula used.

Formula ....

....

Year ending 31 March 2003	Year ending 31 March 2004
....	....
....	....
....	....

(c)   Comment on the results from (b). Give one recommendation to improve the credit control at Lee's Landscapes Ltd.

Trade receivables' collection period ....

....

Trade payables' payment period ....

....

Recommendation ....

....

Assessment and Qualifications Alliance (AQA), 2003

17.4 Robert Adams owns a business manufacturing footballs. At the start of the current year, he introduced a system of budgetary control.

The business operates over 13 four-week periods with five working days in each week.

The sales for the first three periods of the current year were as follows:

	Period 1	Period 2	Period 3
Footballs (units)	13,600	12,400	12,000

Sales for period 4 are expected to be 10,800 footballs at a selling price of £1 per football.

The inventory at the start of period 1 was 3,400 footballs. It is the policy of the business to maintain closing inventory of footballs at a level which is sufficient to cover five days of the next period's sales.

REQUIRED

(a) Prepare the production budget in units for each of the periods 1–3.

(b) Calculate the number of footballs lost during periods 1–3 if, by the end of period 3, there are only 2,500 footballs in inventory.

(c) Explain **two** limitations of introducing a system of budgetary control.

> For periods 1–3, trade receivables as a percentage of sales was 14%. In an attempt to increase sales, the trade receivables' collection period is to be increased to 55 days from period 4 onwards.

REQUIRED

(d) Calculate the trade receivables' collection period for periods 1–3. State the formula used.

(e) Explain how the trade receivables' collection period could be increased and what effect the proposed increase could have on the cash or bank balances.

Assessment and Qualifications Alliance (AQA), 2006

17.5*

(a) Explain the term, 'labour budget'.

(e) Explain **two** uses of a labour budget for a manufacturing company

Assessment and Qualifications Alliance (AQA), Additional Specimen Questions

17.6 Su Ling Ltd has the following production budget for the next quarter:

	Month 1	Month 2	Month 3
Production in units	2,100	2,400	3,000

Each unit takes 6 hours to complete. Each labour hour is paid at a rate of £8 per hour.

There are 15,000 hours of labour available each month.

REQUIRED

(a) A labour budget for the quarter identifying any shortfall or surplus in monthly labour hours.

Part-time labour could be employed to cover each month's shortfall in hours. this would be paid at a rate of £14 per hour.

REQUIRED

(b) Calculate the percentage increase in total cost for the quarter if the part-time labour is employed to cover the shortfall in labour hours compared to the total cost of labour if the part-time labour is not employed.

(c) Describe how the labour budget could be used to prevent the employment of the part-time labour. Explain the limitation of using the labour budget in this manner.

Assessment and Qualifications Alliance (AQA), Additional Specimen Questions

17.7 Wyvern (Medical) Limited is a manufacturer of specialist equipment used in hospitals. The accounts assistant has collected the following information in order to prepare the trade receivables and trade payables budgets for the six months to 30 June 20-5.

- On 1 January 20-5 the figures for trade receivables and trade payables are £65,500 and £42,400 respectively.

- For the six months to 30 June 20-5, the following transactions are forecast:

	January	February	March	April	May	June
	£	£	£	£	£	£
credit purchases	19,500	22,300	22,500	24,000	22,600	23,400
credit sales	38,300	39,500	42,400	45,000	47,400	44,700
cash discount allowed	350	400	450	500	500	400
cash discount received	170	200	220	280	260	270
receipts from trade receivables	42,400	38,100	37,400	40,600	43,200	45,800
payments to trade payables	22,600	20,500	21,600	22,300	24,300	23,200
bad debts written off	500	500	–	–	–	–

REQUIRED

(a)   Prepare the trade receivables budget of Wyvern (Medical) Limited for the six months to 30 June 20-5.

trade receivables budget

	January	February	March	April	May	June	Total
	£	£	£	£	£	£	£

(b)   Prepare the trade payables budget of Wyvern (Medical) Limited for the six months to 30 June 20-5.

trade payables budget

	January	February	March	April	May	June	Total
	£	£	£	£	£	£	£

17.8* Damir Ltd is a small business which manufactures toys.

The following information is available for the next four months.

	January	February	March	April
Expected sales (units)	2,000	2,200	2,300	2,200

Additional information

(1) Each unit sells for £15.

(2) Each month, 20% of the sales are expected to be on a cash basis.

(3) Fifty per cent of trade receivables are expected to pay after one month. The remainder are expected to pay after two months.

(4) Trade receivables on 1 January are expected to be:

£21,600 from December sales, of which £10,800 will be paid in January and the balance in February;

£7,200 from November sales, which will be paid in January.

REQUIRED

(a) Prepare a trade receivables' budget for Damir Ltd for **each** of the four months January to April.

> Damir Ltd continued to trade as expected. Unfortunately, in May, it was discovered that a trade receivable had gone into liquidation and would not be able to settle the debt in full. This trade receivable owed money for 600 units sold in December. Only £1,800 had been received in December for these sales.

(b) Explain how this information will affect Damir Ltd's cash flow.

(c) Explain what measures Damir Ltd should take to improve future trade receivables control.

Assessment and Qualifications Alliance (AQA), 2007

17.9* Corinne Kent plc manufactures two products, A110 and B220.

Information for the two months ending 31 March 2005 is expected to be:

	A110	B220
Purchases – February (units)	1,000	1,600
– March (units)	600	1,800
Opening inventory as at 1 February 2005 (units)	200	300
Cost price	£20	£15
Sales units per month as a percentage of total inventory available	80%	70%
Mark-up on cost	50%	100%

REQUIRED

(a)   Prepare a sales budget for the two months ending 31 March 2005 for **each** of the products.

Sales budget for Corinne Kent for the two months ending 31 March 2005

(i)   Show the number of sales units for each month.

	February units	March units
A110		
B220		

(ii)   Show the monthly sales value.

	February £	March £
A110		
B220		

(b)   Prepare a balance sheet extract to show the forecast inventory for **each** product as at 31 March 2005.

(c)   State the formula used to calculate the rate of inventory turnover.

(d)   Calculate the rate of inventory turnover for **each** product for March 2005.

(e)   Briefly explain the relationship between a sales budget and a master budget.

Assessment and Qualifications Alliance (AQA), 2005

17.10

Marat has been in business for several years manufacturing motor parts. Each year, a small profit is made but there never seems to be enough cash to reinvest in the business. At the year end, the business had a large bank overdraft.

REQUIRED

(a)   Explain the difference between cash and profits.

(b)   Describe **three** possible reasons why Marat has a bank overdraft even though his business is making a profit.

At the beginning of March, Marat decides that he will introduce a system of budgetary control.

The following information is available for March to July.

- Sales in March and April are expected to be 200 parts per month. This is expected to increase from 1 May to 260 parts per month.

- Each part is expected to sell for £24 in March, April and May, but this selling price is expected to increase from 1 June to £26.

- On 1 March, Marat will have 20 parts in inventory.

- In March and April, closing inventory will be maintained at 10% of the following month's sales. At the end of May, this will increase to 15% of the following month's sales.

REQUIRED

(c)   Prepare a sales budget for **each** of the months March to July.

	SALES BUDGET				
	March	April	May	June	July
Parts (units)					
Revenue £					

(d)   Prepare a production budget for **each** of the months March to July. Assume that there are no further increases in sales.

	PRODUCTION BUDGET IN PARTS (UNITS)				
	March	April	May	June	July

(e)   Identify **three** budgets **other than** cash, production and sales budgets, which Marat would find useful.

Marat's business is located in an area of high unemployment. He believes that his labour expenses are too high and he cannot afford to offer his staff a pay rise. Instead he proposes to increase the working day by an extra hour and to reduce breaks to the legal minimum. Overtime rates will be reduced to the same rate as for normal working hours.

REQUIRED

(f)   Explain how the following actions will affect the workforce:

- no pay rise

- an increase in the working day

- a reduction in overtime rates

Assessment and Qualifications Alliance (AQA), 2007

17.11*   Explain **three** benefits to the owner of a new business of using a cash budget.

Assessment and Qualifications Alliance (AQA), 2007

17.12* Peversal Papers Ltd manufactures reams of paper. Each ream is sold for £22 and costs £12 to manufacture.

The company's policy is to maintain inventory levels at the end of each month at 20% of the next month's expected sales.

Sales for 2002 are expected to be:

February	March	April	May	June
£88,000	£99,000	£110,000	£121,000	£110,000

Customers are allowed one month's credit. Only 5% pay immediately and receive a 2% discount for prompt payment.

Inventory as at 1 March 2002 is expected to be 900 units.

Administration and distribution costs which are paid in the month in which they occur are expected to be:

February	March	April	May	June
£26,000	£28,000	£34,000	£38,000	£36,000

The bank balance on 1 March 2002 is expected to be £6,000.

Production costs are paid in the month in which they occur.

REQUIRED

(a) (i) Complete the following cash budget for the 3 months ending 31 May 2002.

<table>
<tr><td colspan="4">Cash Budget for Peversal Papers Ltd
for the three months ending 31 May 2002</td></tr>
<tr><td></td><td>March
£000</td><td>April
£000</td><td>May
£000</td></tr>
<tr><td>Sales   – cash</td><td></td><td></td><td></td></tr>
<tr><td>– credit</td><td></td><td></td><td></td></tr>
<tr><td></td><td></td><td></td><td></td></tr>
<tr><td>Production costs</td><td></td><td></td><td></td></tr>
<tr><td>Admin/distribution</td><td></td><td></td><td></td></tr>
<tr><td></td><td></td><td></td><td></td></tr>
<tr><td>Net inflow/outflow</td><td></td><td></td><td></td></tr>
<tr><td>Opening balance</td><td></td><td></td><td></td></tr>
<tr><td>Closing balance</td><td></td><td></td><td></td></tr>
</table>

(ii)   Complete the following production budget for the 3 months ending 31 May 2002.

Production Budget for Peversal Papers Ltd for the three months ending 31 May 2002			
	March units	April units	May units
Sales Opening inventory Closing inventory			
Production			

(b)   The Managing Director of Peversal Papers Ltd believes that a cash budget is all that is required, however the Production Manager disagrees. He believes that the production budget is vital too. Assess three advantages to Peversal Papers Ltd of using both a cash budget and a production budget.

....

....

....

....

....

....

....

....

....

....

....

Assessment and Qualifications Alliance (AQA), 2002

17.13 Ian hopes to start a new business on 1 March selling surfboards. His balance at the bank on that day will be £3,200.

He intends to sell each surfboard for £160. On 1 June, the price will increase to £190 per surfboard.

The variable cost per surfboard is expected to be £85.

In preparation for the summer season Ian intends his inventory level to be 60 surfboards by 1 June. Thereafter, he will only produce enough to satisfy demand.

Note: Assume each month consists of 4 weeks.

Ian hopes to employ his brother, Malcolm, to help out in the workshop for 3 months from 1 March. Malcolm will be paid £40 per day for 5 days a week.

With Malcolm's help, Ian hopes to make up to a maximum of 10 surfboards a week, whereas he can only make up to 6 surfboards alone.

Expected sales are:

1 March to 30 April	May	1 June onwards
4 surfboards a week	7 surfboards a week	10 surfboards a week

The inventory on 31 July is expected to be 28 surfboards.

His fixed overheads, excluding depreciation, are expected to be £500 per month.

Any bank surplus over £1,000 at the end of each month will be taken as Ian's personal drawings.

All transactions will be on a cash basis.

REQUIRED

(a) Prepare a production budget for each of the 5 months ending 31 July, assuming Malcolm is employed.

	PRODUCTION BUDGET (UNITS/SURFBOARDS)				
	March	April	May	June	July

(b) Prepare a cash budget for each of the 5 months ending 31 July. Include the maximum amount that Ian can withdraw for personal use.

	CASH BUDGET				
	March £	April £	May £	June £	July £

Assessment and Qualifications Alliance (AQA), 2006

17.14 The income statement for the year ended 31 March 2003 for Potter and Son Ltd was:

	£	£
Revenue (250,000 units)		4,000,000
Opening inventory (16,000 units)	120,000	
Purchases (254,000 units)	2,540,000	
Closing inventory (20,000 units)	(200,000)	
Cost of sales		(2,460,000)
Gross profit		1,540,000
Overheads		(1,080,000)
Profit for the year		460,000

Additional information for the year ending 31 March 2004:

1. The unit selling price will *decrease* by 15%. This is expected to *increase* the number of sales units by 25%.

2. The supplier will give a discount of 10% on last year's price.

3. The ratio of units of closing inventory to sales units will be the same in both years. Closing inventory is to be valued at the cost price for the year.

4. The overheads are expected to increase by 6.25%.

REQUIRED

(a) Prepare the forecast income statement for Potter and Son Ltd for the year ending 31 March 2004.

(b) Explain **two** benefits to Potter and Son Ltd of preparing a forecast income statement.

Assessment and Qualifications Alliance (AQA), 2004

18 DECISION-MAKING AND SOCIAL ACCOUNTING

In this book we have looked at various aspects of financial accounting and management accounting. Accounting information is useful in helping the managers of a business to make decisions – for example, we need to replace our existing machinery, so which new machine shall we buy? However, such decisions cannot be made in isolation – a business is part of a wider community, with responsibilities to its employees, the local economy and the environment.

In this chapter we look at the accounting factors, including social accounting factors, which affect decision-making.

DECISION-MAKING IN CONTEXT

A business does not operate in isolation where it can do what it wishes with no thought for others. Even small businesses have responsibilities to others, while large businesses must take great care to consider the effect of their decisions – the public and the media (in the form of television, radio, newspapers) will certainly scrutinise their every move.

The diagram on the next page shows some of the factors which affect business decision-making. This shows that, while the effect on profit and cash is important, other factors need to be considered. These other factors are often referred to as 'social accounting' and we shall be looking at the impact of a variety of social accounting factors later in the chapter.

When we talk about making decisions, there are a variety of levels at which decisions are made. More decisions are made at lower levels than at higher levels – although it is the latter that get most attention in the media. Look at some of these decisions:

- higher level decisions
    - we have decided to close our factory in Scotland
    - our call centre will be transferred to India
    - we will only buy furniture which uses timber from managed forests

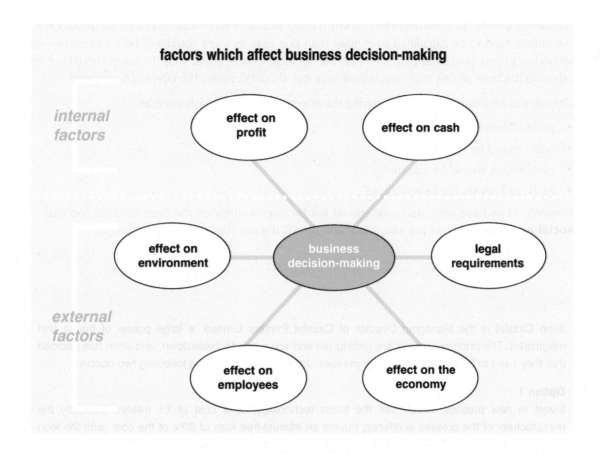

factors which affect business decision-making

- lower level decisions
    - we have instituted a first-aid training programme
    - all our photocopying is done on recycled paper
    - the tea used in our canteen comes from 'fairtrade' suppliers

The conclusion to draw is that we all make decisions – whether at work or in our personal lives. We need to consider not only the financial implications of our decisions, but other factors as well.

DECISION-MAKING: THE EFFECT ON PROFIT AND CASH

- **cash** is the actual amount of money held in the bank or as cash
- **profit** is a calculated figure which shows the surplus of income over expenditure for the year

In studying for your AQA A2 Accounting you will have appreciated the differences between profit and cash. You will have seen that some transactions often have an unequal effect on profit and cash – for example, depreciation is a non-cash expense which reduces profit, but has no effect on the balance of cash in the business.

A business will wish to know the extent to which profit and cash will be affected by its decisions. Often the effects need to be calculated over more than one year, as there could well be initial costs – eg redundancy costs paid to employees – that will not recur in later years. Thus decisions should not be taken on the basis of first year calculations only, but should consider the effect of later years.

The rules to be followed when considering the effect on profit and cash are that:

- profit should be maximised
- costs should be minimised
- cash inflows should be maximised
- cash outflows should be minimised

However, as we have seen, decisions should not be taken entirely on the basis of profit and cash – **social accounting** factors are also important. We will discuss these later in this chapter.

WORKED EXAMPLE: DECISION-MAKING

situation

John Cazalet is the Managing Director of Cazalet Printers Limited, a large printer of books and magazines. The printing presses are getting old and are prone to breakdown, and John has decided that they need to be replaced with new presses. John is considering the following two options:

Option 1
Invest in new presses, which use the latest technology, at a cost of £1 million. Currently the manufacturer of the presses is offering buyers an interest-free loan of 80% of the cost, with the loan repayable at the end of five years. The new presses will require fewer staff to operate them and the cost of redundancies and early retirement will be £140,000 in the first year. After the first year there will be staff cost savings of £60,000 a year. A training programme will have to be set up for remaining staff at a cost of £60,000 spread over the first three years. The new presses will only be able to use paper which is 100% brand new – even a small percentage of recycled content in the paper will cause the presses to break down.

Option 2
Invest in new presses of a lower specification at a cost of £600,000. These presses are able to cope with paper which contains up to 50% of recycled paper. The new presses will be financed with a loan of £400,000, which will be repayable at the end of five years. Interest will be paid annually on the loan at 5%. No staff will need to be made redundant. Retraining costs of £20,000 will be payable in the first year.

Note: under both options the new presses will have a life of ten years and will be depreciated using the straight-line method.

You are to help John Cazalet to evaluate these options by calculating the effect of each on profit and cash for the next financial year. Are there any other factors which John should consider before making a recommendation to the company's board of directors?

solution

	Profit	Cash
	£	£
Option 1		
new presses	–	(1,000,000)
loan	–	800,000
redundancies/early retirement	(140,000)	(140,000)
retraining	(20,000)	(20,000)
depreciation	(100,000)	–
net effect	(260,000)	(360,000)
Option 2		
new presses	–	(600,000)
loan	–	400,000
interest on loan	(20,000)	(20,000)
retraining	(20,000)	(20,000)
depreciation	(60,000)	–
net effect	(100,000)	(240,000)

Note that depreciation is a non-cash expense which affects profit only.

discussion points

- For this first year, option 2 has the smaller effect on both profit and cash.

- If redundancy costs can be avoided in option 1, profit will be (£120,000), which is £20,000 more than option 2 at (£100,000). Cash will be (£220,000), which is £20,000 less than option 2 at (£240,000).

- For years 2 and 3, the effects on profit will be:

	Option 1		Option 2	
	Year 2	Year 3	Year 2	Year 3
	£	£	£	£
retraining	(20,000)	(20,000)	–	–
staff cost savings	60,000	60,000	–	–
interest on loan	–	–	(20,000)	(20,000)
depreciation	(100,000)	(100,000)	(60,000)	(60,000)
net effect	(60,000)	(60,000)	(80,000)	(80,000)

- For years 2 and 3, the effects on cash will be:

	Option 1		Option 2	
	Year 2	Year 3	Year 2	Year 3
	£	£	£	£
retraining	(20,000)	(20,000)	–	–
staff cost savings	60,000	60,000	–	–
interest on loan	–	–	(20,000)	(20,000)
net effect	40,000	40,000	(20,000)	(20,000)

- The company must decide how the loan is to be repaid – either £800,000 for option 1, or £600,000 for option 2.

- There are social factors to consider:

  - redundancy (effect on workforce and local economy)

  - recycling (customers may be lost under option 1 if only non-recycled paper can be used; customers may be gained under option 2 if recycled paper can be used)

- Option 2 is preferred in the short-term because there is less effect on profit and cash. In the longer-term, option 1 is preferable, although the social factors need to be considered. The method of repaying the loan under each option needs to be decided.

SOCIAL ACCOUNTING

The word 'social' is often used but rarely defined. It has a variety of attributes which include:

- living in a group of people
- groups of people that depend on each other
- treating people equally and fairly

The word 'accounting' can relate in a very specific sense to the processes described in the rest of this book, ie financial accounting and management accounting. It can also relate to 'being accountable', ie being responsible to others for what you do.

Social accounting in business can therefore be defined as:

the need for a business to be accountable for its actions to society as a whole

This need for social accountability is recognised by businesses generally. In the case of larger limited companies, solutions to the need – ie 'what we have done to help society' – are formalised in publications and on websites. The term often given to this sense of social responsibility is 'Corporate Social Responsibility' (CSR).

the demands of society: areas of social accounting

As we saw at the beginning of this chapter, social accounting involves a potential conflict of interest within businesses between:

- internal pressures – the need to maximise cash and profit
- external pressures – social accounting – the need to 'take account' of the demands of society

The external pressures involved in social accounting are very wide and varied. They include:

- the requirements of law
- the environment
- economic well-being
- technological improvements
- politics
- ethics

The diagram below shows the main external pressures that are placed on the business decision-making process. Study the diagram and then read the text and Discussion Points that follow. You may wish to debate the issues raised by these Discussion Points with others.

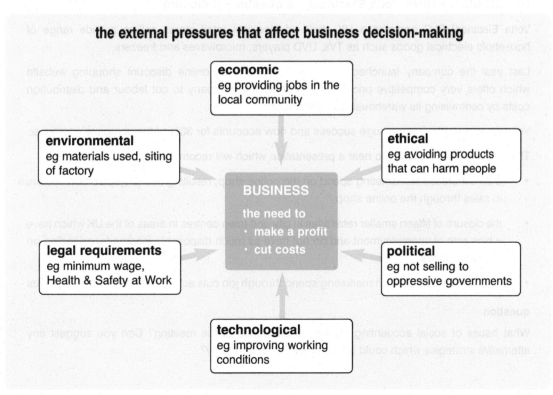

the external pressures that affect business decision-making

economic
eg providing jobs in the local community

environmental
eg materials used, siting of factory

ethical
eg avoiding products that can harm people

BUSINESS
the need to
- make a profit
- cut costs

legal requirements
eg minimum wage, Health & Safety at Work

political
eg not selling to oppressive governments

technological
eg improving working conditions

Social Accounting in Action

The business aim of cash and profit maximisation may get in the way of the'social' needs mentioned previously. In the pages that follow you should read the text and subjects for discussion and write notes on the issues that they raise. These can then be discussed in preparation for the exam.

Note that the individual discussion topics may well involve more than one of the external pressures, and you should look out for this. The first, for example, involves a question of technology in addition to the need to help the Government's economic policy and to benefit local communities.

the demands of economic pressures

A healthy economy is one which should provide, as well as price stability and low interest rates:

- a well-trained and skilled workforce
- support for the less prosperous areas of the country

There are a number of ways in which businesses can help to support this aim. The Government provides through The Department for Business, Innovation & skills (BIS) a wide range of incentives and grants to encourage employment in areas of higher unemployment. It also encourages the development of skills training through the Department for Education and Skills.

DISCUSSION POINT: Volta Electrical – a question of closure

Volta Electrical PLC operates a UK chain of electrical retail stores selling a wide range of household electrical goods such as TVs, DVD players, microwaves and freezers.

Last year the company launched www.voltadirect.com, an online discount shopping website which offers very competitive prices. This enabled the company to cut labour and distribution costs by centralising its warehousing and logistics.

Voltadirect.com has been a huge success and now accounts for 30% of the company's turnover.

The board is meeting today to hear a presentation which will recommend:

- a 25% increase in marketing spend on the online shop, resulting in a projected 30% increase in sales through the online shop

- the closure of fifteen smaller retail sites in city and town centres in areas of the UK which have a high rate of unemployment and do not have as much disposable income for spending on electrical goods

- financing the increase on marketing spend through job cuts achieved through these closures

question

What issues of social accounting should be discussed at the meeting? Can you suggest any alternative strategies which could be adopted by the company?

---

the demands of political pressures

Sometimes businesses may be restricted in their commercial operations by political factors. Are there any restrictions, for example, in exporting goods and services to a country which has an oppressive government? Are there any trade sanctions in place which will restrict exports?

In the example that follows the ethical and political conscience of a company is put to the test.

DISCUSSION POINT: ICO Chemicals PLC – a question of ethics

ICO Chemicals PLC produces a wide range of chemical products, including pharmaceuticals, plastics and paints.

The company has exported raw chemical products to the Government of Maribia for a number of years. Last year there was a military coup in the capital Melba, and the country was taken over by a military dictatorship which operates an autocratic regime and has threatened the neighbouring states with invasion.

The sales director of ICO Chemicals has asked for an urgent board meeting following an order from a Maribian government agency for a large consignment of raw chemicals. The order will be very profitable for ICO Chemicals. Maribia pays cash up front for its orders. The problem is that the chemicals are not only used for fertilisers (Maribia is highly dependent on agriculture), they can also be used in the production of highly effective chemical weapons.

question

What issues are likely to be discussed at the ICO Chemicals meeting? What do you consider to be the right decision?

the demands of the law

All businesses are regulated by the law. By 'law' we mean Statute Law (ie Act of Parliament) and other regulations, some of them required by European Union directives. Areas of law include:

- employment law – anti-discrimination law, for example
- Health and Safety at Work legislation – ensuring a safe and healthy workplace
- law relating to the sale of goods and services
- data protection law – protecting personal details of individuals held on file

Some of these areas are likely to involve business expenditure and may therefore reduce profit.

DISCUSSION POINT: Arbor Sawmills Limited – a question of safety

Arbor Sawmills Limited is a small family-run timber company situated in Dorset. The company has made losses over the last two years and lacks the funds to invest in the new equipment it needs to remain competitive. Its run of bad luck continued last month when as part of a 'risk assessment' required under Health & Safety legislation it was discovered that two of the electric saws operated by the company lacked the necessary guard rail and safety equipment. A supplier has quoted the sum of £25,000 for supply and installation of this equipment. 'It goes against the grain to have to borrow all this', commented Giles Oak, Managing Director. 'We can hardly afford the wages, let alone all this stuff!'

question

What issues are raised here, and how would you advise Mr Oak?

the technological issue

One of the aims of new technology is to improve the working environment, making it cleaner and more efficient. Many manufacturing and service environments have been transformed beyond recognition by the introduction of computing and electronic communications. But technology has its downside and has brought its problems:

- staff redundancies and increased unemployment as technology replaces jobs, eg robotics in manufacturing, computer applications used for accounting
- health problems such as eyestrain, headaches and Repetitive Strain Injury (RSI) through operation of computers

In the Discussion Point that follows, the problems of technological advance are clearly highlighted.

DISCUSSION POINT: Mercia Finance PLC – a question of customer service

Mercia Finance PLC is a Midlands-based finance company which offers financial products (loans, leasing and hire purchase) to a wide range of personal and business customers. Currently all its main functions – including sales and customer service – operate from a central office in Wolverhampton. The Marketing Director has recently been researching the possibility of transferring its sales and customer service operations to a call centre in India. He has calculated that he will be able to cut forty jobs in Wolverhampton, resulting in savings of £600,000 a year.

question

The Marketing Director will have to 'sell' his idea to the Board at a meeting next week. What opposition is he likely to encounter, and what arguments could he use to counter this opposition?

the demands of the environmental lobby

The demands on business practice by environmental pressure groups have become so well known that business has even turned them to advantage – the marketing of organic food, for example. Traditionally, environmental concerns have concentrated on a number of defined needs:

- energy conservation
- restrictions on pollution
- the use of recycled materials
- the use of biodegradable materials
- the use of materials which are not harmful to wildlife

A number of these environmental issues are raised in the Discussion Point that follows.

DISCUSSION POINT: Premier Packaging Limited – a question of going 'green'

Premier Packaging Limited manufactures packaging and labelling for a number of the major UK food producers. The company has recently commissioned a review of its manufacturing processes and the materials it uses. The report produced has highlighted the following issues:

- the plastic wrapping currently used is imported cheaply from overseas, and has been found to contain a substance which has been rumoured (but not proved) to cause cancer when it comes into contact with food

- this imported plastic wrapping is non-biodegradable and can be toxic to animals

- an alternative recycled plastic wrapping is available, but it is more expensive and will add 10% to production costs

question

What issues does this report raise which the management of the company will have to discuss and decide upon?

SOCIAL ACCOUNTING IN THE A2 EXAMINATION

It is likely that social accounting in the examination will be assessed either by a short question or as part of a longer question involving other topics you will have studied as part of Unit 4.

You may be asked to write down a simple definition, or you may be asked to write a short report, in which case you will need to know how to set out a memorandum report. Always remember when writing a report to set out the main points and then make a firm recommendation at the end.

The following two examples are based on past AQA questions involving social accounting.

---

question

Explain what you understand by the term 'social accounting'.

suggested answer

'Social accounting' is the term used to describe the way in which businesses are accountable and responsible to society as a whole. Social accounting requires that businesses should not be driven just by the profit motive but should also consider the wider implications of their decisions. The issues which involve social accounting can be internal, eg the demands of the workforce, or they can be external. External factors can be economic (providing local employment), ethical (not selling high nicotine cigarettes to developing countries), political (not selling goods to oppressive governments), legal (employment law) or environmental (using renewable resources or not polluting the atmosphere).

---

question

Hughes Plc manufactures exclusive premium price, high profit margin sports cars.

The production manager believes that if cheaper filters could be used in the exhaust filtration system, a saving of £20 per car could be made.

The company produces 5,000 cars each year.

Unfortunately, the use of the cheaper filters will mean a 15% increase in carbon dioxide emissions which will obviously affect the atmosphere.

REQUIRED

Write a report to Hughes Plc, explaining whether they should use the cheaper filters.
Consider the effect on the environment as well as financial factors.

suggested answer

To: Hughes Plc

From: A Student

Date: Date of Exam

Subject: The effects of using cheaper filters

The total cost saving to the company will be 5,000 x £20 = £100,000, which will help to increase profitability.

The main question to be asked, however, is whether this saving will offset the fall in sales which could result from the increase in carbon dioxide emissions. The factors involved are:

1   Hughes Plc would be seen by the environmental lobby as being irresponsible and environmentally unfriendly. Bad publicity could result.

2   Customers would be put off by the higher emissions, not only because of the environmental issue but also because they are likely to have to pay a higher rate of car tax.

3   Customers may consequently chose to buy a new car from one of our competitors.

4   As Hughes Plc sells exclusive cars at a premium price, price sensitivity is not an issue; an extra £20 in cost may not seriously affect our profit margin.

On the basis of these factors I recommend that we do not cut costs by using cheaper filters.

CHAPTER SUMMARY

- Businesses cannot make decisions in isolation – they need to consider their responsibilities to others.

- There may be a conflict between internal factors (what the business wants to do) and external factors (what other people want the business to do).

- Internal factors affecting decision-making include the need to maximise profitability and the advisability of maximising cash.

- External pressures influencing business decision-making include

  – environmental pressures, eg the choice of materials used, the siting of a manufacturing plant

  – the needs of the local economy, eg the need to support local employment

  – the opportunities offered by new technology, eg improving working conditions and efficiency

  – legal requirements such as the Health & Safety at Work regulations

  – ethical issues such as making profits from the sale of tobacco and alcohol which may cause damage to health

  – political issues such as selling goods and services to countries which are known to have oppressive governments

QUESTIONS

visit
www.osbornebooks.co.uk
to take an online test

An asterisk (*) after the question number means that the answer is given at the end of this book.

18.1*   Jack Smart is the manager of a factory which produces cardboard boxes from recycled paper.

The current production process needs to be replaced.

Jack has the following two options:

Option 1. Invest in new recycling machinery at a cost of £450,000. In order to finance this purchase a loan of £600,000 will need to be taken out. This will be repayable at the end of five years. Interest is paid annually at 10%. Also 15% of the staff will no longer be needed and will have to be made redundant or take early retirement in the first year at a cost of £160,000. Most of the remaining staff will need to be retrained to use the new machinery, which is expected to cost £60,000 and is payable over 2 years.

Option 2. To make cardboard boxes from paper which has not been recycled. This will involve investing in new machinery at a cost of £250,000. This will be financed by a loan of £300,000, repayable at the end of five years. Interest is paid annually at 10%. No staff will need to be made redundant. The retraining costs are expected to be £80,000 and are payable in the first year. Jack is unsure how customers will react to boxes which are not made from recycled paper. However, he believes that this is the better option as it will have less of an effect on cash resources and therefore profitability.

Both machines will be depreciated using the straight-line method over 10 years.

REQUIRED

(a)   Explain the difference between profit and cash.

(b)   Calculate the effect of each option on profit and cash for the next financial year.

(c)   State which option you would recommend. Justify your choice.

Assessment and Qualifications Alliance, (AQA), 2003

18.2   Sanderson Sheds Supplies has been trading for many years. The business is expected to manufacture 12,000 sheds a year. Each shed is sold for £190 and costs £140 to make.

In an attempt to reduce costs the business has changed its supplier of paint. This will save £22 per shed. The new paint is rumoured to be harmful to wildlife.

REQUIRED

(a)   Calculate the increase in total contribution which will result from the change in paint supplier.

(b)   Discuss whether Sanderson Sheds Supplies should have changed its paint supplier.

Assessment and Qualifications Alliance, (AQA), 2003

18.3* Poseidon Porcelain PLC operates a production plant in a socially deprived area in the UK. The plant is unprofitable and one way to keep it running and make it competitive is to reduce its local workforce by 40%, which will achieve a similar reduction in annual manufacturing wages.

J Woodwedge, the finance director, believes that the main factor to be considered when making business decisions is profitability: this is what the shareholders will be looking for.

REQUIRED

Write a report to J Woodwedge explaining three factors, other than profitability, which will need to be considered before reducing the workforce Use the format shown below. Conclude your report with a firm recommendation.

REPORT

To ....

From ....

Date ....

Subject ....

18.4 Explain in your own words what you understand by the term 'social accounting'.

Answers to Chapter Questions

Answers to asterisked (*) questions follow in chapter order over the pages that follow. Answers are given in fully displayed form; this will assist by showing the correct layouts, which is important in accounting.

Where answers are given to questions from the past examination papers, these answers are the responsibility of the author and not of the examining board. They have not been provided by or approved by AQA and may not necessarily constitute the only possible solutions.

These resources are available to tutors in a password-protected area – a **Tutor Zone** – on the Osborne Books website. Tutors who would like access to this material should complete the online application form for membership; this form can be found on the tutor section of www.osbornebooks.co.uk

1.1   (a)   The two main sources of internal finance are funds from the owner(s) and family and funds generated from profits made by the business:

- Funds from the owners are normally savings and other money invested as capital. Funds from the family can take the form of loans provided at a low or nil rate of interest. This form of financing is relatively cheap.

- Funds generated from the profits of the business are useful if the business wishes to purchase assets. Funds generated from profits are useful because they do not attract an interest charge.

(b)   Funds from the owners are very valuable when the business is starting up for the first time and has no profit to call upon. Funds generated from profit are useful when the business has been up and running for a while and wishes to expand and needs a cheap source of financing (there is no interest involved).

(c)   Funds from the owner(s) may be limited in supply, loans from family may need repaying unexpectedly; also the family member(s) involved may want to have a say in the way the business is run.

1.3   (a)   A 'business angel' is a wealthy investor (often an active or retired entrepreneur) who provides finance for a business, and in return receives a percentage ownership stake in the business and an active role in helping to run it.

(b)   'Private equity finance' is provided by an independent company to private limited companies. In return for financing the private equity company receives shares in the private limited company and is likely to take an active role in running the company.

These two forms of financing differ significantly from bank lending. The bank is an independent body which takes security and can demand repayment of the finance and realise the security if the business runs into trouble. The business angel and private equity company, on the other hand, have an investment and an active role in running the business. Their commitment and expertise mean that the business should be less likely to run into financial difficulties.

1.4   (a)   Ordinary shares are issued to 'shareholders' of a limited company in return for their investment. They are paid dividends out of the profits of the company. The dividend will vary according to the amount of profit made. If the company does not make a profit shareholders may not receive a dividend.

(b)   Preference shares are issued to investors in a limited company. The dividend is normally set at a fixed percentage rate. Holders of preference shares receive their dividends in 'preference' to the ordinary shareholders, ie they take 'first cut' of the profits.

(c)   Debenture stock represents a loan to the company rather than an investment in shares. Fixed interest is payable whether a profit is made or not, and so ranks ahead of shareholder dividends (see [a] and [b] above).

2.1   £260,000

2.3   £21,100

2.4

JAMES HARVEY
CALCULATION OF INVENTORY LOSS FOR THE YEAR ENDED 30 JUNE 20-8

	£	£
Opening inventory		21,500
Purchases		132,000
Cost of inventory available for sale		153,500
Sales	180,000	
Less normal gross profit margin (30%)	54,000	
Cost of sales		126,000
Estimated closing inventory		27,500
Less Actual closing inventory		26,000
Value of inventory loss		1,500

2.6   (a)

		£
Inventory at 31 December 2006		?
– sales at cost price	2,429 ÷ 1.4	1,735
+ sales returns at cost price	350 ÷ 1.4	250
+ purchases		1,320
– purchases returns		56
– owner's drawings at cost price	84 ÷ 1.4	60
– goods stolen at cost price	322 ÷ 1.4	230
Inventory valuation at 8 January 2007		14,569

By working up the calculation (adding the minuses and deducting the pluses), the inventory valuation at 31 December 2006 is found to be **£15,080.**

(b)

Correct gross profit:	£
profit calculated by Mary	168,530
– Mary's estimated inventory valuation	12,000
+ actual inventory valuation, shown in (a) above	15,080
Gross profit for year ended 31 December 2006	171,610

Tutorial note:

- Because closing inventory is deducted from opening inventory and purchases to calculate cost of sales, an increase in the value of closing inventory reduces cost of sales which then increases gross profit.
- Remember the rules: "higher closing inventory = higher gross profit; lower closing inventory = lower gross profit."

2.9

(a)
- receipts from trade receivables — 153,500
- add trade receivables at year end — 2,500
- **sales for year** — 156,000

(b)
- payments to trade payables — 95,000
- add trade payables at year end — 65,000
- **purchases for year** — 160,000

(c)
- payments for rent — 8,750
- less rent prepaid at 31 Dec 20-4 — 250
- **rent for year** — 8,500

- payments for wages — 15,000
- add wages accrued at 31 Dec 20-4 — 550
- **wages for year** — 15,550

(d)

JANE PRICE

INCOME STATEMENT FOR THE YEAR ENDED 31 DECEMBER 20-4

	£	£
Revenue		156,000
Purchases	160,000	
Less Closing inventory	73,900	
Cost of sales		86,100
Gross profit		69,900
Less expenses:		
Advertising	4,830	
Rent	8,500	
Wages	15,550	
General expenses	5,000	
Provision for depreciation: shop fittings	10,000	
		43,880
Profit for the year		26,020

(e)

JANE PRICE

BALANCE SHEET AS AT 31 DECEMBER 20-4

	Cost £	Provision for depreciation £	Net book value £
Non-current Assets			
Shop fittings	50,000	10,000	40,000
Current Assets			
Inventory		73,900	
Trade receivables		2,500	
Prepayment: rent		250	
Bank*		19,900	
		96,550	
Less Current Liabilities			
Trade payables	65,000		
Accrual: wages	550		
		65,550	
Net Current Assets			31,000
NET ASSETS			71,000
FINANCED BY			
Capital			
Opening capital (introduced at start of year)			60,000
Add Profit for the year			26,020
			86,020
Less Drawings			15,020
			71,000

* Cash book summary:

	£
• total receipts for year	213,500
• less total payments for year	193,600
• **balance at year end**	19,900

2.12 (a) Tutorial note: this part of the question requires accounts to be prepared; you will not achieve full marks if you provide only a vertical calculation of the figures.

(i)

Cash Account

Dr		£				Cr £
2005/06			2005/06			
1 Apr	Balance b/d	260		Bank		253,641
	Cash sales for year			Drawings	1,500 x 12	18,000
	(missing figure)	303,501		Staff wages	2,650 x 12	31,800
			31 Mar	Balance c/d		320
		303,761				303,761
2006/07			2006/07			
1 Apr	Balance b/d	320				

(ii)

Sales Ledger Control Account

Dr		£				Cr £
2005/06			2005/06			
1 Apr	Balance b/d	458		Receipts from trade receivables		2,356
	Sales (missing figure)	2,374	31 Mar	Balance c/d		476
		2,832				2,832
2006/07			2006/07			
1 Apr	Balance b/d	476				

(iii)

Purchases Ledger Control Account

Dr		£				Cr £
2005/06			2005/06			
	Payments to trade payables	178,943	1 Apr	Balance b/d	12,403	
31 Mar	Balance c/d	11,987		Purchases		178,527
				(missing figure)		
		190,930				190,930
2006/07			2006/07			
			1 Apr	Balance b/d		11,987

(iv)

Vehicles Account

Dr		£				Cr £
2005/06			2005/06			
1 Apr	Balance b/d	20,000		Disposals		12,000
	Bank	30,000	31 Mar	Depreciation		9,500
				(missing figure)		
			31 Mar	Balance c/d		28,500
		50,000				50,000
2006/07			2006/07			
1 Apr	Balance b/d	28,500				

Note: the business does not keep a separate provision for depreciation account.

(b)

MICHAEL WONG

INCOME STATEMENT FOR THE YEAR ENDED 31 MARCH 2006

		£	£	£
Revenue	cash			303,501
	credit			2,374
Net revenue				305,875
Opening inventory			4,562	
Purchases		178,527		
– Goods for own use		368		
– Goods written off		1,560		
			176,599	
			181,161	
Less Closing inventory			4,328	
Cost of sales				176,833
Gross profit				129,042
Less expenses:				
Rent 7,800 – 700 accrual at 1 April 2005			7,100	
Advertising and wrapping materials			12,340	
Rates and insurances		11,870		
+ prepayment at 1 April 2006		760		
– prepayment at 31 March 2006		840		
Motor expenses			11,790	
General expenses			12,659	
Staff wages (see cash account)			7,562	
Provision for depreciation:			31,800	
property 103,600 – 100,800			2,800	
fixtures and fittings 12,000 – 10,000			2,000	
vehicles (see vehicles account)			9,500	
Loss on sale of vehicle 12,000 – 7,200			4,800	
Goods written off			*1,560	
				103,911
Profit for the year				25,131

* Goods written off are deducted from purchases and shown as an expense: in this way, double-entry book-keeping is completed, ie credit purchases account, debit income statement.

	Lysa £	Mark £			Lysa £	Mark £
20-4			20-4			
31 Dec Drawings	13,000	12,250	1 Jan Balances b/d		420	1,780
31 Dec Balance c/d	–	830	31 Dec Interest on capital	2,500	2,000
			31 Dec Share of profits	9,300	9,300
			31 Dec Balance c/d	780	–
	13,000	13,080		13,000	13,080
20-5			20-5			
1 Jan Balance b/d	780	–	1 Jan Balance b/d	–	830

3.7

SIGRID AND TOMASCZ IN PARTNERSHIP, TRADING AS "S & T PLUMBERS"
INCOME STATEMENT APPROPRIATION ACCOUNT FOR THE YEAR ENDED 30 JUNE 20-2

	£	£
Profit for the year		50,500
Add interest charged on partners' drawings:		
Sigrid	1,280	
Tomascz	920	
		2,200
		52,700
Less appropriation of profit:		
Salary: Tomascz		12,000
Interest allowed on partners' capitals:		
Sigrid £40,000 x 10%	4,000	
Tomascz £30,000 x 10%	3,000	
		7,000
		33,700
Share of remaining profit:		
Sigrid (60%)	20,220	
Tomascz (40%)	13,480	
		33,700

(c) Michael Wong wishes to know whether or not he should sell his business and retire. The points he should consider are:

For retirement	Against retirement
Gross margin is declining and, for 2006, is 42.19% (129,042 ÷ 305,875): this indicates that the gap between his buying and selling prices is narrowing.	Drawings are currently £1,500 per month = £18,000 per year, plus goods for own use £368 = £18,368 in total.
Net margin is declining and, for 2006, is 8.22% (25,131 ÷ 305,875).	Profit for 2006 is £25,131 giving a return on capital employed (ROCE) of 19.50% (£25,131 ÷ net assets of £128,884 at 31 March 2006).
The gap between gross margin and net margin has widened from 26% in 2003 to 34% (42% − 8%) in 2006. This indicates that expenses as a proportion of sales are increasing.	He is being offered £150,000 for a business with net assets of £128,884 (at 31 March 2006). This values his goodwill at £21,116 which he may not consider high enough for a going concern business.
Other non-financial factors: he would have less stress and more leisure time.	If he invested the £150,000 being offered at 5% he would earn £7,500 per year, which is well under half what he is earning currently.

Conclusion

From a financial viewpoint he should not retire yet. However, he could investigate running his business more efficiently (eg increasing the gap between buying and selling prices, reducing expenses), and seeing if he can increase the price offered for the business. His decision will depend on how stressful he finds running the business and how much he values his leisure time.

CHAPTER 3   Partnership final accounts

3.1 (b)

3.2 (c)

3.5

Dr   Partners' Capital Accounts   Cr

	Lysa £	Mark £			Lysa £	Mark £
20-4			20-4			
31 Dec Balances c/d	50,000	40,000	1 Jan Balances b/d	50,000	40,000
			20-5			
			1 Jan Balances b/d	50,000	40,000

(b)

Partners' Capital Accounts

Dr					Cr	
		Sigrid £	Tomascz £		Sigrid £	Tomascz £
20-2				20-1		
30 Jun	Balances c/d	40,000	30,000	1 Jul Balances b/d	40,000	30,000
				20-2		
		40,000	30,000	1 Jul Balances b/d	40,000	30,000

Partners' Current Accounts

Dr		Sigrid £	Tomascz £			Cr Sigrid £	Tomascz £
20-1				20-1			
1 Jul	Balance b/d	–	2,500	1 Jul	Balance b/d	1,200	–
20-2				20-2			
30 Jun	Interest on drawings	1,280	920	30 Jun	Salary	–	12,000
30 Jun	Drawings	26,000	21,500	30 Jun	Interest on capital	4,000	3,000
30 Jun	Balance c/d	–	3,560	30 Jun	Share of profits	20,220	13,480
				30 Jun	Balance c/d	1,860	–
		27,280	28,480			27,280	28,480
20-2				20-2			
1 Jul	Balance b/d	1,860	–	1 Jul	Balance b/d	–	3,560

3.8 (a)

Partners' Capital Accounts

Dr		James £	Hill £			Cr James £	Hill £
20-4				20-4			
31 Dec	Balances c/d	38,000	32,000	1 Jan	Balances b/d	38,000	32,000
				20-5			
		38,000	32,000	1 Jan	Balances b/d	38,000	32,000

Partners' Current Accounts

Dr		James £	Hill £			Cr James £	Hill £
20-4				20-4			
1 Jan	Balance b/d	3,000	–	1 Jan	Balance b/d	–	1,000
31 Dec	Drawings	10,000	22,000	31 Dec	Salary	–	15,000
31 Dec	Balances c/d	800	7,200	31 Dec	Interest on capital	3,800	3,200
				31 Dec	Share of profits	10,000	10,000
		13,800	29,200			13,800	29,200
				20-5			
				1 Jan	Balances b/d	800	7,200

(b)

JOHN JAMES AND STEVEN HILL IN PARTNERSHIP, TRADING AS "GRAPES"
INCOME STATEMENT FOR THE YEAR ENDED 31 DECEMBER 20-4

	£	£	£
Gross profit			89,000
Less expenses:			
Rent and rates		7,500	
Advertising		12,000	
Heat and light		3,500	
Wages and salaries		18,000	
Sundry expenses		4,000	
Provision for depreciation: shop fittings		2,000	
			47,000
Profit for the year			42,000
Less appropriation of profit:			
Salary: Hill		15,000	
Interest allowed on partners' capitals			
James £38,000 x 10%	3,800		
Hill £32,000 x 10%	3,200	7,000	
			20,000
Share of remaining profit:			
James		10,000	
Hill		10,000	
			20,000

BALANCE SHEET AS AT 31 DECEMBER 20-4

	Cost £	Provision for depreciation £	Net book value £
Non-current Assets			
Shop fittings	20,000	2,000	18,000
Current Assets			
Inventory		35,000	
Trade receivables		6,000	
Bank		29,000	
		70,000	
Less Current Liabilities			
Trade payables		10,000	
Net Current Assets			60,000
NET ASSETS			78,000
FINANCED BY			
Capital Accounts			
James		38,000	
Hill		32,000	
			70,000
Current Accounts			
James		800	
Hill		7,200	
			8,000
			78,000

(c) • The balance on the partners' current accounts represents the balance owed or owing between the business and the individual partners after transactions such as salaries, interest on capital, share of profits, and drawings have been taken into account.

• A debit balance on a partner's current account means that the partner has drawn out more than his/her entitlement of salary, interest on capital and share of profits.

• A credit balance on a partner's current account means that the partner has drawn out less than his/her entitlement of salary, interest on capital and share of profits.

3.10 (a)

Partners' Capital Accounts

Dr		Clark £	Pearce £			Clark £	Pearce £	Cr
20-4				20-3				
30 Jun	Balances c/d	60,000	30,000	1 Jul	Balances b/d	60,000	30,000	
				20-4				
		60,000	30,000	1 Jul	Balances b/d	60,000	30,000	

Partners' Current Accounts

Dr		Clark £	Pearce £			Clark £	Pearce £	Cr
20-4				20-3				
30 Jun	Drawings	20,600	15,700	1 Jul	Balances b/d	430	300	
30 Jun	Balance c/d	–	4,840	20-4				
				30 Jun	Salary	–	12,000	
				30 Jun	Share of profits	16,480	8,240	
				30 Jun	Balance c/d	3,690	–	
		20,600	20,540			20,600	20,540	
20-4				20-4				
1 Jul	Balance b/d	3,690	–	1 Jul	Balance b/d	–	4,840	

(b)

CLARK AND PEARCE, IN PARTNERSHIP
INCOME STATEMENT FOR THE YEAR ENDED 30 JUNE 20-4

	£	£
Gross profit		105,000
Less expenses:		
Salaries	30,400	
Electricity	2,420	
Telephone	3,110	
Rent and rates	10,000	
Discount allowed	140	
Office expenses	10,610	
Bad debts written off	1,200	
Provision for depreciation: office equipment	10,400	
		68,280
Profit for the year		36,720
Less appropriation of profit:		
Salary: Pearce		12,000
		24,720
Share of remaining profit:		
Clark (two-thirds)	16,480	
Pearce (one-third)	8,240	
		24,720

BALANCE SHEET AS AT 30 JUNE 20-4

	Cost £	Provision for depreciation £	Net book value £
Non-current Assets			
Office equipment	52,000	31,200	20,800
Current Assets			
Inventory			41,570
Trade receivables	20,000		
Less provision for doubtful debts	780		
			19,220
Bank			21,750
			82,540
Less Current Liabilities			
Trade payables			12,190
Net Current Assets			70,350
NET ASSETS			91,150
FINANCED BY			
Capital Accounts			
Clark			60,000
Pearce			30,000
			90,000
Current Accounts			
Clark			(3,690)
Pearce			4,840
			1,150
			91,150

3.13

(a)

(i) Effect on the draft profit for the year ended 30 April 2006:

- **Item (1)**

  As these two costs have been used in the building of an office for business use, they must be treated as capital expenditure. The accounting entries to adjust this are:

  – debit property, £30,690
  – credit purchases, £12,450
  – credit wages, £18,240

  Thus profit is increased by £12,450 + £18,240 = £30,690.

- **Item (2)**

  This amount of £2,780 is to be treated as goods for own use, which is added to Geraldine's drawings.

  The accounting entries to adjust this are:

  – debit Geraldine's drawings, £2,780
  – credit purchases/materials, £2,780

  Thus profit is increased by £2,780.

- **Item (3)**

  This amount of £600 is a business cost, which should be debited to wages or salaries account, rather than Tom's drawings. The accounting entries to adjust this are:

  – debit wages/salaries, £600
  – credit Tom's drawings, £600

  Thus profit is reduced by £600.

- **Item (4)**

  The net book value of the equipment at the date of sale was £5,000 (cost £20,000, less three years' depreciation at £5,000 per year = £15,000). As the equipment has been sold for £8,000, a profit on sale of £3,000 has been made. The £8,000 sale proceeds should have been credited to disposals account. The accounting entries to adjust this and which affect profit are:

  – debit sales, £8,000
  – credit disposals, £8,000
  – credit income statement, £3,000
  – debit disposals, £3,000

  Note that other accounting entries will be needed to complete the disposal of the equipment.

  Thus profit is reduced by £8,000 – £3,000 = £5,000.

(ii) Change in profit for the year ended 30 April 2006:

	£	
item 1	30,690	increase
item 2	2,780	increase
item 3	600	decrease
item 4	5,000	decrease
net change in profit	27,870	increase, ie £13,935 per partner

(b)

Partners' Current Accounts

Dr						Cr
		Tom	Geraldine		Tom	Geraldine
2006		£	£	2006	£	£
30 Apr	Balance b/d	–	1,450	30 Apr Balance b/d	3,720	–
30 Apr	Drawings (item 2)	–	2,780	30 Apr Wages (item 3)	600	–
30 Apr	Balances c/d	18,255	9,705	30 Apr Share of profit	13,935	13,935
		18,255	13,935		18,255	13,935
				1 May Balances b/d	18,255	9,705

(c) The benefits of maintaining separate capital and current accounts are:

- the capital account remains fixed except for capital introduced or withdrawn

- the current account is a working account dealing with all aspects of the distribution of profits and drawings of profits

- the distinction between the two amounts shows whether or not partners are maintaining their permanent capital in the business, while the fluctuating current account shows whether or not partners have withdrawn more profit from the business than they are earning

- the fixed capital account makes calculation of interest on capital – where permitted by the partnership agreement – easy to calculate

However, it should be pointed out that separate capital and current accounts require more work and are, therefore, more time-consuming for the book-keeper than using the partners' capital accounts for all transactions. As to which is used will depend on the size and complexity of the partnership business.

4.2 (a)

4.3 (b)

4.4

Partners' Capital Accounts

Dr		Jim £	Maisie £	Matt £			Cr Jim £	Maisie £	Matt £
20-4					20-4				
1 Jan	Goodwill written off	24,000	16,000	8,000	31 Dec	Balances b/d	60,000	40,000	—
31 Dec	Drawings	12,000	12,000	8,000	20-5				
31 Dec	Balances c/d	82,800	51,200	22,000	1 Jan	Goodwill created	28,800	19,200	
					1 Jan	Bank			28,000
					31 Dec	Share of profit	30,000	20,000	10,000
		118,800	79,200	38,000			118,800	79,200	38,000
					20-6				
					1 Jan	Balances b/d	82,800	51,200	22,000

4.6

Revaluation Account

Dr		£			Cr £
2005			2005		
30 Sep	Current assets, excl. bank (£28,000 – £27,000)	1,000	30 Sep	Non-current assets (£130,000 – £60,000)	70,000
30 Sep	Capital accounts:				
	Mei (3/6)	34,500			
	Janet (2/6)	23,000			
	Michael (1/6)	11,500			
		70,000			70,000

Goodwill Account

Dr		£			Cr £
2005			2005		
30 Sep	Capital accounts:		30 Sep	Capital accounts:	
	Mei (3/6)	37,500		Mei (2/3)	50,000
	Janet (2/6)	25,000		Michael (1/3)	25,000
	Michael (1/6)	12,500			
		75,000			75,000

4.2 (a)

4.3 (b)

4.4

Partners' Capital Accounts

Dr		Mei £	Janet £	Michael £			Cr Mei £	Janet £	Michael £
2005					2005				
30 Sep	Goodwill written off	50,000	—	25,000	30 Sep	Balances b/d	40,000	20,000	5,000
30 Sep	Loan account		68,000	—	30 Sep	Revaluation	34,500	23,000	11,500
30 Sep	Balances c/d	62,000		4,000	30 Sep	Goodwill created	37,500	25,000	12,500
		112,000	68,000	29,000			112,000	68,000	29,000
					1 Oct	Balances b/d	62,000	—	4,000

4.8 (a)

Partners' Capital Accounts

Dr		Dave £	Elsa £			Cr Dave £	Elsa £
20-4				20-4			
1 Oct	Goodwill written off	30,000	15,000	1 Oct	Balances b/d	80,000	50,000
1 Oct	Balances c/d	72,500	57,500	1 Oct	Goodwill created	22,500	22,500
		102,500	72,500			102,500	72,500
				1 Oct	Balances b/d	72,500	57,500

(b)

BALANCE SHEET OF DAVE AND ELSA AS AT 1 OCTOBER 20-4

	£
Net assets	130,000
Capital accounts:	
Dave	72,500
Elsa	57,500
	130,000

4.11

Dr		Revaluation Account		Cr
20-9	£	20-9		£
1 Jan Inventory write-off	3,000	1 Jan Property		30,000
1 Jan Bad debts written off	2,000			
1 Jan Capital accounts:				
Henry (3/5)	15,000			
Jenny (2/5)	10,000			
	30,000			30,000

Dr		Goodwill Account		Cr
20-9	£	20-9		£
1 Jan Capital accounts:		1 Jan Capital accounts:		
Henry (3/5)	24,000	Henry (2/5)		16,000
Jenny (2/5)	16,000	Jenny (2/5)		16,000
		Kylie (1/5)		8,000
	40,000			40,000

Dr				Partners' Capital Accounts				Cr
	Henry	Jenny	Kylie			Henry	Jenny	Kylie
20-9	£	£	£	20-9		£	£	£
1 Jan Goodwill written off	16,000	16,000	8,000	1 Jan Balances b/d		100,000	90,000	–
				1 Jan Revaluation		15,000	10,000	–
				1 Jan Goodwill created		24,000	16,000	–
1 Jan Balances c/d	123,000	100,000	42,000	1 Jan Bank		–	–	50,000
	139,000	116,000	50,000			139,000	116,000	50,000
				1 Jan Balances b/d		123,000	100,000	42,000

BALANCE SHEET OF HENRY, JENNY AND KYLIE AS AT 1 JANUARY 20-9

	£	£
Non-current Assets		
Property (revaluation)		180,000
Vehicles (net book value)		30,000
		210,000
Current Assets		
Inventory	17,000	
Trade receivables	23,000	
Bank 3,000 + 50,000	53,000	
	93,000	
Less Current Liabilities		
Trade payables	28,000	
Net Current Assets		65,000
NET ASSETS		275,000
FINANCED BY		
Capital Accounts		
Henry		123,000
Jenny		100,000
Kylie		42,000
		265,000
Current Accounts		
Henry	8,500	
Jenny	1,500	
		10,000
		275,000

4.12

Realisation Account

Dr		£			Cr £
20-5			20-5		
30 Jun	Property	100,000	30 Jun	Trade payables	25,000
30 Jun	Plant and equipment	30,000	30 Jun	Bank: property	160,000
30 Jun	Vehicles	20,000	30 Jun	Bank: plant and equipment	26,000
30 Jun	Inventory	25,000	30 Jun	Bank: vehicles	18,000
30 Jun	Trade receivables	20,000	30 Jun	Bank: inventory and trade receivables	38,000
30 Jun	Bank: trade payables	23,000			
30 Jun	Bank: realisation expenses	4,000			
30 Jun	Profit on realisation:				
	Amy (4/10)	18,000			
	Briony (3/10)	13,500			
	Clarissa (2/10)	9,000			
	Daljit (1/10)	4,500			
		45,000			45,000

Partners' Capital Accounts

Dr		A £	B £	C £	D £			A £	B £	C £	D £
20-5						20-5					
30 Jun	Bank	78,000	63,500	49,000	29,500	30 Jun	Balances b/d	60,000	50,000	40,000	25,000
							Realisation acc: profit	18,000	13,500	9,000	4,500
		78,000	63,500	49,000	29,500			78,000	63,500	49,000	29,500

Bank Account

Dr		£			Cr £
20-5			20-5		
30 Jun	Balance b/d	5,000	30 Jun	Trade payables	23,000
30 Jun	Property	160,000	30 Jun	Realisation account: expenses	4,000
30 Jun	Plant and equipment	26,000	30 Jun	Capital accounts:	
30 Jun	Vehicles	18,000		Amy	78,000
30 Jun	Inventory and trade receivables	38,000		Briony	63,500
				Clarissa	49,000
				Daljit	29,500
		247,000			247,000

4.13

(a)
- When a partnership is dissolved, any partner with a debit balance remaining on capital account must pay in monies from private funds to clear the balance.
- If a partner is unable to settle his or her debt because of insolvency, then the other partners must share the loss in the ratio of their last agreed capital balances, ie the balances of their capital accounts before the dissolution began. This rule was established in the legal case of Garner v Murray (1904).

(b) As Liz cannot pay any of the debt to the partnership, it must be shared between Keith and Mina, the solvent partners, in the ratio of their last agreed capitals.

- Keith will have to pay: $\dfrac{£80,000}{£80,000 + £20,000} \times £15,000 = £12,000$

- Mina will have to pay: $\dfrac{£20,000}{£80,000 + £20,000} \times £15,000 = £3,000$

Partners' Capital Accounts

Dr		Keith £	Liz £	Mina £			Keith £	Liz £	Mina £
20-2					20-2				
30 Jun	Balance b/d		15,000		30 Jun	Balances b/d	55,000		10,000
30 Jun	Liz	12,000		3,000	30 Jun	Keith		12,000	
30 Jun	Bank	43,000	-	7,000	30 Jun	Mina		3,000	
		55,000	15,000	10,000			55,000	15,000	10,000

The amounts paid to Keith and Mina from the bank are £43,000 + £7,000 = £50,000, which is the amount of the bank balance shown on the partnership balance sheet.

CHAPTER 5   Published accounts of limited companies

5.2 A statement of changes in equity is important to shareholders because it shows the changes that have taken place to their stake in the company. It includes not only the *realised* profit or loss from the income statement, but also *unrealised* profits (such as the gain on the upwards revaluation of property) which are taken directly to reserves.

5.4 Explanation of the words 'true' and 'fair':
- 'true' means that if any of the financial statements states that a transaction has taken place then, in reality, it has taken place; likewise, if an asset is shown on a balance sheet, then the asset actually exists
- 'fair' implies that transactions and assets are shown using generally accepted accounting rules and principles

5.5 Items to be included in a directors' report (four items required for the answer):

- the principal activities of the company
- a review of the activities of the company over the past year
- likely developments that will affect the company in the future, including research and development activity
- directors' names and their shareholdings in the company
- proposed dividends
- any significant differences between the book value and market value of property
- political and charitable contributions
- the company's policies on:
  – employment of disabled people
  – health and safety at work of employees
  – actions taken on employee involvement and consultation
  – payment of suppliers

5.8 (a) (i) *Intangible non-current assets*, eg goodwill, patents, trademarks

Assets which do not have material substance but which belong to the company.

(ii) *Current assets*, eg trade receivables, inventories, cash or cash equivalents

Assets which are:
- cash or cash equivalent
- those to be realised, sold or used within the normal operating cycle
- assets held for trading and expected to be realised within twelve months

(iii) *Current liabilities*, eg trade payables, tax liabilities, bank overdraft

Liabilities which are:
- those expected to be settled within the normal operating cycle
- liabilities held for trading and expected to be settled within twelve months
- where the company does not have the right to defer payment beyond twelve months

(b) (i) Dividends; activities; review of business; list of directors and their shareholdings; employees; charity/political contributions; health and safety; payment of suppliers, etc.

(ii) The directors are responsible for producing financial statements that give a true and fair view of the company's financial position, with regard to company law and accounting standards, and maintaining the supporting accounting records.

Auditors are responsible for ensuring that the accounts give a true and fair view and comply with company law and accounting standards.

5.11 This answer may be set out either vertically or horizontally.

Non-current Assets	£000
Property, plant and equipment	
Net book value at start of year	3,832
Additions at cost	722
Disposals during year (£1,076 – £695)	(381)
Depreciation for year *(missing figure)*	(589)
Net book value at end of year	3,584

Non-current Assets	Net book value at start £000	Additions at cost £000	Disposals during year £000	Depreciation for year £000	Net book value at end £000
Property, plant and equipment	3,832	722	(381)	(589)	3,584

5.13

- **shareholders**
  - dividends
  - profits

  Dividends enable shareholders to see how much cash they are receiving from their investment and to enable comparison with previous years/other investments.

  Profits enable shareholders to see how much was retained in the company for investment and to assess the future prospects of the company.

- **loan stock holders**
  - total loans
  - profits

  There may be other lenders which need to be repaid, so reducing the ability of the company to repay its lending.

  Profits enable the loan providers to assess the likelihood of receiving their interest payments and loan repayments.

- **trade payables**
  - current assets, net current assets
  - profits

  The current assets/net current assets will enable trade payables to look at the liquidity of the company (ie the stability of the company on a short-term basis) and to assess its ability to pay trade payables as they fall due.

  A company that is generating profits is likely to be able to pay its trade payables. Also, the company may be expanding, so creating an increased level of purchases from its suppliers; comparison of profits with previous years.

- **employees**
  - profits
  - net assets

  A profitable company may be able to afford pay rises; comparison of profits with previous years.

  The net assets show the financial strength of the company and indicate its ability to continue in business, so assuring future employment prospects.

5.15

CRANTOCK PLC

INCOME STATEMENT FOR THE YEAR ENDED 31 MARCH 20-2

	£000	£000
Revenue		2,295
Opening inventories	160	
Purchases	1,200	
	1,360	
Less Closing inventories	180	
Cost of sales		(1,180)
Gross profit		1,115
Overheads:		
Distribution expenses	(500)	
Administrative expenses	(240)	
		(740)
Profit/(loss) from operations		375
Finance costs		—
Profit/(loss) before tax		375
Tax		(65)
Profit/(loss) for the year attributable to equity holders		310

STATEMENT OF CHANGES IN EQUITY (EXTRACT)

Retained earnings	
Balance at 1 April 20-1	350
Profit for the year	310
	660
Dividends paid	(140)
Balance at 31 March 20-2	520

CRANTOCK PLC
BALANCE SHEET AS AT 31 MARCH 20-1

	Valuation £000	Cost £000	Aggregate Depreciation £000	Net £000
Non-current Assets				
Property, plant and equipment				
Plant and machinery	–	1,600	500	1,100
Current Assets				
Inventories			180	
Trade receivables			525	
Cash and cash equivalents			75	
			780	
Total assets				1,880
Current Liabilities				
Trade payables			(395)	
Tax liabilities			(65)	
			(460)	
Net Current Assets				320
Total liabilities				460
Net Assets				1,420
EQUITY				
Issued Share Capital				
Ordinary shares of £1 each				700
Capital Reserves				
Share premium				200
Revenue Reserve				
Retained earnings				520
TOTAL EQUITY				1,420

6.1

Transaction	Inflow of cash	Outflow of cash	No effect on cash
(a) Cash purchases		✓	
(b) Sold goods on credit			✓
(c) Bought goods on credit			✓
(d) Bought a non-current asset paying by cheque		✓	
(e) A trade receivable pays by cheque	✓		
(f) Paid expenses in cash		✓	
(g) Paid a trade payable by cheque		✓	

6.6

(a) •   The cash flow statement links profit from the income statement with changes in assets and liabilities in the balance sheet, and shows the effect on the cash flows of the company over a period of time.

   •   It gives information that is not found in the income statement and balance sheet, eg the *change* in inventories, trade receivables and trade payables.

   •   It is an objective accounting statement which focuses on cash inflows and cash outflows.

   •   For the current year it shows:
       –   cash flow from operating activities, investing activities and financing activities
       –   taxes paid
       –   dividends paid
       –   interest paid and received
       –   non-current assets purchased and sold
       –   loans received and repaid
       –   shares issued

(b) •   income statement
   •   balance sheet

6.8

(a)

(i) *profit from operations*

Profit from the normal trading activities of the company, before deduction of interest and tax.

(ii) *cash flow from operations*

Amount of cash generated by the trading activities of the company, taking into account non-cash items such as depreciation, and changes in inventories, trade receivables and trade payables.

(b)

(i) *depreciation – added*

Depreciation is a non-cash item and is added back as the cash has not left the company.

(ii) *increase in inventories – subtracted*

An increase in inventories uses cash, ie the company spends money, so it is subtracted

(iii) *increase in trade receivables – subtracted*

An increase in trade receivables means that the company is allowing its customers longer to pay, or has increased its credit sales business. Either way, the company is financing the increase and therefore has less cash available, so it is subtracted.

(iv) *increase in trade payables – added*

An increase in trade payables means that the company is paying its suppliers more slowly, or has increased its credit purchases. Either way, the company has more cash available, so it is added.

6.9 Advantages of producing a cash flow statement include:

* Cash is often described as the 'life blood' of any business, and the survival of a company will depend on its ability to generate sufficient cash in order to fund its activities and meet its day-to-day obligations.

* The level of cash is an important indicator of business performance.

* Users of financial statements can easily identify with cash (often more so than profit) - for example, managers may be helped with decision-making and development of the company, employees may look at the level of cash when negotiating the next pay award.

* Cash flow accounting can be used by shareholders to compare business performance against previous periods or against other companies.

* Loan stock holders/debenture holders will look at the cash available at the year end as a demonstration of the security of their loan stock and debentures.

* Trade payables will look at the liquidity of the company as a demonstration of the likelihood of being paid for goods and services supplied.

6.12

HALL PLC

CASH FLOW STATEMENT FOR THE YEAR ENDED 30 SEPTEMBER 20-5

	£000	£000
Cash flows from operating activities		
Profit from operations		24
Adjustments for:		
Depreciation for year	318	
Increase in inventories	(251)	
Increase in trade receivables	(152)	
Increase in trade payables	165	
Cash (used in)/from operations		104
Interest paid	(218)	
Income taxes paid	(75)	
Net cash (used in)/from operating activities		(189)
Cash flows from investing activities		
Purchase of non-current assets	(358)	
Proceeds from sale of non-current assets	132	
Net cash (used in)/from investing activities		(226)
Cash flows from financing activities		
Proceeds from issue of share capital	150	
Proceeds from long-term borrowings	200	
Dividends paid	(280)	
Net cash (used in)/from financing activities		70
Net increase/(decrease) in cash and cash equivalents		(345)
Cash and cash equivalents at beginning of year		395
Cash and cash equivalents at end of year		50

6.13 (a)

PANCHOLI PLC

CASH FLOW STATEMENT FOR THE YEAR ENDED 31 DECEMBER 20-3

	£000	£000
Cash flows from operating activities		
Profit from operations	104	
Adjustments for:		
Depreciation for year	30	
Increase in inventories (203–175)	(28)	
Increase in trade receivables (141–127)	(14)	
Increase in trade payables (142–118)	24	
Cash (used in)/from operations	116	
Interest paid	(5)	
Income taxes paid*	(19)	
Net cash (used in)/from operating activities		92
Cash flows from investing activities		
Net cash (used in)/rom investing activities		–
Cash flows from financing activities		
Repayment of long-term borrowings	(50)	
Dividends paid	(20)	
Net cash (used in)/from financing activities		(70)
Net increase/(decrease) in cash and cash equivalents		22
Cash and cash equivalents at beginning of year		(16)
Cash and cash equivalents at end of year		6

* Tax liability of £19,000 for 20-2 paid in 20-3.

(b) From the point of view of the company's shareholders, the following points are highlighted by the cash flow statement of Pancholi plc for 20-3:

- a good cash flow has been generated from operations, £116,000, which is well above the amounts paid for tax, £19,000, and dividends, £20,000

- inventories, trade receivables and trade payables have increased during the year, with a net increase of £18,000 – an indication of an expanding business

- loans and debentures of £50,000 have been repaid which has reduced the company's gearing to nil

- interest paid is a low amount and will be even less next year following repayment of the loans and debentures

- during the year there has been no investment in non-current assets

- the bank balance – cash and cash equivalents – has increased during the year from an overdraft of £16,000 to a credit balance of £6,000.

Conclusion:

The cash flow statement shows that Pancholi plc is a profitable company which is generating cash. There has been an expansion of net current assets and the company has repaid debt and eliminated its gearing. The company is in a strong financial position and, although it has not invested in non-current assets this year, it has the ability to do so in the future. Shareholders should hold their existing shares and should consider buying more as profits and dividends seem likely to increase in the future.

6.14 (a)

SHEEHAN PLC

RECONCILIATION OF PROFIT FROM OPERATIONS TO NET CASH FLOW FROM OPERATING ACTIVITIES

	£000
Profit from operations	2,520
Adjustments for:	
Depreciation for year[1]	318
Loss on sale of non-current assets[2]	3
Increase in inventories (84–69)	(15)
Decrease in trade receivables (270–255)	15
Increase in trade payables (108–81)	27
Cash (used in)/from operations	2,868
Interest paid	(168)
Income taxes paid	(744)
Net cash (used in)/from operating activities	1,956

(b)

SHEEHAN PLC

CASH FLOW STATEMENT FOR THE YEAR ENDED 31 OCTOBER 20-3

	£000	£000
Net cash (used in)/from operating activities		1,956
Cash flows from investing activities		
Purchase of non-current assets[3]	(629)	
Proceeds from sale of non-current assets	8	
Net cash (used in)/from investing activities		(621)
Cash flows from financing activities		
Proceeds from issue of share capital[4]	627	
Repayment of long-term borrowings	(1,800)	
Dividends paid	(144)	
Net cash (used in)/from financing activities		(1,317)
Net increase/(decrease) in cash and cash equivalents		18
Cash and cash equivalents at beginning of year		30
Cash and cash equivalents at end of year		48

Working notes

1

Accumulated Depreciation

		£000				£000
20-3			20-2			
31 Oct	Disposal	18	1 Nov	Balance b/d		1,500
31 Oct	Balance c/d	1,800	20-3			
			31 Oct	Income statement (bal fig)		318
		1,818				1,818
			20-3			
			1 Nov	Balance b/d		1,800

2

Non-current Asset disposals

		£000			£000
20-3			20-3		
31 Oct	At cost	29	31 Oct	Accumulated depreciation	18
			31 Oct	Sale proceeds	8
			31 Oct	Income statement (bal fig)	*3
		29			29

* Denotes a loss on sale

3

Non-current Assets

		£000			£000
20-2			20-3		
1 Nov	Balance b/d	8,400	31 Oct	Disposals	29
20-3			31 Oct	Balance c/d	9,000
31 Oct	Additions (bal fig)	629			
		9,029			9,029
20-3					
1 Nov	Balance b/d	9,000			

4

Proceeds from issue of share capital

	£000
Issue of shares (3,000–2,550)	450
At a premium	177
Total proceeds from issue	627

7.1 The **reasons** for using international accounting standards are:

- to provide a framework for preparing and presenting financial statements – the 'rules' of accounting

- to ensure that accountants follow the same set of rules

- to reduce the number of different accounting treatments and so make 'window dressing' more difficult

- to meet with the duty of the directors to ensure that financial statements comply with accounting standards

- to meet with the auditors' report requirement to state that the financial statements have been prepared in accordance with accounting standards

The **benefits** of international accounting standards are:

- to standardise financial statements internationally – thus a company operating in several countries knows that the same accounting rules have been applied to all parts of its business

- to reduce the variations of accounting treatments used in financial statements – thus making 'window dressing' the accounts more difficult

- to allow users of financial statements to make inter-firm comparisons in the knowledge that all the financial statements have been prepared using the same standards.

7.4 (a) £120,000 (£250,000 less £25,000 depreciation over five years = £225,000 net book value, compared with £345,000 revaluation)

(b) £7,500 (£345,000 revaluation ÷ 46 years)

7.5 (a) IAS 38, *Intangible Assets*, defines an intangible asset as *'an identifiable non-monetary asset without physical substance'*.

(b) The three key elements of an intangible asset set out in IAS 38 are:

- *identifiability* – the asset is either separate from the business so that it is capable of being sold or transferred, or it arises from contractual rights

- *control* – the business has the power to obtain future economic benefits from the asset

- *future economic benefits* – include revenue from the sale of products or services, cost savings, or other benefits

(c) • At acquisition, intangible assets are recorded at cost.

    • After acquisition, a company can choose either the cost model or the revaluation model:

        – cost, the intangible asset is shown in the balance sheet at cost less accumulated amortisation (depreciation) and impairment losses

        – revaluation, the intangible asset is shown in the balance sheet at a revalued amount, being its fair value less subsequent amortisation and impairment losses

        Intangible assets are amortised – usually using the straight-line method.

7.9 A **provision** is a liability of uncertain timing or amount at the time of preparing the financial statements. A provision is to be shown as a liability in the financial statements where:

• the company has a present obligation as a result of a past event

• it is probable that the company will have to settle the obligation (eg payment will be made)

• a reliable financial estimate can be made of the obligation

The word 'probable' is used as this represents a more than 50% likelihood that an outflow of economic benefits will take place.

A **contingent liability** is *either*:

• a possible obligation arising from past events whose outcome is based on uncertain future events; *or*

• an obligation that is not recognised because it is not probable or cannot be measured reliably.

The word 'possible' is used to indicate a less than 50% likelihood of its occurrence. Therefore a contingent liability is not recognised in the financial statements; however, it should be disclosed as a note to the statements to include:

• a description of the contingent liability

• an estimate of its financial effect

• an indication of the uncertainties regarding the amount or timing of any resulting expenditure

7.10 These are uncertainties that must be accounted for consistently in financial statements, if users are to achieve a full understanding.

The purpose of IAS 37, *Provisions, Contingent Liabilities and Contingent Assets*, is to ensure a consistent accounting treatment for provisions, contingent liabilities and contingent assets, and that sufficient information is disclosed in the notes to the financial statements, to enable users to understand their nature, timing and amount.

IAS 37 states that a **provision** is to be recognised as a liability in the financial statements where:

• the company has a present obligation as a result of a past event

• it is probable (more then 50% likely) that the company will have to settle the obligation (eg payment will be made)

• a reliable financial estimate can be made of the obligation

The amount of a provision is shown as an expense in the income statement, and as a liability in the balance sheet (either as a current or non-current liability).

Disclosure in the notes to the financial statements requires:

• movements in the amount of provisions during the financial year

• a description of the provisions and expected timings of any resulting expenditure

• an indication of the uncertainties regarding the amount or timing of any resulting expenditure

A **contingent liability** is *either*:

• a possible obligation, ie less than 50% likelihood of its occurrence, arising from past events whose outcome is based on uncertain future events; *or*

• an obligation that is not recognised because it is not probable or cannot be measured reliably.

A contingent liability is not recognised in the financial statements but should be disclosed as a note to include:

• a description of the contingent liability

• an estimate of its financial effect

• an indication of the uncertainties regarding the amount or timing of any resulting expenditure

Thus in summary:

Provision = probable = more than 50% likely, recognised in financial statements and disclosed in notes.

Contingent liability = possible = less than 50% likely, not recognised in financial statements, but disclosed in notes.

7.11 Quite often there will be events occurring after the reporting period which will provide new evidence about the value of assets and liabilities at that time. Changes can be made to these valuations up until the time the financial statements are authorised for issue (usually by the board of directors). After this time it becomes impossible to alter them.

IAS 10, *Events after the Reporting Period*, identifies adjusting and non-adjusting events.

Adjusting events provide evidence of conditions that existed at the end of the reporting period. If the amount(s) involved are material, then the amounts shown in the financial statements should be changed. Examples of adjusting events include:

– the settlement after the end of the reporting period of a court case which confirms that a liability existed at the year end

– where a customer has become insolvent after the end of the reporting period and the debt has been included in the balance sheet figure of year end trade receivables

Non-adjusting events are conditions that arose after the reporting period. No adjustment is made to the financial statements. If such events are material, then they are disclosed by way of notes. The notes would explain the nature of the event and, if possible, give the likely financial consequences of the event. Examples of non-adjusting events include:

– major purchase of assets
– a major restructuring of the business
– significant business commitments entered into after the end of the reporting period

7.13 (a) IAS 18, *Revenue*, states that revenue is the inflow of economic benefits arising from the ordinary activities of a business. Revenue is to be recorded at the fair value of the monies received or receivable.

(b) Examples:
- sale of goods and services
- receipt of interest, royalties and dividends

STORES LEDGER RECORD: wholewheat flour

Date	Receipts Quantity kgs	Cost per kg £	Total Cost £	Issues Quantity kgs	Cost per kg £	Total Cost £	Balance Quantity kgs	Total Cost £
20-7								
Balance at 1 May							10,000	2,500
6 May	20,000	0.30	6,000				30,000	8,500
10 May				10,000	0.25	2,500	10,000	3,000
				10,000	0.30	3,000		
17 May	10,000	0.35	3,500				10,000	3,000
							10,000	3,500
							20,000	6,500
20 May				10,000	0.30	3,000	5,000	1,750
				5,000	0.35	1,750		

8.7 International Accounting Standard (IAS) No 2, *Inventories*, states that each category of inventory must be valued at the lower of cost and net realisable value.

'X1X': cost = £40; net realisable value = £30; therefore they are valued at £30 each

'X-TRA-G': cost = £56; net realisable value = £90; therefore they are valued at £56 each

'X-TREME 2': cost = £35; net realisable value = £42; therefore they are valued at £35 each

The total value of these items is therefore:

		£
'X1X'	300 at £30 each	9,000
'X-TRA-G'	260 at £56 each	14,560
'X-TREME 2'	100 at £35 each	3,500
TOTAL VALUE		27,060

CHAPTER 8   Inventory valuation

8.1 (a) stores ledger record

(b) inventory reconciliation

(c) IAS 2, *Inventories*

(d) cost and net realisable value

8.8 Using the lower of cost and net realisable value for each category of inventory separately gives the following value:

	£
Replica strip (old version)	2,500 (net realisable value)
Replica strip (new version)	8,400 (cost)
TOTAL VALUE	10,900

8.9 (a) GROSS PROFIT OF DENISE WATSON FOR APRIL 2008

		£	£
Sales			44,600
Opening inventory (2 at £1,200)		2,400	
Purchases		20,200	
		22,600	
Less Closing inventory (2 at £1,400)		2,800	
Cost of sales			19,800
Gross profit			24,800

Tutorial note:	inventory at start	2	
	purchases	15	
		17	
	sales	(15)	
	inventory at end	2	at £1,400 each

(b) Note: the question asks for one advantage and one disadvantage of AVCO.

Advantages

- AVCO is one of the two inventory valuation methods which IAS 2, *Inventories*, allows companies to use.
- AVCO is acceptable for tax purposes
- over a number of accounting periods reported profits are smoothed
- fluctuations in purchase costs are evened out so that issue prices do not vary greatly
- AVCO is logical – it assumes that identical units, even when purchased at different times, have the same value
- closing inventory valuation is close to current market values
- AVCO calculations are easy to computerise

Disadvantages

- with AVCO, a new weighted average has to be calculated after each receipt
- calculations may be to several decimal places
- issues and inventory valuations are usually at costs which never existed
- issues may not be at current costs and, in times of rising prices, will be below current costs

Advice to Denise Watson

- if prices are rising, her profits will be higher under FIFO than AVCO – this could be an advantage if she is thinking of selling the business in the near future, but a disadvantage because she will pay more tax
- FIFO and AVCO are both methods of inventory valuation and, over the life of her business, total profit will be the same under both – there will be no effect on the cash generated by the business
- FIFO is logical and relatively easy to calculate; however, if she uses a computer accounting system, this can be used for AVCO calculations
- to meet the accounting concept of consistency, if she changes to AVCO she will need to adjust her financial statements to show comparability
- both FIFO and AVCO are acceptable for tax purposes and under IAS 2

Conclusion

Denise is currently using AVCO, which is an acceptable inventory valuation method under IAS2, *Inventories*. Although her profits will be higher under FIFO when prices are rising, there will be no effect on the cash generated by the business. All-in-all, there do not appear to be compelling reasons to make the change.

8.11 (a) Closing inventory valuations:

			£
FIFO	350	toys at £1.40	490.00
	1,050	toys at £1.62	1,701.00
	1,400		2,191.00
AVCO	1,400	toys at £1.57*	2,198.00

* 7 April AVCO = £1.42; 27 April AVCO = £1.57

9.1

(a) manufacturing account	(e) income statement
(b) manufacturing account	(f) manufacturing account
(c) manufacturing account	(g) income statement
(d) income statement	

9.2

(a)

BARBARA FRANCIS
MANUFACTURING ACCOUNT
FOR THE YEAR ENDED 31 DECEMBER 20-8

	£	£	£
Opening inventory of raw materials			31,860
Add Purchases of raw materials			237,660
			269,520
Less Closing inventory of raw materials			44,790
COST OF RAW MATERIALS USED			224,730
Direct labour			234,630
PRIME COST			459,360
Add Production (factory) overheads:			
Rent and rates		24,690	
Power		7,650	
Heat and light		2,370	
Sundry expenses and maintenance		7,355	
Depreciation of plant and machinery		7,450	
			49,515
PRODUCTION (OR MANUFACTURING) COST OF GOODS COMPLETED			508,875

INCOME STATEMENT FOR THE YEAR ENDED 31 DECEMBER 20-8

	£	£
Revenue		796,950
Opening inventory of finished goods		42,640
Production (or manufacturing) cost of goods completed		508,875
		551,515
Less Closing inventory of finished goods		96,510
COST OF SALES		455,005
Gross profit		341,945
Less Non-production overheads:		
Rent and rates	8,230	
Administrative salaries	138,700	
Advertising	22,170	
Office expenses	7,860	
		176,960
Profit for the year		164,985

(b)   **GROSS PROFIT OF GERRY GALLAGHER FOR APRIL**

	FIFO		AVCO	
	£	£	£	£
Sales†		2,995		2,995
Purchases††	3,851		3,851	
Less Closing inventory	2,191		2,198	
Cost of sales		1,660		1,653
Gross profit		1,335		1,342

	£
† 250 toys at £2.50	625.00
600 toys at £2.60	1,560.00
300 toys at £2.70	810.00
	2,995.00
†† 500 toys at £1.50	750.00
1,000 toys at £1.40	1,400.00
1,050 toys at £1.62	1,701.00
	3,851.00

(c)

- The difference in profit for April is £7 with AVCO showing the higher profit. The reason for this is that, here, AVCO gives a higher closing inventory, which means that cost of sales is lower and profit is higher; by contrast, FIFO gives a lower closing inventory, which means that cost of sales is higher and profit is lower.

- Any change in profit will be only temporary as, over the life of his business, total profits will be the same under both methods.

- In times of rising prices, FIFO gives the higher profit. (Note that, here, the purchase made on 7 April was at a lower price than on 1 April.)

- Higher profit results in more tax to pay.

- The bank manager will not be impressed because, whichever of the two methods is chosen, there is no more money in the bank account – FIFO and AVCO are simply valuation techniques.

9.3

(b) Unit cost = $\dfrac{\text{Production cost}}{\text{Number of units}}$ = $\dfrac{£508,875}{575 \text{ units}}$ = <u>£885 per unit</u>

(c) *Explanation to Barbara Francis*

A manufacturing account has been prepared in order to show the main elements of cost which make up the manufacturing cost. In your business, the main elements of cost are:

- *direct materials* – the raw materials used to make the product
- *direct labour* – the wages of the workforce engaged in manufacturing the product
- *production overheads* – the other costs of manufacture; here rent and rates, power, heat and light, etc

The first two of these make up *prime cost*, the basic cost of manufacturing the product. Prime cost plus production overheads gives the production cost. The figure for production cost is carried down to the income statement where it is used to calculate *cost of sales*. The income statement then goes on to show *gross profit* and, after deduction of non-production overheads, *profit for the year*.

(a) NORIV PLC

MANUFACTURING ACCOUNT – PRIME COST FOR THE YEAR ENDED 31 MAY 2003

	£	£
Opening inventory of raw materials		21,450
Add Purchases of raw materials	234,090	
Add Carriage inward	750	
	234,840	
Less Returns outward	980	
	233,860	
Less Closing inventory of raw materials	22,170	
		211,690
COST OF RAW MATERIALS USED		233,140
Direct labour*		266,000
Manufacturing royalties		6,560
PRIME COST		505,700

* 260,000 + (8,000 x three-quarters)

(b) Partly finished goods in course of manufacture, at a stage between raw materials and finished products.

9.5

(a) £11,200 – £12,100* = £900 increase in provision for unrealised profit
* £60,500 x 25/125

(b) BALANCE SHEET EXTRACT AS AT 31 DECEMBER 20-8

	£	£
Current Assets		
Inventory of finished goods	60,500	
Less Provision for unrealised profit	12,100	
Adjusted inventory of finished goods		48,400

(c) Provision for unrealised profit is made to reduce the closing inventory value of finished goods to cost price. This enables the balance sheet valuation to comply with IAS 2, *Inventories*, and the concept of prudence.

9.9

(a) OSBORNE MELBOURNE LIMITED

MANUFACTURING ACCOUNT FOR THE YEAR ENDED 31 DECEMBER 2006

	£	£
Opening inventory of raw materials	48,560	
Add Purchases of raw materials	188,360	
	236,920	
Less Closing inventory of raw materials	50,120	
COST OF RAW MATERIALS USED		186,800
Direct labour (factory wages)	*400,000	
Royalties	10,080	
		410,080
PRIME COST		596,880
Add Production (factory) overheads:		
Factory canteen expenses	**36,000	
Factory machinery depreciation	***14,400	
Machine maintenance	12,000	
Machine set-up costs	40,000	
		102,400
		699,280
Add Opening inventory of work-in-progress		28,420
		727,700
Less Closing inventory of work-in-progress		31,400
PRODUCTION COST OF GOODS COMPLETED		696,300

* Direct labour: £390,500 + £9,500 accrual
** Factory canteen expenses: £37,150 – £1,150 prepaid
*** Factory machinery depreciation: £720,000 x 2%

(b) Manufacturing cost per hedge cutter = $\dfrac{\text{Production cost of goods completed}}{\text{Number of units completed}}$

$= \dfrac{£696,300}{30,000} = \underline{£23.21 \text{ per unit}}$

9.11 (a)

	£
Provision for unrealised profit at 30 November 2003	3,900
Provision for unrealised profit at 1 December 2002	3,700
Increase in provision for unrealised profit	200

In income statement the increase is deducted from factory profit in order to remove the profit element from inventory so that profit is not overstated.

(b)

TECYL PRODUCTS
BALANCE SHEET EXTRACT AS AT 30 NOVEMBER 2003

	£	£
Current Assets		
Inventory – raw materials		28,000
– work-in-progress		8,500
– finished goods	23,400	
less provision for unrealised profit	3,900	
adjusted inventory of finished goods		19,500
		56,000

(c) Reasons for making a provision for unrealised profit:

- A provision is always required when production is increased with the addition of a factory profit, ie the transfer price to income statement is higher than production cost.

- As a result of the transfer price, the valuation of finished goods inventory is higher than cost price.

- Following the prudence concept, the profit element needs to be removed from the valuation of finished goods inventory.

- IAS 2, *Inventories*, requires that inventory is valued at the lower of cost and net realisable value.

10.1 (a) See text, pages 249-254.

(b)
- raw materials: variable
- factory rent: fixed
- telephone bill: semi-variable
- direct labour: variable
- indirect labour: fixed
- commission to sales staff: variable

Analysing costs by behaviour identifies them as being fixed, or semi-variable, or variable. This helps with decision making – the business might be able to alter the balance between fixed and variable costs in order to increase profits. For example, a furniture manufacturing business will have to make decisions on whether to use direct labour (variable cost) or machinery (fixed cost) for many of the production processes. The decision will be based very much on the expected level of sales, ie for lower sales it is likely to make greater use of direct labour, while for higher sales a more machine-intensive method of production might be used.

10.2 **Graph A**
- shows a *fixed cost*, which remains constant over a range of output levels
- as output increases, the *cost per unit* falls

Graph B
- shows a *variable cost*, which alters directly with changes in output levels
- as output increases then the cost increases, ie the cost per unit remains the same

Graph C
- shows a *semi-variable cost*
- here, a part of the cost acts as a variable cost, and a part acts as a fixed cost

Graph D
- shows a *stepped fixed cost*
- here, as the business expands, the fixed cost of rent increases as another factory needs to be rented

	fixed	semi-variable	variable
(a)	✓		
(b)			✓
(c)		✓	
(d)			✓
(e)	✓		
(f)			✓
(g)		✓	
(h)	✓		

(a) rates of business premises

(b) royalty paid to designer for each unit of output

(c) car hire with fixed rental and charge per mile

(d) employees paid on piecework basis

(e) straight-line depreciation

(f) direct materials

(g) telephone bill with fixed rental and charge per call unit

(h) office salaries

10.6 (a)
(i) fixed costs do not vary with the level of output
(ii) variable costs vary directly with the level of output
(iii) semi-variable costs are part fixed and part variable

(b) *Formula*

(selling price less variable cost) per unit = contribution per unit

Contribution per unit

$$\text{Variable cost} = \frac{£360,000}{40,000} = £9 \text{ per unit}$$

$$\text{Semi-variable cost} = \frac{£280,000 - £80,000}{40,000} = £5 \text{ per unit}$$

Therefore, contribution is £32 – (£9 + £5) = £18 per unit

(c)

		£
	sales revenue £32 x 46,000 units	1,472,000
less	variable costs £9 x 46,000 units	(414,000)
less	semi-variable costs £5 x 46,000 units	(230,000)
equals	total contribution	828,000
less	fixed costs	(80,000)
less	fixed costs	(340,000)
equals	profit for the year	408,000

10.9 (a) Variable costs vary directly with the level of output, eg direct labour

Fixed costs do not vary with the level of output, eg rent

(b) Total cost of 650 pumps:

		£
Materials:	£20 x 400 pumps	8,000
	£18 x 250 pumps	4,500
Labour:	£15 x 650 pumps	9,750
	£3 x 50 pumps	150
Other variable costs:	£9,750* ÷ 5	1,950
Fixed costs:		2,400
Total costs:		26,750

* 'other variable costs' are one-fifth of the labour cost (excluding any bonus) of £9,750

CHAPTER 11 Break-even analysis

11.2 Graphical method

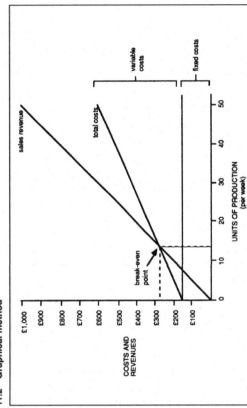

Calculation method

The contribution per unit is:

		£
	selling price per unit	20
less	variable costs* per unit	9
equals	contribution per unit	11

* materials £4 + direct labour £5

The break-even calculation is:

$$\frac{\text{fixed costs (£)}}{\text{contribution per unit (£)}} = \frac{£154^{**}}{£11} = 14 \text{ units (teddy bears) per week}$$

** factory rent and rates £100 + fuel and power £20 + other costs £20

11.3 (a) table method

units of output	fixed costs	variable costs	total cost	sales revenue	profit/(loss)*
	£	£	£	£	£
100	12,000	2,000	14,000	3,500	(10,500)
200	12,000	4,000	16,000	7,000	(9,000)
300	12,000	6,000	18,000	10,500	(7,500)
400	12,000	8,000	20,000	14,000	(6,000)
500	12,000	10,000	22,000	17,500	(4,500)
600	12,000	12,000	24,000	21,000	(3,000)
700	12,000	14,000	26,000	24,500	(1,500)
800	12,000	16,000	28,000	28,000	nil
900	12,000	18,000	30,000	31,500	1,500
1,000	12,000	20,000	32,000	35,000	3,000
1,100	12,000	22,000	34,000	38,500	4,500
1,200	12,000	24,000	36,000	42,000	6,000

* brackets indicate a loss

(b) graph method

(c) calculation method

Fixed costs of £12,000 ÷ contribution of £15 per bat = 800 bats to break-even.

(d) profit/(loss)

• 200 bats

	£
Sales revenue (£35 per bat)	7,000
Less variable costs (£20 per bat)	4,000
Contribution	3,000
Less fixed costs	12,000
Loss for month	(9,000)

• 1,200 bats

	£
Sales revenue (£35 per bat)	42,000
Less variable costs (£20 per bat)	24,000
Contribution	18,000
Less fixed costs	12,000
Profit for month	6,000

(d)
- At a reduced selling price of £47, the contribution is reduced to £47 – £35 = £12 per unit
  - Break-even point is higher at £450,000 ÷ £12 per unit = 37,500 units (and sales revenue of 37,500 x £47 = £1,762,500)
  - As 37,500 units is the maximum capacity of Suddley Limited, no profit can be achieved
- The margin of safety is zero
- The reduction in selling price is not recommended

(e) **margin of safety**

$$\frac{\text{current output} - \text{break-even output}}{\text{current output}} \times \frac{100}{1} = \frac{1,000 - 800}{1,000}$$

= 20 per cent, or 200 units

11.6

(a) (i) *Formula*: contribution per unit = selling price per unit – variable costs per unit

Definition: the amount that each unit contributes, firstly, to cover total fixed costs and, when they have been covered, secondly, contributes to profit

Calculation: £50 – £35* = £15 contribution per unit

* variable costs £12 + £16 + £7

(ii) *Formula*: break-even point (units) = $\dfrac{\text{fixed costs (£)}}{\text{contribution per unit (£)}}$

break-even point (sales) = $\dfrac{\text{fixed costs (£)}}{\text{contribution per unit (£)}}$ x selling price per unit (£)

Definition: the point at which neither a profit nor a loss is made

Calculation: $\dfrac{£450,000}{£15}$ = 30,000 units to break-even

30,000 units x £50 = £1,500,000 sales revenue to break-even

(b)

Line or term	A, B, C or D
Fixed costs	B
Total sales revenue	D
Break-even point	C
Margin of safety	A

(c) From the graph (see page 280), at sales of 35,000 units:

	£
sales revenue	1,750,000
less costs	1,675,000
equals profit	75,000

Check: margin of safety is 5,000 units (35,000 – 30,000) x £15 contribution per unit = £75,000 profit

11.7 The limitations of break-even analysis are that:

– the assumption is made that all output is sold
– the presumption is that there is only one product
– costs and revenues are expressed in straight lines
– fixed costs do not remain fixed at all levels of output
– it is not possible to extrapolate the break-even graph or calculation
– the profit or loss is probably only true for figures close to current output levels
– external factors are not considered
– it concentrates too much on the break-even point

See text, page 270, for a fuller explanation of these points.

11.10 (a) A = the break-even point of 5,000 books
B = the total costs at 10,000 books
C = fixed costs of £40,000
D = sales value and total costs at break-even point
Area E = area of profit
Area F = area of loss
G = margin of safety, between 5,000 and 10,000 books

(b) (i) Point D: 5,000 books x £15 per book = £75,000

(ii)

	£
Sales: revenue at break-even	75,000
less fixed costs	40,000
equals marginal cost	35,000

marginal cost per unit = £35,000 ÷ 5,000 books = £7 per book

(iii) Contribution per unit: selling price – marginal cost = £15 – £7 = £8 per book

12.3

(a)

Marginal cost per coffee machine

	£
Direct materials (per machine)	25.00
Direct labour (per machine)	20.00
MARGINAL COST (per machine)	45.00

(b)

Absorption cost per coffee machine

	£
Direct materials (per machine)	25.00
Direct labour (per machine)	20.00
PRIME COST (per machine)	45.00
Overheads (fixed) £270,000 ÷ 15,000 machines	18.00
TOTAL COST (per machine)	63.00

(c)

COFFEEWORKS LIMITED

PROFIT STATEMENT: 15,000 COFFEE MACHINES

	£	£
Sales revenue (15,000 x £80)		1,200,000
Direct materials (15,000 x £25)	375,000	
Direct labour (15,000 x £20)	300,000	
PRIME COST	675,000	
Overheads (fixed)	270,000	
TOTAL COST		945,000
PROFIT		255,000

MAXXA LIMITED

PROFIT STATEMENT FOR THE YEAR ENDED 31 JANUARY 20-7

	MARGINAL COSTING		ABSORPTION COSTING	
	£	£	£	£
Sales revenue 3,000 units at £8 each		24,000		24,000
Variable costs				
Direct materials at £1.25 each	5,000		5,000	
Direct labour at £2.25 each	9,000		9,000	
	14,000			
Fixed production overheads			6,000	
			20,000	
Less Closing inventory (marginal cost)				
1,000 units at £3.50 each	3,500			
		10,500		
CONTRIBUTION		13,500		
Fixed production overheads		6,000		
Less Closing inventory (absorption cost)				
1,000 units at £5 each			5,000	
Less Cost of sales				15,000
PROFIT		7,500		9,000

Working notes:

Closing inventory is calculated on the basis of this year's costs:

marginal costing, variable costs only, ie £1.25 + £2.25 = £3.50 per unit

absorption costing, variable and fixed costs, ie £20,000 ÷ 4,000 units = £5 per unit

The difference in the profit is caused only by the closing inventory figures: £3,500 under marginal costing, and £5,000 under absorption costing. With marginal costing, the full amount of the fixed production overheads has been charged in this year's profit statement; by contrast, with absorption costing, part of the fixed production overheads (here £6,000 x 25%* = £1,500) has been carried forward in the inventory valuation.

* 1,000 units in inventory out of 4,000 units manufactured

12.8

(a) Absorption cost per unit: £53.00, includes both production and selling/administrative overheads.

(b) Marginal cost per unit:

	£
Direct labour	12.25
Direct material	16.25
Variable production overhead	*12.50
	41.00

* £18.00 x 9,000 units = £162,500 – fixed production overhead £49,500 = £112,500.
£112,500 ÷ 9,000 units = £12.50 per unit

(c) (i) *Marginal costing*

		£	£
	Sales revenue 9,000 units @ £60		540,000
less	Marginal cost 9,000 units @ £41		369,000
equals	Contribution		171,000
less	Fixed production overhead	49,500	
	Selling and administrative overhead	*58,500	
			108,000
equals	Profit for the quarter		63,000

* £6.50 x 9,000 units = £58,500

(ii) *Absorption costing*

		£
	Sales revenue	540,000
less	Absorption cost 9,000 units @ £53	477,000
equals	Profit for the quarter	63,000

12.10

(a) Activity based costing is a costing method which charges overheads to output on the basis of activities. The cost per unit of a product can be calculated based on its use of activities.

(b) A cost driver is an activity which causes costs to be incurred.

12.12 Benefits of activity based costing (ABC) over marginal costing:

- produces more accurate cost information as cost drivers are used to identify the activity which causes costs to be incurred
- is more objective than marginal costing because it is able to identify the overhead costs relating to different products; marginal costing focuses on variable costs and does not analyse fixed costs between products
- focuses on overhead costs; marginal costing focuses on variable costs and does not analyse overhead costs
- gives the management of a business a good understanding of why costs are incurred and how they will be altered by changes in production
- leads to the more accurate calculation of selling prices because overhead costs are analysed to the products which use the activities

CHAPTER 13 Overheads and overhead absorption

13.1

- allocation of overheads – the charging to a cost centre of those overheads that have been directly incurred by that cost centre
- apportionment of overheads – the charging to a cost centre of a proportion of overheads

13.2 (a)

OVERHEAD ANALYSIS SHEET		
	MOULDING	FINISHING
Budgeted total overheads (£)	9,338	3,298
Budgeted machine hours	1,450	680
Budgeted overhead absorption rate (£)	6.44*	4.85**

* £9,338 ÷ 1,450 hours
** £3,298 ÷ 680 hours

(b)

JOB 1234: OVERHEAD ANALYSIS SHEET		
	MOULDING	FINISHING
Job machine hours	412	154
Budgeted overhead absorption rate (£)	6.44	4.85
Overhead absorbed by job (£)	2,653.28*	746.90**

* 412 hours x £6.44 per hour
** 154 hours x £4.85 per hour

(c) Labour hour

- With this method, production overhead is absorbed on the basis of the number of direct labour hours worked.

- While this is a commonly-used method, it is inappropriate where some output is worked on by hand while other output passes quickly through a machinery process and requires little direct labour time.

- This method may be appropriate for Wyvern Fabrication; however, much depends on the balance between direct labour hours and machine hours in the two production departments.

13.4 (a)

Cost	Basis of apportionment	Total £	Dept A £	Dept B £	Dept C £
Rent and rates	Floor area	7,210	3,090	1,545	2,575
Depn. of machinery	Value of machinery	10,800	5,400	3,240	2,160
Supervisor's salary	Production-line employees	12,750	6,800	3,400	2,550
Machinery insurance	Value of machinery	750	375	225	150
		31,510	15,665	8,410	7,435

(b) 37 hours x 48 weeks   =   1,776 labour hours per employee

Dept A: 8 employees   =   14,208 hours   =   £1.10 per labour hour

Dept B: 4 employees   =   7,104 hours   =   £1.18 per labour hour

Dept C: 3 employees   =   5,328 hours   =   £1.40 per labour hour

---

13.6

	total	business studies £	general studies £	administration £	technical support £
Overheads	81,600	40,000	20,000	9,600	12,000
Technical support	–	6,000	3,000	3,000	(12,000)
				12,600	
Administration	–	8,400	4,200	(12,600)	–
	81,600	54,400	27,200	–	–

13.7

(a) $\dfrac{\text{total overheads}}{\text{total hours}}$ $= \dfrac{£59,900}{3,290}$ = £18.21 per partner hour

(b) $\dfrac{£59,900 + £100,000}{3,290}$ = £48.60 per partner hour

(c) 2 hours x 47 weeks x £18.21 = £1,711.74 per partner (ie £3,423.48 in total)

13.15 Tutorial note: the calculations can be made either in total or per operation

(a) *percentage mark-up on absorption cost*

Selling price is calculated as:

	£
total cost (£400 per operation)	1,000,000
20 per cent mark-up (£80 per operation)	200,000
selling price	1,200,000

The price per minor operation will be:
£1,200,000 ÷ 2,500 operations = £480 per operation

(b) *percentage mark-up on marginal cost*

The variable costs are £300 per operation (materials £100, labour £200).
To achieve a price of £480 per minor operation, the marginal cost must be marked up by 60%, ie

$$\frac{\text{profit}}{\text{marginal cost}} = \frac{£180}{£300} = 60\%$$

CHAPTER 14 Costing in decision-making

14.3 The marginal cost per unit of Exe is £5 (direct materials £3 + direct labour £2), and so any contribution, ie selling price less marginal cost, will be profit:

- *200 units at £6 each*

The offer price of £6 is above the marginal cost of £5 and increases profit by the amount of the £1 extra contribution, ie (£6 – £5) x 200 units = £200 extra profit.

- *500 units at £4 each*

This offer price is below the marginal cost of £5; therefore there will be a fall in profit if this order is undertaken of (£4 – £5) x 500 units = £500 reduced profit.

13.9 (a)

Fixed overheads for November 20-7	Basis	Total £	Warehouse £	Manufacturing £	Sales £	Administration £
Depreciation of non-current assets	Net book value	9,150	1,830	6,100	305	915
Rent	Floor space	11,000	1,650	6,600	1,100	1,650
Other property overheads	Floor space	6,200	930	3,720	620	930
Administration overheads	Allocated	13,450				13,450
Staff costs	Allocated	27,370	3,600	9,180	8,650	5,940
		67,170	8,010	25,600	10,675	22,885

(b) Budgeted fixed overhead absorption rate for the manufacturing department:

£25,600 ÷ 10,000 hours = £2.56 per machine hour

The offer from the supermarket chain should be accepted because:

- the marginal cost of producing each can is 14p (direct materials 5p, direct labour 5p, variable production overheads 4p)
- the offer price is 18p per can, which is above marginal cost, and gives a contribution of 4p
- profits increase by the amount of the extra contribution, ie (18p – 14p) x 50,000 cans = £2,000 extra profit

14.7

(a)
- Check the scarce resources listed on page xxx against the organisation you are investigating.
- Which one do you see as being the main scarce resource?
- Can it be overcome by maximising contribution from some sections of the business or organisation to the detriment of others? How will this affect the business or organisation as a whole?

(b)
- Consider the relevance of the use of marginal costing. For example, consider the application of:
  – make or buy decisions
  – acceptance of additional work
  – optimum use of scarce resources
- If marginal costing is used, what problems will be created? See page 349 for possible points.

14.8 Production of Aye and Bee

- Materials used in the production of both products are in short supply and the company can only obtain 500 kgs each week. These materials need to be used to the best advantage of the company.
- With insufficient direct materials there is a scarce resource (or a limiting factor). To make best use of this scarce resource to produce profits for the company, the contribution (selling price – variable costs) from each kg of direct material must be maximised.
- The contribution from producing each unit of Aye is £30. As this product requires two kgs of material, the contribution per kg is £30 ÷ 2 kgs = £15.
- The contribution from producing each unit of Bee is £50. As this product requires four kgs of material, the contribution per kg is £50 ÷ 4 kgs = £12.50.
- To make best use of the scarce resource of direct material, the company should produce all of product Aye that can be sold, ie 200 per week. This will take 400 kgs of materials (200 units x 2 kgs each) and will leave 100 kgs available to produce 25 of product Bee (25 units x 4 kgs each).
- If this production plan is followed, insufficient of product Bee will be produced to meet demand. This may make it difficult to re-establish it in the market when full production of this product can be resumed, once the shortage of direct materials has been resolved.

WESTFIELD LIMITED
monthly profit statements

	Existing production of 2,000 units £	Existing production + 200 units @ £6 each £	Existing production + 500 units @ £4 each £
Sales revenue (per month):			
2,000 units at £12 each	24,000	24,000	24,000
200 units at £6 each	–	1,200	–
500 units at £4 each	–	–	2,000
	24,000	25,200	26,000
Less production costs:			
Direct materials (£3 per unit)	6,000	6,600	7,500
Direct labour (£2 per unit)	4,000	4,400	5,000
Production overheads (fixed)	8,000	8,000	8,000
PROFIT	6,000	6,200	5,500

The conclusion is that the first special order should be accepted, and the second declined.

14.4

POPCAN LIMITED
monthly profit statements

	Existing production of 150,000 cans at 18p each £	Existing production + 50,000 cans £
Sales revenue (per month):		
150,000 cans at 25p each	37,500	37,500
50,000 cans at 18p each	–	9,000
	37,500	46,500
Less production costs:		
Direct materials (5p per can)	7,500	10,000
Direct labour (5p per can)	7,500	10,000
Production overheads – variable (4p per can)	6,000	8,000
– fixed*	9,000	9,000
PROFIT	7,500	9,500

* 6p x 150,000 cans = £9,000

Conclusion

- Based on the concept of maximising the contribution from each kg of material (the scarce resource), the optimum production plan for next week should be:

  200 units of product Aye

  25 units of product Bee

- This will give a forecast profit statement for next week as follows:

	Aye £	Bee £	Total £
Sales revenue:			
200 product Aye at £150 per unit	30,000		30,000
25 product Bee at £200 per unit		5,000	5,000
	30,000	5,000	35,000
less Variable costs:			
200 product Aye at £120 per unit	24,000		24,000
25 product Bee at £150 per unit		3,750	3,750
equals Contribution	6,000	1,250	7,250
less Fixed overheads			4,000
equals Profit			3,250

14.9

(a)

Product	'Madrid' £	'Paris' £	'Rome' £
Selling price per unit	30	40	60
Less: Unit variable costs			
Direct materials	10	15	20
Direct labour	5	8	12
Variable overheads	2	3	2.50
Contribution per unit	13	14	25.50

(b) Break-even point for the 'Madrid' range is:

$$\frac{\text{fixed costs (£)}}{\text{contribution per unit (£)}} = \frac{£72,800}{£13} = 5,600 \text{ units}$$

(c)

Product	'Madrid' £	'Paris' £	'Rome' £
Contribution per unit	£13	£14	£25.50
Machine hours per unit	0.5	0.4	0.75
Contribution per machine hour	£26	£35	£34

(d)

- Machine hours are the scarce resource here, with 3,000 hours available.
- To maximise profits, the company should maximise the contribution from each machine hour.
- The preferred order is 'Paris' (at £35 contribution per machine hour), 'Rome' (at £34), and 'Madrid' (at £26).
- Optimum production plan:

	Total hours available per month	3,000
less	'Paris', 3,000 units x 0.4 hours per unit	1,200
		1,800
less	'Rome', 500 units x 0.75 hours per unit	375
equals	hours remaining to produce 'Madrid'	1,425

Therefore production of 'Madrid' at 0.5 hours per unit will be 2,850 units. This production plan does not allow for full production of the 'Madrid' range.

14.11

(a)

- Direct costs can be identified directly with each unit of output.
- Indirect costs (overheads) cannot be identified directly with specific units of output.

(b) Total cost per unit if 560 units are produced:

		£
Materials	2 metres @ £3 per metre x 560 units	3,360
Labour	2 hours @ £8 per hour x 500 units	8,000
	2 hours @ £10 per hour x 60 units	1,200
PRIME COST		12,560
Indirect fixed costs		2,840
TOTAL COST		15,400

Total cost per unit £15,400 ÷ 560 units = £27.50

(c) Original unit selling price:

	£
Materials per unit	6.00
Labour per unit	16.00
Indirect fixed costs per unit £2,840 ÷ 400 units	7.10
TOTAL COST PER UNIT	29.10
Profit 20%	5.82
SELLING PRICE PER UNIT	34.92

New selling price:

	£
Total cost per unit – see (b) above	27.50
Profit 20%	5.50
SELLING PRICE PER UNIT	33.00

∴ the new selling price is £1.92 less than the original selling price.

(d) Effect on company's present customers:

- will be pleased with reduction in the price they pay to buy the product
- will be concerned to ensure that, with the increase in production, quality of the product is maintained
- will wish to be assured that supplies will be maintained and may question the ability of Mark Maxmus Ltd to use overtime as a solution in the medium term

14.15

(a) Labour hours to achieve budgeted production:

Meton	40,000 units x 1 labour hour	=	40,000	hours
Nevon	30,000 units x 0.5 labour hours	=	15,000	hours
Obon	15,000 units x 0.25 labour hours	=	3,750	hours
TOTAL LABOUR HOURS			58,750	hours

(b) Overhead absorption rate:

£822,500 ÷ 58,750 = £14.00 per direct labour hour

(c)

Product	Meton	Nevon	Obon
	£	£	£
Direct materials per unit	20.00	18.00	16.50
Direct labour per unit	8.00	4.00	2.00
DIRECT COST PER UNIT	28.00	22.00	18.50
Overheads	14.00	7.00	3.50
TOTAL COST PER UNIT	42.00	29.00	22.00

(d)

Product		Meton	Nevon	Obon
	Selling price per unit	£48.00	£49.00	£54.00
less	Unit variable costs	£28.00	£22.00	£18.50
equals	Contribution per unit	£20.00	£27.00	£35.50
	Direct labour hours per unit	1 hour	0.50 hour	0.25 hour
	Contribution per direct labour hour	£20.00	£54.00	£142.00
	Ranking	3	2	1

Optimum production plan:

	Total hours available for year	50,000
less	15,000 units of Obon at 0.25 hours each	3,750
		46,250
less	30,000 units of Nevon at 0.50 hours each	15,000
equals	hours remaining to produce units of Meton	31,250

Therefore production of Meton at 1 hour per unit will be 31,250 units. This production plan does not allow for full production of the Meton.

Tutorial note: this part of the question does not require total contribution and/or profit to be calculated.

15.2

	Sheet steel	Alloy	Flour	Gelling fluid
	£ p	£ p	£ p	£ p
material price variance	0.50 ADV	–	0.06 FAV	1.25 ADV
material usage variance	–	0.75	0.05 ADV	0.75 FAV
material variance	0.50 ADV	0.75 ADV	0.01 FAV	0.50 ADV

15.3

	Casting	Machining	Finishing	Packing
	£ p	£ p	£ p	£ p
labour rate variance	–	4.00 ADV	1.00 ADV	0.60 FAV
labour efficiency variance	10.00 ADV	–	3.00 ADV	2.00 FAV
labour variance	10.00 ADV	4.00 ADV	4.00 ADV	2.60 FAV

15.7

(a) A variance is the calculated difference between the standard cost/expected revenue and the actual cost/revenue.

(b) Material price variance:

actual quantity x (standard price – actual price)

1,250 metres x (£4.00 – £3.50)   = £625   FAVOURABLE

Material usage variance:

standard price x (standard quantity – actual quantity)

£4.00 x (1,200 metres – 1,250 metres)   = £200   ADVERSE

(c) Labour rate variance:

actual labour hours x (standard rate – actual rate)

520 hours x (£12 – £13)   = £520   ADVERSE

Labour efficiency variance:

standard rate x (standard hours – actual hours)

£12 x (600 hours – 520 hours)   = £960   FAVOURABLE

(d)

MIHAIL MANUFACTURING LTD
PROFIT RECONCILIATION STATEMENT FOR THE YEAR ENDED 31 MARCH 2007

	£ ADV	£ FAV	£
Forecast profit			72,100
Material price variance		625	
Material usage variance	200		
Labour rate variance	520		
Labour efficiency variance		960	
	720	1,585	865
Actual profit			72,965

Remember: favourable variances increase profit; adverse variances reduce profit.

15.9

(a) A variance is the calculated difference between the standard cost/expected revenue and the actual cost/revenue.

(b) Material price – adverse:

A higher price has been paid for materials than the standard price. Possible causes include using a different, more expensive supplier, or using better quality, more expensive materials, or a shortage of materials which has increased the price, or a seasonal increase in the price, or a failure to secure a discount on the price paid, or adverse exchange rate fluctuations.

Material usage – favourable:

Fewer materials have been used than the standard quantity. Possible causes include using better quality materials with less wastage, or better production processes with no machine breakdowns, or a more highly skilled workforce.

(a)

HANDLEY LTD
PROFIT RECONCILIATION STATEMENT FOR THE YEAR ENDED 31 MARCH 2007

	ADV £	FAV £	£
Budgeted profit			123,450
Material price variance	1,400		
Material usage variance		2,600	
Labour rate variance	750		
Labour efficiency variance		600	
	2,150	3,200	1,050
Actual profit			124,500

(b) Material price – adverse:

A higher price has been paid for materials than the standard price. Possible causes include using a different, more expensive supplier, or using better quality, more expensive, materials, or a shortage of materials which has increased the price, or a seasonal increase in prices, or a failure to secure a discount on the price paid, or adverse exchange rate fluctuations.

Material usage – favourable:

Fewer materials have been used than the standard quantity. Possible causes include using better quality materials with less wastage, or better production processes with no machine breakdowns, or a more highly skilled workforce.

Labour rate – adverse:

A higher rate has been paid per hour to the workforce. Possible causes include using more skilled, more expensive, employees, or an increase in wage rates because of inflationary pressures.

Labour efficiency – favourable:

The workforce has been more efficient than expected. Possible causes include using more skilled employees, or using better quality materials which are quicker to process, or a period with few machine breakdowns.

(c) •   The largest sub-variance is material usage at £2,600 favourable.

•   The reasons why this may have occurred are given in (b), and the precise cause needs to be identified so tht it can be replicated for future periods. In particular, as material price is adverse, it might be that better quality, but more expensive materials, are being used – the net benefit to the business is £1,200 favourable (£2,600 – £1,400).

•   If a permanent improvement can be achieved, the budget will need to be reviewed for future periods.

(Note also that there may well be a link between the adverse labour rate variance and the favourable labour efficiency variance – paying higher wage rates, or using a more skilled workforce, or using better quality materials has led to a more efficient workforce; however, here, there is a net deficit to the business of £150 adverse, ie £750 – £600.)

Labour rate – favourable:

A lower rate has been paid per hour to the workforce. Possible causes include using less skilled employees, or a reduction in wage rates because of poor economic circumstances.

Labour efficiency – adverse:

The workforce has been less efficient than expected. Possible causes include using less skilled employees, using poor quality materials which are slower to process, or a production stoppage caused, perhaps, by a machine breakdown.

Sales price – adverse:

The product has been sold at a lower price than expected. Possible causes include increased competition, or a strategy of the business to gain market share by reducing the selling price, or larger discounts have been offered to customers, or adverse exchange rate fluctuations.

Sales volume – favourable:

More of the product has been sold than expected. Possible causes include a lower price being charged than competitors, or a lower price/better product is more attractive to customers.

(c)

DOUNES LTD
COST RECONCILIATION STATEMENT FOR THE YEAR ENDED 31 DECEMBER 2004

	ADV £	FAV £	£
Budgeted total cost			124,600
Material price variance	1,400		
Material usage variance		600	
Labour rate variance		2,400	
Labour efficiency variance	900		
	2,300	3,000	(700)
Actual total cost			123,900

Remember: because we are dealing with costs, adverse variances are added and favourable variances are deducted.

Tutorial note: the sales price and volume variances are not used in the calculation of actual total cost.

15.12

(a) Sales price variance:

actual quantity x (standard price – actual price)

14,000 units x (£6 – *£5) = £14,000 **ADVERSE**

* £70,000 ÷ 14,000 units

(b) Sales volume variance:

standard price x (standard quantity – actual quantity)

£6 x (12,000 – 14,000) = £12,000 **FAVOURABLE**

(c) Sales price variance:

– lower selling price than expected
– increased competition, or
– a strategy to gain market share by reducing the selling price, or
– larger discounts offered to customers

Sales volume variance:

– more sold than expected
– either lower price has been charged than competitors
– or a lower price/better product is more attractive to customers

---

(a) payback period

Year	Cash Flow £	Cumulative Cash Flow £
0	(95,000)	(95,000)
1	30,000	(65,000)
2	40,000	(25,000)
3	50,000	25,000 ∴ £25,000 required
4	50,000	75,000
5	25,000	100,000

The design costs are recovered half-way through year 3: £30,000 + £40,000 + (£25,000/£50,000 x 12 months). Thus the payback period is 2 years and 6 months. Note that these assume even cash flows during the year.

(b) net present value

Year	Cash Flow £		Discount Factor		Discounted Cash Flow £
0	(95,000)	x	1.000		(95,000)
1	30,000	x	0.909		27,270
2	40,000	x	0.826		33,040
3	50,000	x	0.751		37,550
4	50,000	x	0.683		34,150
5	25,000	x	0.621		15,525
			Net Present Value		52,535

CHAPTER 16 Capital investment appraisal

16.1

The net cash flows are:

	£
year 0	(95,000)
year 1	30,000
year 2	40,000
year 3	50,000
year 4	50,000
year 5	25,000

16.2

(a) payback period

PROJECT EXE

Year	Cash Flow £	Cumulative Cash Flow £
0	(80,000)	(80,000)
1	40,000	(40,000)
2	40,000	–
3	20,000	20,000
4	10,000	30,000
5	10,000	40,000

PROJECT WYE

Year	Cash Flow £	Cumulative Cash Flow £
0	(100,000)	(100,000)
1	20,000	(80,000)
2	30,000	(50,000)
3	50,000	–
4	50,000	50,000
5	40,000	90,000

net present value

PROJECT EXE

Year	Discount Factor	Cash Flow £	Discounted Cash Flow £
0	1.000	(80,000)	(80,000)
1	0.893	40,000	35,720
2	0.797	40,000	31,880
3	0.712	20,000	14,240
4	0.636	10,000	6,360
5	0.567	10,000	5,670
Net Present Value			13,870

PROJECT WYE

Year	Cash Flow £	Discounted Cash Flow £
0	(100,000)	(100,000)
1	20,000	17,860
2	30,000	23,910
3	50,000	35,600
4	50,000	31,800
5	40,000	22,680
		31,850

(b)

REPORT

To: Robert Smith

From: A2 Accounting Student

Date: Today

Capital investment projects: Exe and Wye

This report carries out an appraisal of these two projects, based on the information provided. Two techniques are used:

- payback
- net present value

The first of these, payback, sees how long it takes for the initial outlay of the project to be repaid by the net cash flow coming in. For Project Exe, the payback period is two years; for Project Wye, it is three years. Using this technique, Project Exe is more favourable.

Payback is an easy technique both to calculate and understand. However, it does have the disadvantage of ignoring all cash flows after the payback period. With these two projects, Wye has strong cash inflows in years 4 and 5, after the payback period (however, these could be a disadvantage if the project is likely to go out-of-date soon).

The net present value technique relies on discounting relevant cash flows at an appropriate rate of return, which is 12 per cent for these projects. Net present value is a more sophisticated technique than payback in that it uses all cash flows and takes the timing of cash flows into account. However, the meaning of Net Present Value is not always clear, and the rate of return required on the projects may vary over their life.

Project Wye has a higher net present value (but also a higher initial cost) at £31,850, when compared with Exe at £13,870. The fact that both figures are positive means that either project will be worthwhile. However, Project Exe is to be preferred because:

- it has the faster payback
- the initial capital outlay is smaller
- it has strong cash flows in the early years, which are likely to be more accurate than the amounts for later years.

16.3 (a)   The net cash flows are:

	£
year 0	(40,000)
year 1	(60,000)
year 2	45,000
year 3	54,000
year 4	90,000
year 5	60,000

payback period

Year	Cash Flow		Cumulative Cash Flow
	£		£
0	(40,000)		(40,000)
1	(60,000)		(100,000)
2	45,000		(55,000)
3	54,000		(1,000)
4	90,000		89,000 ∴ £1,000 required
5	60,000		149,000

The development costs are recovered in the very early part of year 4: £45,000 + £54,000 + (£1,000/£90,000). Thus the payback period is 3 years and 0.13 months/3 years and 0.6 weeks/3 years and 4.1 days. Note that these assume even cash flows during the year.

net present value

Year	Cash Flow		Discount Factor	Discounted Cash Flow
	£			£
0	(40,000)	×	1.000	(40,000)
1	(60,000)	×	0.893	(53,580)
2	45,000	×	0.797	35,865
3	54,000	×	0.712	38,448
4	90,000	×	0.636	57,240
5	60,000	×	0.567	34,020
			Net Present Value	71,993

(b)

REPORT

To:	Managing Director
From:	A2 Accounting Student
Date:	Today

Introduction of a new range of bikes

This report carries out an appraisal on the project, based on the information provided.

The net present value technique relies on discounting relevant cash flows at an appropriate rate of return. It would be helpful to know:

1. whether there are any additional cash flows beyond year 5

2. whether the introduction of a new range of bikes will affect sales of our existing bikes

On the basis of the information provided, the project has a positive net present value of £71,993 and should be carried out.

16.8 (a)   Payback is the length of time it takes for the initial cost to be repaid by net cash inflows.

(b)   **Machine 1**

£60,000 ÷ 4 years payback period = £15,000 cash flow per year.

∴ £15,000 × 10 years = £150,000 total cash flow

Machine 2

£90,000 ÷ 5 years payback period = £18,000 cash flow per year.

∴ £18,000 × 10 years = £180,000 total cash flow

(c)   • Machine 1
   - costs less than machine 2
   - will require less finance
   - has a shorter payback period than Machine 2
   • Machine 2
   - costs 50% more than machine 1
   - generates 20% more cash flow
   - will require more finance
   - takes one year longer to pay back than Machine 1

- The calculations are based on estimated figures, which may prove to be incorrect
- The effects of inflation are ignored
- The time value of money is ignored
- Conclusion: Machine 1 is to be preferred because:
  - the cost is lower and Tom Drake will need £30,000 less finance
  - the extra cash flow of £30,000 over 10 years for Machine 2 only covers the extra cost of the machine
  - in uncertain economic times, the cheaper machine with the quicker payback is to be preferred so that Tom Drake's capital expenditure is at risk for the shortest possible time

16.10 (a) **Payback period**

$$\frac{\text{cost of machine}}{\text{cash flow per year}} = \frac{£60,000}{£26,000} \times 365 \text{ days} = 842.3 \text{ days}$$

842.3 days = 2 years and 112.3 days (or 2 years and 16 weeks/2 years and 4 months)

(b) **Net present value**

Year	Cash Flow £		Discount Factor		Discounted Cash Flow £
0	(60,000)	×	1.000	=	(60,000)
1	26,000	×	0.926	=	24,076
2	26,000	×	0.857	=	22,282
3	26,000	×	0.794	=	20,644
			Net Present Value	=	7,002

(c) Usefulness of the net present value method of capital investment appraisal:

Advantages
- all cash flows are considered
- the time value of money is used
- the timing of cash flows is taken into account
- more complex to calculate than payback, but a table of factors can be used

Disadvantages
- the cost of capital may be difficult to ascertain and may vary over the life of the project
- the meaning of net present value is not always clear to users of the information
- the estimates of cash flows may be inaccurate

16.11 (a) **Payback period**

Machine cost is £180,000 + delivery/installation charge £20,000 = £200,000

		£
Year 1 cash flow	£60,000 − £40,000 =	20,000
Year 2 cash flow	£80,000 − £40,000 =	40,000
Year 3 cash flow	£120,000 − £40,000 =	80,000
Year 4 cash flow	£120,000 − (£40,000 + £20,000*) =	60,000
Year 5 cash flow	£80,000 − £40,000 =	40,000
		240,000

* cost of machine overhaul in year 4

The payback period, shaded, is 4 years: cost of machine £200,000; cash inflows £20,000 + £40,000 + £80,000 + £60,000.

(b) **Net present value**

Year	Cash Flow £		Discount Factor		Discounted Cash Flow £
0	(200,000)	×	1.000	=	(200,000)
1	20,000	×	0.893	=	17,860
2	40,000	×	0.797	=	31,880
3	80,000	×	0.712	=	56,960
4	60,000	×	0.636	=	38,160
5	40,000	×	0.567	=	22,680
			Net Present Value	=	(32,460)

(c) On the basis of net present value, this machine should not be purchased.

Reasons:

- There is a negative net present value over the five-year life of the machine.
- The cost of capital is high at 12% – is lower cost finance available?
- Payback is 4 years, leaving only year 5's cash flow as profit.
- After year 4, cash flows are declining rapidly.
- The estimates of cash flows may be inaccurate.

CHAPTER 17 Further aspects of budgeting

17.2

Davidson Reproductions Ltd: Production budget

	Month 1 (tables)	Month 2 (tables)	Month 3 (tables)	Month 4 (tables)
Sales	1,200	1,080	1,134	1,191
Opening inventory	(100)	(216)	(227)	(239)
Closing inventory	216	227	239	240
Production	1,316	1,091	1,146	1,192

17.5

(a) A labour budget is used to plan and control the labour hours and labour costs of production-line employees.

(b) Any two uses of a labour budget for a manufacturing company:

- it can be used to plan and control the cost of labour
- it identifies any surplus or shortfall in the number of labour hours available for planned production, allowing corrective action to be taken and changes made to overtime and shift working
- it can be used to plan labour requirements for future production, identifying when more or fewer labour hours will be needed, and linking to recruitment or redundancy issues for the Human Resources Department

17.8

(a)

DAMIR LTD

Trade receivables budget for January to April

	January £	February £	March £	April £
Opening trade receivables	28,800	34,800	38,400	40,800
Credit sales*	24,000	26,400	27,600	26,400
Receipts: 50% from 1 month ago	(10,800)	(12,000)	(13,200)	(13,800)
50% from 2 months ago	(7,200)	(10,800)	(12,000)	(13,200)
Closing trade receivables	34,800	38,400	40,800	40,200

* Credit sales =

January	2,000 units x £15 each x 80%
February	2,200 units x £15 each x 80%
March	2,300 units x £15 each x 80%
April	2,200 units x £15 each x 80%

(b)

	£	
Sales to trade receivables in December	9,000	600 units x £15 each
Less payment received in December	1,800	
Balance outstanding	7,200	

Expected to be received:

January	3,600
February	3,600
	7,200

These amounts will not now be received because the customer has gone into liquidation. This means that less cash will be received than was expected in January and February and will affect the cash budget. This will reduce the bank balance or increase the bank overdraft by these amounts. The profitability of the business will also be affected as £7,200 will have to be written off in income statement as a bad debt.

(c) To improve future trade receivables control:

- take two credit references from new customers
- use 'pro forma' invoices – where the customer pays before the goods are delivered – until credit references received
- set credit limits for each customer
- offer cash discounts for prompt settlement
- issue statements of account to customers regularly, eg monthly
- chase up overdue accounts with letters/phone calls/emails
- threaten to charge interest on overdue accounts
- legal action to be taken only when cost effective

17.9 (a) (i)

	February units	March units
A110	960	672
B220	1,330	1,659

Workings

	A110 units	B220 units
Opening inventory at 1 February	200	300
Purchases in February	1,000	1,600
	1,200	1,900
80%/70% sold in February	960	1,330
Opening inventory at 1 March	240	570
Purchases in March	600	1,800
	840	2,370
80%/70% sold in March	672	1,659
Closing inventory at 31 March	168	711

(ii)

	February £	March £
A110	28,800	20,160
B220	39,900	49,770

A110: cost price £20 + 50% mark-up, ie £10 = £30
B220: cost price £15 + 100% mark-up, ie £15 = £30

(b)

Balance sheet (extract) as at 31 March 2005

Current Assets	£
Inventory	*14,025

* A110: 168 units at £20 each	=	£3,360
B220: 711 units at £15 each	=	£10,665
		£14,025

(c)

$$\frac{\text{Average inventory}}{\text{Cost of sales}} \times 365 \text{ days} \quad \text{or} \quad \frac{\text{Cost of sales}}{\text{Average inventory}}$$

(d) Rate of inventory turnover for A110 for March 2005

Average inventory: (240 units + 168 units) ÷ 2 = 204 units x £20 = £4,080
Cost of sales: 240 units + 600 units – 168 units = 672 units x £20 = £13,440

$$\frac{£4,080}{£13,440} \times 365 \text{ days} = 111 \text{ days} \quad \textbf{or} \quad \frac{£13,440}{£4,080} = 3.29 \text{ times per year}$$

Rate of inventory turnover for B220 for March 2005

Average inventory: (570 units + 711 units) ÷ 2 = 640.5 units x £15 = £9,607.50
Cost of sales: 570 units + 1,800 units – 711 units = 1,659 units x £15 = £24,885

$$\frac{£9,607.50}{£24,885} \times 365 \text{ days} = 141 \text{ days} \quad \textbf{or} \quad \frac{£24,885}{£9,607.50} = 2.59 \text{ times per year}$$

(e)

- A sales budget estimates future sales in terms of units and revenue.
- The figures from the sales budget contribute to the master budget which takes the form of a forecast operating statement – forecast income statement – and a forecast balance sheet.

17.11 *Benefits of a cash budget:*

- to plan future expenditure, eg the financing of new non-current assets
- to control costs and revenues to ensure that either
  - a bank overdraft is avoided (so saving interest and charges payable), or
  - a bank overdraft or loan can be arranged in advance
- to reschedule payments where necessary to avoid bank borrowing, eg delay the purchase of non-current assets
- to co-ordinate the activities of the various sections of the business, eg the production department buys in materials not only to meet the expected sales of the sales department but also at a time when there is available cash
- to communicate the overall aims of the business to the various sections and to check that the cash will be available to meet their needs
- to identify any possible cash surpluses in advance and take steps to invest the surplus on a short-term basis (so earning interest)

17.12 (a) (i)

Cash Budget for Peversal Papers Ltd for the three months ending 31 May 2002	March	April	May
	£000	£000	£000
Sales – cash	4,851	5,390	5,929
– credit	83,600	94,050	104,500
	88,451	99,440	110,429
Production* costs (at £12 each)	55,200	61,200	64,800
Admin/distribution	28,000	34,000	38,000
	83,200	95,200	102,800
Net cash inflow/outflow	5,251	4,240	7,629
Opening balance	6,000	11,251	15,491
Closing balance	11,251	15,491	23,120

* see production budget, which follows

(ii)

Production Budget for Peversal Papers Ltd for the three months ending 31 May 2002	March	April	May
	units	units	units
Sales	4,500	5,000	5,500
Opening inventory	(900)	(1,000)	(1,100)
Closing inventory	1,000	1,100	1,000
Production	4,600	5,100	5,400

(b)

- Planning ahead
  - future receipts (from sales) and payments (for production costs and administration)
  - production of reams of paper, and inventory position to meet next month's sales
- Monitoring and control
  - of cash resources
  - of production
- Co-ordination of resources to ensure that cash is available to pay for planned production
- Decision-making about production costs and administration expenses
- Communicating the budgets to managers and staff
- Motivating staff to ensure that the budgets are met
- Evaluation of systems and staff

18.1 (a) • Profit is a calculated figure which shows the surplus of income over expenditure for the year; it takes note of adjustments for accruals and prepayments and non-cash items such as depreciation and provision for doubtful debts.

• Cash is the actual amount of money held in the bank or as cash.

(b)

	Profit	Cash
	£	£
Option 1		
new machinery	–	(450,000)
loan	–	600,000
interest on loan	(60,000)	(60,000)
redundancy	(160,000)	(160,000)
retraining	(30,000)	(30,000)
depreciation	(45,000)	–
net effect	(295,000)	(100,000)
Option 2		
new machinery	–	(250,000)
loan	–	300,000
interest on loan	(30,000)	(30,000)
retraining	(80,000)	(80,000)
depreciation	(25,000)	–
net effect	(135,000)	(60,000)

Note that depreciation is a non-cash expense which affects profit only

(c) • For this first year, option 2 has the smaller effect on both profit and cash.

• If redundancy costs of £160,000 could be avoided in option 1 the effect on profit would be (£135,000), which is the same as option 2, and the effect on cash would be £60,000, compared with option 2 (£60,000).

• In subsequent years option 1 will have the larger effect on both profit and cash, with interest, retraining (year 2 only) and depreciation (affecting profit only); there will also be cost savings from employing fewer staff (affecting both profit and cash equally)

• There are social factors to consider:

  – redundancy (effect on workforce and local economy)

  – recycling (customers may be lost if non-recyclable paper is used)

• Making the assumption that sales will be the same under both options, then option 2 is to be preferred in the short-term. However, in the longer term, option 1 may be preferable, despite its higher costs, because it has the benefits of recycling.

18.3

To: J Woodwedge, Finance Director
From: A student
Date: Date of exam
Subject: Analysis of factors that need to be considered before making redundancies

Three factors from:

1 Unemployment in the community where the workforce is based will affect the local economy.

2 Negative publicity may cause customers to buy products from competitors.

3 Negative effect on remaining staff (internal factor) which may affect productivity.

4 Loss of skilled workforce, which may affect productivity.

5 If business picks up it may be difficult to recruit suitable skilled workers.

A firm recommendation should be made whichever option is chosen.

Index